Save **50% OFF** the cover price

SHONEN JUMP
THE WORLD'S MOST POPULAR MANGA ™

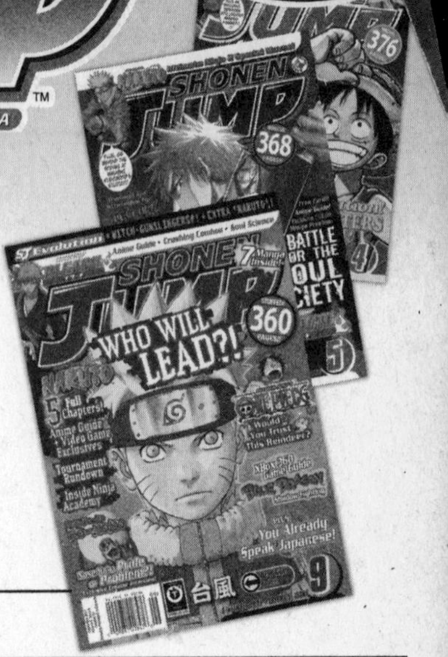

Each issue of SHONEN JUMP contains the coolest manga available in the U.S., anime news, and info on video & card games, toys AND more!

☑ **YES!** Please enter my one-year subscription (12 HUGE issues) to **SHONEN JUMP** at the LOW SUBSCRIPTION RATE of **$29.95!**

NAME

ADDRESS

CITY   STATE   ZIP

E-MAIL ADDRESS   P7GNC1

☐ MY CHECK IS ENCLOSED (PAYABLE TO SHONEN JUMP) ☐ BILL ME LATER

CREDIT CARD: ☐ VISA   ☐ MASTERCARD

ACCOUNT #   EXP. DATE

SIGNATURE

CLIP AND MAIL TO ➡

SHONEN JUMP
Subscriptions Service Dept.
P.O. Box 515
Mount Morris, IL 61054-0515

Make checks payable to: **SHONEN JUMP**. Canada price for 12 issues: $41.95 USD, including GST, HST and QST. US/CAN orders only. Allow 6-8 weeks for delivery.

RATED **T** TEEN
ratings.viz.com

BLEACH © 2001 by Tite Kubo/SHUEISHA Inc. NARUTO © 1999 by Masashi Kishimoto/SHUEISHA Inc. ONE PIECE © 1997 by Eiichiro Oda/SHUEISHA Inc.

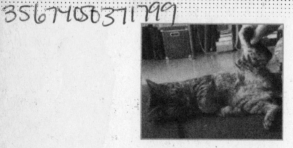

My beloved Coro is a cat with a birth defect and has a hard time walking. Even so, the cat does its best to move around the house and rolls around a lot on the floor. Seeing the cat walking around and not giving up cheers me up, especially when the editor yells at me. By the way, I think Coro looks a lot like Timcanpy.

—Katsura Hoshino

Shiga Prefecture native Katsura Hoshino's hit manga series *D.Gray-man* has been serialized in *Weekly Shonen Jump* since 2004. Katsura's debut manga, "Continue," appeared for the first time in *Weekly Shonen Jump* in 2003.

Katsura adores cats.

D.GRAY-MAN

VOL. 9

The SHONEN JUMP ADVANCED Manga Edition

STORY AND ART BY

KATSURA HOSHINO

English Adaptation/Lance Caselman
Translation/Toshifumi Yoshida
Touch-up Art & Lettering/Kelle Han
Design/Matt Hinrichs
Editor/Gary Leach

Editor in Chief, Books/Alvin Lu
Editor in Chief, Magazines/Marc Weidenbaum
VP of Publishing Licensing/Rika Inouye
VP of Sales/Gonzalo Ferreyra
Sr. VP of Marketing/Liza Coppola
Publisher/Hyoe Narita

Printed in the U.S.A.

Published by VIZ Media, LLC
P.O. Box 77010
San Francisco, CA 94107

SHONEN JUMP ADVANCED Manga Edition
10 9 8 7 6 5 4 3 2 1
First printing, May 2008

RATED T+ FOR OLDER TEEN

PARENTAL ADVISORY
D.GRAY-MAN is rated T+ for Older Teen and is recommended for ages 16 and up. This volume contains fantasy violence.

ratings.viz.com

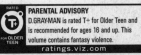

SHONEN JUMP ADVANCED MANGA EDITION

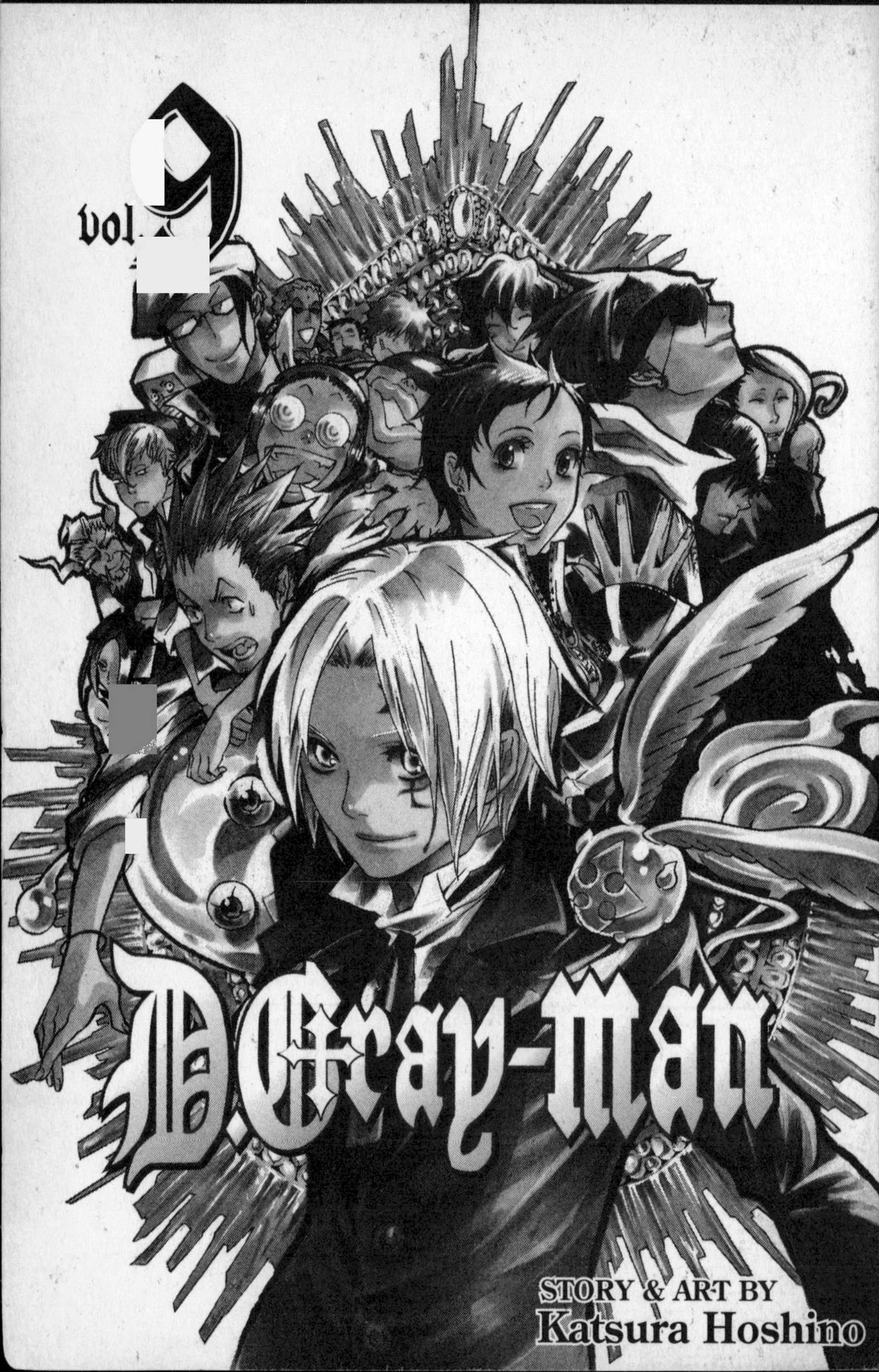
vol. 9
D.Gray-man
STORY & ART BY
Katsura Hoshino

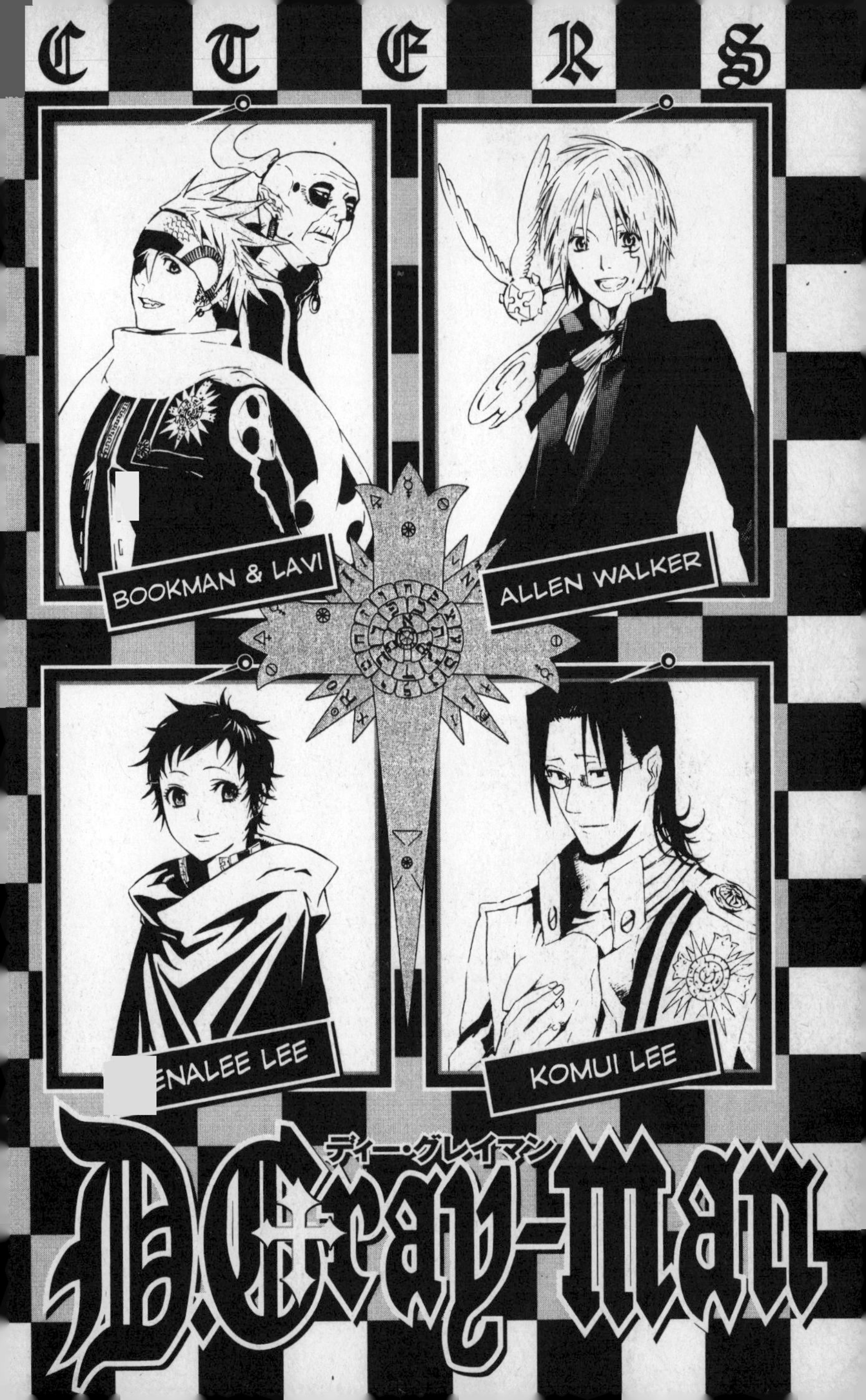
C T E R S
BOOKMAN & LAVI
ALLEN WALKER
ENALEE LEE
KOMUI LEE
ディー・グレイマン
D.Gray-man

CHARA

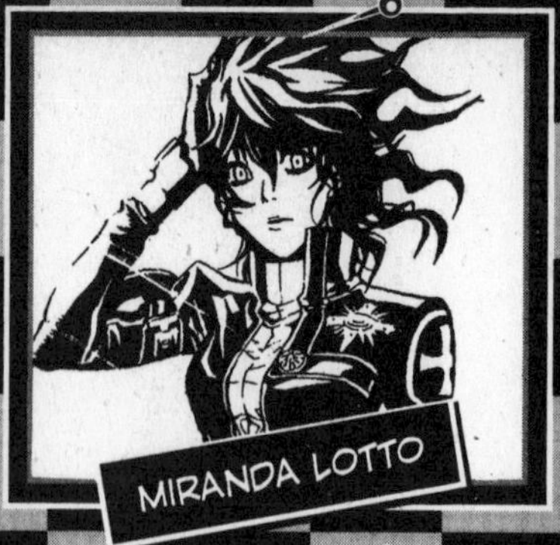
MIRANDA LOTTO

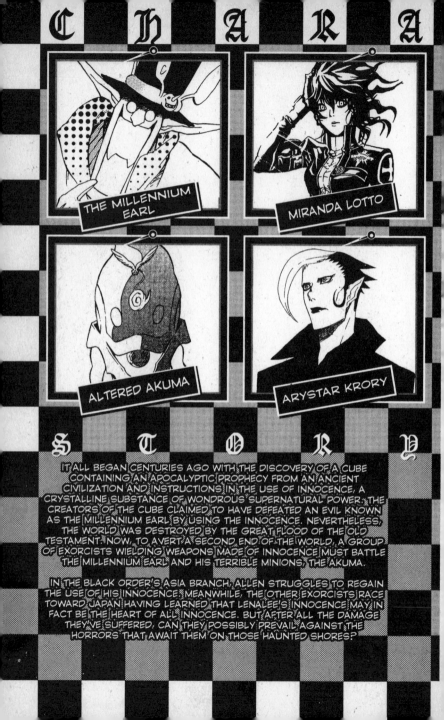

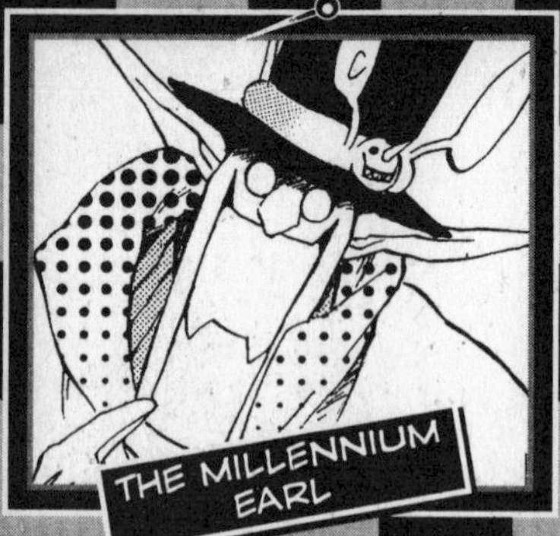
THE MILLENNIUM EARL

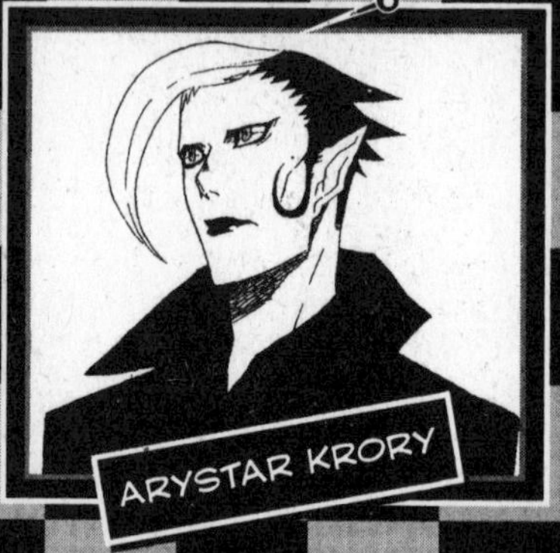
ARYSTAR KRORY

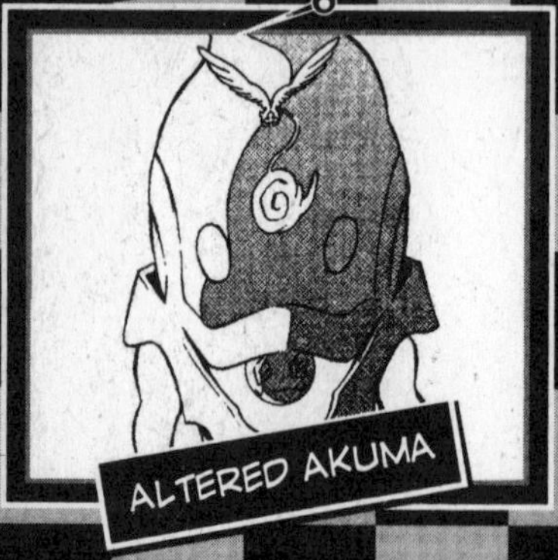
ALTERED AKUMA

STORY

IT ALL BEGAN CENTURIES AGO WITH THE DISCOVERY OF A CUBE CONTAINING AN APOCALYPTIC PROPHECY FROM AN ANCIENT CIVILIZATION AND INSTRUCTIONS IN THE USE OF INNOCENCE, A CRYSTALLINE SUBSTANCE OF WONDROUS SUPERNATURAL POWER. THE CREATORS OF THE CUBE CLAIMED TO HAVE DEFEATED AN EVIL KNOWN AS THE MILLENNIUM EARL BY USING THE INNOCENCE. NEVERTHELESS, THE WORLD WAS DESTROYED BY THE GREAT FLOOD OF THE OLD TESTAMENT. NOW, TO AVERT A SECOND END OF THE WORLD, A GROUP OF EXORCISTS WIELDING WEAPONS MADE OF INNOCENCE MUST BATTLE THE MILLENNIUM EARL AND HIS TERRIBLE MINIONS, THE AKUMA.

IN THE BLACK ORDER'S ASIA BRANCH, ALLEN STRUGGLES TO REGAIN THE USE OF HIS INNOCENCE. MEANWHILE, THE OTHER EXORCISTS RACE TOWARD JAPAN HAVING LEARNED THAT LENALEE'S INNOCENCE MAY IN FACT BE THE HEART OF ALL INNOCENCE. BUT AFTER ALL THE DAMAGE THEY'VE SUFFERED, CAN THEY POSSIBLY PREVAIL AGAINST THE HORRORS THAT AWAIT THEM ON THOSE HAUNTED SHORES?

D.GRAY-MAN
Vol. 9

CONTENTS

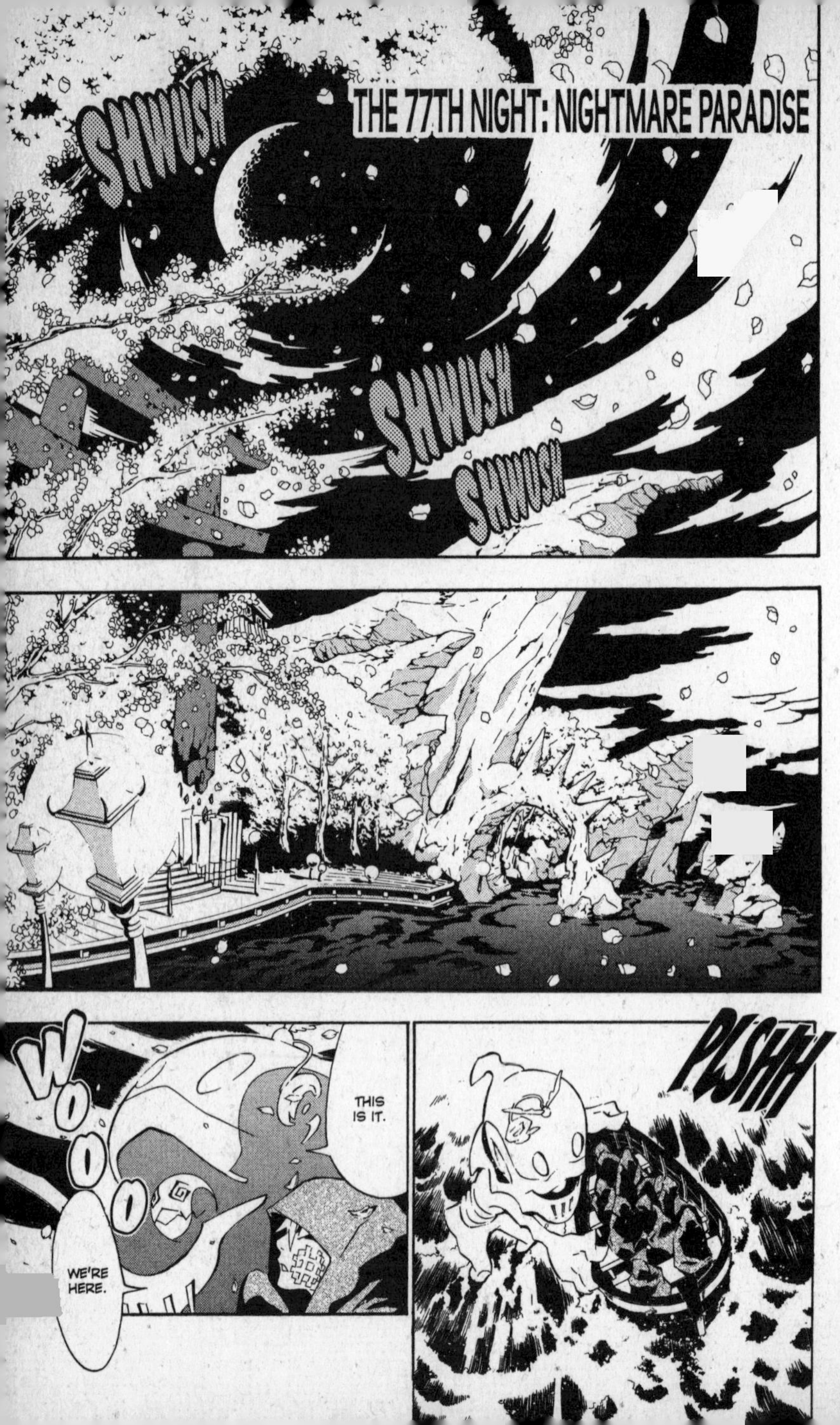
THE 77TH NIGHT: NIGHTMARE PARADISE
SHWUSH
SHWUSH
SHWUSH
PLSHH
THIS IS IT.
WOOO
WE'RE HERE.

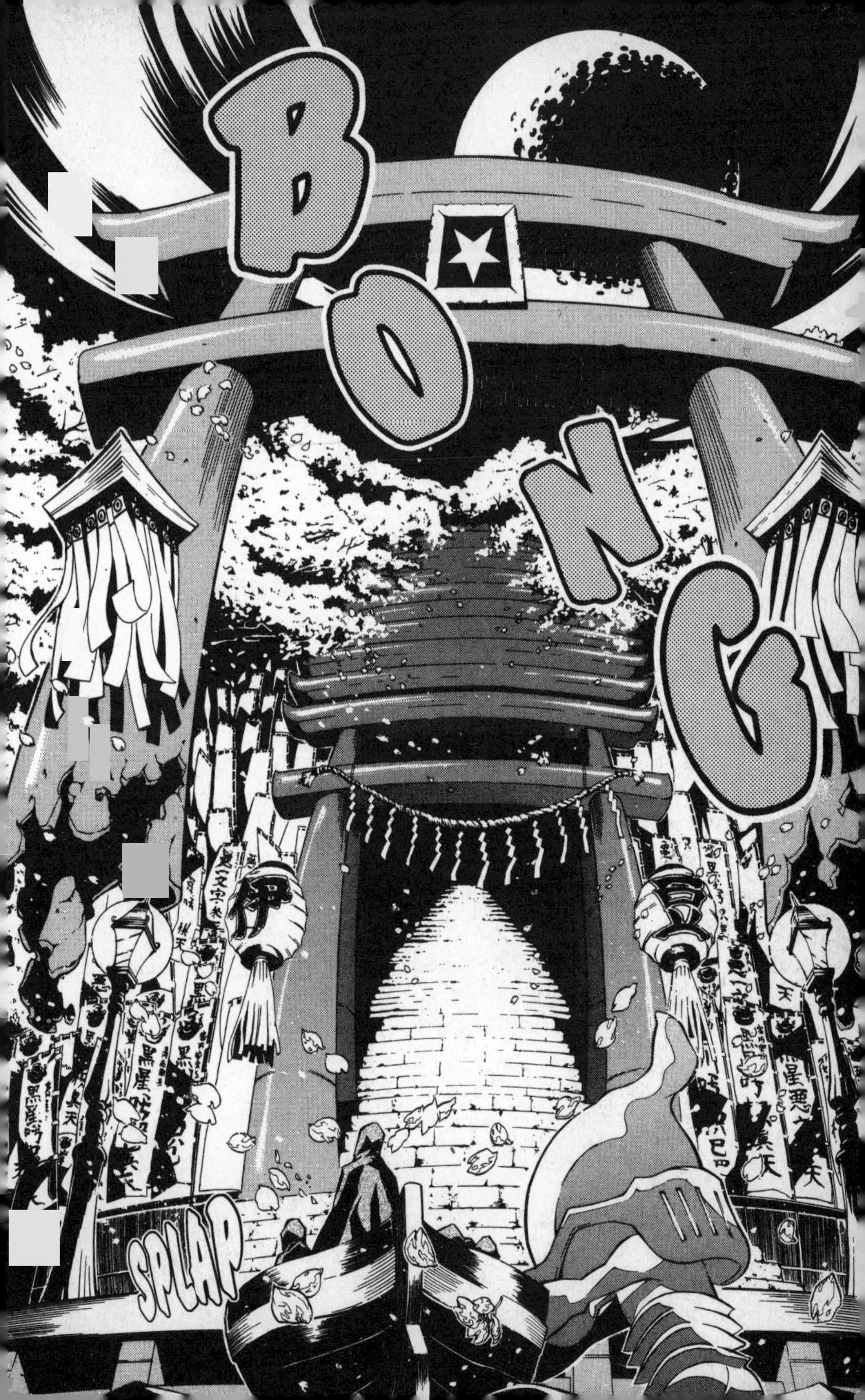
BONG
SPLAP

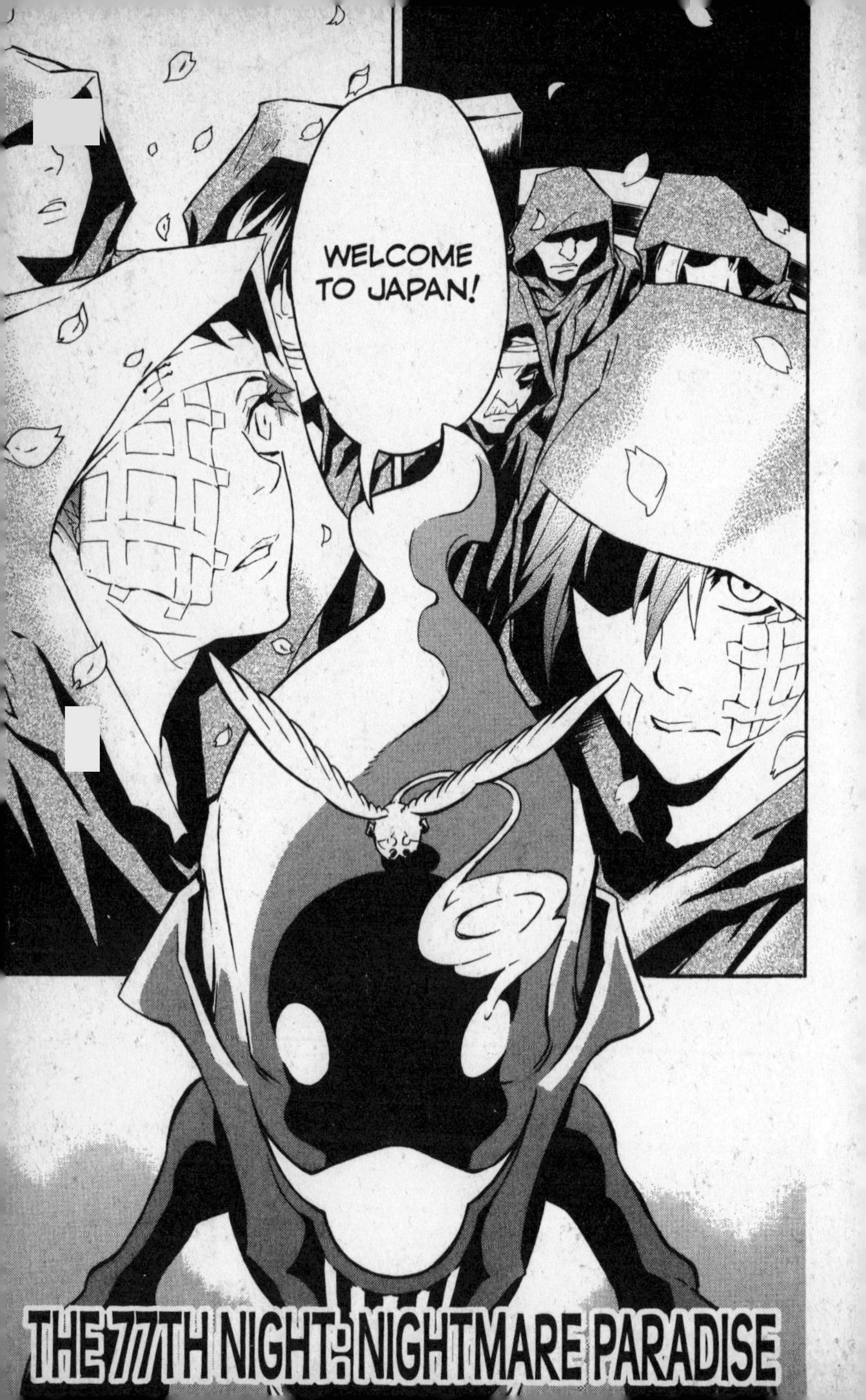
WELCOME TO JAPAN!
THE 77TH NIGHT: NIGHTMARE PARADISE

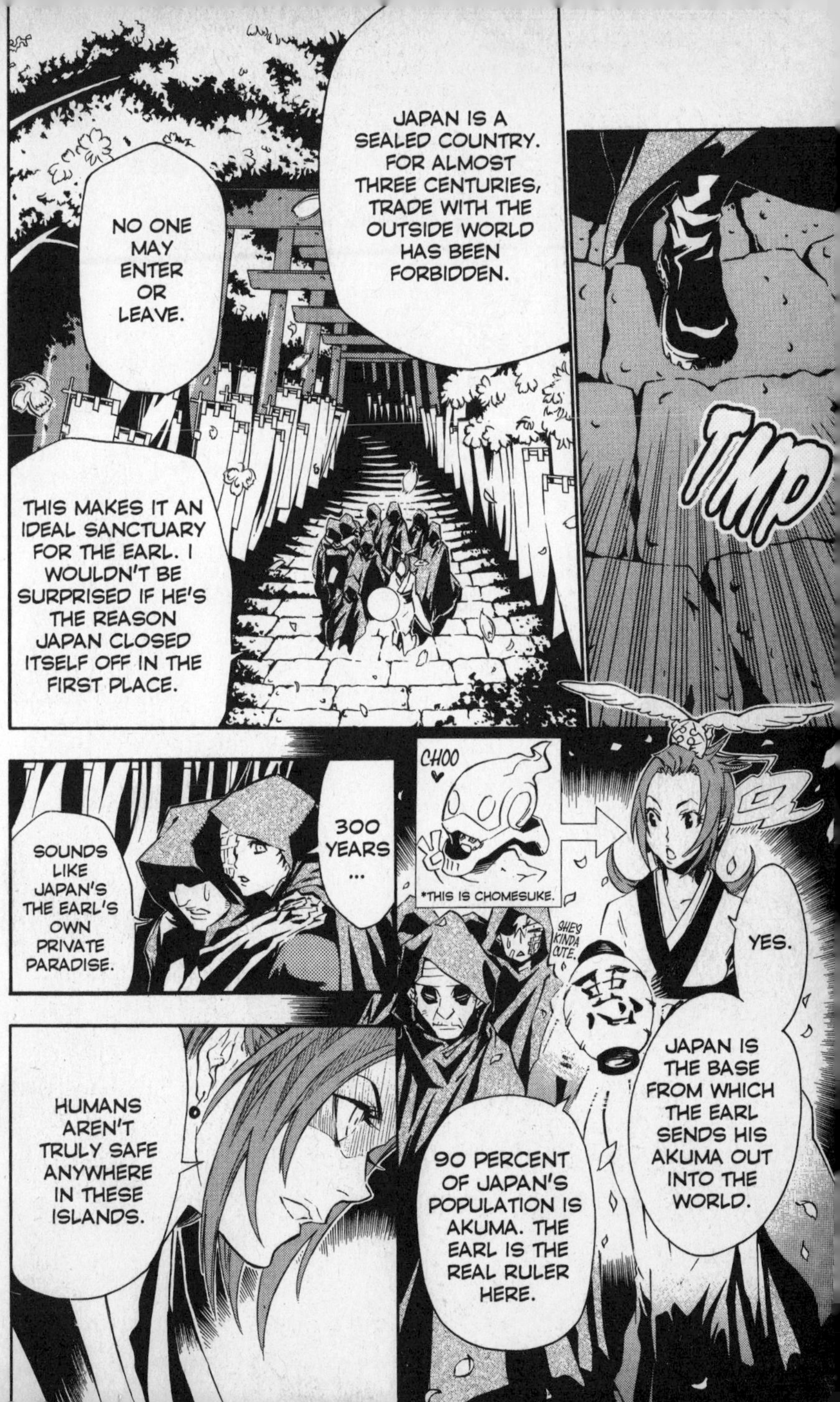
TMP
JAPAN IS A SEALED COUNTRY. FOR ALMOST THREE CENTURIES, TRADE WITH THE OUTSIDE WORLD HAS BEEN FORBIDDEN.
NO ONE MAY ENTER OR LEAVE.
THIS MAKES IT AN IDEAL SANCTUARY FOR THE EARL. I WOULDN'T BE SURPRISED IF HE'S THE REASON JAPAN CLOSED ITSELF OFF IN THE FIRST PLACE.
300 YEARS ...
SOUNDS LIKE JAPAN'S THE EARL'S OWN PRIVATE PARADISE.
CHOO ♥
*THIS IS CHOMESUKE.
SHE'S KINDA CUTE.
YES.
JAPAN IS THE BASE FROM WHICH THE EARL SENDS HIS AKUMA OUT INTO THE WORLD.
90 PERCENT OF JAPAN'S POPULATION IS AKUMA. THE EARL IS THE REAL RULER HERE.
HUMANS AREN'T TRULY SAFE ANYWHERE IN THESE ISLANDS.

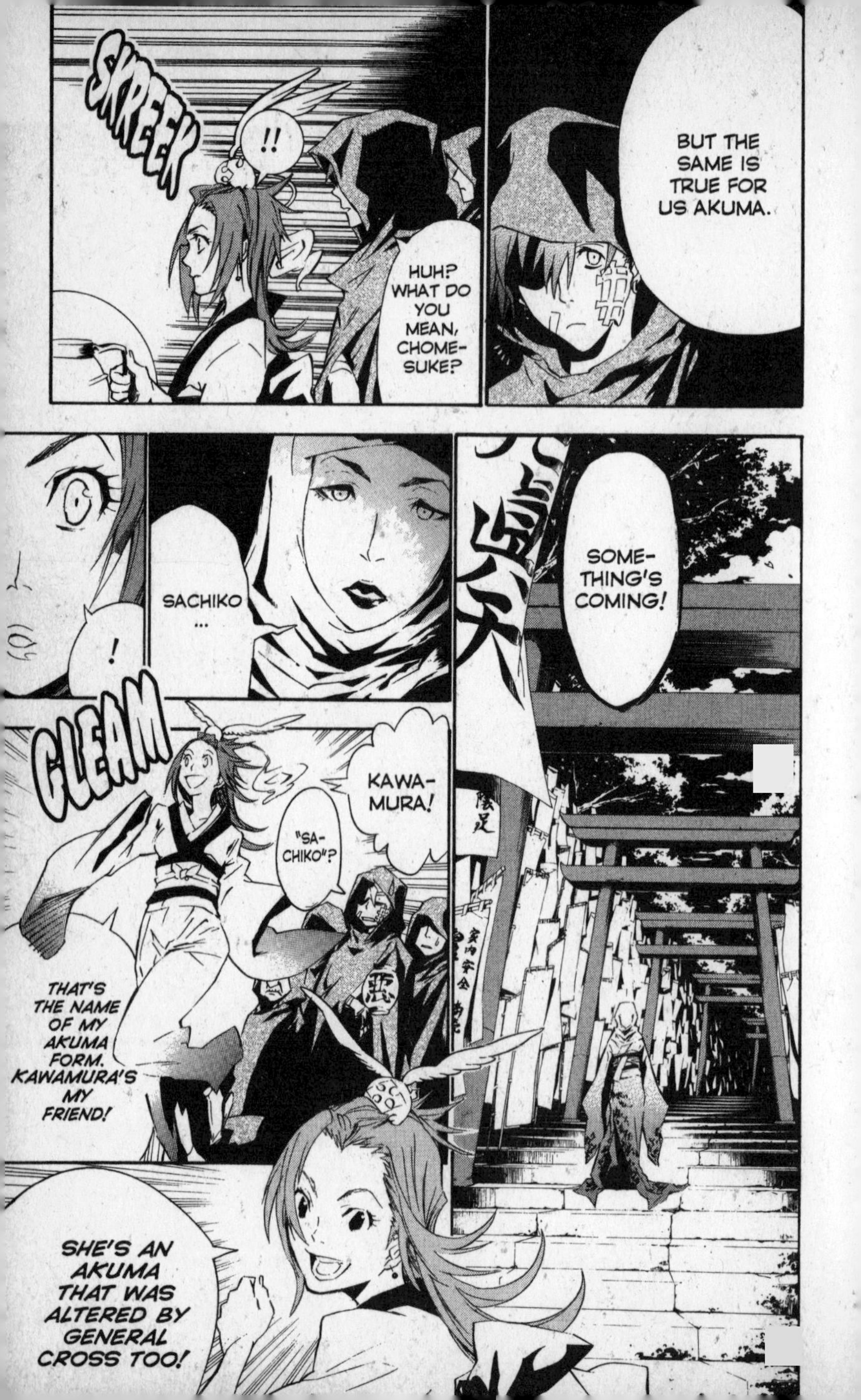
BUT THE SAME IS TRUE FOR US AKUMA.
HUH? WHAT DO YOU MEAN, CHOME-SUKE?
!!
SKREEK
SOME-THING'S COMING!
SACHIKO ...
!
KAWA-MURA!
"SA-CHIKO"?
CLEAM
THAT'S THE NAME OF MY AKUMA FORM. KAWAMURA'S MY FRIEND!
SHE'S AN AKUMA THAT WAS ALTERED BY GENERAL CROSS TOO!

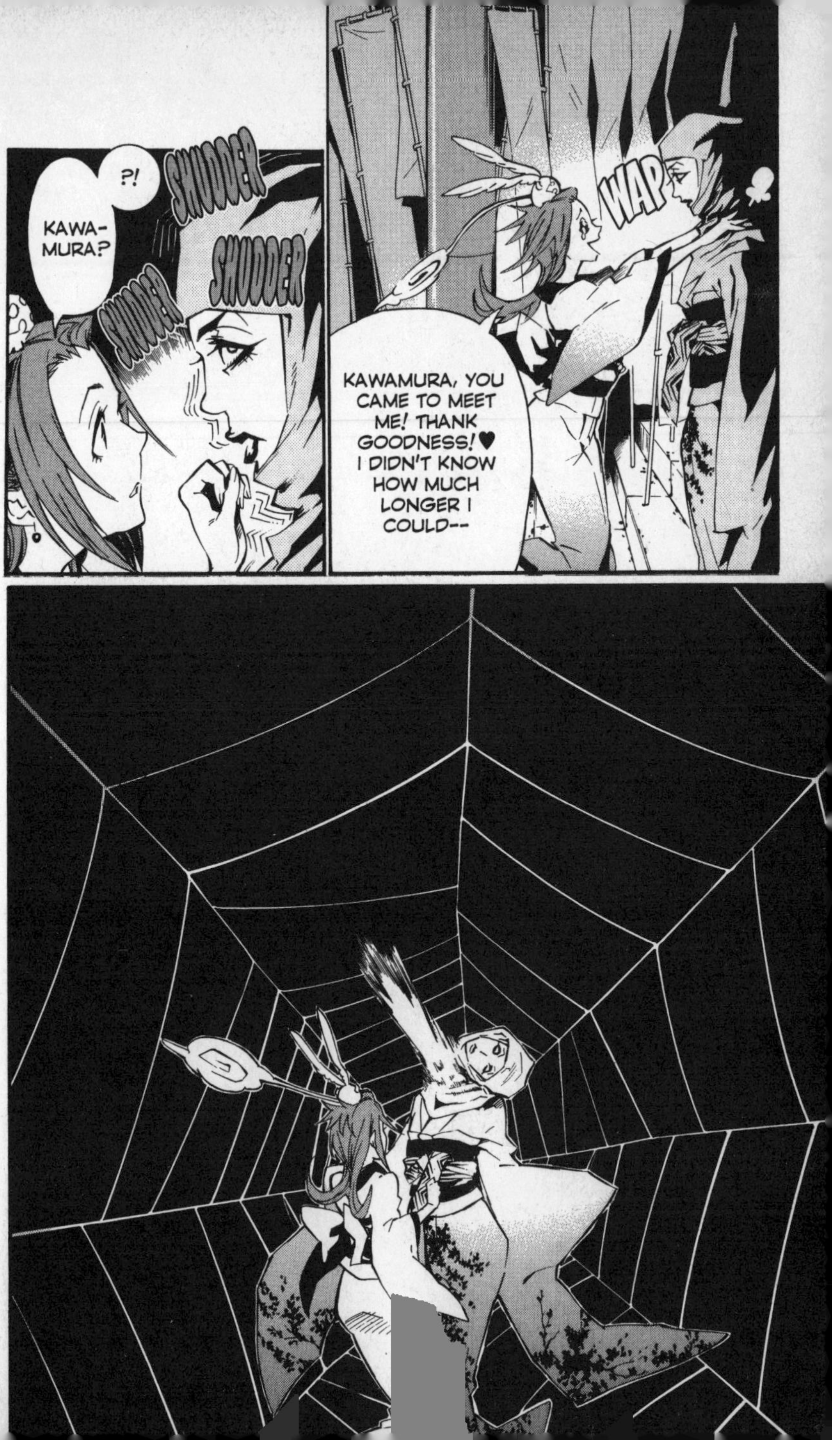
WAP
KAWAMURA, YOU CAME TO MEET ME! THANK GOODNESS!♥ I DIDN'T KNOW HOW MUCH LONGER I COULD--
SHUDDER
?!
KAWA-MURA?
SHUDDER
SHUDDER

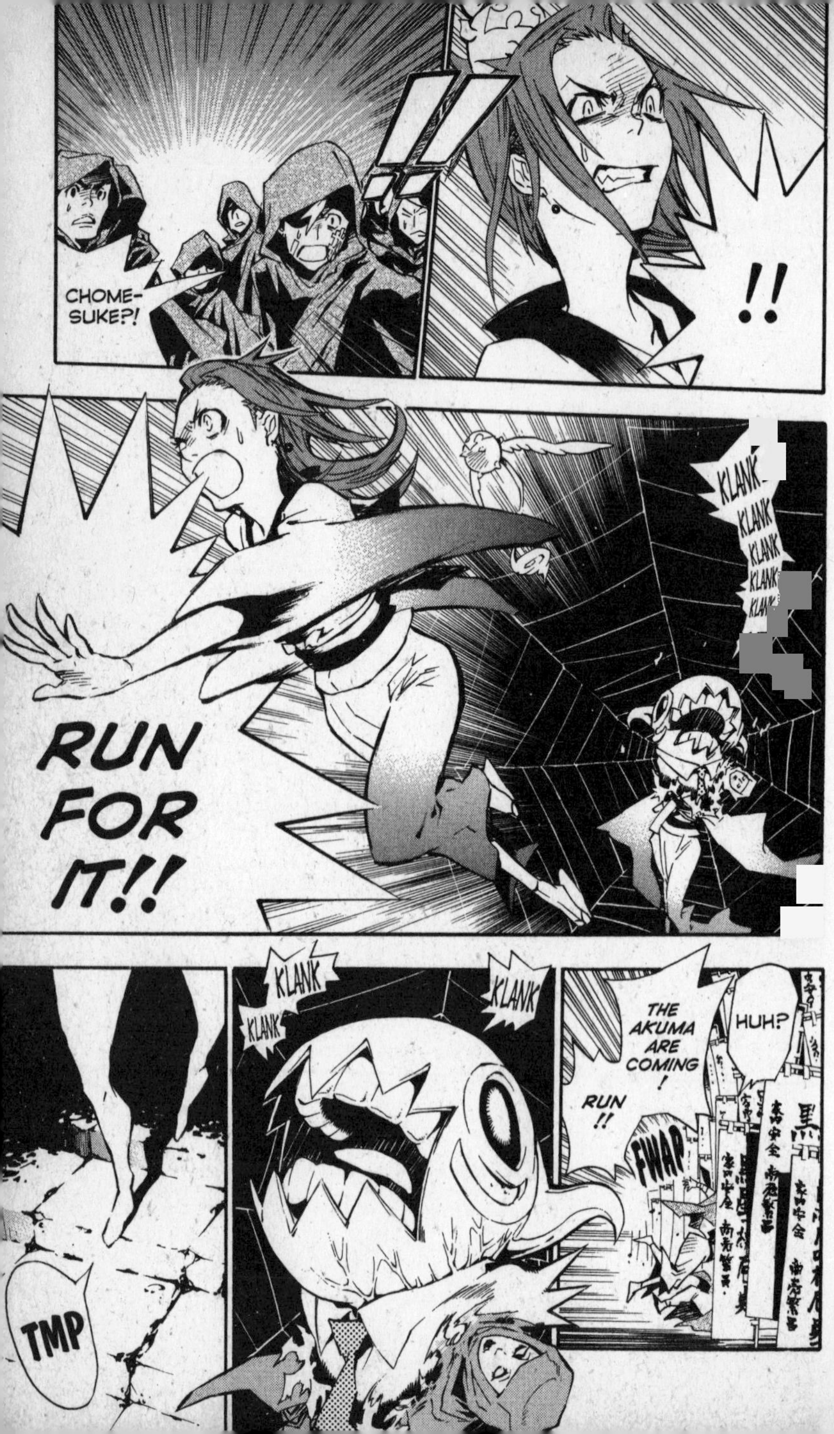

!!
!!
CHOME-SUKE?!
KLANK
KLANK
KLANK
KLANK
KLANK
RUN FOR IT!!
HUH?
THE AKUMA ARE COMING!
RUN!!
FWAP
KLANK
KLANK
KLANK
TMP

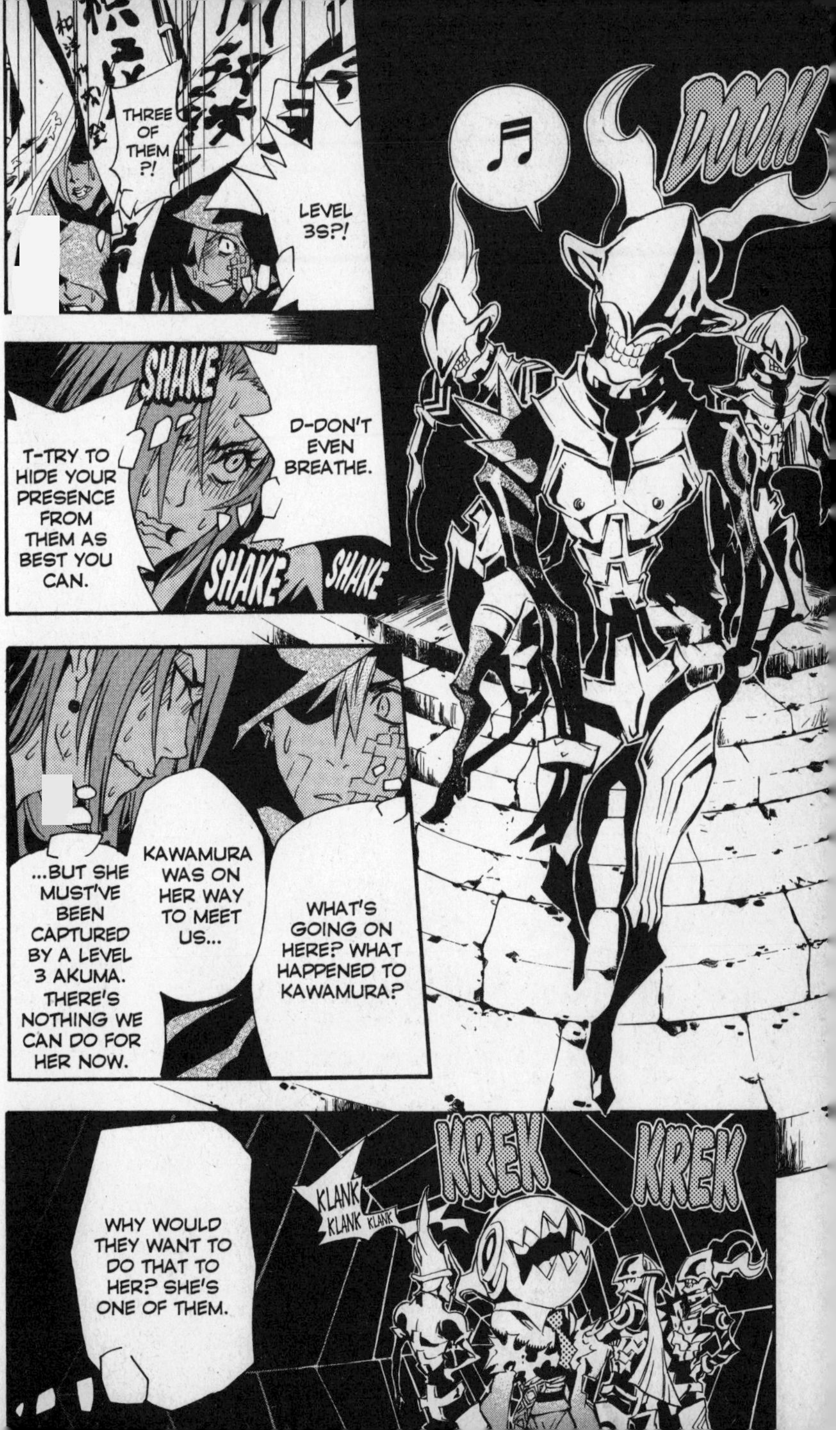
♫
DOOM
LEVEL 3S?!
THREE OF THEM ?!
D-DON'T EVEN BREATHE.
SHAKE
T-TRY TO HIDE YOUR PRESENCE FROM THEM AS BEST YOU CAN.
SHAKE
SHAKE
WHAT'S GOING ON HERE? WHAT HAPPENED TO KAWAMURA?
KAWAMURA WAS ON HER WAY TO MEET US...
...BUT SHE MUST'VE BEEN CAPTURED BY A LEVEL 3 AKUMA. THERE'S NOTHING WE CAN DO FOR HER NOW.
KREK
KREK
KLANK
KLANK
KLANK
WHY WOULD THEY WANT TO DO THAT TO HER? SHE'S ONE OF THEM.

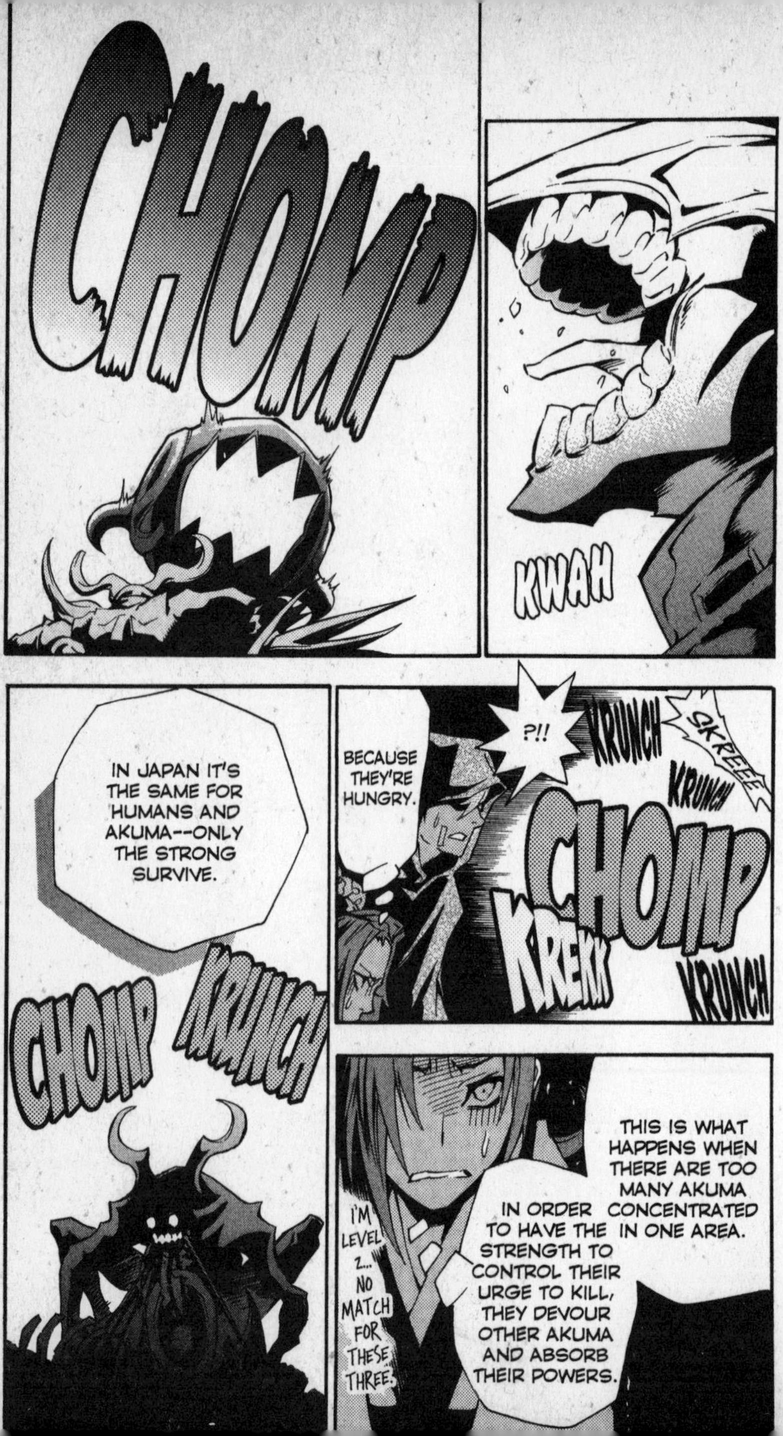
KWAH
CHOMP
SKREEE
KRUNCH
?!!
KRUNCH
BECAUSE THEY'RE HUNGRY.
CHOMP
KRUNCH
KREKK
THIS IS WHAT HAPPENS WHEN THERE ARE TOO MANY AKUMA CONCENTRATED IN ONE AREA.
IN ORDER TO HAVE THE STRENGTH TO CONTROL THEIR URGE TO KILL, THEY DEVOUR OTHER AKUMA AND ABSORB THEIR POWERS.
I'M LEVEL 2... NO MATCH FOR THESE THREE.
IN JAPAN IT'S THE SAME FOR HUMANS AND AKUMA--ONLY THE STRONG SURVIVE.
KRUNCH
CHOMP

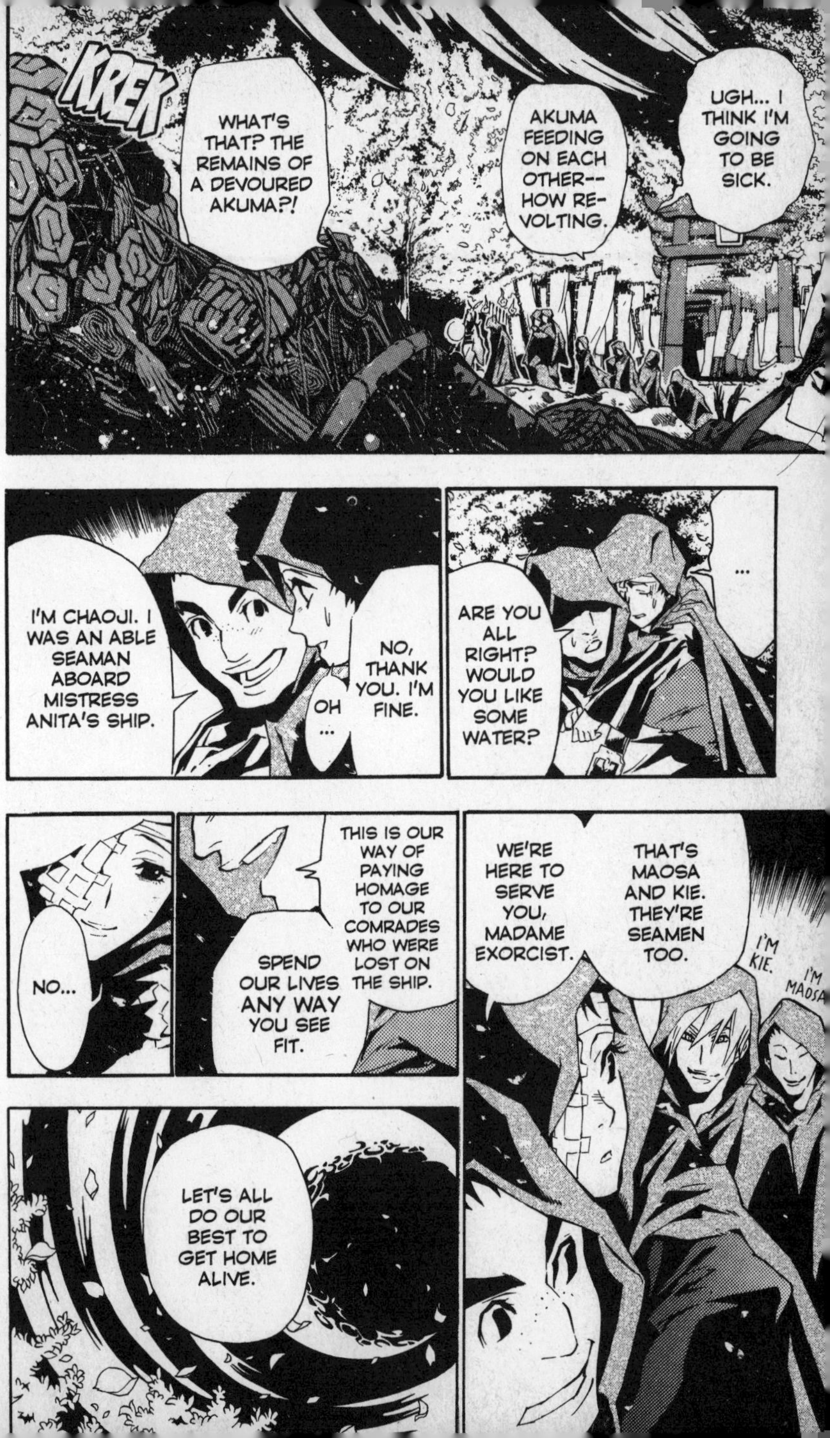
UGH... I THINK I'M GOING TO BE SICK.
AKUMA FEEDING ON EACH OTHER-- HOW RE-VOLTING.
WHAT'S THAT? THE REMAINS OF A DEVOURED AKUMA?!
KREK
...
ARE YOU ALL RIGHT? WOULD YOU LIKE SOME WATER?
NO, THANK YOU. I'M FINE.
OH ...
I'M CHAOJI. I WAS AN ABLE SEAMAN ABOARD MISTRESS ANITA'S SHIP.
THAT'S MAOSA AND KIE. THEY'RE SEAMEN TOO.
WE'RE HERE TO SERVE YOU, MADAME EXORCIST.
I'M KIE.
I'M MAOSA
THIS IS OUR WAY OF PAYING HOMAGE TO OUR COMRADES WHO WERE LOST ON THE SHIP.
SPEND OUR LIVES ANY WAY YOU SEE FIT.
NO...
LET'S ALL DO OUR BEST TO GET HOME ALIVE.

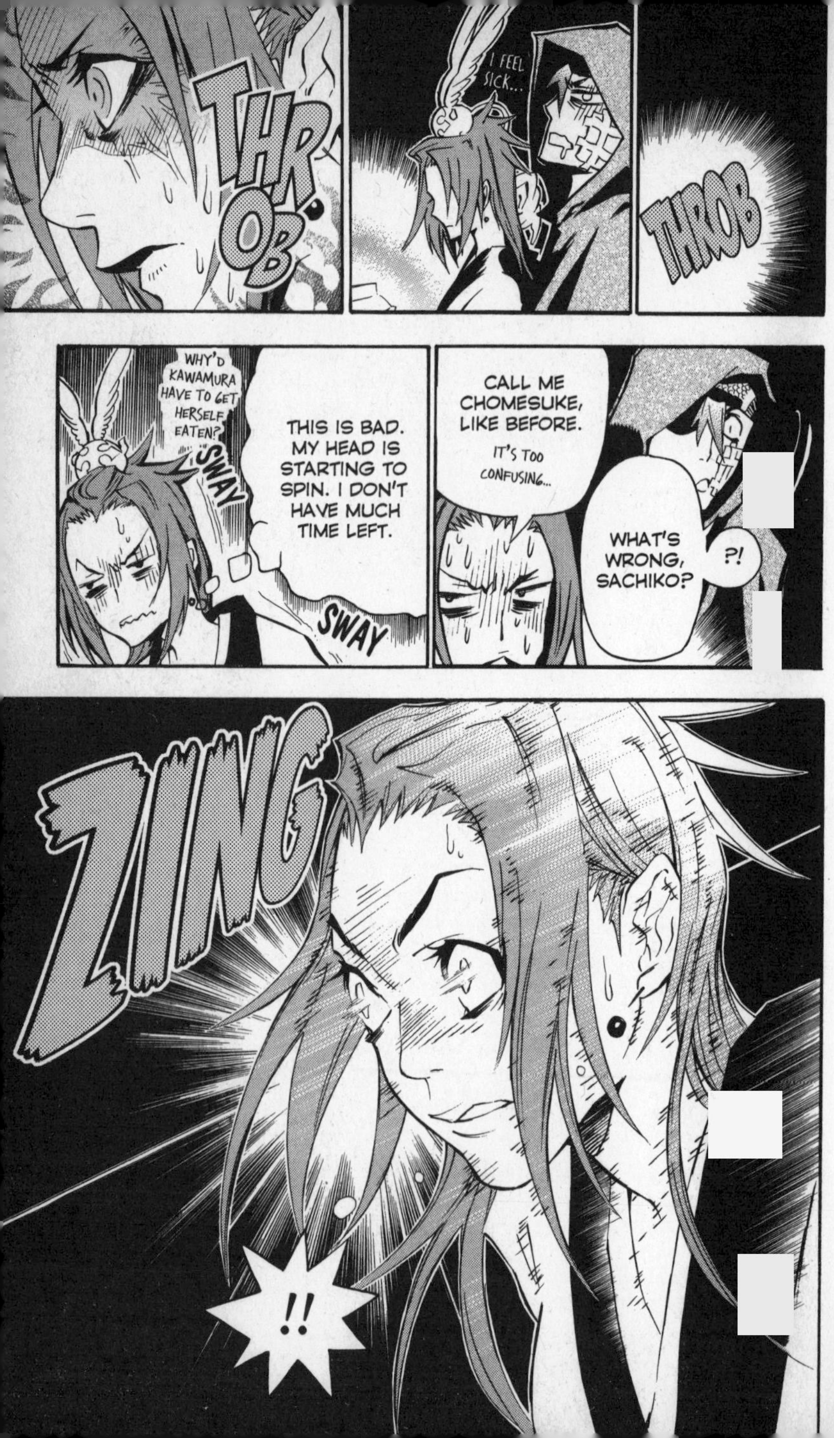
THROB
I FEEL SICK...
THROB
WHAT'S WRONG, SACHIKO?
?!
CALL ME CHOMESUKE, LIKE BEFORE.
IT'S TOO CONFUSING...
THIS IS BAD. MY HEAD IS STARTING TO SPIN. I DON'T HAVE MUCH TIME LEFT.
SWAY
WHY'D KAWAMURA HAVE TO GET HERSELF EATEN?
SWAY
ZIING
!!

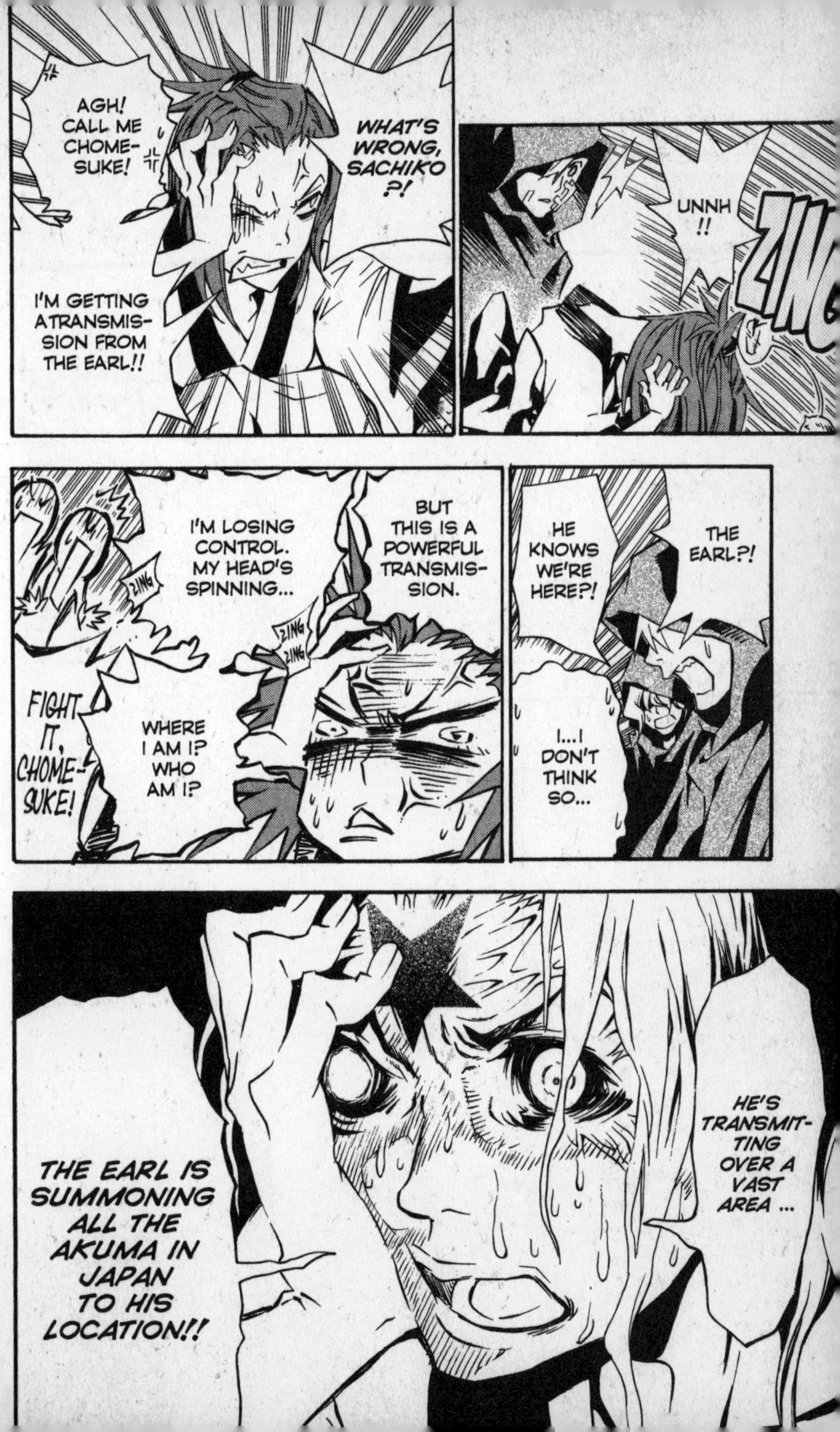
UNNH!!
ZING
WHAT'S WRONG, SACHIKO?!
AGH! CALL ME CHOME-SUKE!
I'M GETTING ATRANSMISSION FROM THE EARL!!
THE EARL?!
HE KNOWS WE'RE HERE?!
I...I DON'T THINK SO...
BUT THIS IS A POWERFUL TRANSMISSION.
I'M LOSING CONTROL. MY HEAD'S SPINNING...
ZING
ZING ZING
WHERE I AM I? WHO AM I?
FIGHT IT, CHOME-SUKE!
HE'S TRANSMITTING OVER A VAST AREA ...
THE EARL IS SUMMONING ALL THE AKUMA IN JAPAN TO HIS LOCATION!!

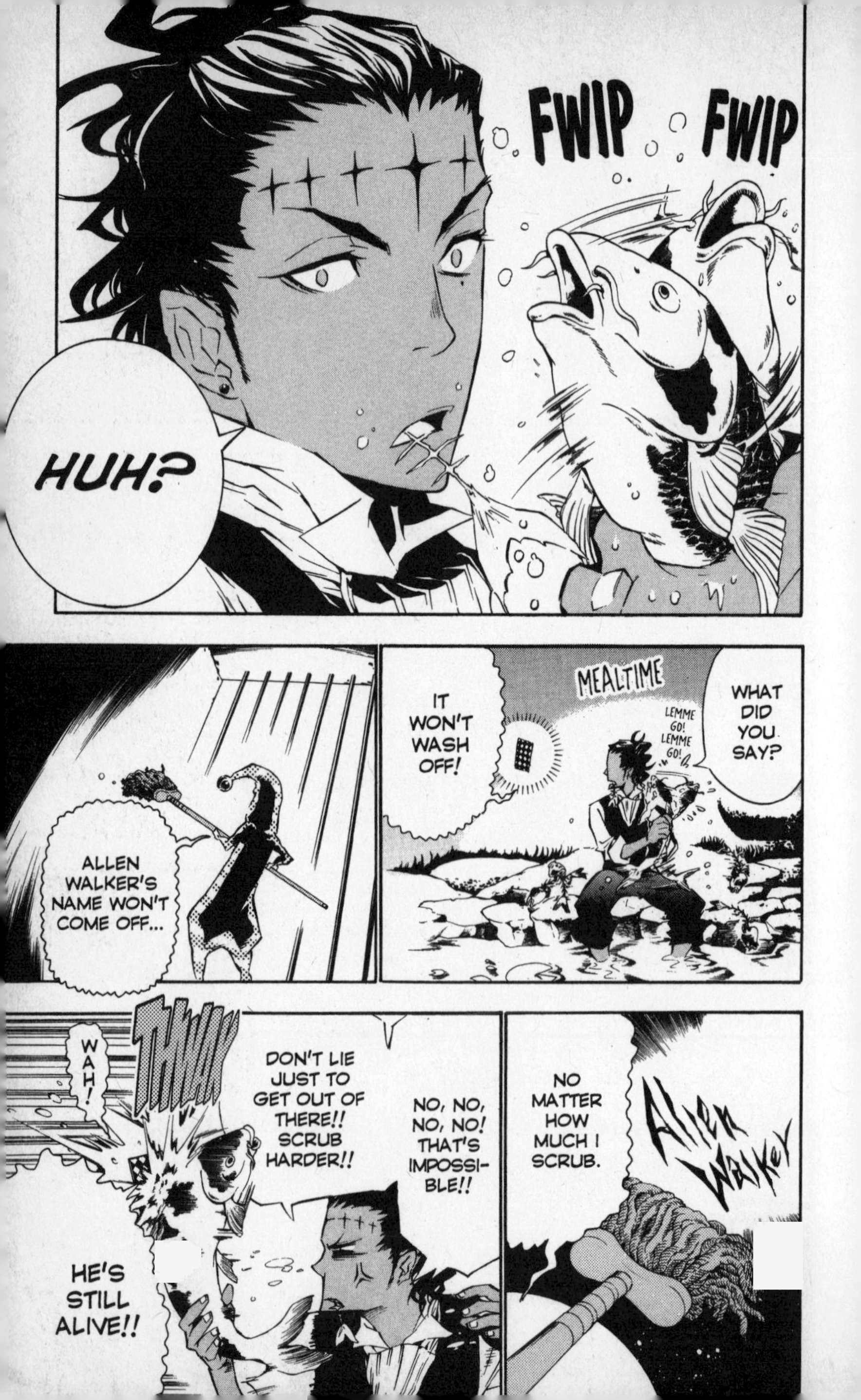
FWIP FWIP
HUH?
WHAT DID YOU SAY?
LEMME GO! LEMME GO!
MEALTIME
IT WON'T WASH OFF!
ALLEN WALKER'S NAME WON'T COME OFF...
NO MATTER HOW MUCH I SCRUB.
Allen Walker
NO, NO, NO, NO! THAT'S IMPOSSIBLE!!
DON'T LIE JUST TO GET OUT OF THERE!! SCRUB HARDER!!
THWAK
WAH!
HE'S STILL ALIVE!!

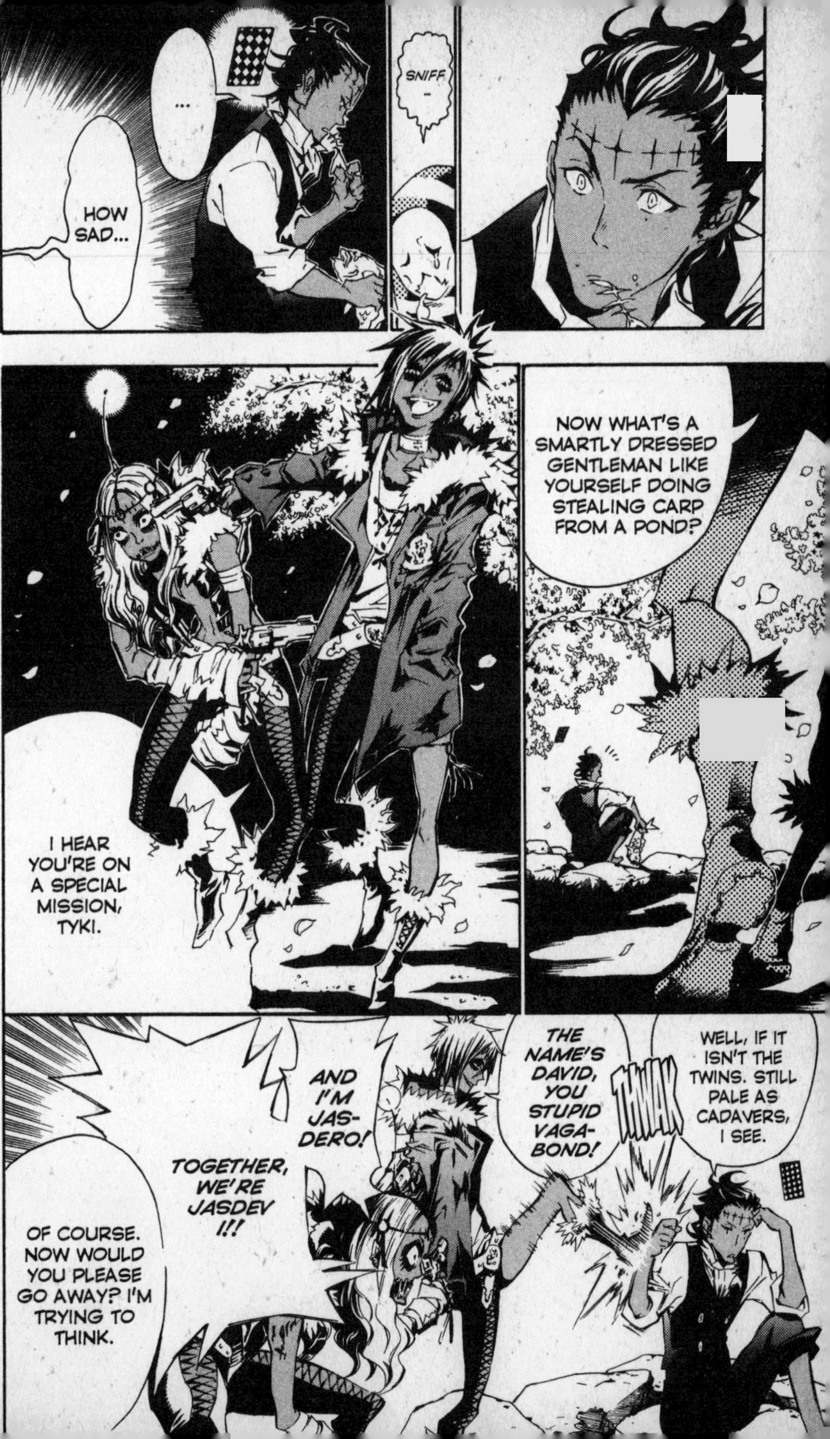
SNIFF –
...
HOW SAD...
NOW WHAT'S A SMARTLY DRESSED GENTLEMAN LIKE YOURSELF DOING STEALING CARP FROM A POND?
I HEAR YOU'RE ON A SPECIAL MISSION, TYKI.
WELL, IF IT ISN'T THE TWINS. STILL PALE AS CADAVERS, I SEE.
THWAK
THE NAME'S DAVID, YOU STUPID VAGA-BOND!
AND I'M JAS-DERO!
TOGETHER, WE'RE JASDEV I!!
OF COURSE. NOW WOULD YOU PLEASE GO AWAY? I'M TRYING TO THINK.

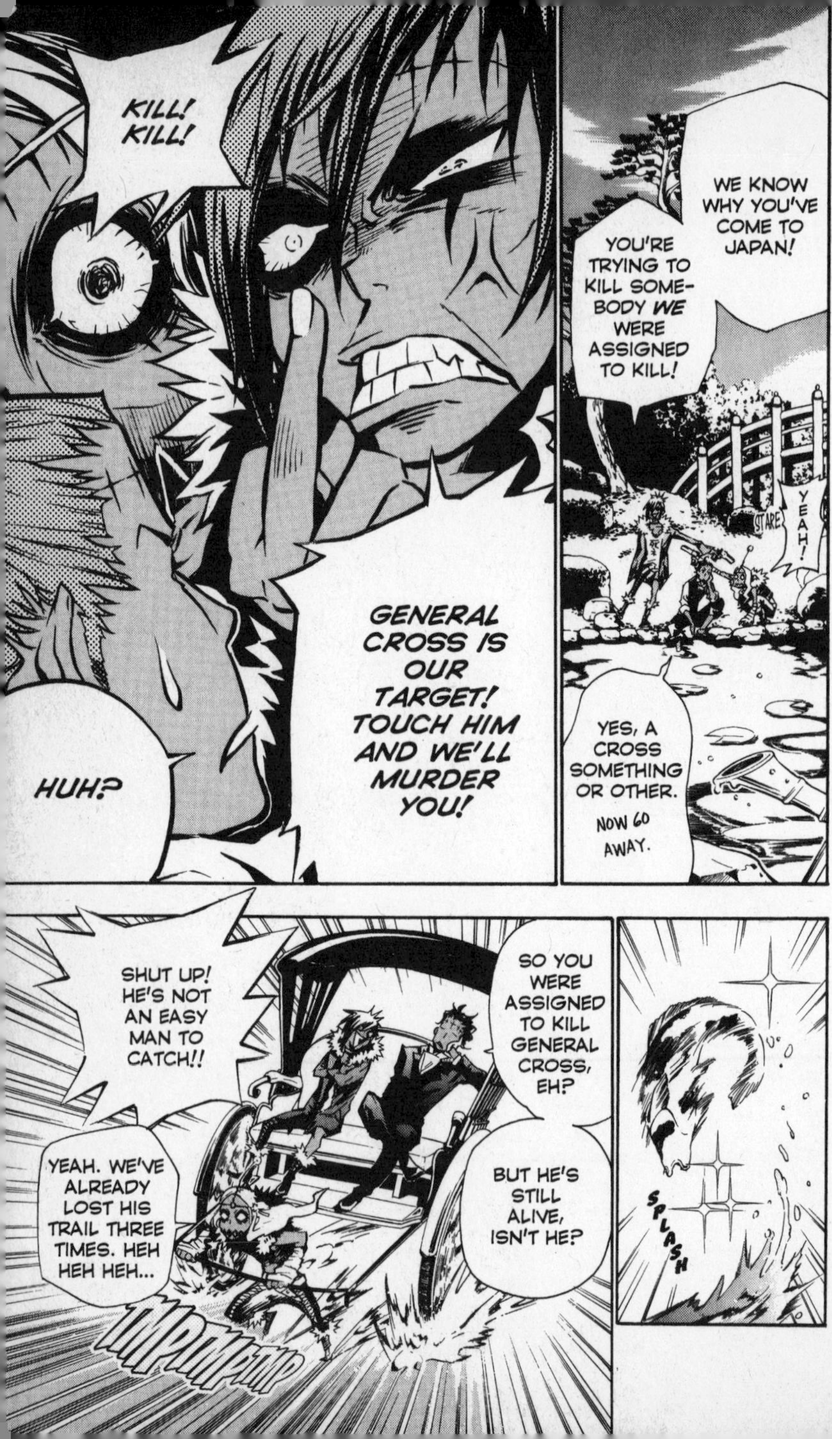
WE KNOW WHY YOU'VE COME TO JAPAN!
YOU'RE TRYING TO KILL SOMEBODY WE WERE ASSIGNED TO KILL!
YEAH!
STARE
YES, A CROSS SOMETHING OR OTHER.
NOW GO AWAY.
KILL! KILL!
GENERAL CROSS IS OUR TARGET! TOUCH HIM AND WE'LL MURDER YOU!
HUH?
SPLASH
SO YOU WERE ASSIGNED TO KILL GENERAL CROSS, EH?
SHUT UP! HE'S NOT AN EASY MAN TO CATCH!!
BUT HE'S STILL ALIVE, ISN'T HE?
YEAH. WE'VE ALREADY LOST HIS TRAIL THREE TIMES. HEH HEH HEH...

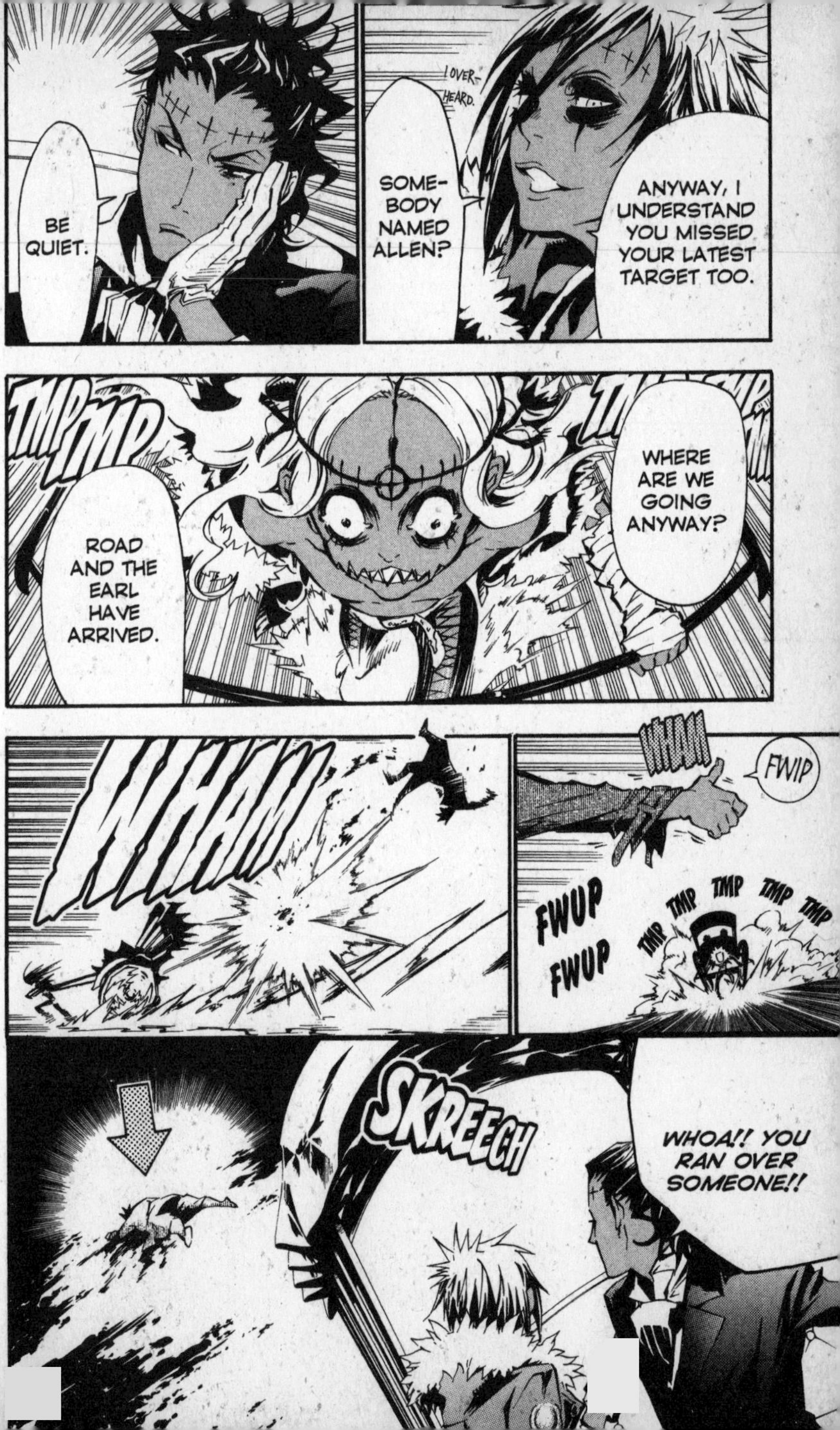
ANYWAY, I UNDERSTAND YOU MISSED YOUR LATEST TARGET TOO.
SOME-BODY NAMED ALLEN?
I OVER-HEARD.
BE QUIET.
WHERE ARE WE GOING ANYWAY?
ROAD AND THE EARL HAVE ARRIVED.
TMPTMP
WHAM
FWIP
FWUP
FWUP
TMP TMP TMP TMP TMP
WHAM
WHOA!! YOU RAN OVER SOMEONE!!
SKREECH

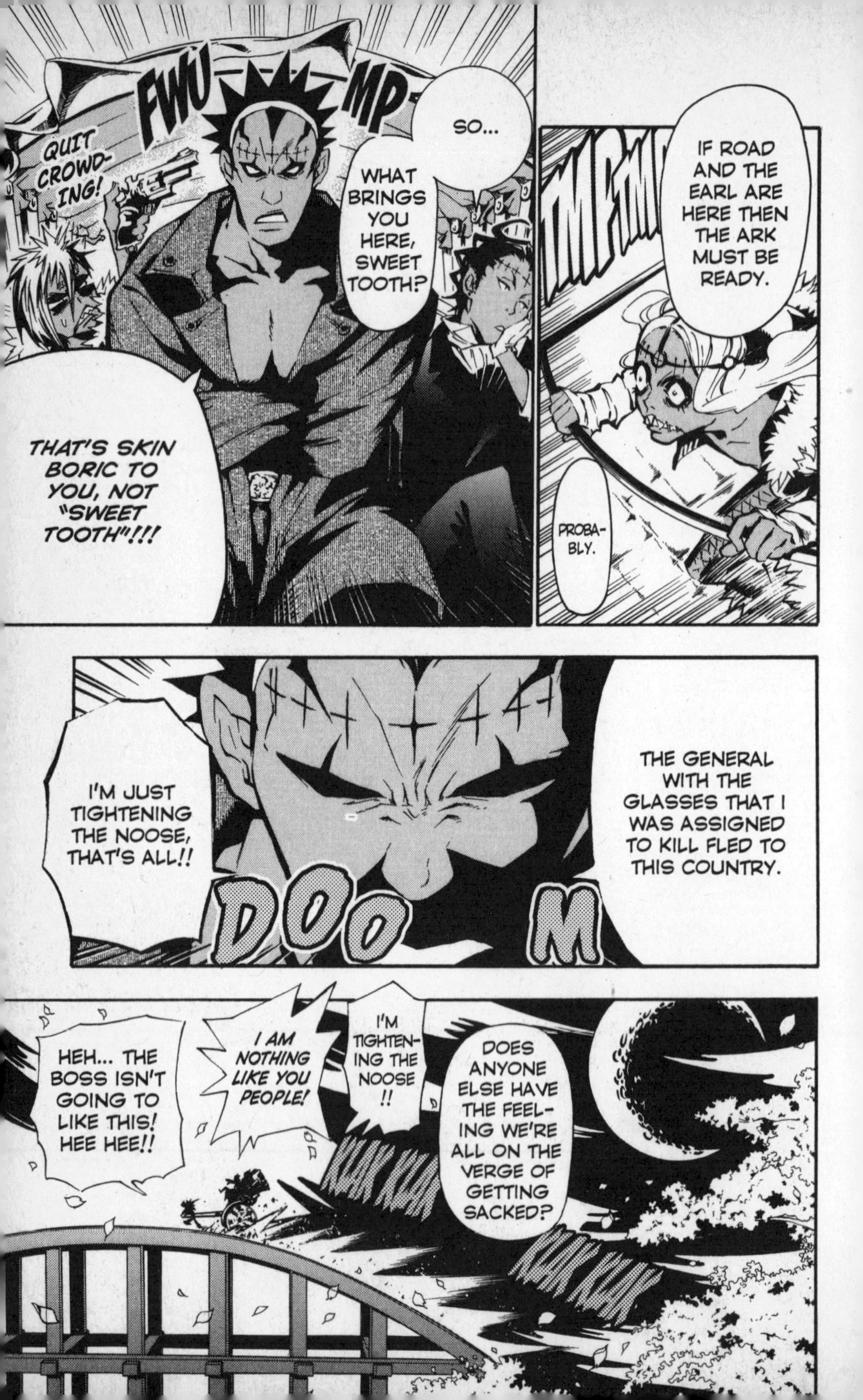
IF ROAD AND THE EARL ARE HERE THEN THE ARK MUST BE READY.
PROBABLY.
SO...
WHAT BRINGS YOU HERE, SWEET TOOTH?
FWUMP
QUIT CROWDING!
THAT'S SKIN BORIC TO YOU, NOT "SWEET TOOTH"!!!
THE GENERAL WITH THE GLASSES THAT I WAS ASSIGNED TO KILL FLED TO THIS COUNTRY.
DOOM
I'M JUST TIGHTENING THE NOOSE, THAT'S ALL!!
DOES ANYONE ELSE HAVE THE FEELING WE'RE ALL ON THE VERGE OF GETTING SACKED?
I'M TIGHTENING THE NOOSE!!
I AM NOTHING LIKE YOU PEOPLE!
HEH... THE BOSS ISN'T GOING TO LIKE THIS! HEE HEE!!

KOMUI'S DISCUSSION ROOM SPECIAL EDITION: NOAH'S ARK, VOL. 1

GOOD EVENING, EVERYONE.♥ THIS IS D. GRAY-MAN'S PORTLY AND LOVEABLE MILLENNIUM EARL.♥ TODAY WE'RE GOING TO ANSWER SOME QUESTIONS REGARDING THE CLAN OF NOAH IN THIS SPECIAL FORUM WE CALL "NOAH'S ARK."♥ GET TO IT, MY DEAR MINIONS.♥

Q: WHY DOES EVERYTHING THE MILLENNIUM EARL SAYS END WITH A HEART?
(TYKI) HUH? WHERE'D THE EARL GO?
(ROAD) HE WENT SHOPPING. WE'RE HAVING HAMBURGERS TONIGHT.
(JASDERO) HEE HEE! THE BOSS IS THE BEST!!
(DAVID) BUT THAT MEANS WE'LL HAVE TO DO THIS OURSELVES! IT'S TOO HARD! TAKE CHARGE, TYKI, YOU'RE THE GROWNUP HERE.
(TYKI) WHAT ABOUT SWEET TOOTH?
(ROAD) HE DOESN'T HAVE THE BRAINS FOR IT, DAVID.
(EVERYBODY BUT TYKI) GA HA HA HA HA HA!!
(ROAD) THE HEARTS ARE THE EARL'S TRADEMARK. HEY, WHERE ARE YOU GOING, TYKI?
(TYKI) CAN I GO HOME NOW?
(ROAD) NO, YOU CAN'T.♡

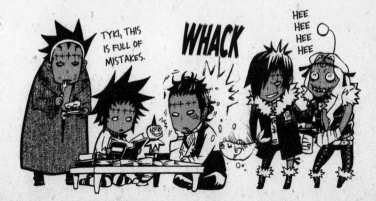

HEE HEE HEE HEE
WHACK
TYKI, THIS IS FULL OF MISTAKES.

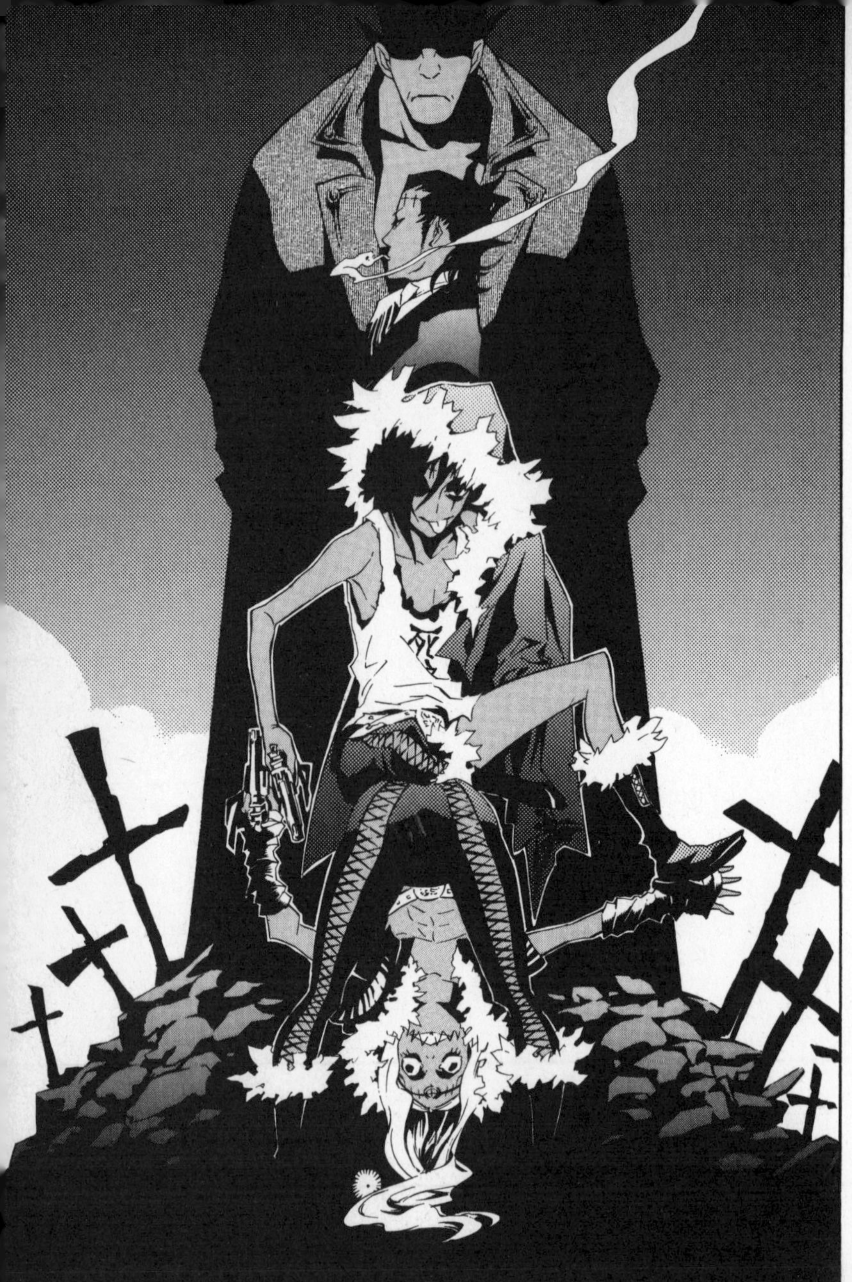

THE 78TH NIGHT: THE JUDGMENT

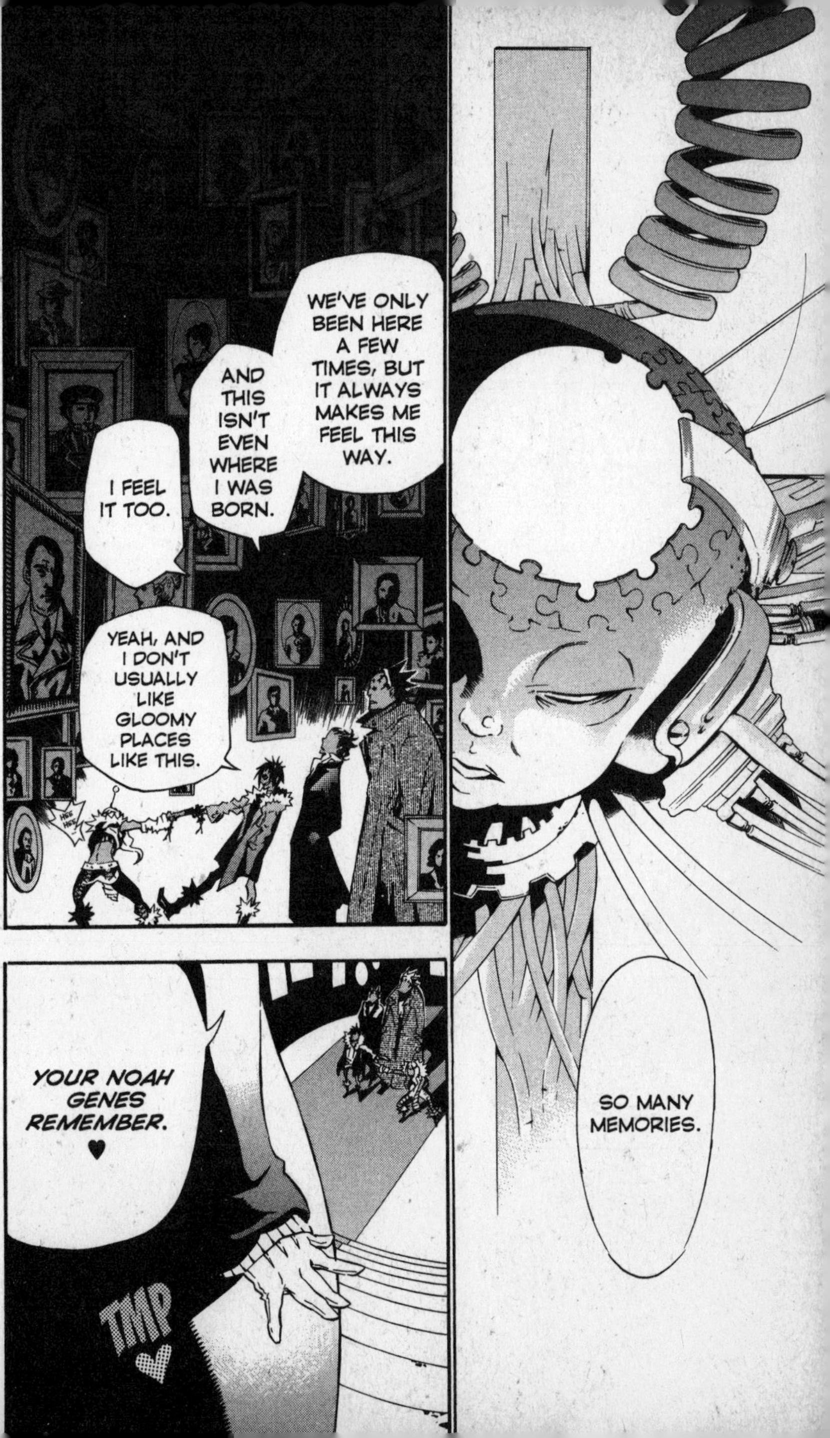
SO MANY MEMORIES.
WE'VE ONLY BEEN HERE A FEW TIMES, BUT IT ALWAYS MAKES ME FEEL THIS WAY.
AND THIS ISN'T EVEN WHERE I WAS BORN.
I FEEL IT TOO.
YEAH, AND I DON'T USUALLY LIKE GLOOMY PLACES LIKE THIS.
HEE HEE
YOUR NOAH GENES REMEMBER. ♥
TMP ♥

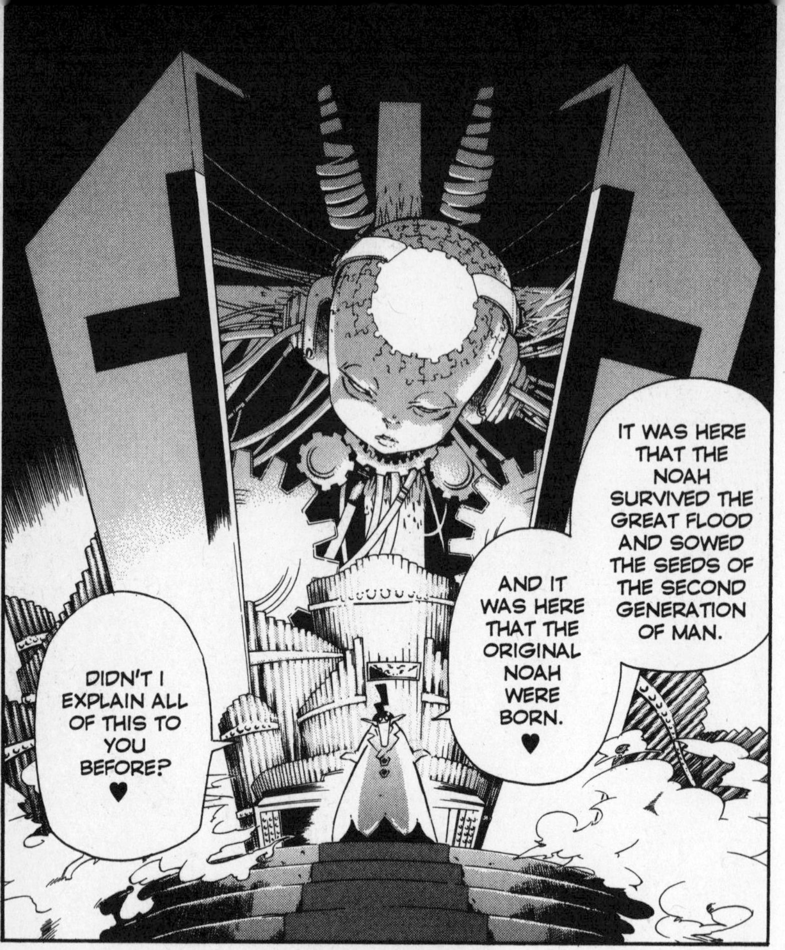
IT WAS HERE THAT THE NOAH SURVIVED THE GREAT FLOOD AND SOWED THE SEEDS OF THE SECOND GENERATION OF MAN.
AND IT WAS HERE THAT THE ORIGINAL NOAH WERE BORN. ♥
DIDN'T I EXPLAIN ALL OF THIS TO YOU BEFORE? ♥

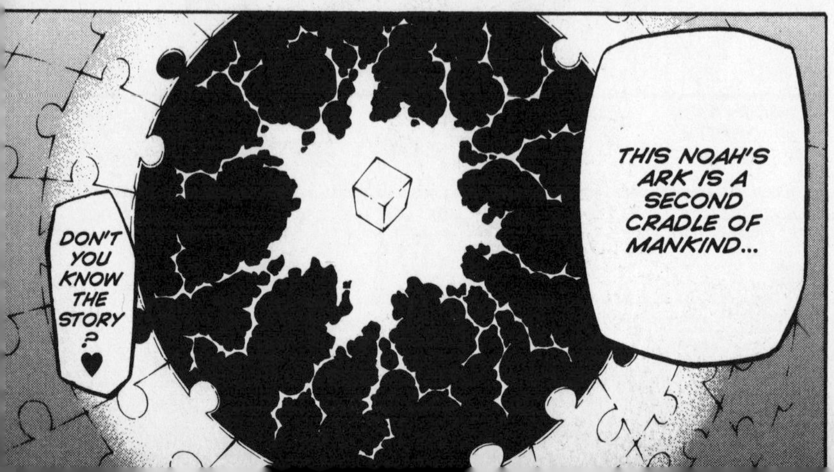
THIS NOAH'S ARK IS A SECOND CRADLE OF MANKIND...
DON'T YOU KNOW THE STORY? ♥

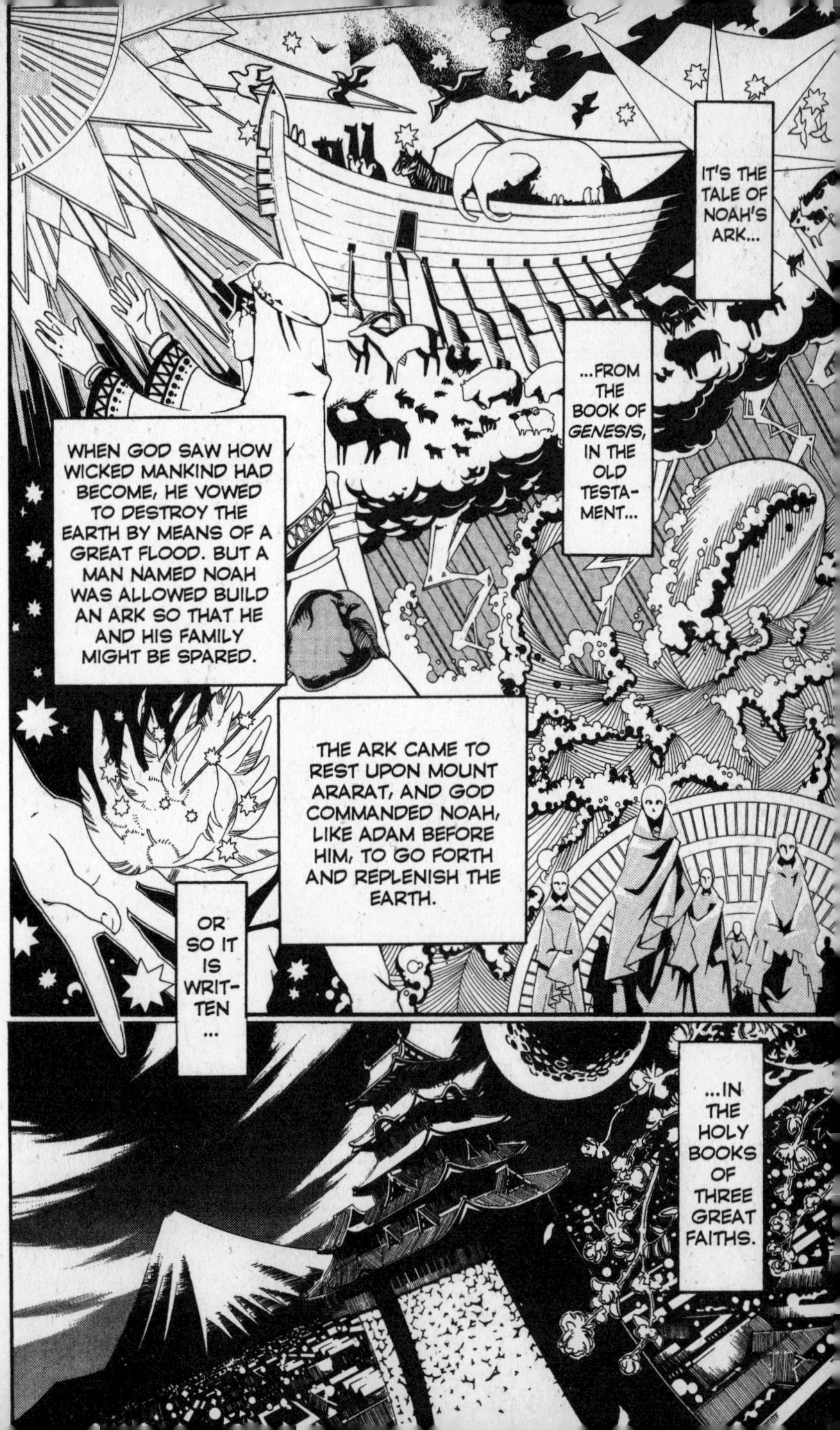
IT'S THE TALE OF NOAH'S ARK...
...FROM THE BOOK OF *GENESIS*, IN THE OLD TESTAMENT...
WHEN GOD SAW HOW WICKED MANKIND HAD BECOME, HE VOWED TO DESTROY THE EARTH BY MEANS OF A GREAT FLOOD. BUT A MAN NAMED NOAH WAS ALLOWED BUILD AN ARK SO THAT HE AND HIS FAMILY MIGHT BE SPARED.
THE ARK CAME TO REST UPON MOUNT ARARAT, AND GOD COMMANDED NOAH, LIKE ADAM BEFORE HIM, TO GO FORTH AND REPLENISH THE EARTH.
OR SO IT IS WRITTEN...
...IN THE HOLY BOOKS OF THREE GREAT FAITHS.

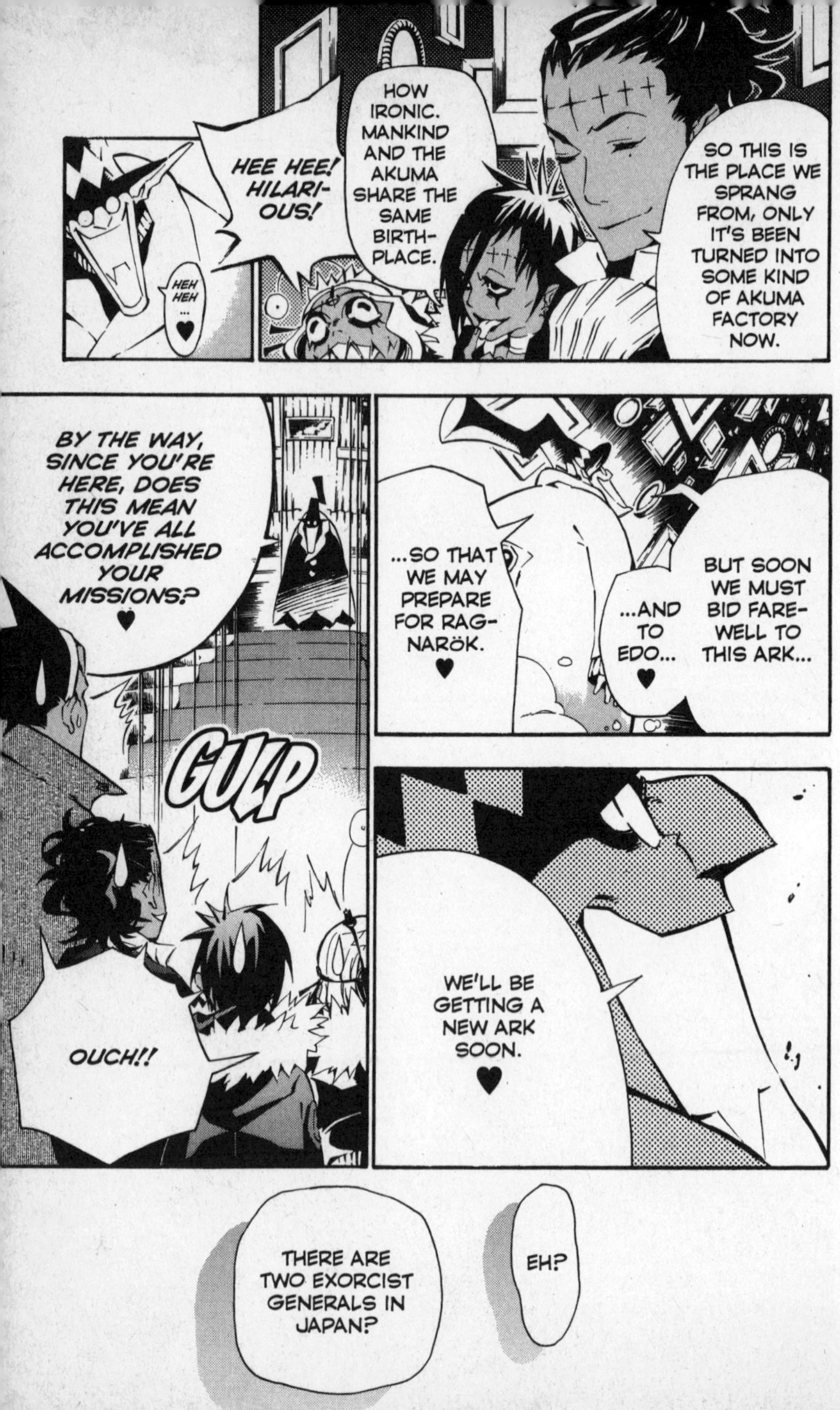
SO THIS IS THE PLACE WE SPRANG FROM, ONLY IT'S BEEN TURNED INTO SOME KIND OF AKUMA FACTORY NOW.
HOW IRONIC. MANKIND AND THE AKUMA SHARE THE SAME BIRTH-PLACE.
HEE HEE! HILARI-OUS!
HEH HEH ... ♥
BUT SOON WE MUST BID FARE-WELL TO THIS ARK...
...AND TO EDO... ♥
...SO THAT WE MAY PREPARE FOR RAG-NARÖK. ♥
WE'LL BE GETTING A NEW ARK SOON. ♥
BY THE WAY, SINCE YOU'RE HERE, DOES THIS MEAN YOU'VE ALL ACCOMPLISHED YOUR MISSIONS? ♥
GULP
OUCH!!
EH?
THERE ARE TWO EXORCIST GENERALS IN JAPAN?

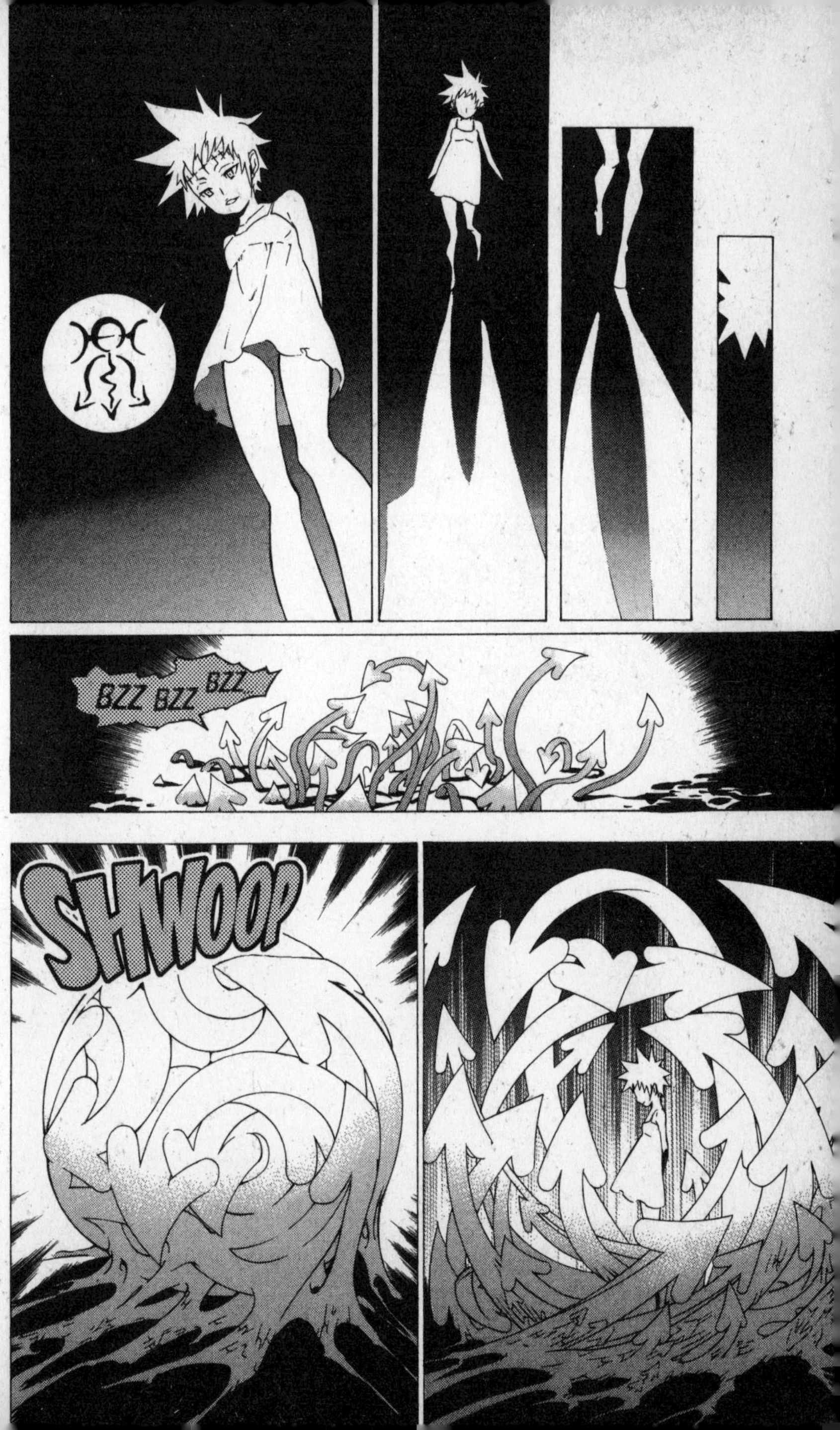
BZZ BZZ BZZ
SHWOOP

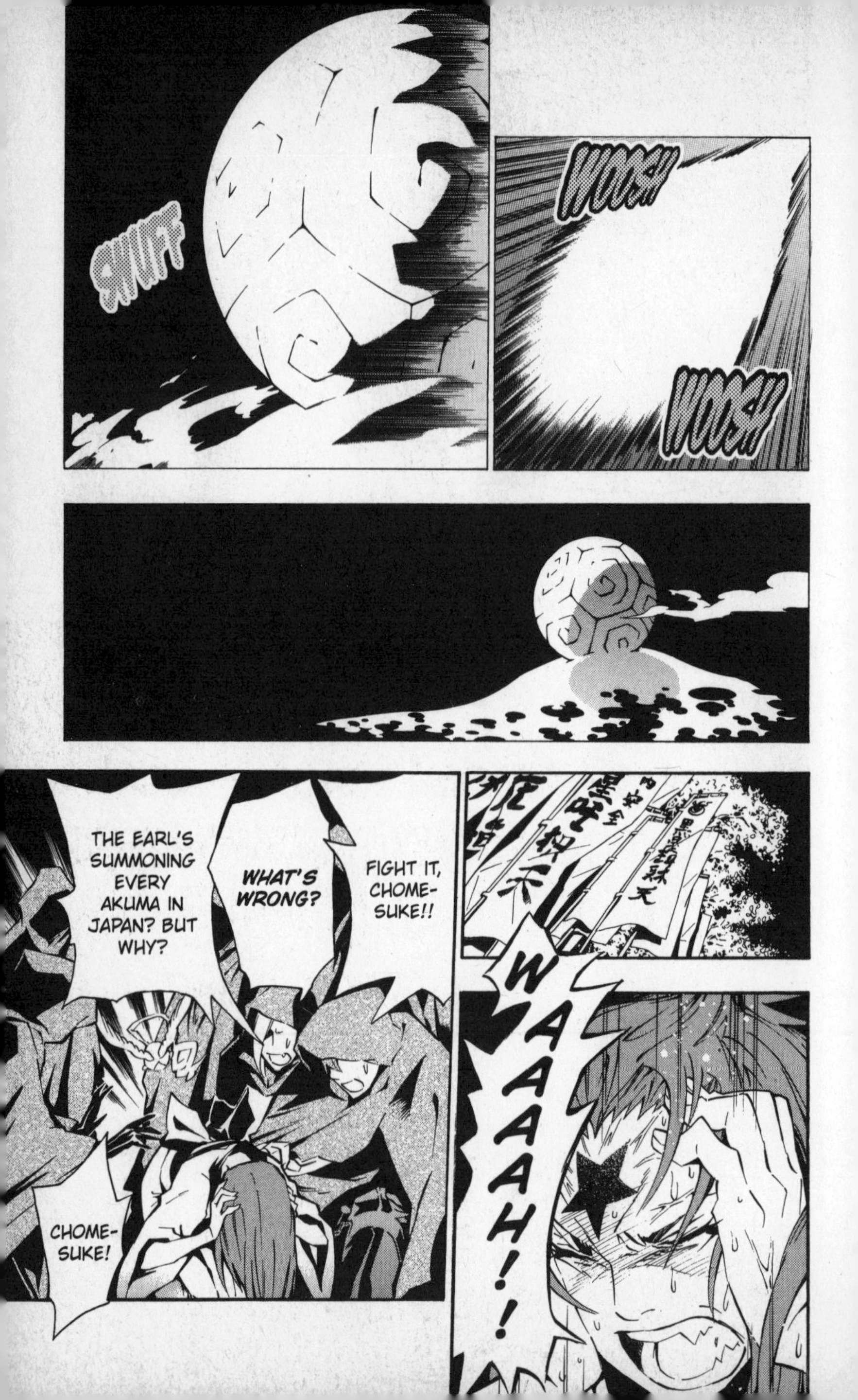
WOOSH
WOOSH
SNIFF
WAAAAAH!!!
FIGHT IT, CHOME-SUKE!!
WHAT'S WRONG?
THE EARL'S SUMMONING EVERY AKUMA IN JAPAN? BUT WHY?
CHOME-SUKE!

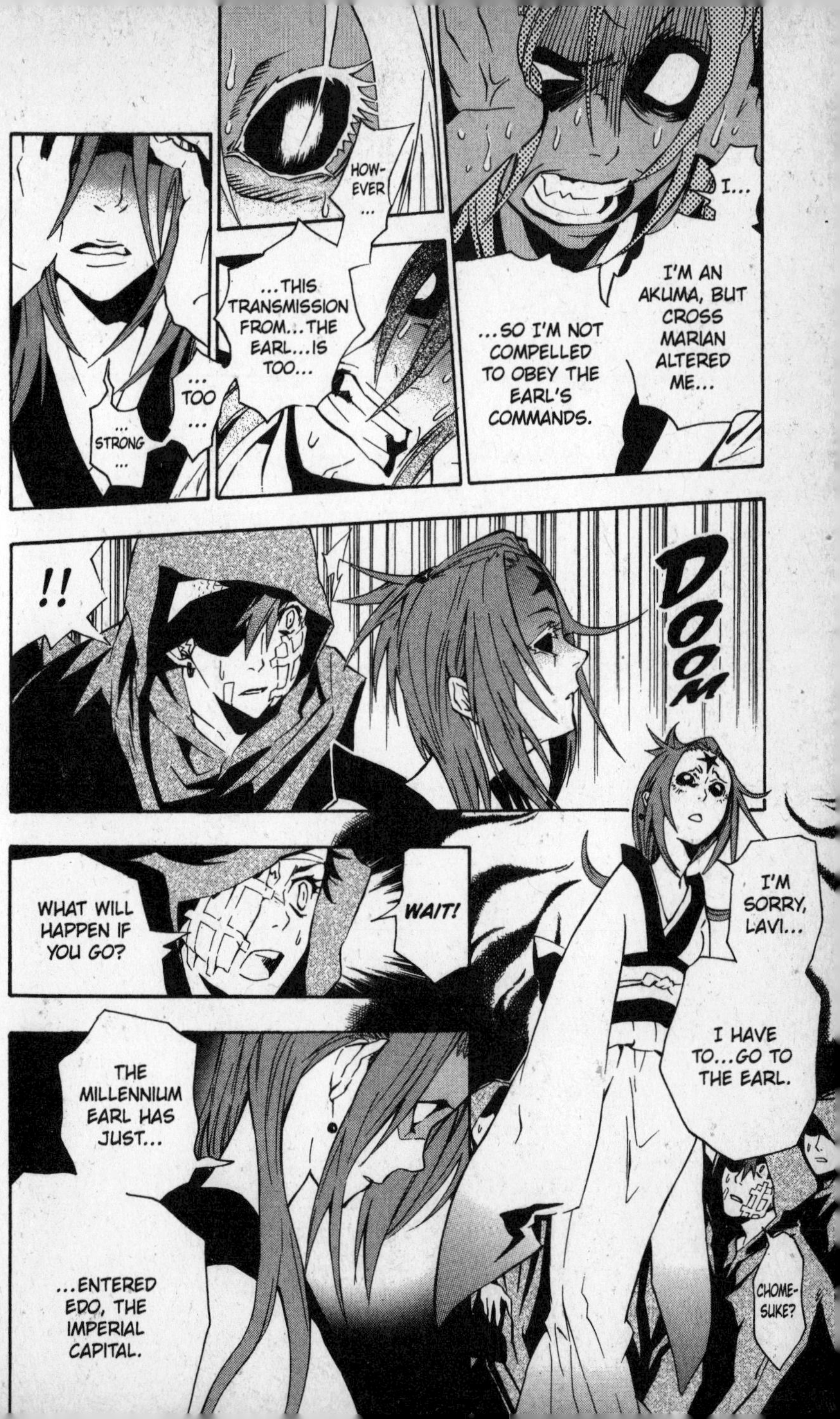
I...
I'M AN AKUMA, BUT CROSS MARIAN ALTERED ME...
...SO I'M NOT COMPELLED TO OBEY THE EARL'S COMMANDS.
HOW-EVER...
...THIS TRANSMISSION FROM...THE EARL...IS TOO...
...TOO...
...STRONG...
DOOM
!!
I'M SORRY, LAVI...
I HAVE TO...GO TO THE EARL.
WAIT!
WHAT WILL HAPPEN IF YOU GO?
CHOME-SUKE?
THE MILLENNIUM EARL HAS JUST...
...ENTERED EDO, THE IMPERIAL CAPITAL.

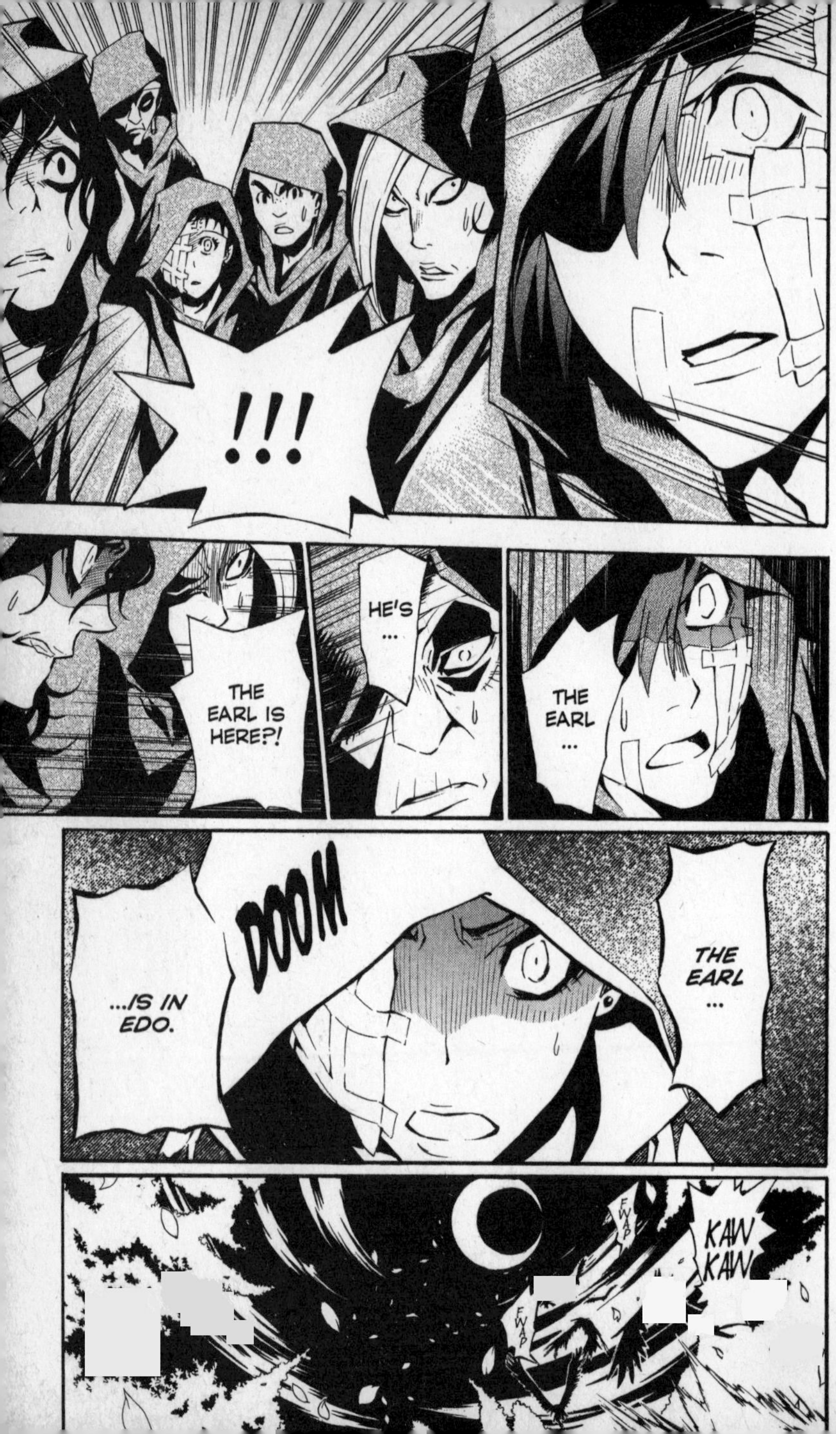
!!!
THE EARL ...
HE'S ...
THE EARL IS HERE?!
THE EARL ...
DOOM
...IS IN EDO.
KAW KAW
FWAP
FWAP

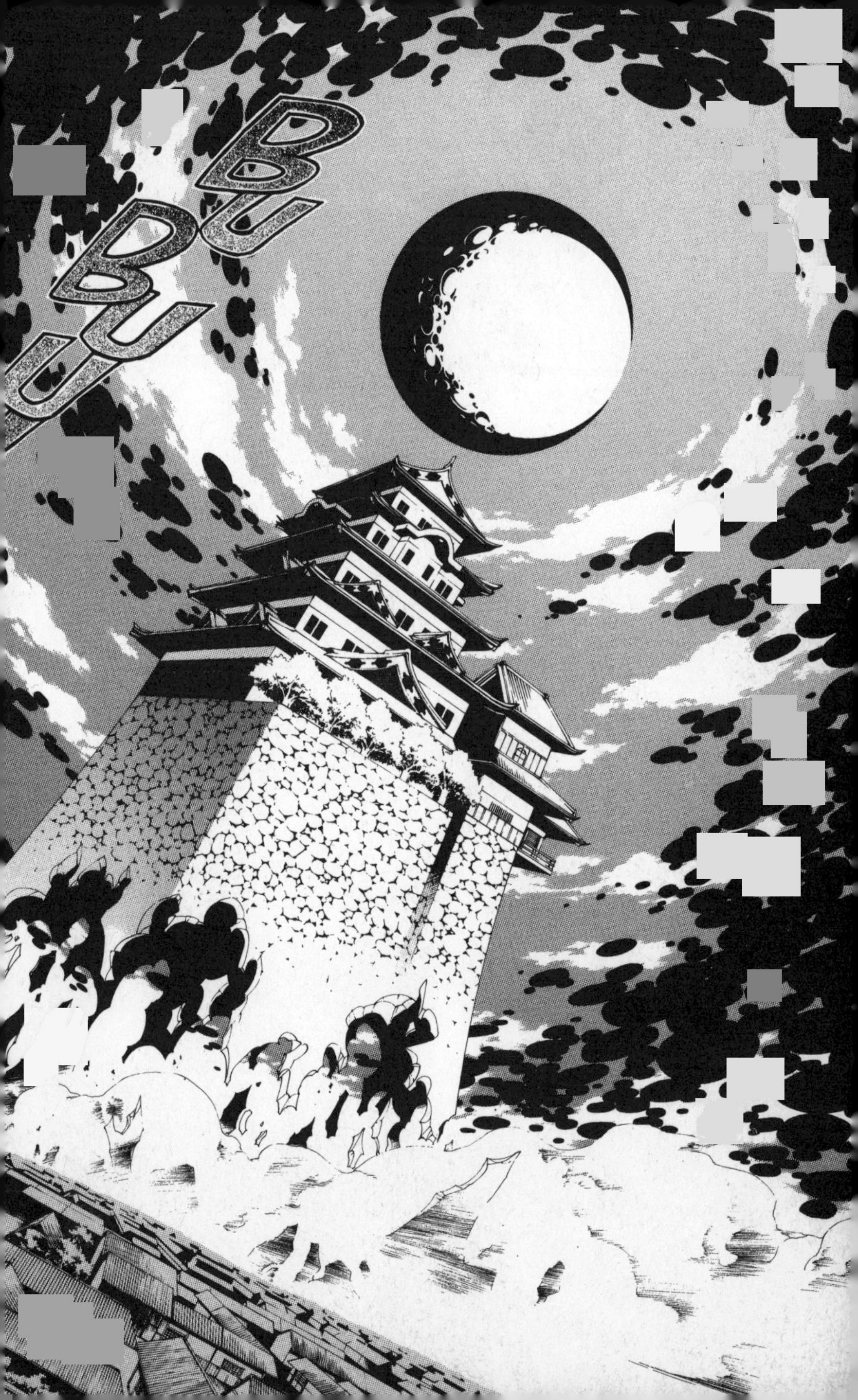
BUBU

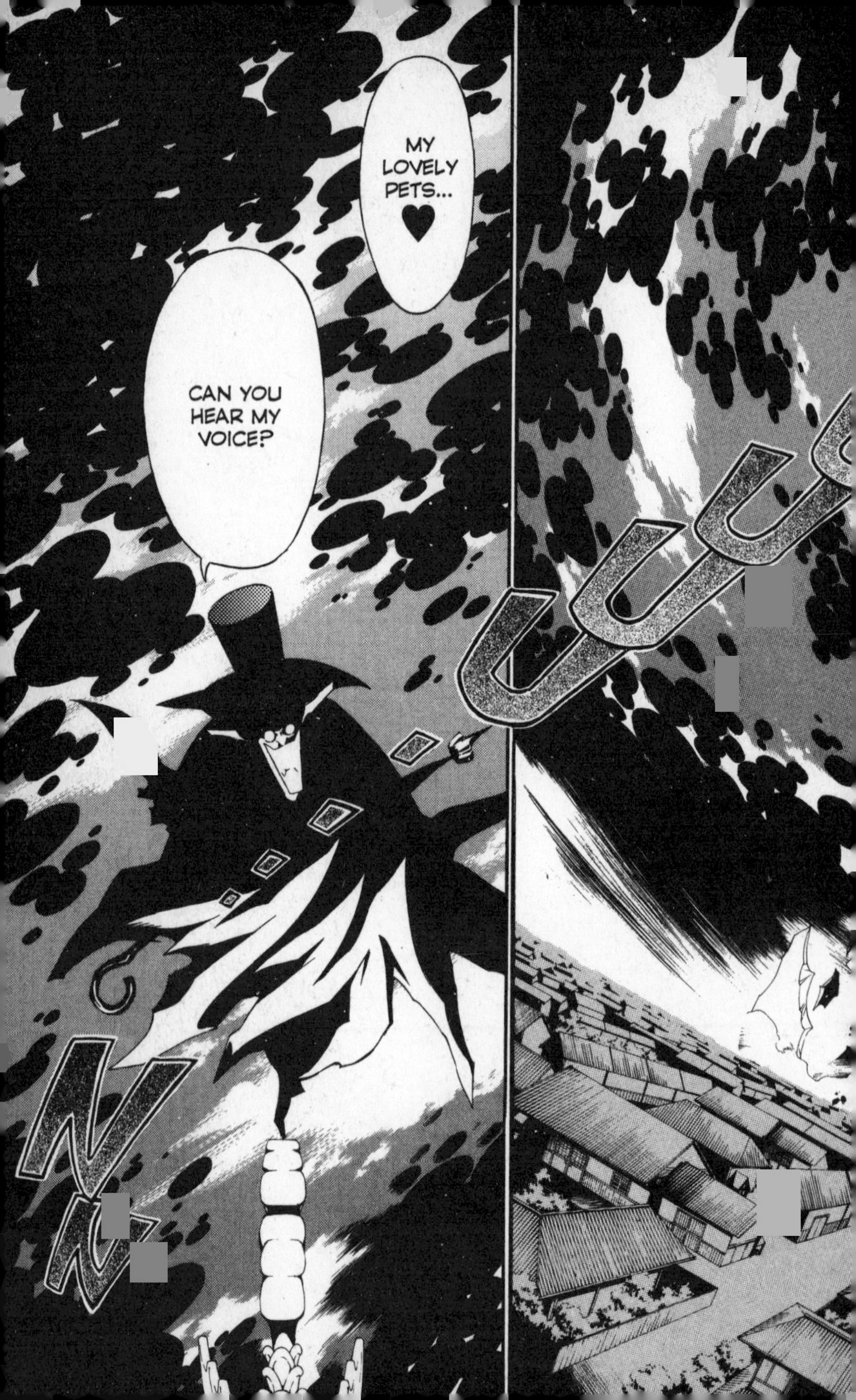
MY LOVELY PETS... ♥
CAN YOU HEAR MY VOICE?

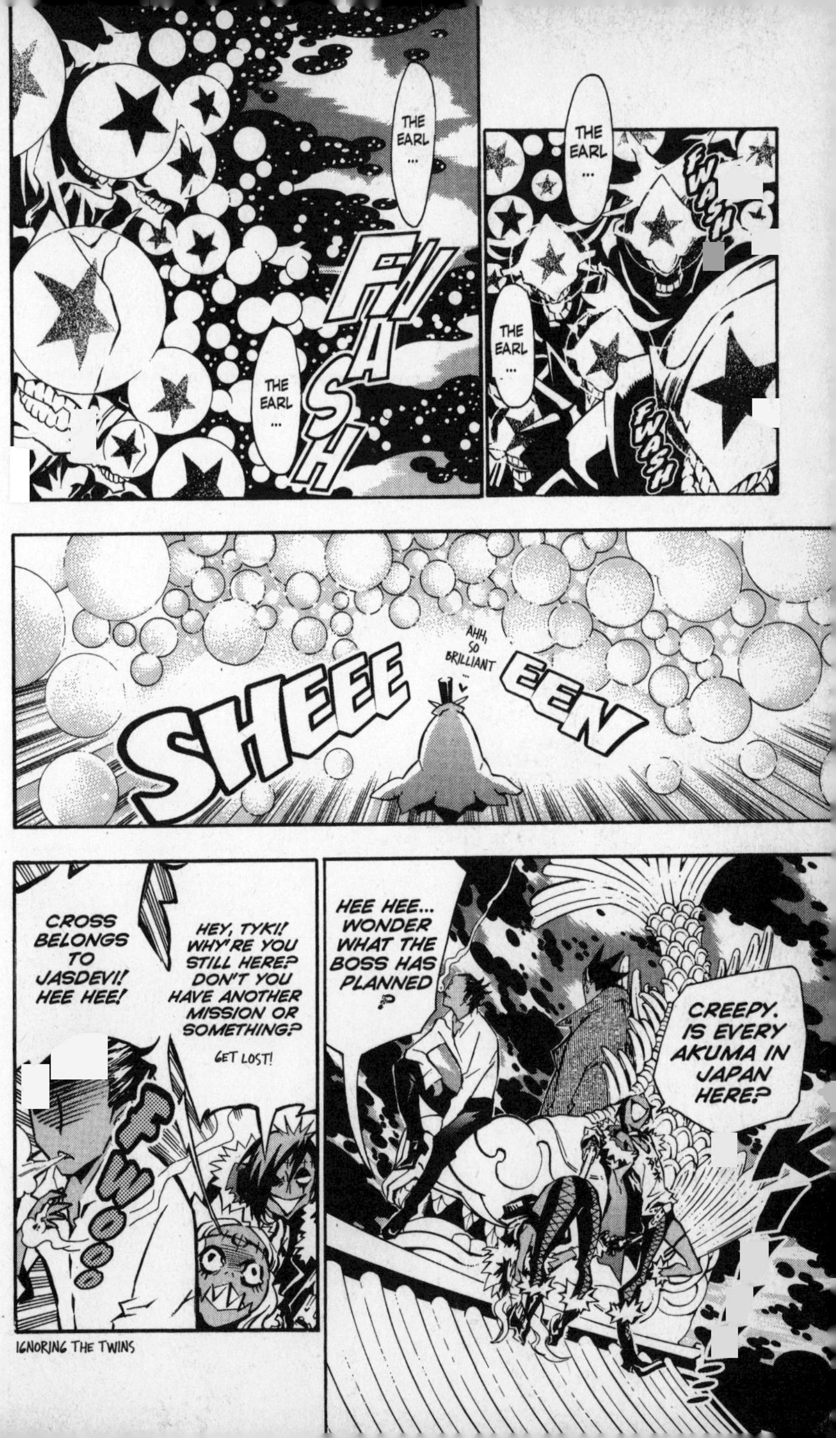
THE EARL...
FWASH
THE EARL...
FWASH
THE EARL...
FWASH
THE EARL...
AHH, SO BRILLIANT...
SHEEE EEN
CREEPY. IS EVERY AKUMA IN JAPAN HERE?
HEE HEE... WONDER WHAT THE BOSS HAS PLANNED?
HEY, TYKI! WHY'RE YOU STILL HERE? DON'T YOU HAVE ANOTHER MISSION OR SOMETHING?
GET LOST!
CROSS BELONGS TO JASDEVI! HEE HEE!
IGNORING THE TWINS

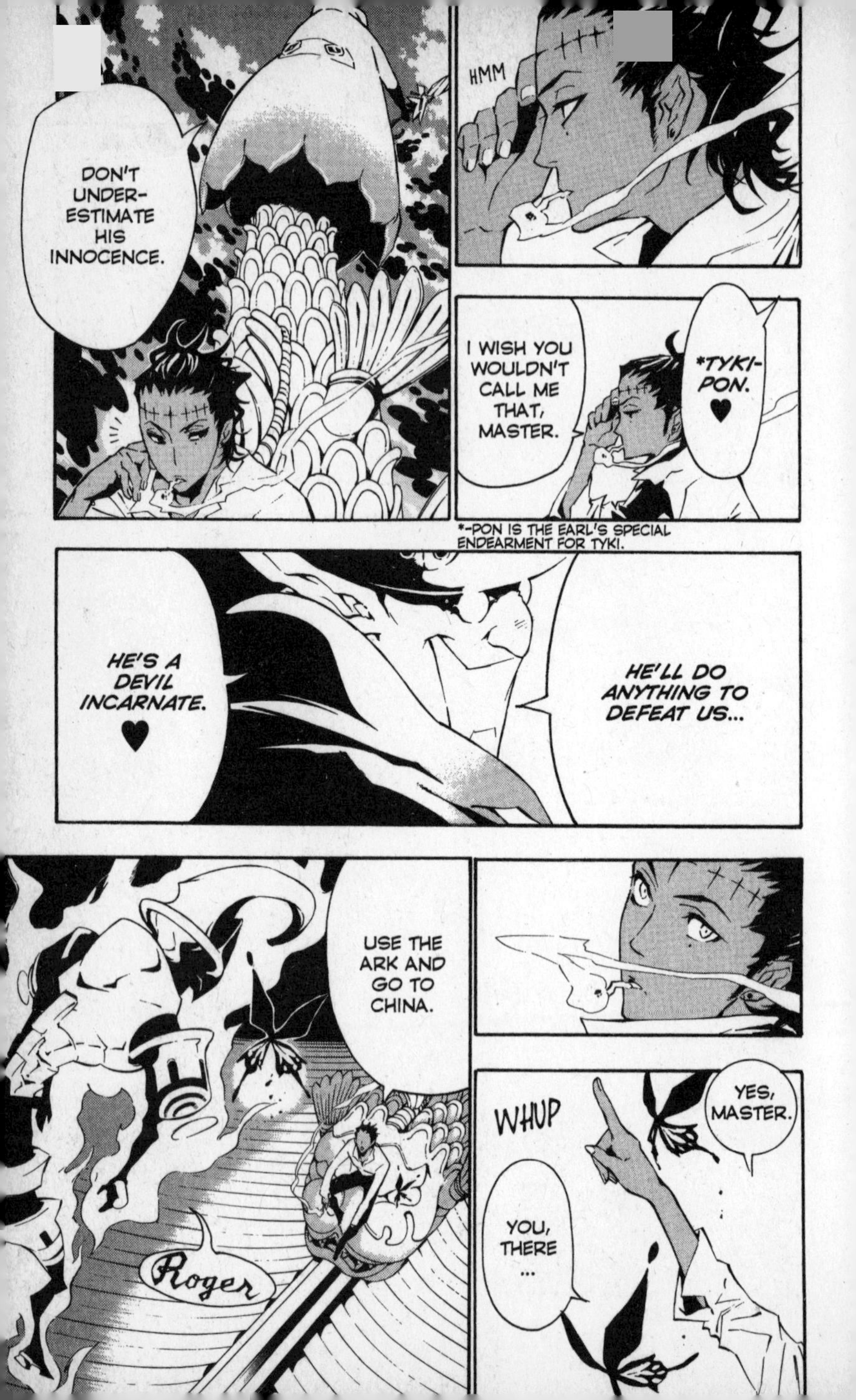
HMM
*TYKI-PON. ♥
I WISH YOU WOULDN'T CALL ME THAT, MASTER.
DON'T UNDER-ESTIMATE HIS INNOCENCE.
HE'LL DO ANYTHING TO DEFEAT US...
HE'S A DEVIL INCARNATE. ♥
YES, MASTER.
WHUP
YOU, THERE ...
USE THE ARK AND GO TO CHINA.
Roger

*-PON IS THE EARL'S SPECIAL ENDEARMENT FOR TYKI.

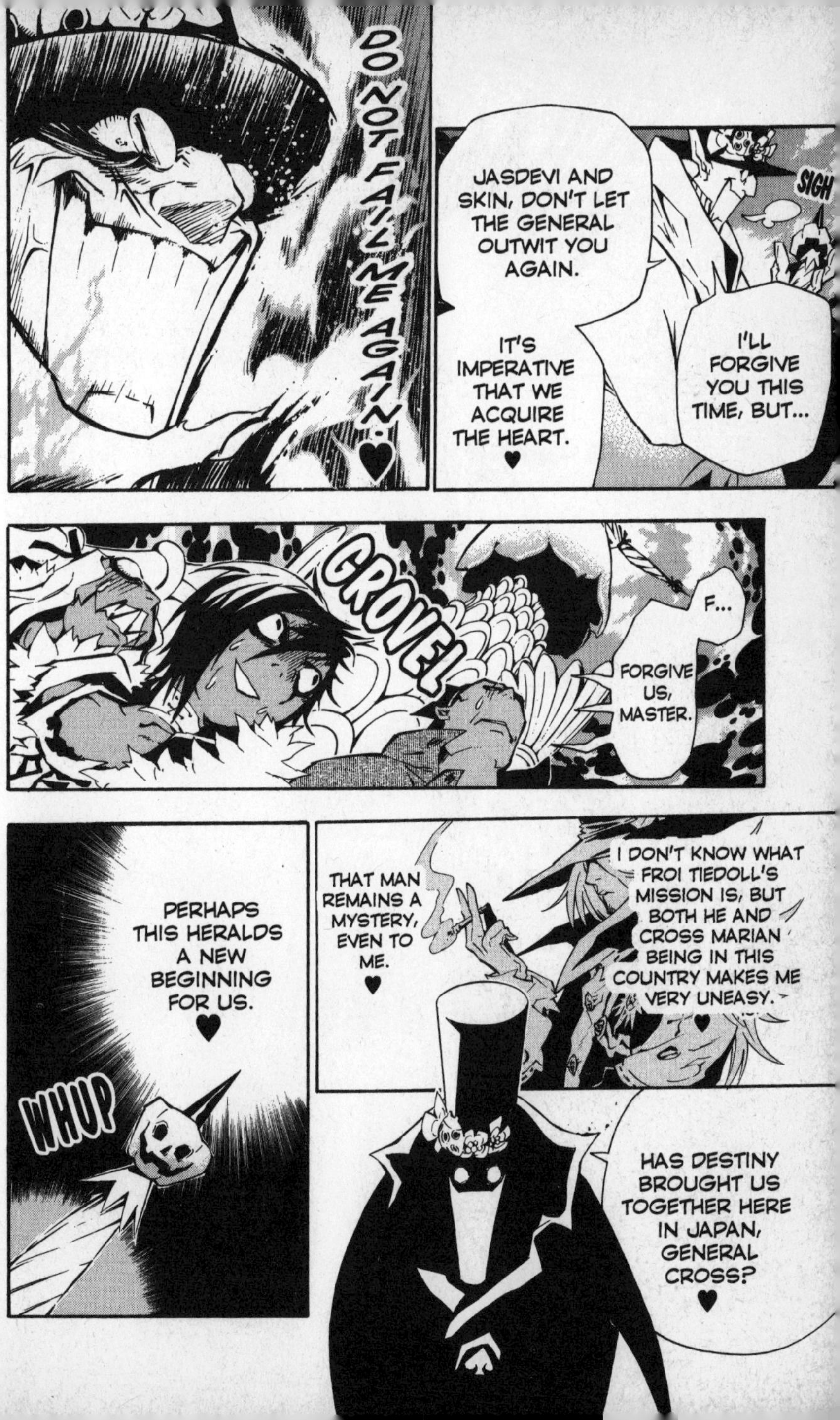
SIGH
I'LL FORGIVE YOU THIS TIME, BUT...
JASDEVI AND SKIN, DON'T LET THE GENERAL OUTWIT YOU AGAIN.
IT'S IMPERATIVE THAT WE ACQUIRE THE HEART. ♥
DO NOT FAIL ME AGAIN. ♥
F...
FORGIVE US, MASTER.
GROVEL
I DON'T KNOW WHAT FROI TIEDOLL'S MISSION IS, BUT BOTH HE AND CROSS MARIAN BEING IN THIS COUNTRY MAKES ME VERY UNEASY. ♥
THAT MAN REMAINS A MYSTERY, EVEN TO ME. ♥
PERHAPS THIS HERALDS A NEW BEGINNING FOR US. ♥
WHUP
HAS DESTINY BROUGHT US TOGETHER HERE IN JAPAN, GENERAL CROSS? ♥

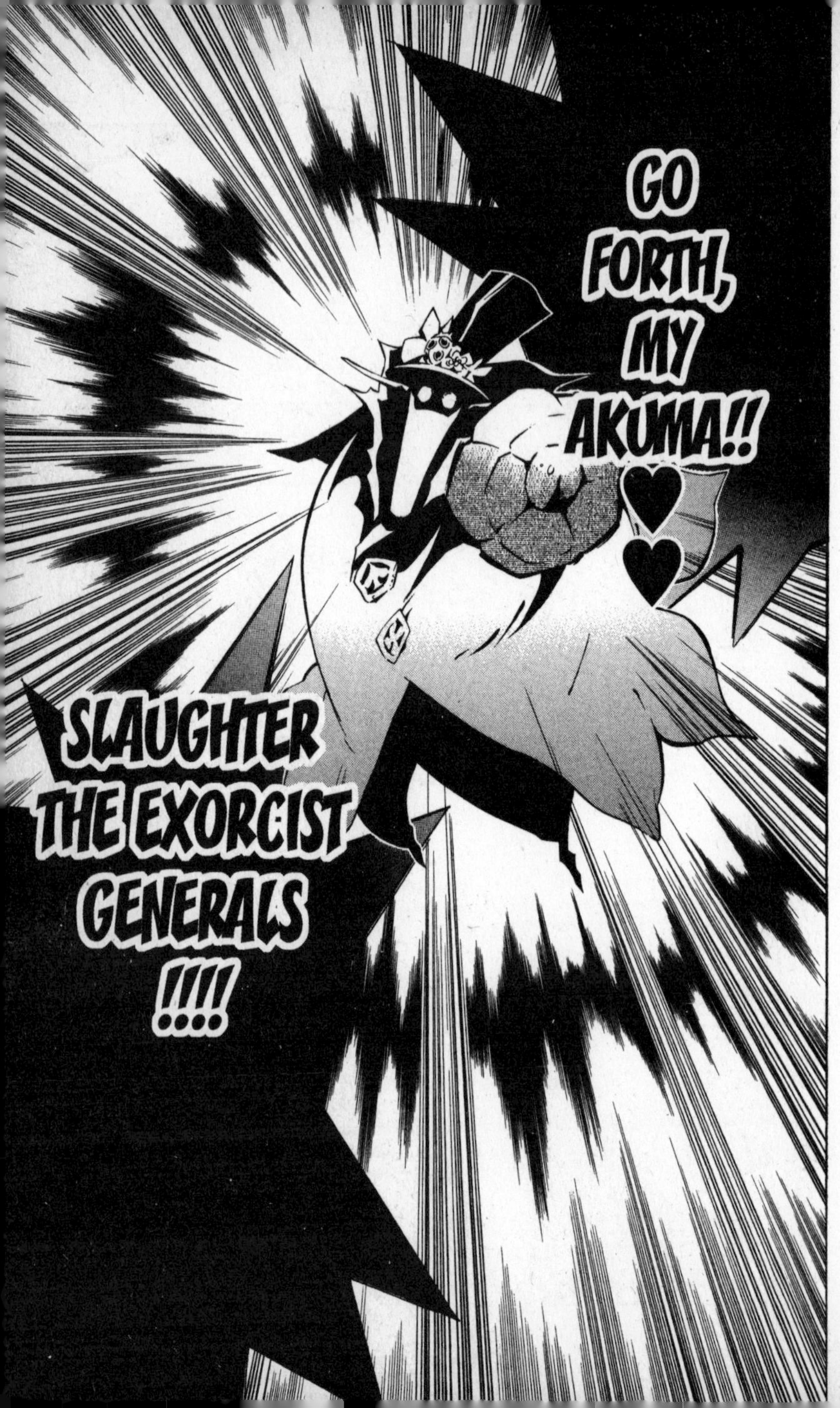
GO FORTH, MY AKUMA!! ♥♥
SLAUGHTER THE EXORCIST GENERALS !!!!

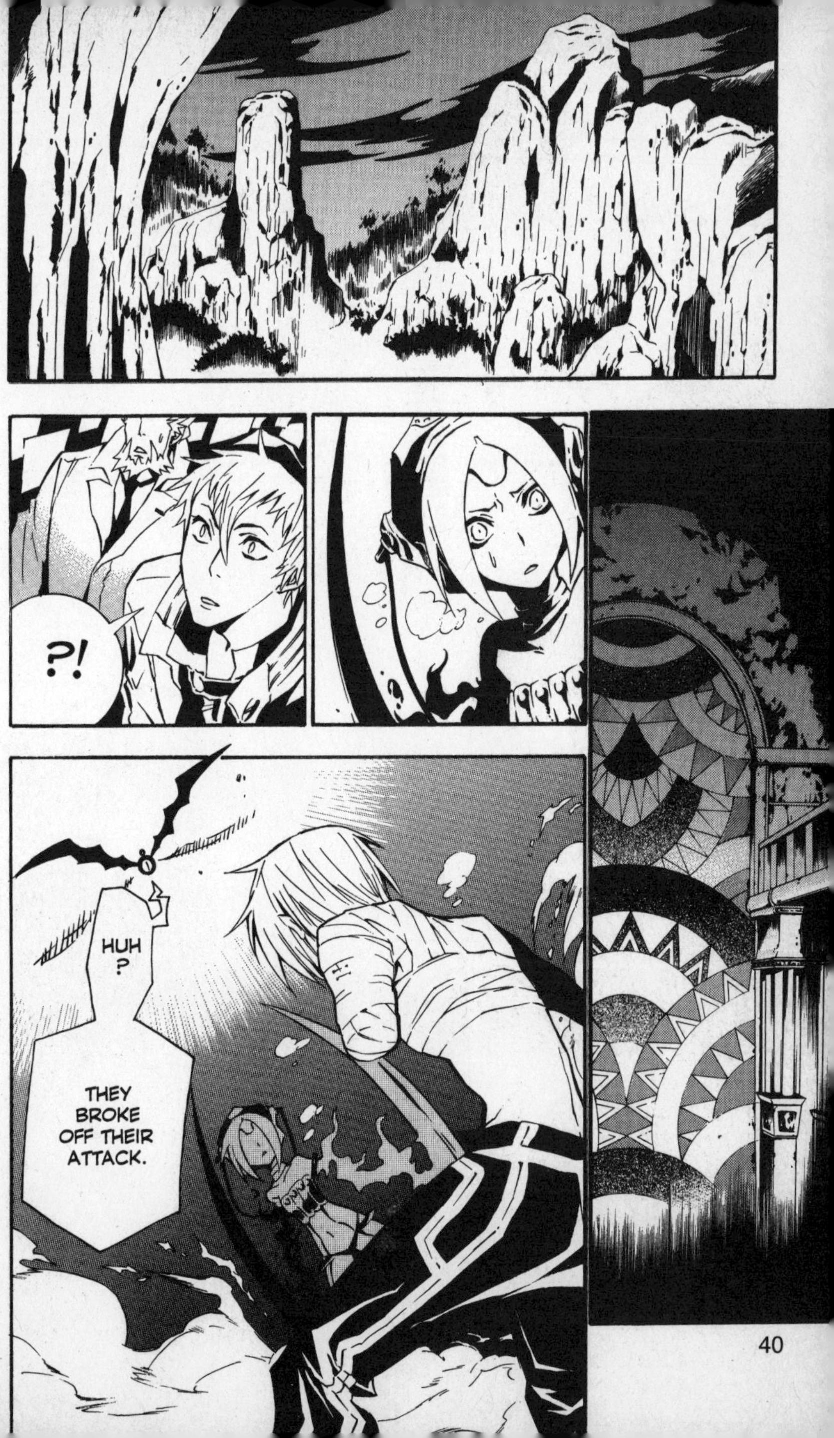
?!
HUH ?
THEY BROKE OFF THEIR ATTACK.

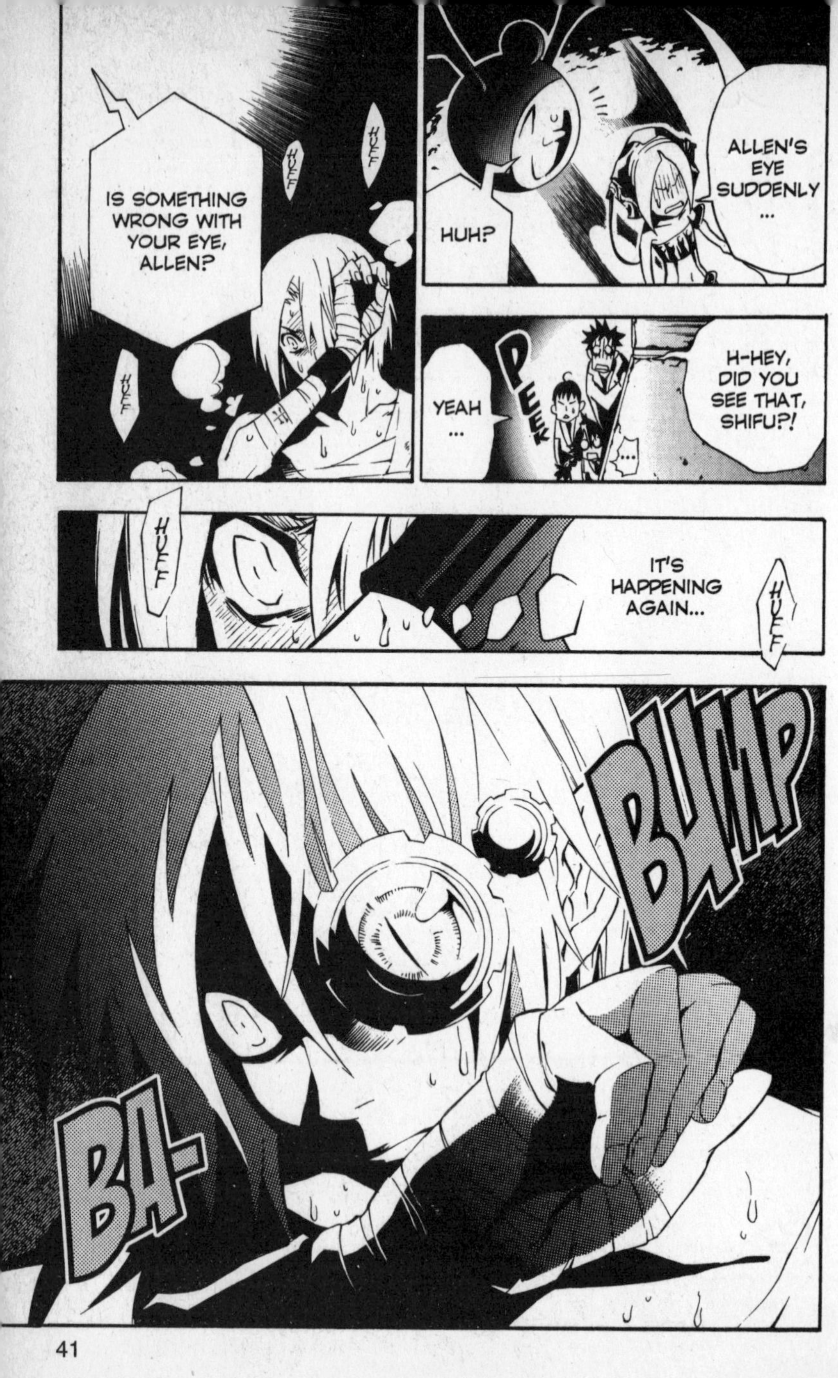
ALLEN'S EYE SUDDENLY ...
HUH?
H-HEY, DID YOU SEE THAT, SHIFU?!
PEEK
YEAH ...
...
HUFF
HUFF
IS SOMETHING WRONG WITH YOUR EYE, ALLEN?
HUFF
HUFF
IT'S HAPPENING AGAIN...
HUFF
BUMP
BA-

KOMUI'S DISCUSSION ROOM SPECIAL EDITION: NOAH'S ARK, VOL. 2

Q: WHERE DOES ROAD KAMELOT GO TO SCHOOL? IS IT A HUMAN SCHOOL OR AN AKUMA SCHOOL?
(ROAD) IT'S A NORMAL HUMAN SCHOOL. THE OUTFIT I WAS WEARING IN VOL. 5 IS MY SCHOOL UNIFORM.
(DAVID) I HAPPEN TO KNOW THAT IT'S AN EXPENSIVE PRIVATE SCHOOL, AND THE EARL'S PAYING HIS TUITION!
(JASDERO) HEE HEE! NO FAIR!! THE EARL ALWAYS DOES SPECIAL STUFF FOR ROAD!
(TYKI) THE EARL IS SWEET ON ROAD. OR COULD SHE BE BLACKMAILING HIM?
(SKIN) SWEET...

Q: IF TYKI AND KANDA WERE TO DO PROBLEMS DESIGNED FOR THIRD GRADERS, WHICH WOULD EMERGE THE BIGGER IDIOT?
(ROAD, JASDEVI) GA HA HA HA HA HA HA HA!!
(DAVID) HA HA!! I'M LAUGHING SO HARD MY STOMACH HURTS!!
(JASDERO) THAT'S A GOOD ONE!!
(ROAD) COME ON, TYKI, ANSWER THE QUESTION!
(TYKI) I WANNA GO HOME.
(ROAD) NO WAY!

Q: DOES TYKI-PON HAVE A GIRLFRIEND?
(TYKI) NO, I DON'T!
(ROAD) WHAT ARE YOU GETTING SO MAD ABOUT?
(JASDEVI) DON'T TAKE OUT YOUR FRUSTRATIONS ON THE READERS. TALK ABOUT BEING CHILDISH! (TYKI) ...

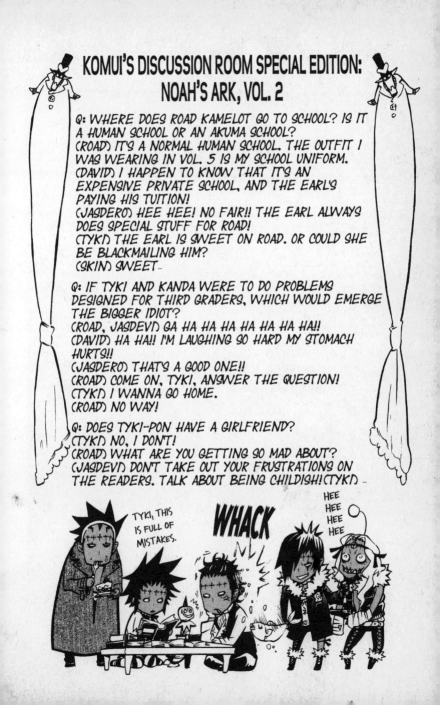

HEE HEE HEE HEE
WHACK
TYKI, THIS IS FULL OF MISTAKES.

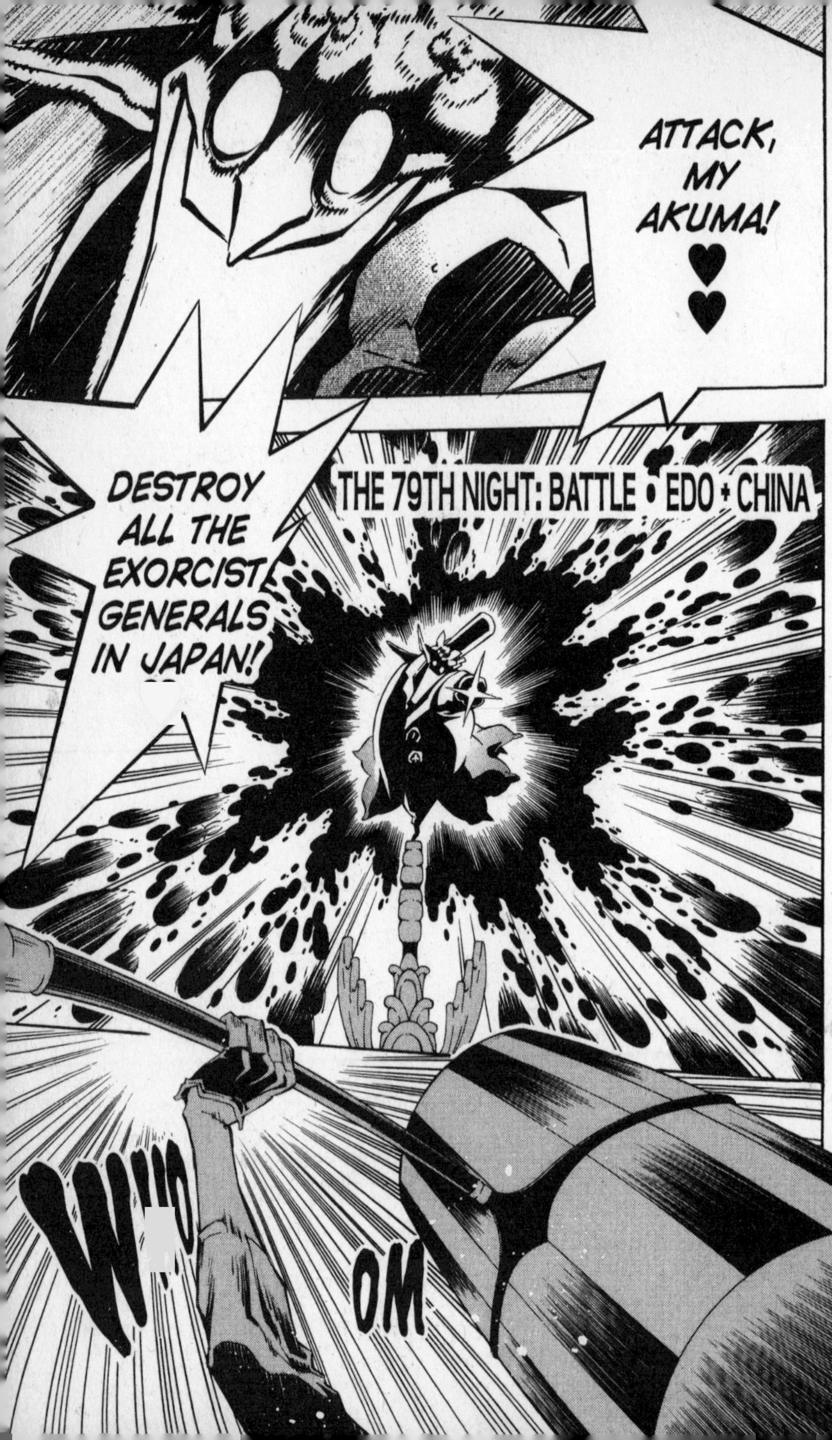
ATTACK, MY AKUMA! ♥♥
THE 79TH NIGHT: BATTLE • EDO + CHINA
DESTROY ALL THE EXORCIST GENERALS IN JAPAN!
WHO
OM

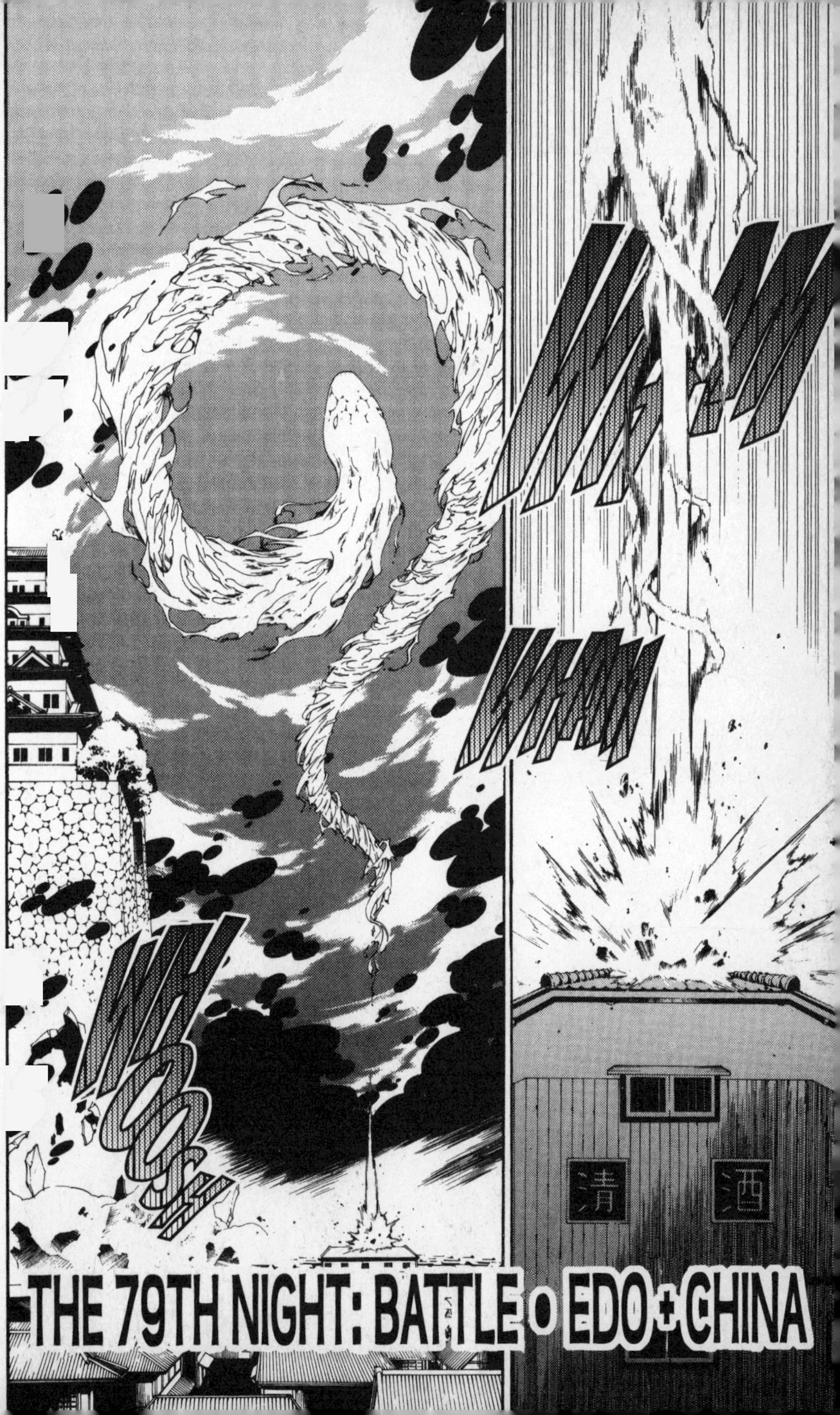
清 酒
WHOOSH
THE 79TH NIGHT: BATTLE • EDO + CHINA

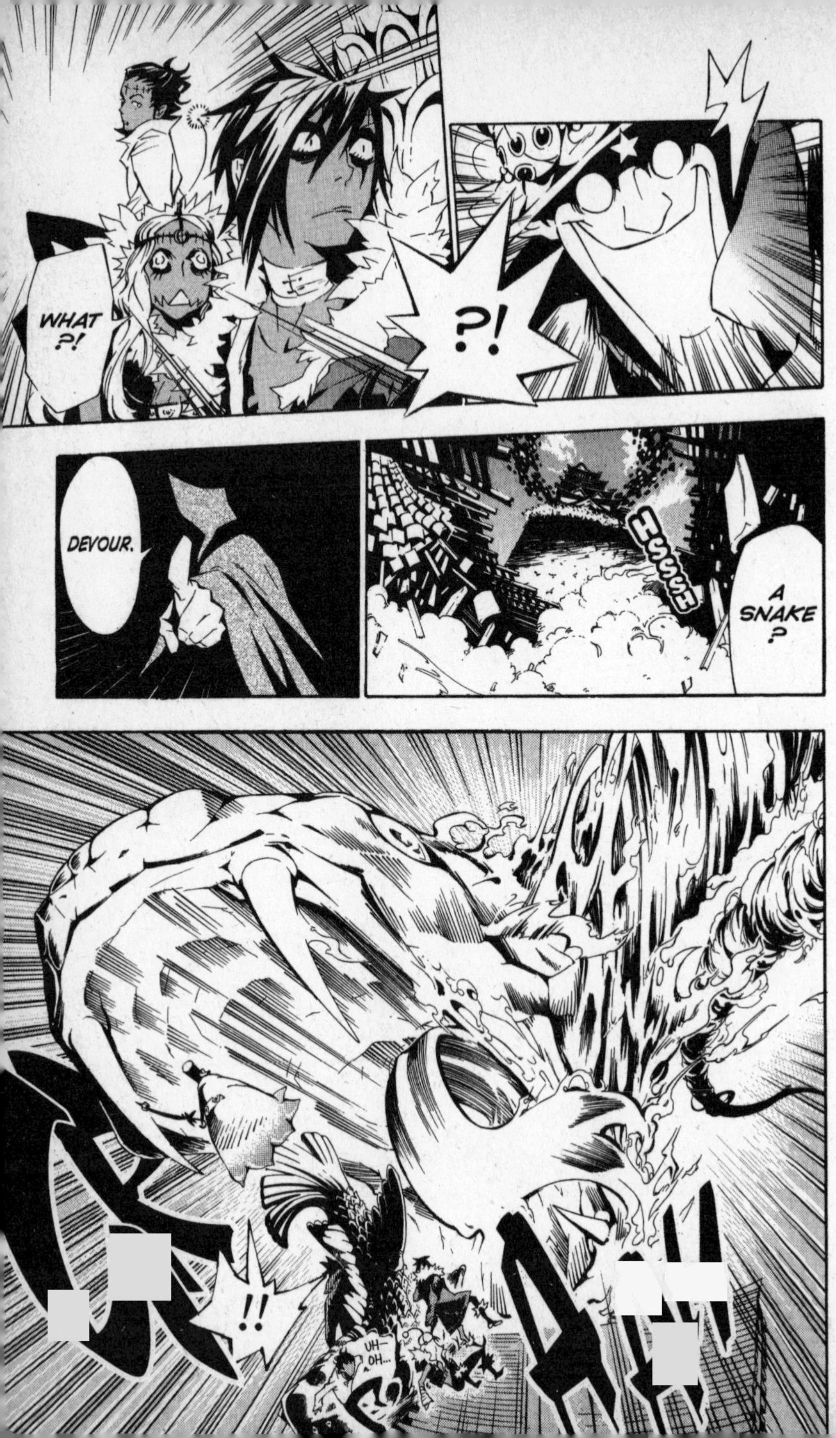
?!
WHAT ?!
HSSSSH
A SNAKE ?
DEVOUR.
!!
UH-OH...

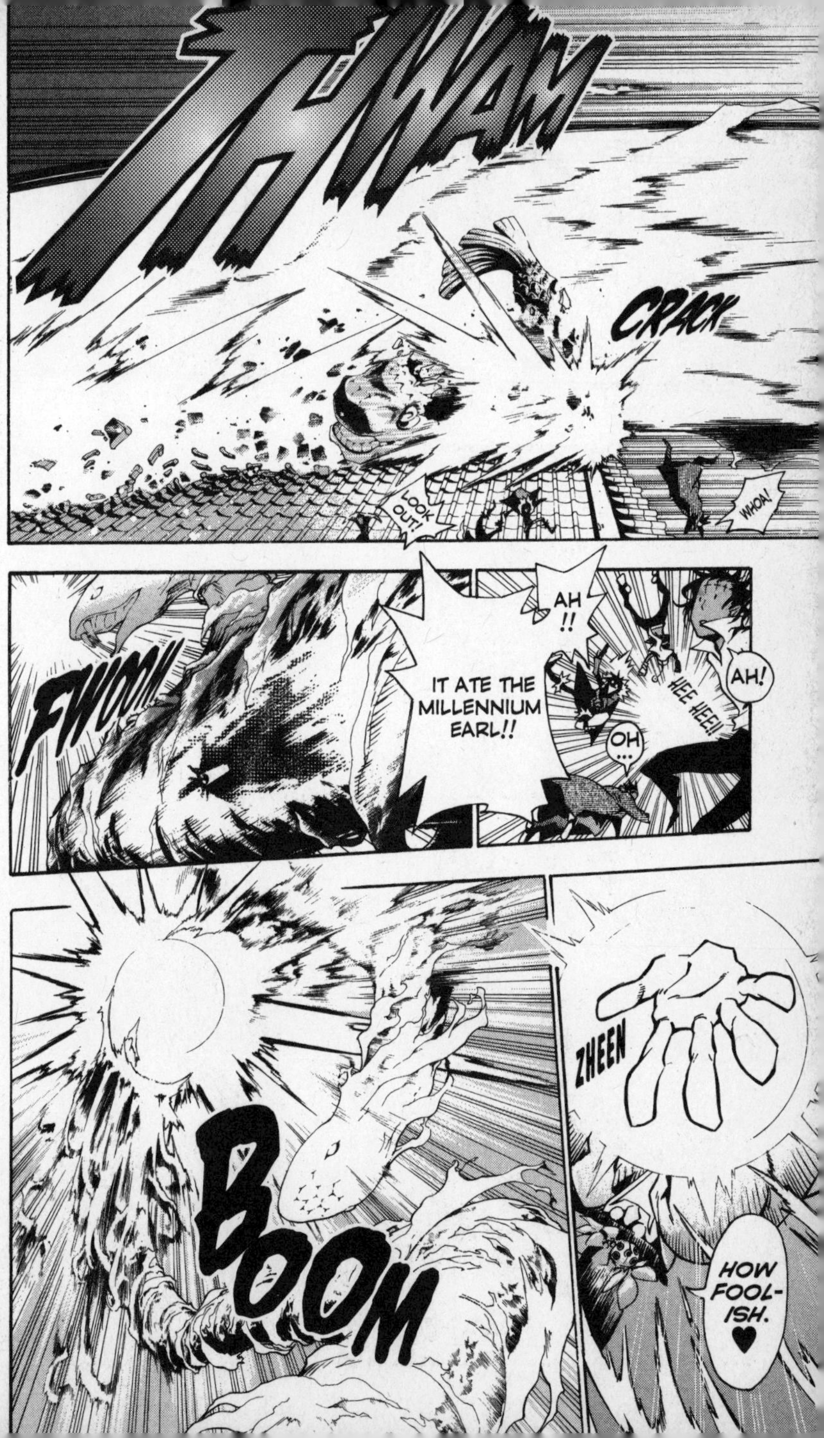
THWAM
CRACK
WHOA!
LOOK OUT!
AH !!
AH!
HEE HEE!!
OH ...
IT ATE THE MILLENNIUM EARL!!
FWOOM!!
ZHEEN
HOW FOOL-ISH. ♥
BOOM

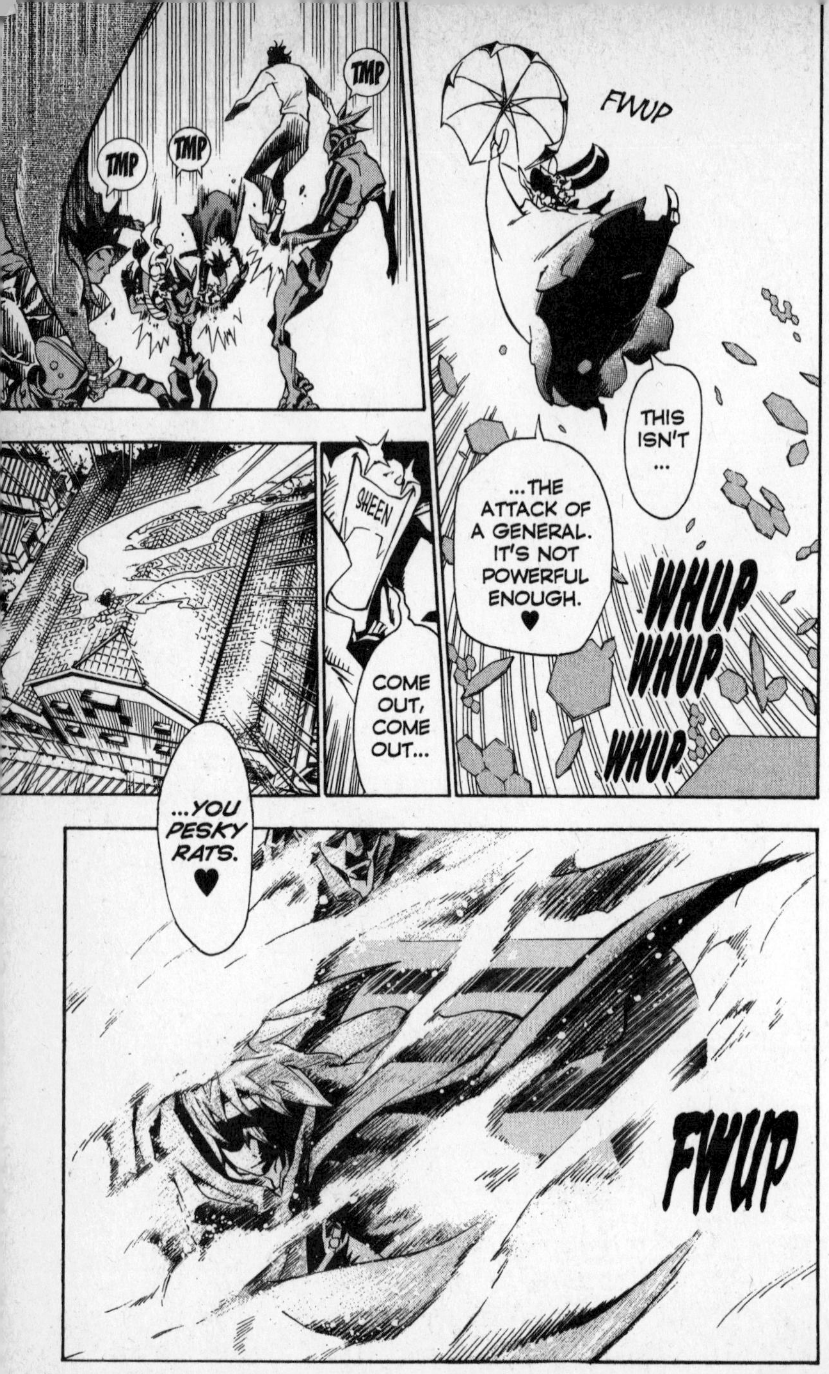
FWUP
THIS ISN'T ...
...THE ATTACK OF A GENERAL. IT'S NOT POWERFUL ENOUGH. ♥
WHUP WHUP WHUP
TMP
TMP
TMP
SHEEN
COME OUT, COME OUT...
...YOU PESKY RATS. ♥
FWUP

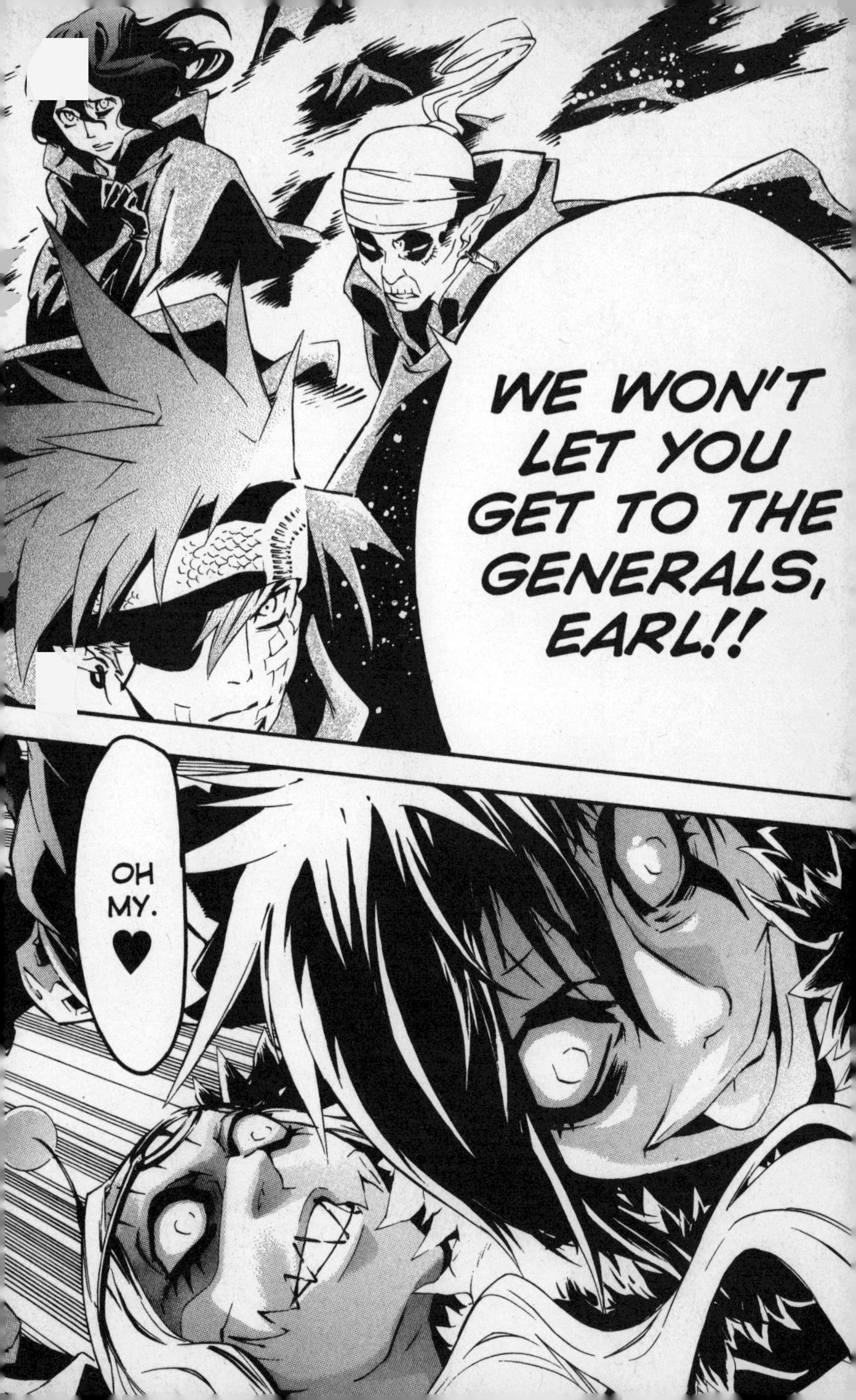
WE WON'T LET YOU GET TO THE GENERALS, EARL!!
OH MY. ♥

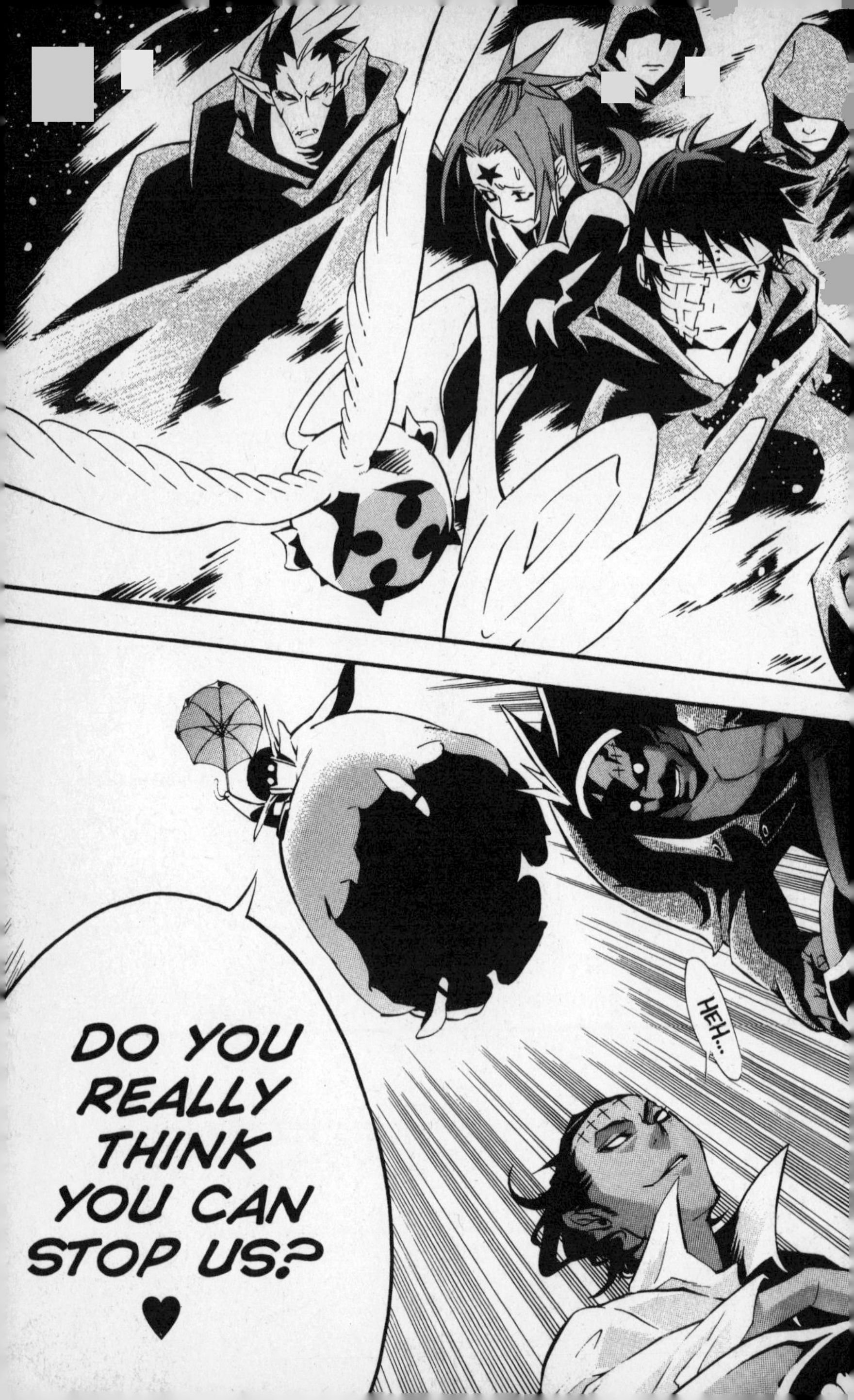
HEH...
DO YOU REALLY THINK YOU CAN STOP US? ♥

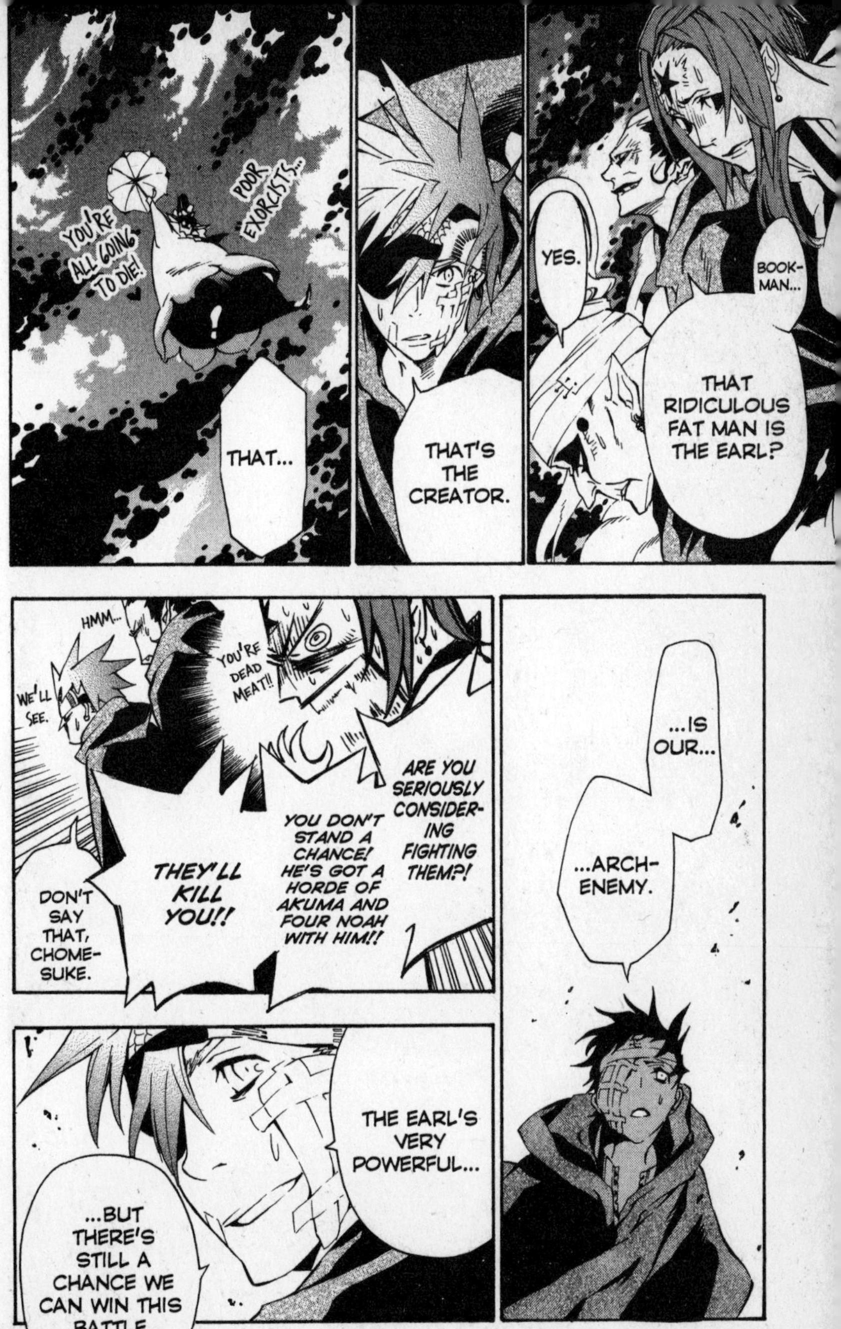
BOOK-MAN...
THAT RIDICULOUS FAT MAN IS THE EARL?
YES.
THAT'S THE CREATOR.
POOR EXORCISTS...
YOU'RE ALL GOING TO DIE!
THAT...
...IS OUR...
...ARCH-ENEMY.
YOU'RE DEAD MEAT!!
HMM...
WE'LL SEE.
ARE YOU SERIOUSLY CONSIDER-ING FIGHTING THEM?!
YOU DON'T STAND A CHANCE! HE'S GOT A HORDE OF AKUMA AND FOUR NOAH WITH HIM!!
THEY'LL KILL YOU!!
DON'T SAY THAT, CHOME-SUKE.
THE EARL'S VERY POWERFUL...
...BUT THERE'S STILL A CHANCE WE CAN WIN THIS BATTLE.

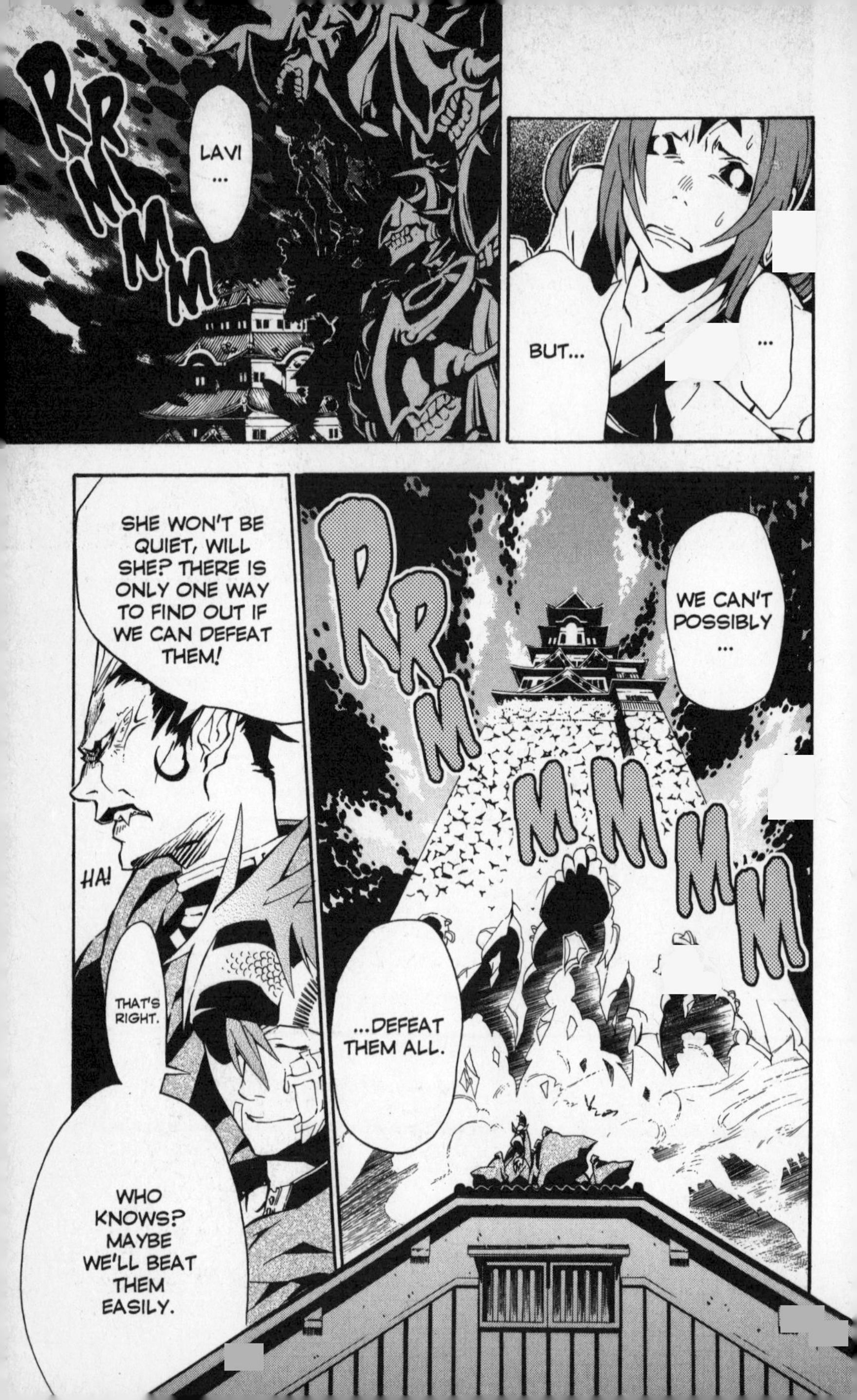

...
BUT...
RRMMMM
LAVI ...
WE CAN'T POSSIBLY ...
RRMMMMMM
...DEFEAT THEM ALL.
SHE WON'T BE QUIET, WILL SHE? THERE IS ONLY ONE WAY TO FIND OUT IF WE CAN DEFEAT THEM!
HA!
THAT'S RIGHT.
WHO KNOWS? MAYBE WE'LL BEAT THEM EASILY.

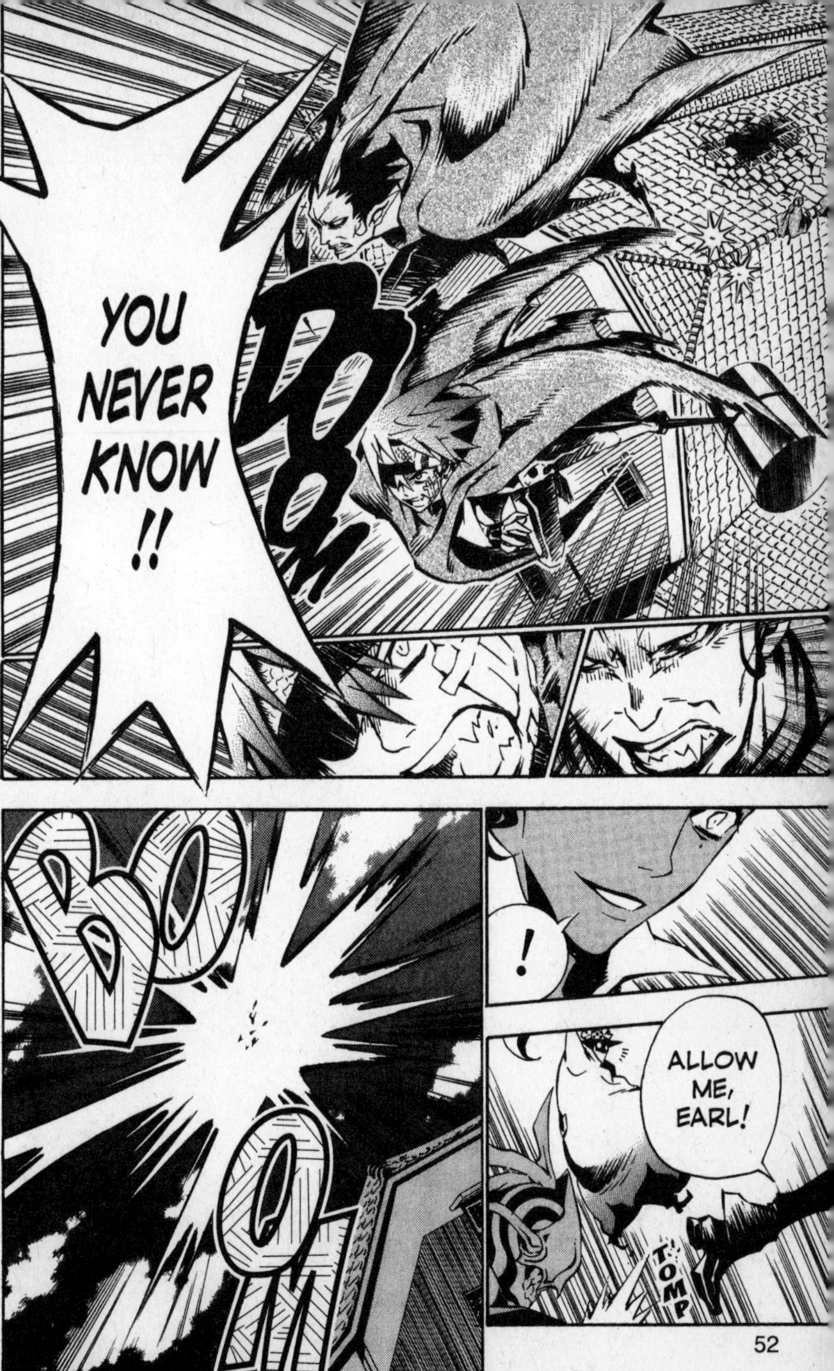
YOU NEVER KNOW!!
!
ALLOW ME, EARL!
TOMP

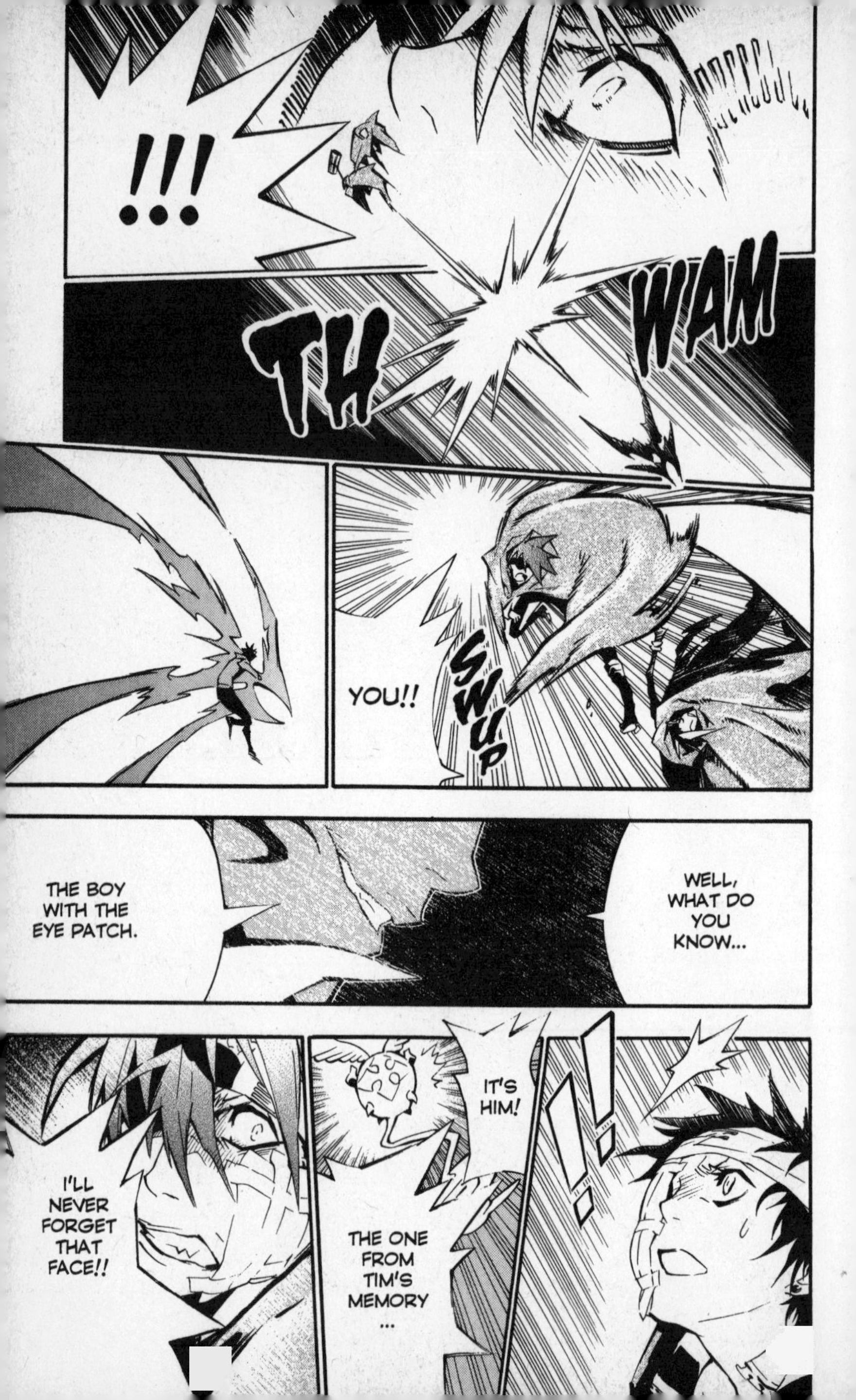
!!!
TH
WAM
YOU!!
SWUP
WELL, WHAT DO YOU KNOW...
THE BOY WITH THE EYE PATCH.
!!
IT'S HIM!
THE ONE FROM TIM'S MEMORY ...
I'LL NEVER FORGET THAT FACE!!

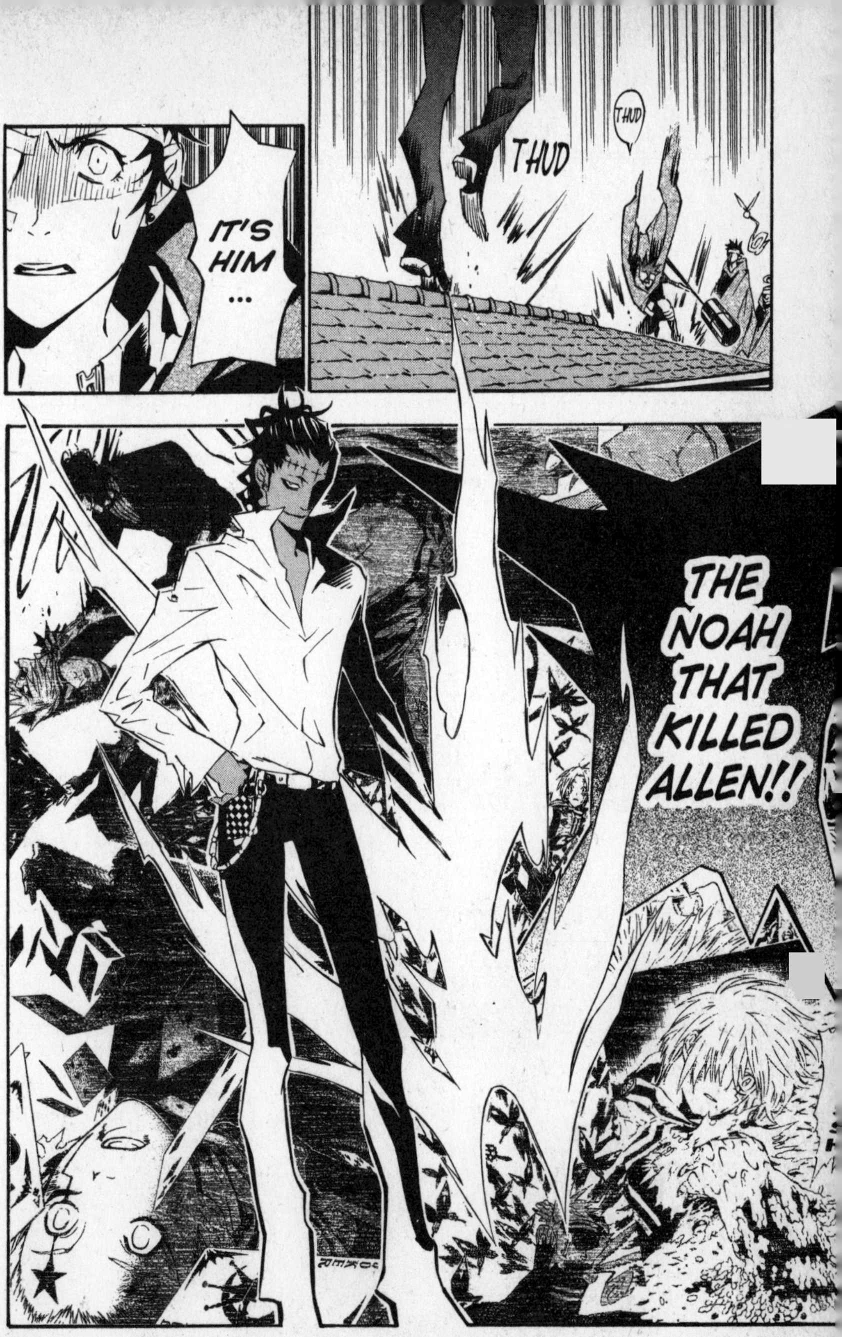
THUD
THUD
IT'S HIM ...
THE NOAH THAT KILLED ALLEN!!

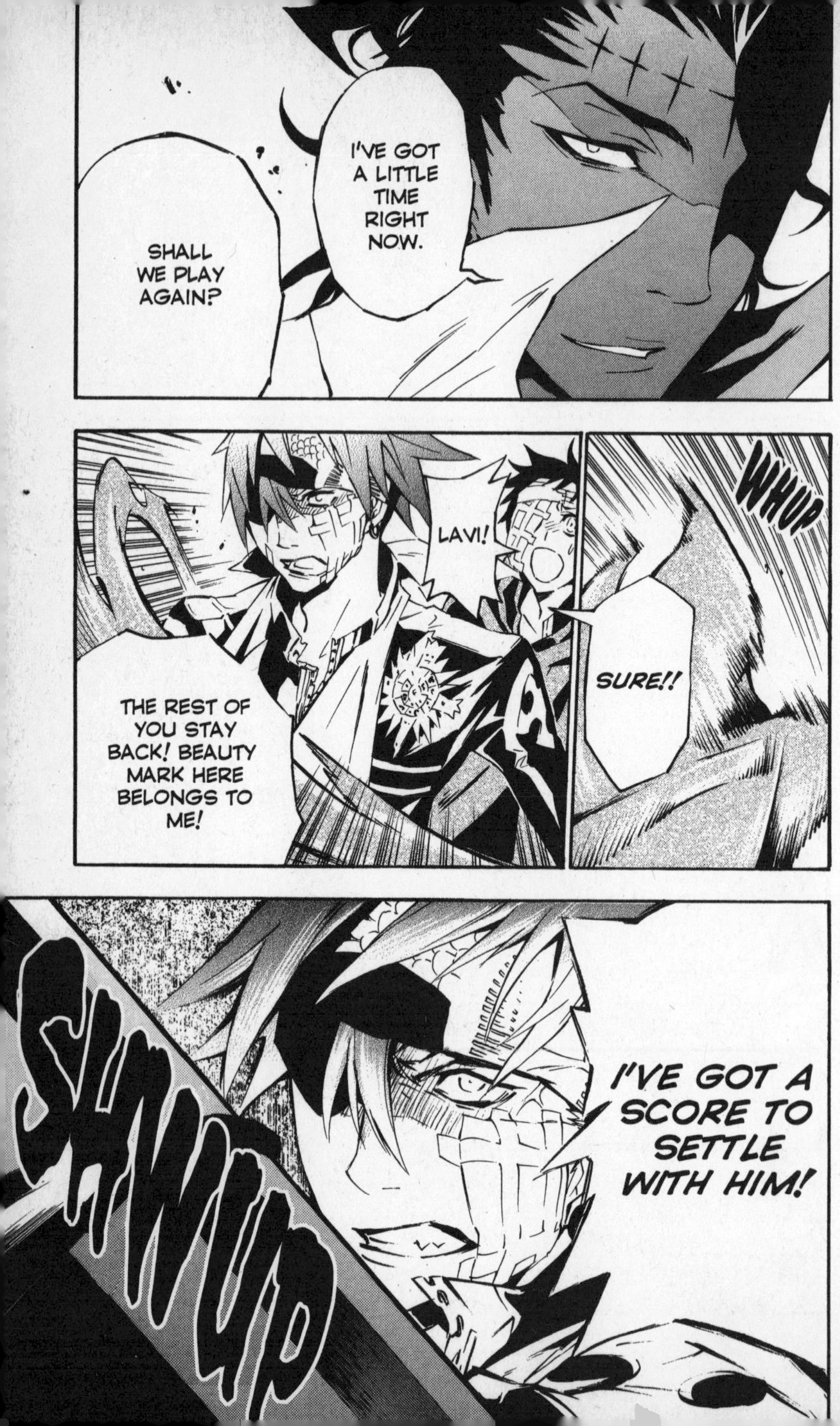
I'VE GOT A LITTLE TIME RIGHT NOW.
SHALL WE PLAY AGAIN?
WHUP
SURE!!
LAVI!
THE REST OF YOU STAY BACK! BEAUTY MARK HERE BELONGS TO ME!
I'VE GOT A SCORE TO SETTLE WITH HIM!
SHWUP

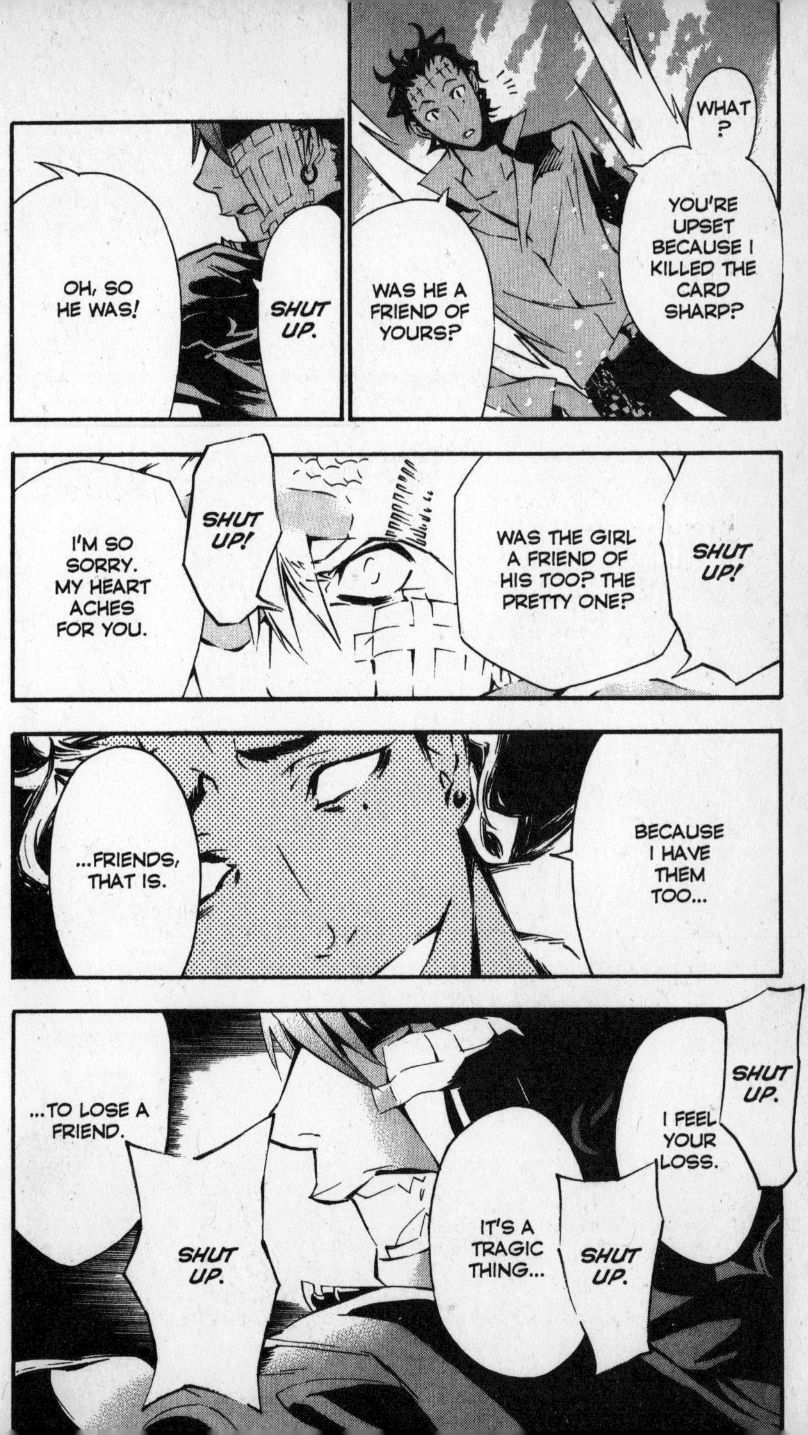

WHAT ?
YOU'RE UPSET BECAUSE I KILLED THE CARD SHARP?
WAS HE A FRIEND OF YOURS?
SHUT UP.
OH, SO HE WAS!
SHUT UP!
WAS THE GIRL A FRIEND OF HIS TOO? THE PRETTY ONE?
SHUT UP!
I'M SO SORRY. MY HEART ACHES FOR YOU.
BECAUSE I HAVE THEM TOO...
...FRIENDS, THAT IS.
SHUT UP.
I FEEL YOUR LOSS.
SHUT UP.
IT'S A TRAGIC THING...
SHUT UP.
...TO LOSE A FRIEND.

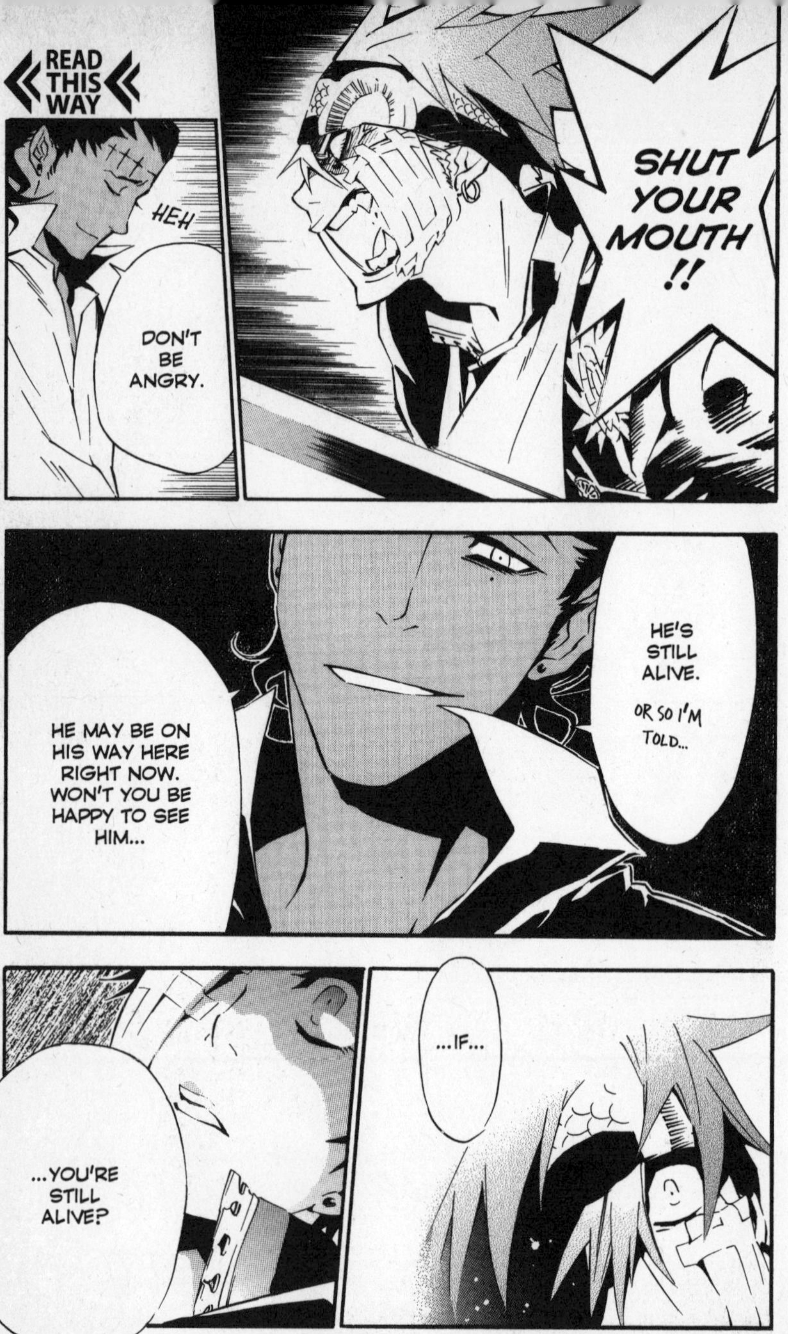
READ THIS WAY
SHUT YOUR MOUTH!!
HEH
DON'T BE ANGRY.
HE'S STILL ALIVE.
OR SO I'M TOLD...
HE MAY BE ON HIS WAY HERE RIGHT NOW. WON'T YOU BE HAPPY TO SEE HIM...
...IF...
...YOU'RE STILL ALIVE?

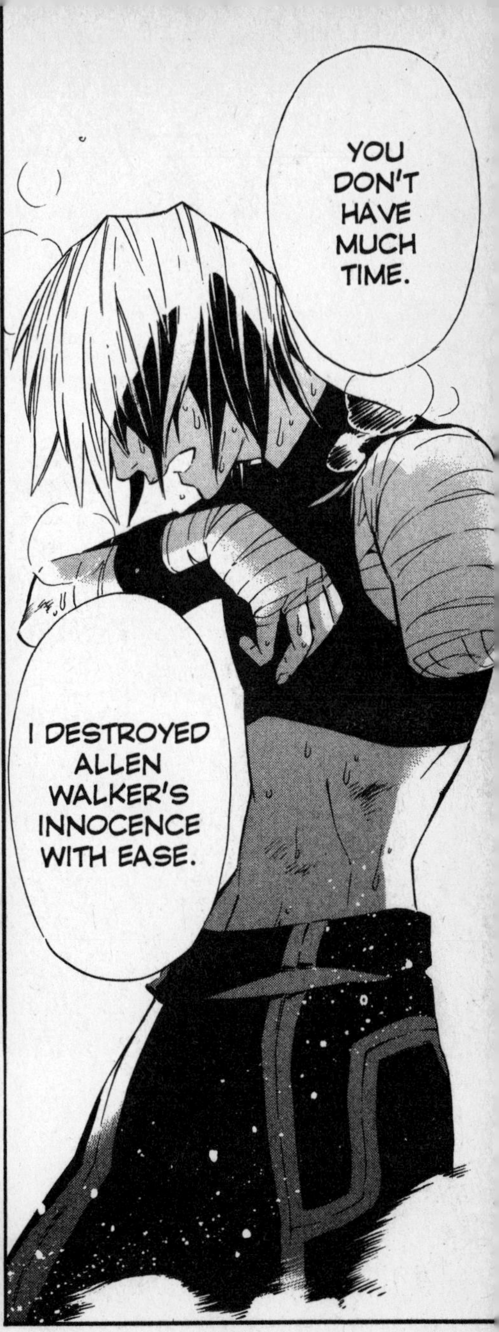
YOU DON'T HAVE MUCH TIME.
I DESTROYED ALLEN WALKER'S INNOCENCE WITH EASE.
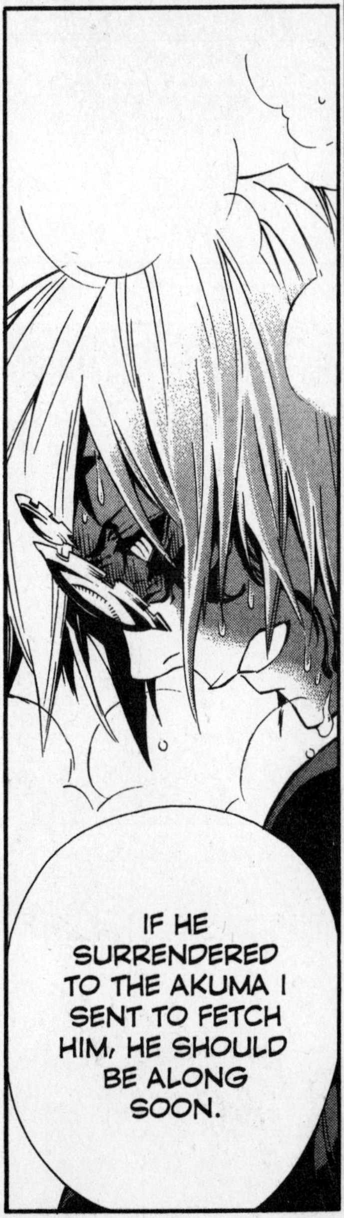
IF HE SURRENDERED TO THE AKUMA I SENT TO FETCH HIM, HE SHOULD BE ALONG SOON.

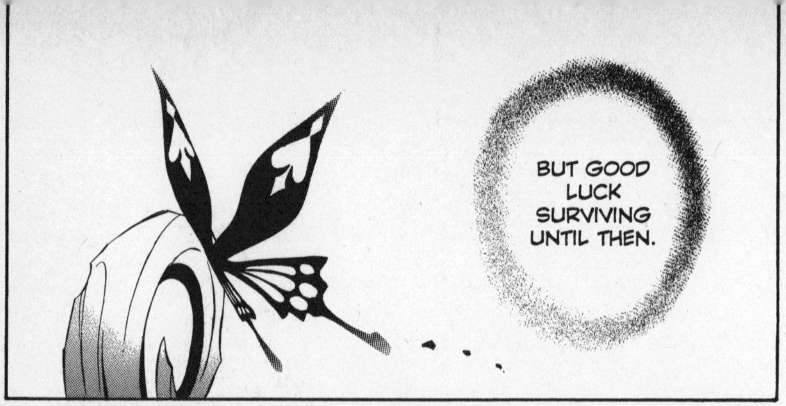
BUT GOOD LUCK SURVIVING UNTIL THEN.

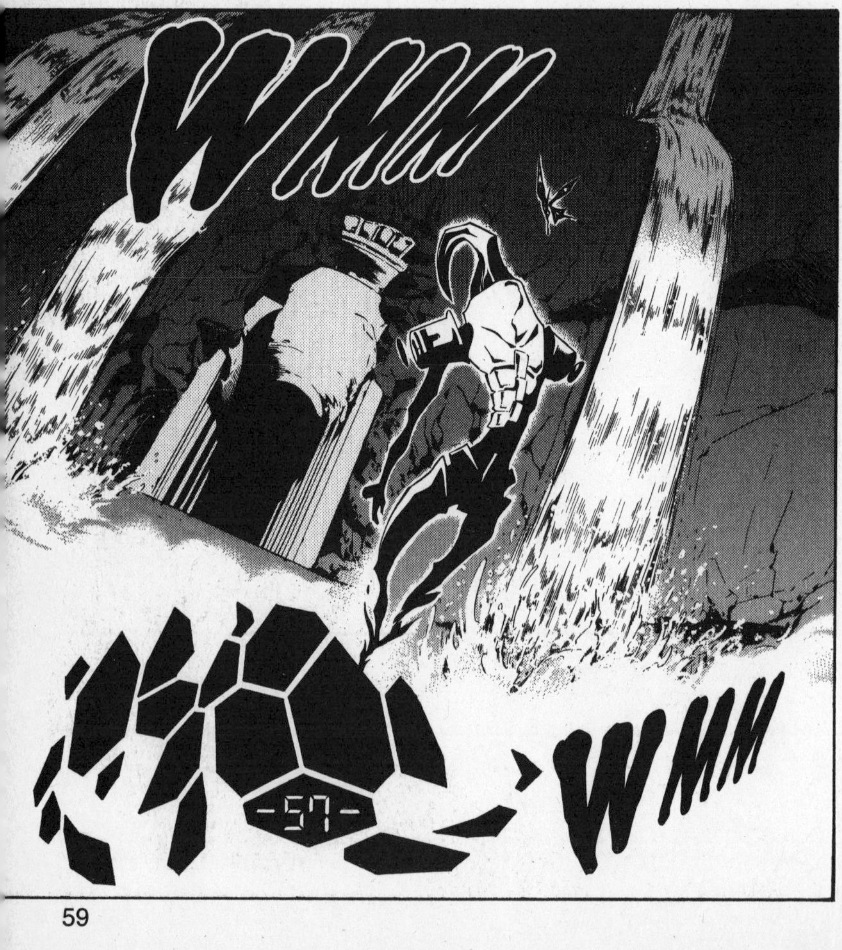
WMMM
-57-
WMM

KOMUI'S DISCUSSION ROOM SPECIAL EDITION: NOAH'S ARK, VOL. 3

Q: HOW MANY ARE THERE IN THE CLAN OF NOAH?
(ROAD) THERE ARE MORE OF US THAN THIS. LET'S SEE, ALTOGETHER, THERE ARE--
(LERO) NO!! MISTRESS ROAD, YOU MUSTN'T REVEAL ANYTHING ABOUT THE FAMILY TO STRANGERS!! (SWEATING)
(ROAD) OH, POOH. YOU'RE NO FUN, LERO.
Q: WHY DOES TYKI WEAR THOSE GLASSES? (SEE VOL. 5 P. 94)
(ROAD) THOSE THINGS ARE HIDEOUS!
(DAVID) YEAH, THEY COULDN'T BE MORE UNFASHIONABLE.
(JASDERO) YEAH, BAD! REALLY BAD! BAD STYLE TOO!
(TYKI) WILL YOU ALL GIVE IT A REST?! IT'S NOT LIKE I BOUGHT THEM. I FOUND THEM IN THE TRASH.
(ROAD, DAVID, JASDERO) !!!!!
TEXT:Q: THE EARL KNITS, HELPS ROAD WITH HER HOMEWORK AND CREATES THINGS LIKE THE TEEZ. IS THERE ANYTHING HE CAN'T DO?
(THE EARL) I'M PRACTICALLY PERFECT.♥
(ROAD) YAY!! WELCOME BACK, MASTER! (RUBBING TUMMY)
(DAVID) MOMMY! THAT MAN (POINTING AT TYKI) IS FILTHY!
(JASDERO) PLEASE DON'T WASH MY CLOTHES WITH HIS!
(EARL) NOW, NOW?♥ IT'S NORMAL FOR TEENS TO GET UPSET WITH THEIR FATHERS AT SOME POINT.♥
TYKI-PON, BE A GOOD DADDY AND GO TAKE A BATH BEFORE DINNER.♥
(TYKI) WHEN DID I BECOME THEIR FATHER?
(EARL) NOW THEN, CHILDREN, ARE YOU ALL HUNGRY?♥
(ROAD) COME ON, TYKI, ANSWER THE QUESTION!
(ALL BUT TYKI) YES, WE ARE!

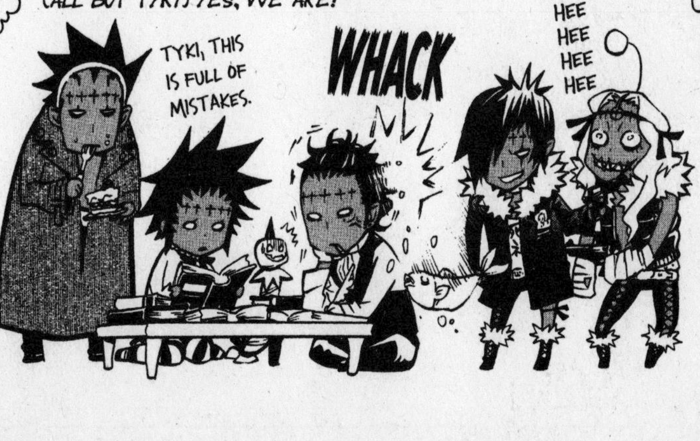
HEE HEE HEE HEE
WHACK
TYKI, THIS IS FULL OF MISTAKES.

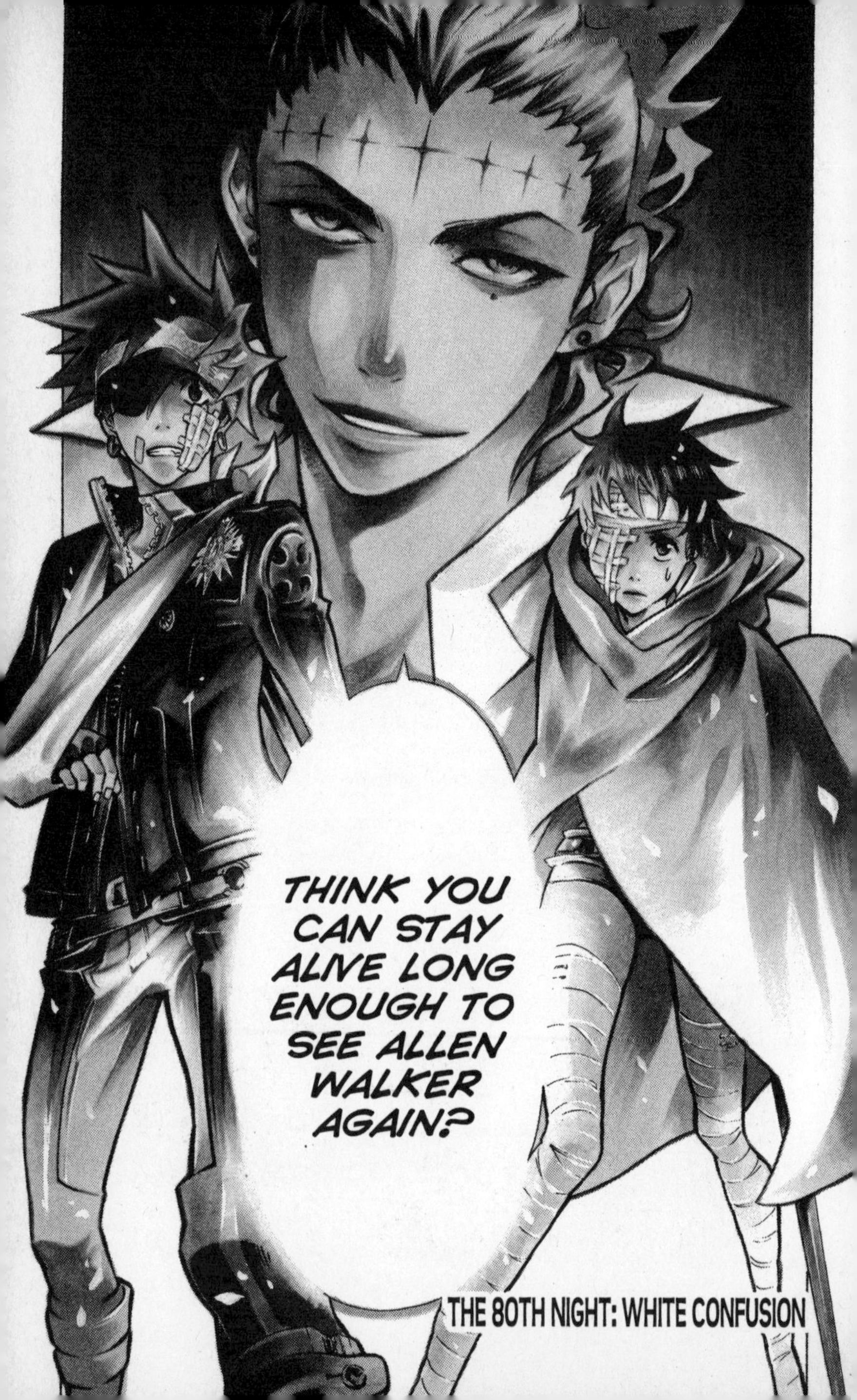
THINK YOU CAN STAY ALIVE LONG ENOUGH TO SEE ALLEN WALKER AGAIN?

THE 80TH NIGHT: WHITE CONFUSION

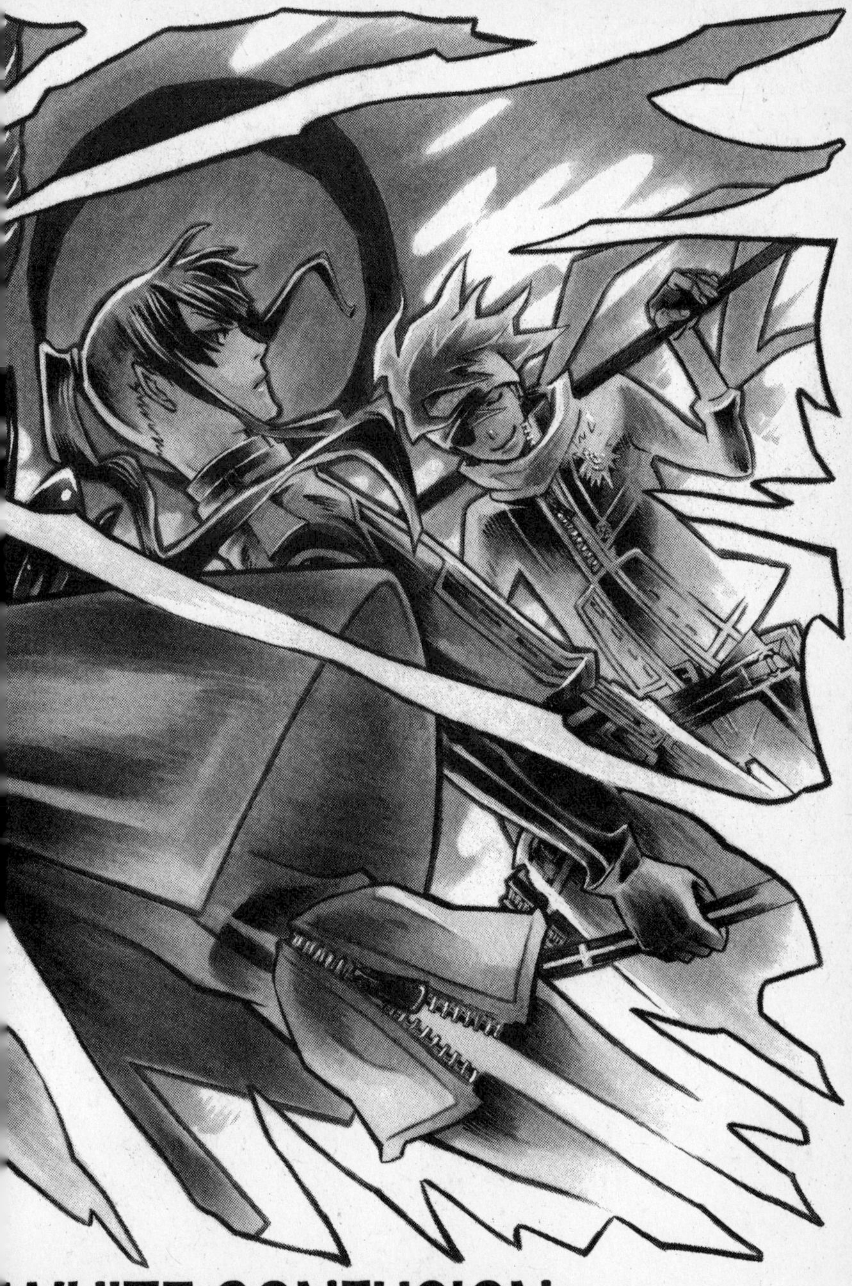

WHITE CONFUSION

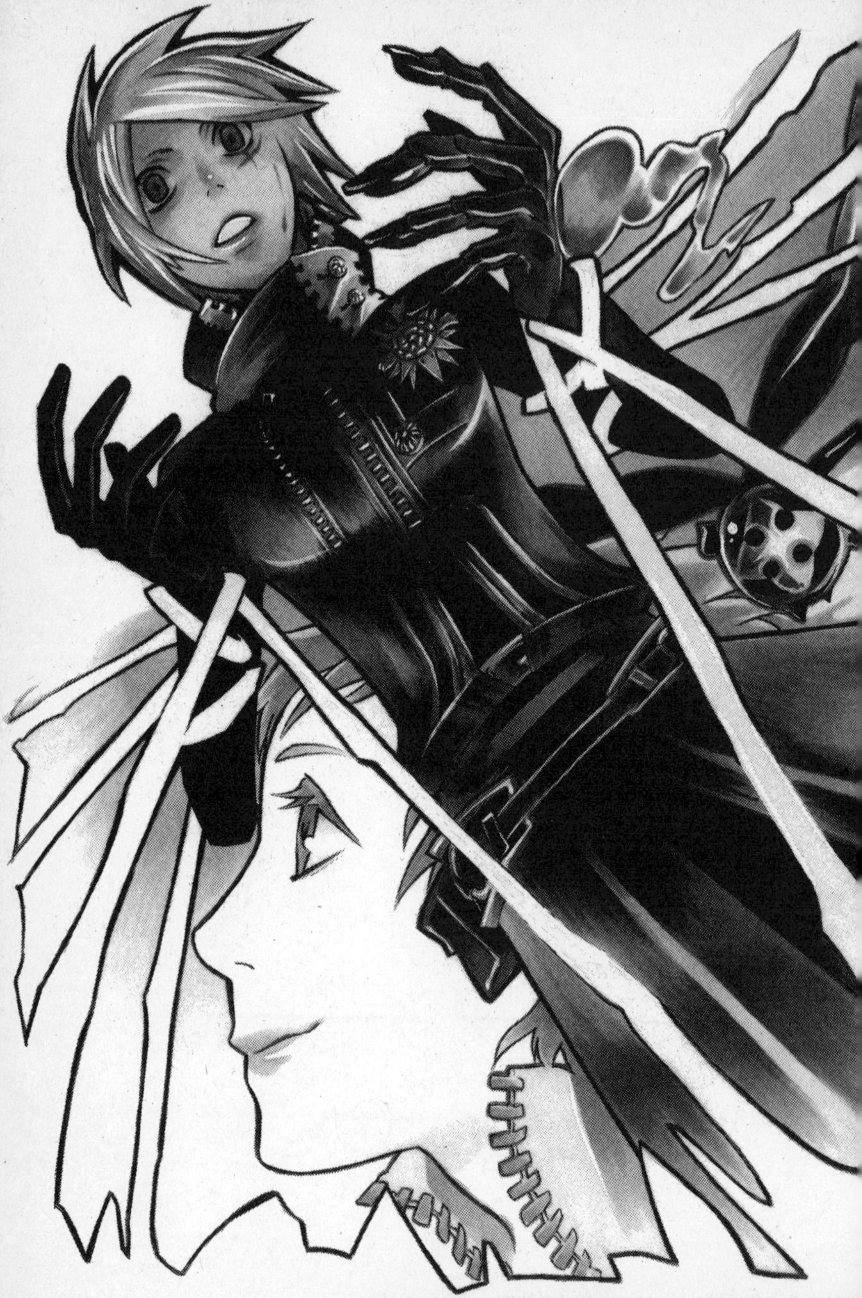

THE 80TH NIGHT:

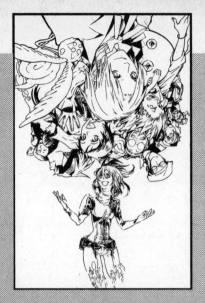

THESE TWO ILLUSTRATIONS WERE COVER
IDEAS FOR VOLUME 8. UNFORTUNATELY,
EDITOR Y REJECTED THEM BOTH.

DARN IT!!!
(HOSHINO)

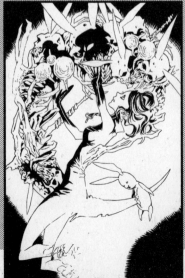

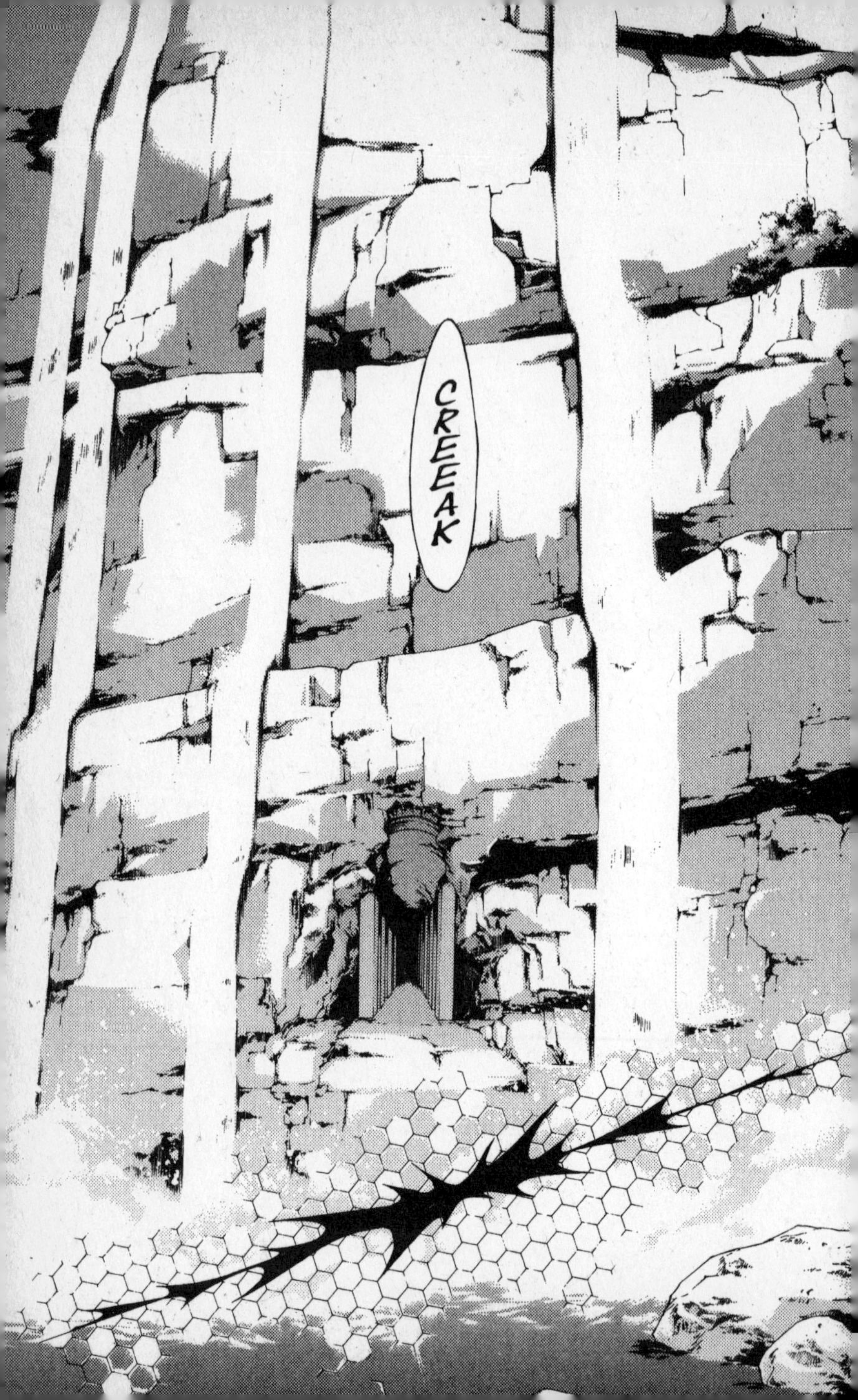
CREEEAK

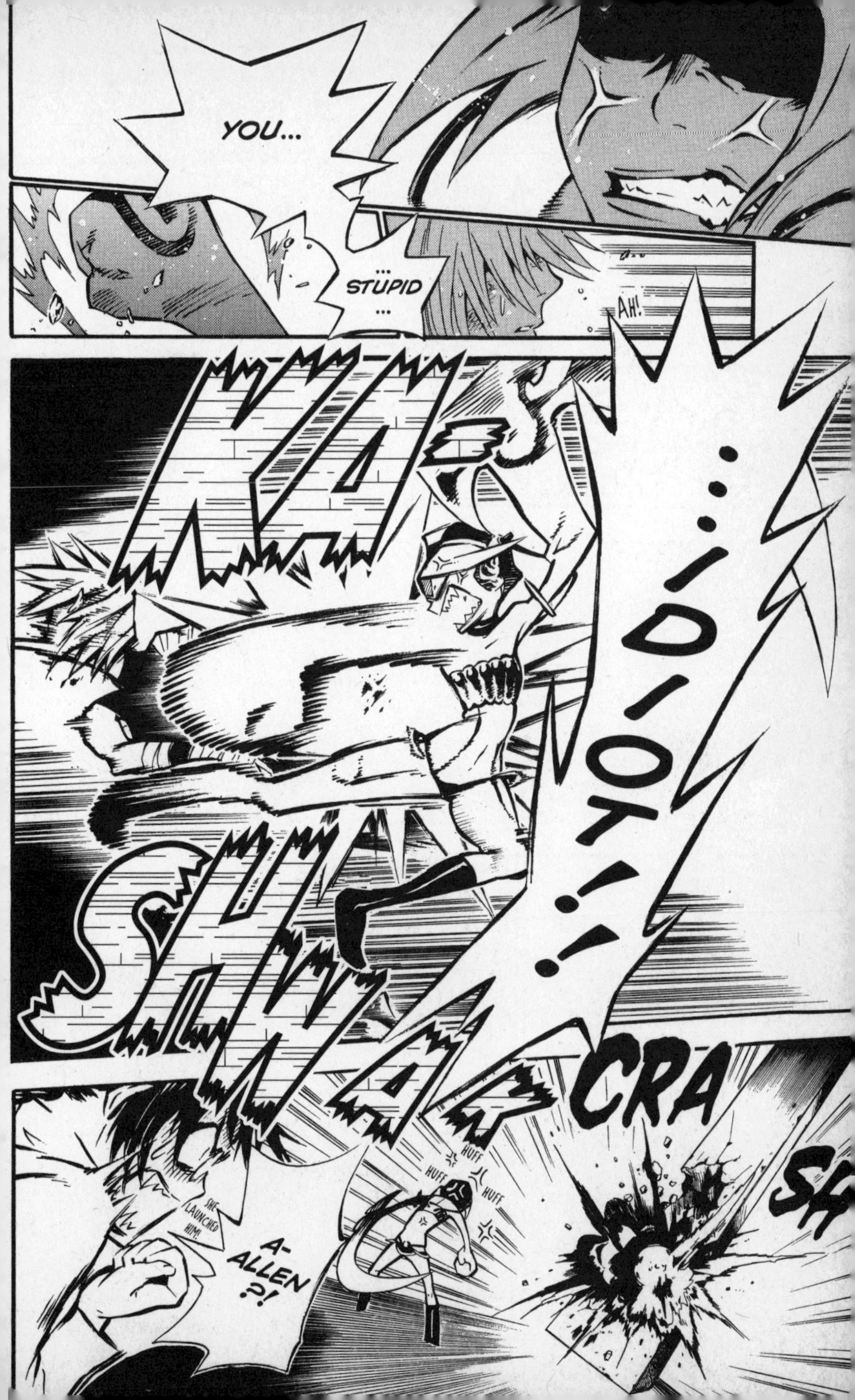
YOU...
... STUPID ...
AH!
...IDIOT!!!
KA SHWAK
CRA SH
HUFF
HUFF
HUFF
SHE LAUNCHED HIM!
A-ALLEN ?!

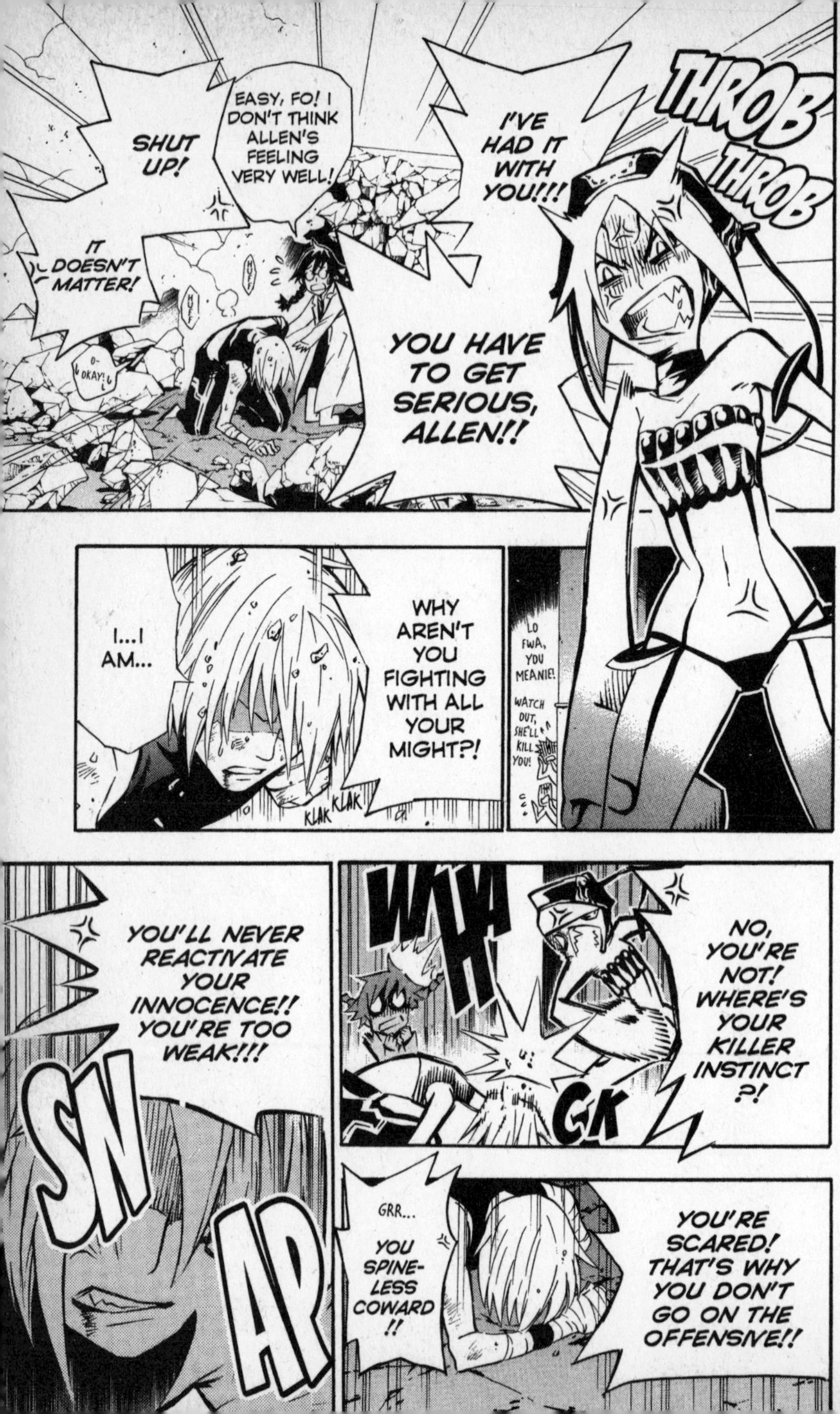
THROB THROB
I'VE HAD IT WITH YOU!!!
YOU HAVE TO GET SERIOUS, ALLEN!!
EASY, FO! I DON'T THINK ALLEN'S FEELING VERY WELL!
SHUT UP!
IT DOESN'T MATTER!
HUFF
HUFF
O-OKAY!
LO FWA, YOU MEANIE!
WATCH OUT, SHE'LL KILL YOU!
WHY AREN'T YOU FIGHTING WITH ALL YOUR MIGHT?!
I...I AM...
KLAK KLAK
NO, YOU'RE NOT! WHERE'S YOUR KILLER INSTINCT?!
WHA
CK
YOU'RE SCARED! THAT'S WHY YOU DON'T GO ON THE OFFENSIVE!!
GRR...
YOU SPINELESS COWARD!!
YOU'LL NEVER REACTIVATE YOUR INNOCENCE!! YOU'RE TOO WEAK!!!
SNAP

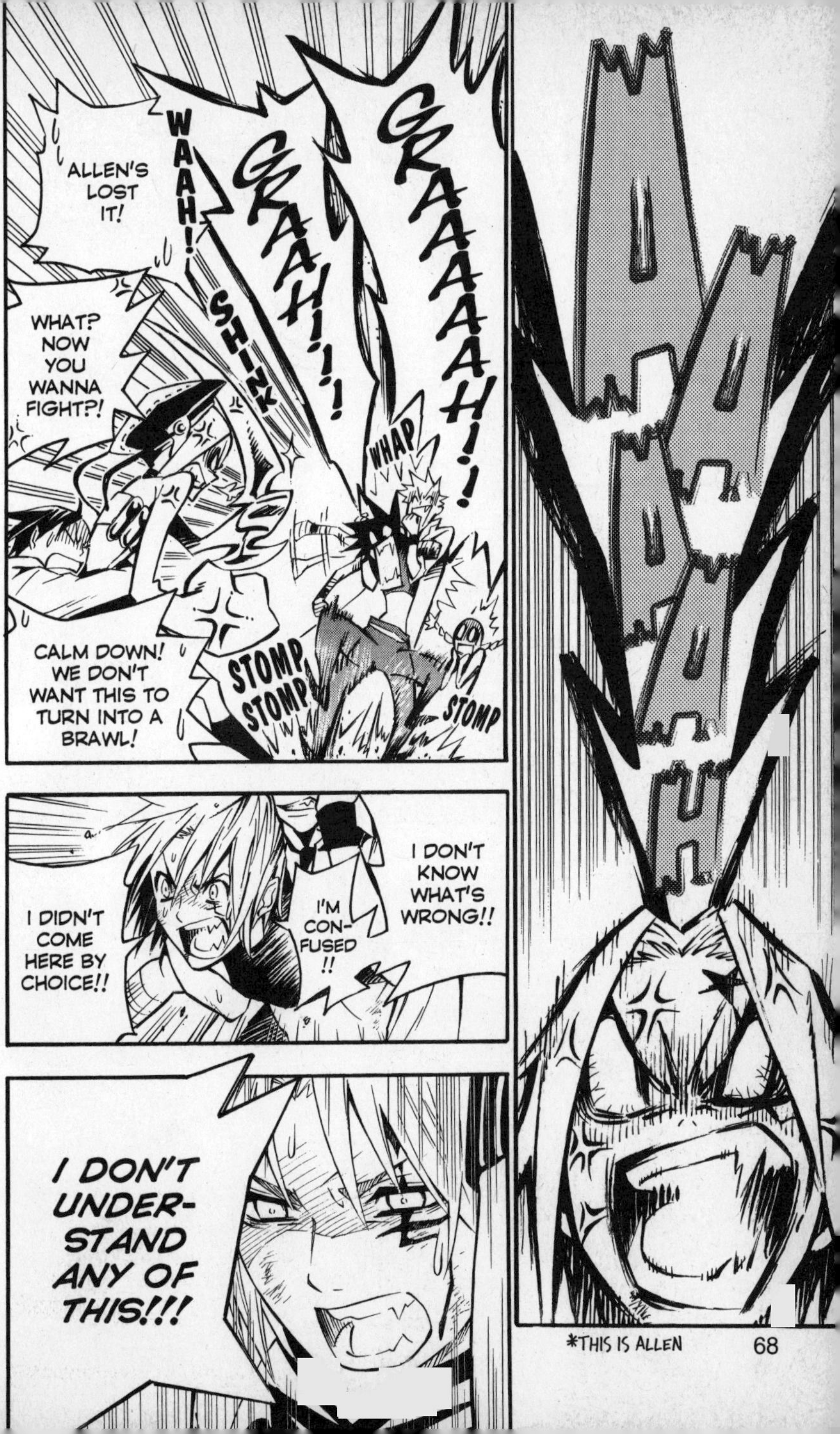
WAAAH
GRAAAAAAH!!!
GRAAH!!!
WAAAH!!
SHINK
ALLEN'S LOST IT!
WHAP
WHAT? NOW YOU WANNA FIGHT?!
STOMP
STOMP STOMP
CALM DOWN! WE DON'T WANT THIS TO TURN INTO A BRAWL!
I DON'T KNOW WHAT'S WRONG!!
I'M CONFUSED!!
I DIDN'T COME HERE BY CHOICE!!
I DON'T UNDERSTAND ANY OF THIS!!!

*THIS IS ALLEN

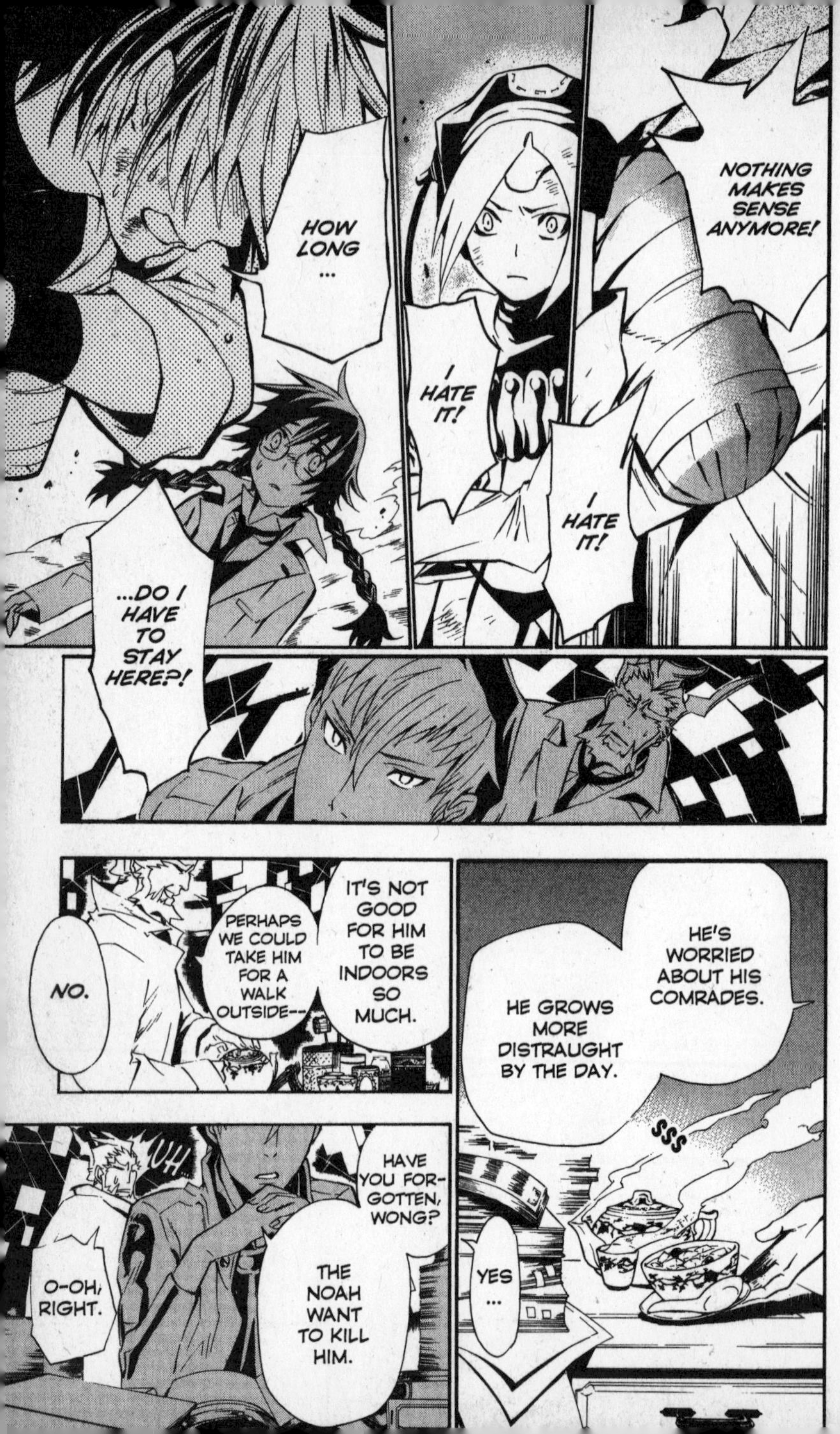
NOTHING MAKES SENSE ANYMORE!
I HATE IT!
I HATE IT!
HOW LONG ...
...DO I HAVE TO STAY HERE?!
HE'S WORRIED ABOUT HIS COMRADES.
HE GROWS MORE DISTRAUGHT BY THE DAY.
SSS
YES ...
IT'S NOT GOOD FOR HIM TO BE INDOORS SO MUCH.
PERHAPS WE COULD TAKE HIM FOR A WALK OUTSIDE--
NO.
HAVE YOU FOR-GOTTEN, WONG?
THE NOAH WANT TO KILL HIM.
O-OH, RIGHT.

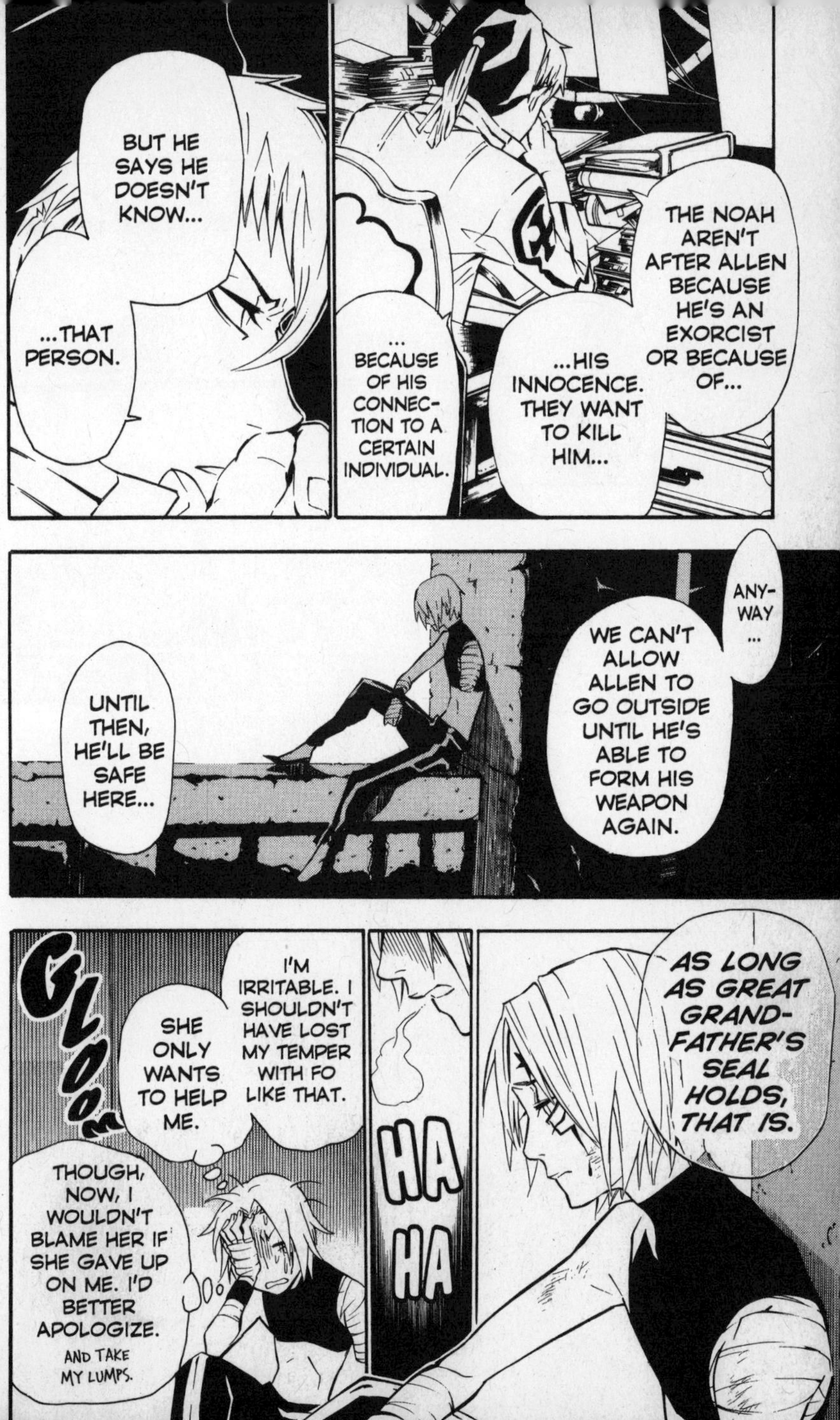
THE NOAH AREN'T AFTER ALLEN BECAUSE HE'S AN EXORCIST OR BECAUSE OF...
...HIS INNOCENCE. THEY WANT TO KILL HIM...
...BECAUSE OF HIS CONNECTION TO A CERTAIN INDIVIDUAL.
BUT HE SAYS HE DOESN'T KNOW...
...THAT PERSON.
ANYWAY...
WE CAN'T ALLOW ALLEN TO GO OUTSIDE UNTIL HE'S ABLE TO FORM HIS WEAPON AGAIN.
UNTIL THEN, HE'LL BE SAFE HERE...
AS LONG AS GREAT GRANDFATHER'S SEAL HOLDS, THAT IS.
HA HA
GLOOM
I'M IRRITABLE. I SHOULDN'T HAVE LOST MY TEMPER WITH FO LIKE THAT.
SHE ONLY WANTS TO HELP ME.
THOUGH, NOW, I WOULDN'T BLAME HER IF SHE GAVE UP ON ME. I'D BETTER APOLOGIZE.
AND TAKE MY LUMPS.

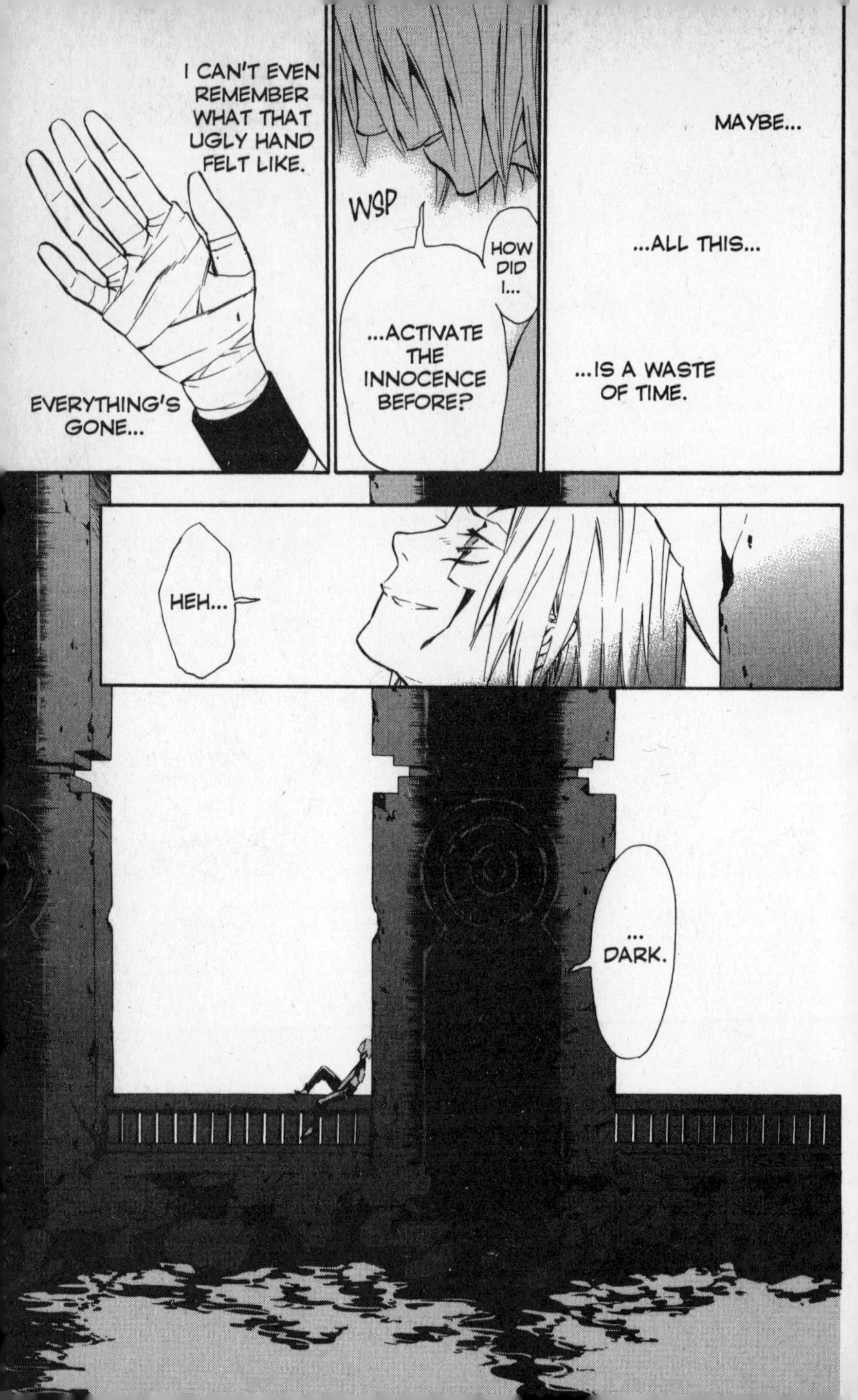
MAYBE...
...ALL THIS...
...IS A WASTE OF TIME.
WSP
HOW DID I...
...ACTIVATE THE INNOCENCE BEFORE?
I CAN'T EVEN REMEMBER WHAT THAT UGLY HAND FELT LIKE.
EVERYTHING'S GONE...
HEH...
... DARK.

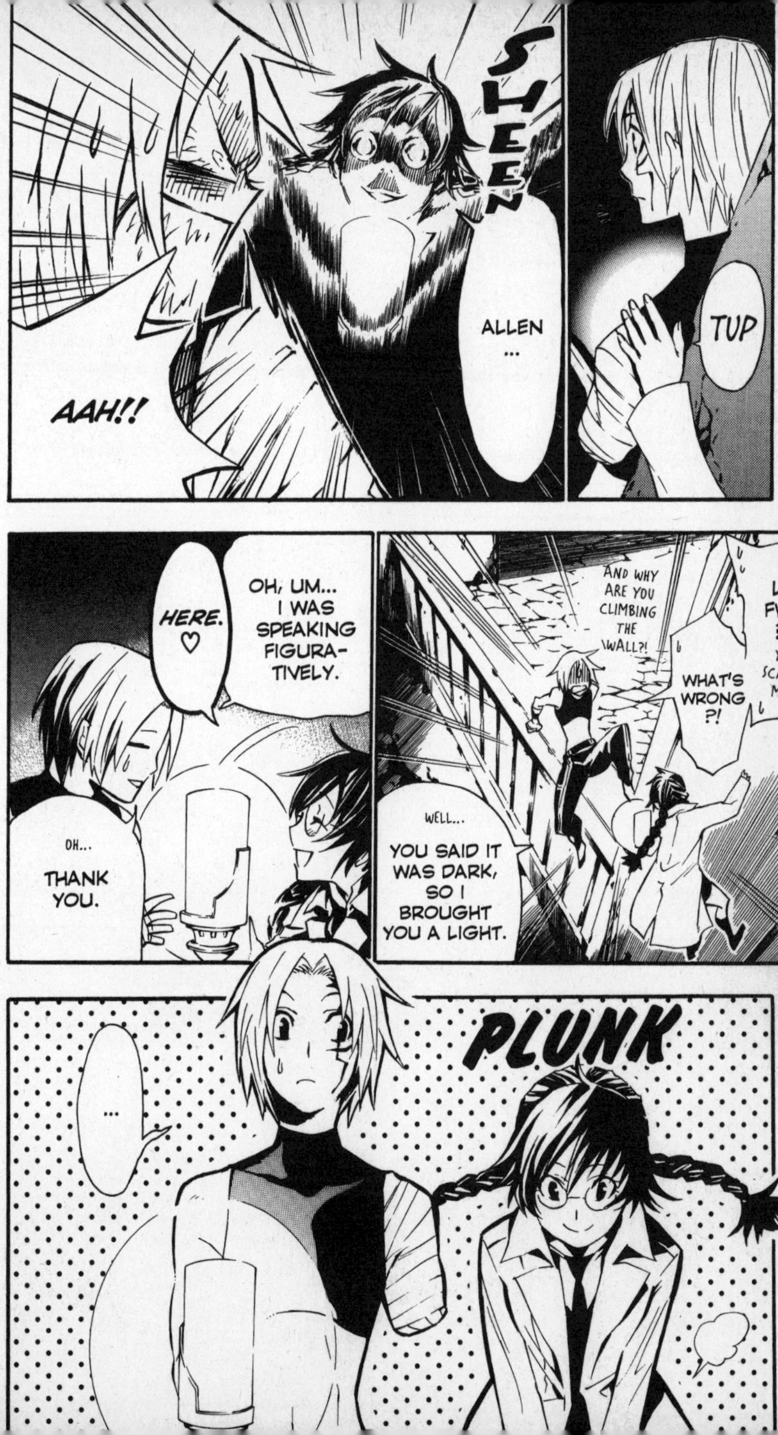
TUP
ALLEN ...
SHEEN
AAH!!
LO FWA?!
YOU SCARED ME!
WHAT'S WRONG?!
AND WHY ARE YOU CLIMBING THE WALL?!
WELL...
YOU SAID IT WAS DARK, SO I BROUGHT YOU A LIGHT.
OH, UM... I WAS SPEAKING FIGURA-TIVELY.
HERE. ♡
OH...
THANK YOU.
PLUNK
...

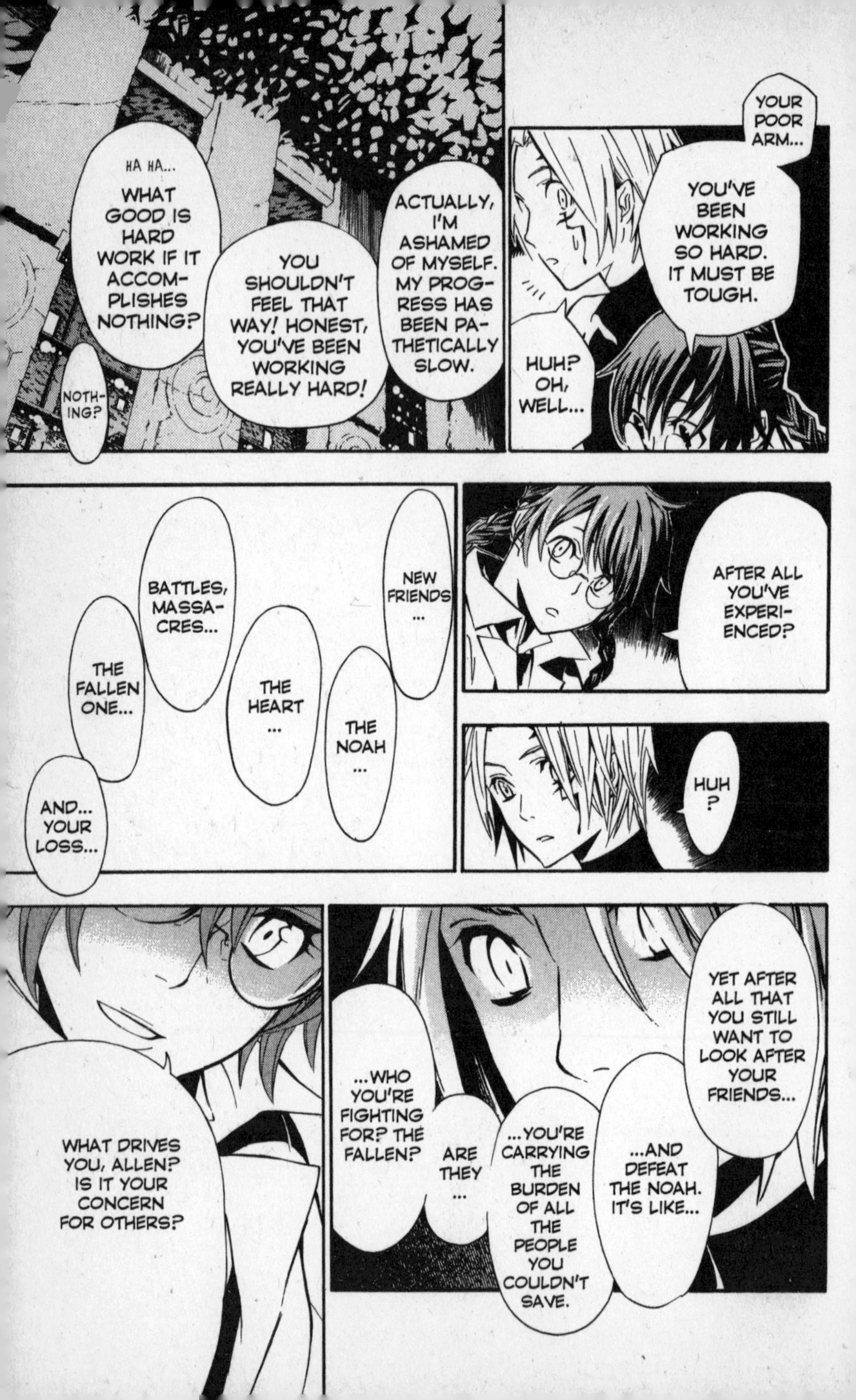

YOUR POOR ARM...
YOU'VE BEEN WORKING SO HARD. IT MUST BE TOUGH.
HUH? OH, WELL...
ACTUALLY, I'M ASHAMED OF MYSELF. MY PROG-RESS HAS BEEN PA-THETICALLY SLOW.
YOU SHOULDN'T FEEL THAT WAY! HONEST, YOU'VE BEEN WORKING REALLY HARD!
HA HA... WHAT GOOD IS HARD WORK IF IT ACCOM-PLISHES NOTHING?
NOTH-ING?
AFTER ALL YOU'VE EXPERI-ENCED?
HUH?
NEW FRIENDS...
THE NOAH...
THE HEART...
BATTLES, MASSA-CRES...
THE FALLEN ONE...
AND... YOUR LOSS...
YET AFTER ALL THAT YOU STILL WANT TO LOOK AFTER YOUR FRIENDS...
...AND DEFEAT THE NOAH. IT'S LIKE...
...YOU'RE CARRYING THE BURDEN OF ALL THE PEOPLE YOU COULDN'T SAVE.
ARE THEY...
...WHO YOU'RE FIGHTING FOR? THE FALLEN?
WHAT DRIVES YOU, ALLEN? IS IT YOUR CONCERN FOR OTHERS?

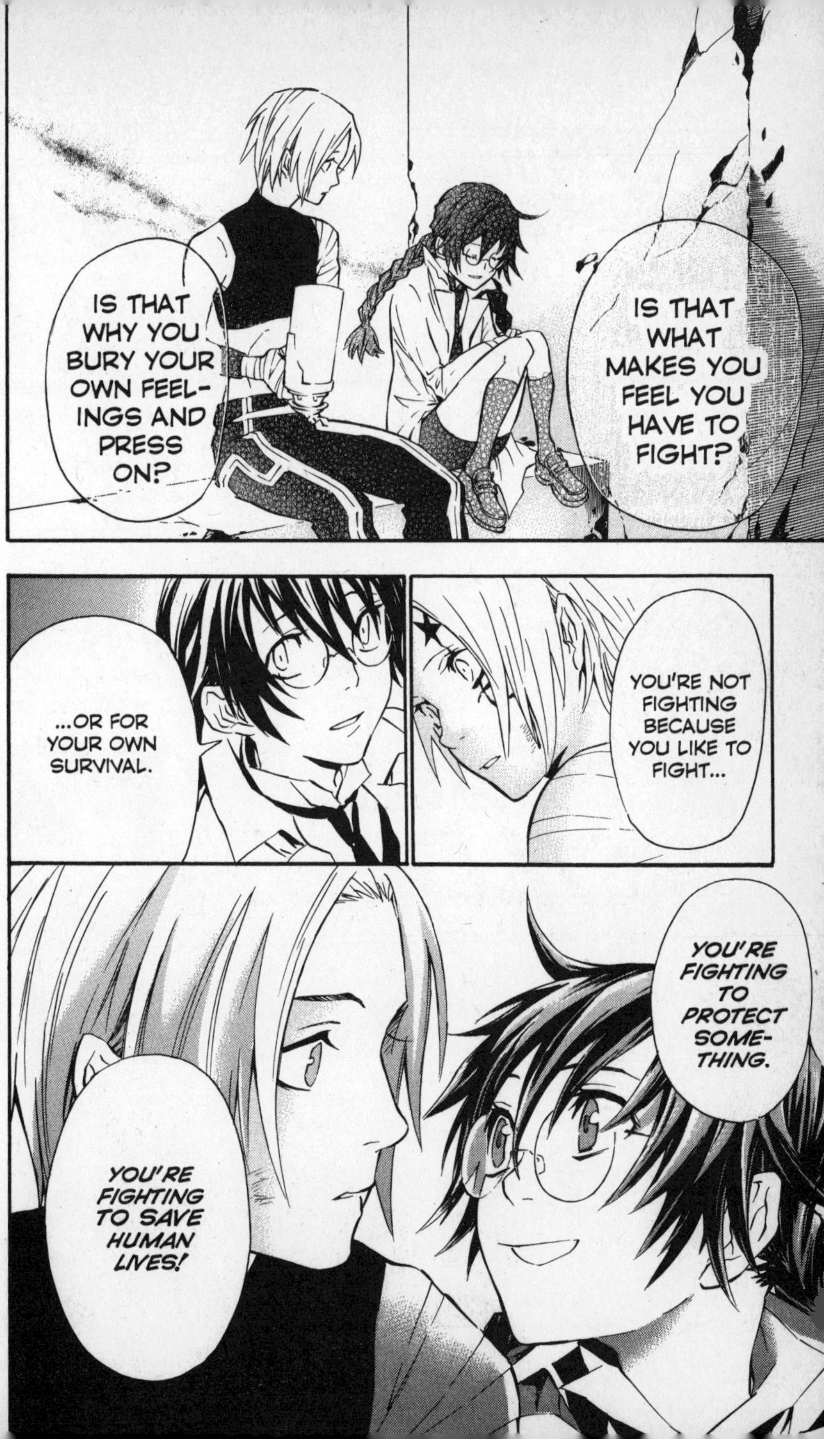
IS THAT WHAT MAKES YOU FEEL YOU HAVE TO FIGHT?
IS THAT WHY YOU BURY YOUR OWN FEEL-INGS AND PRESS ON?
YOU'RE NOT FIGHTING BECAUSE YOU LIKE TO FIGHT...
...OR FOR YOUR OWN SURVIVAL.
YOU'RE FIGHTING TO PROTECT SOME-THING.
YOU'RE FIGHTING TO SAVE HUMAN LIVES!

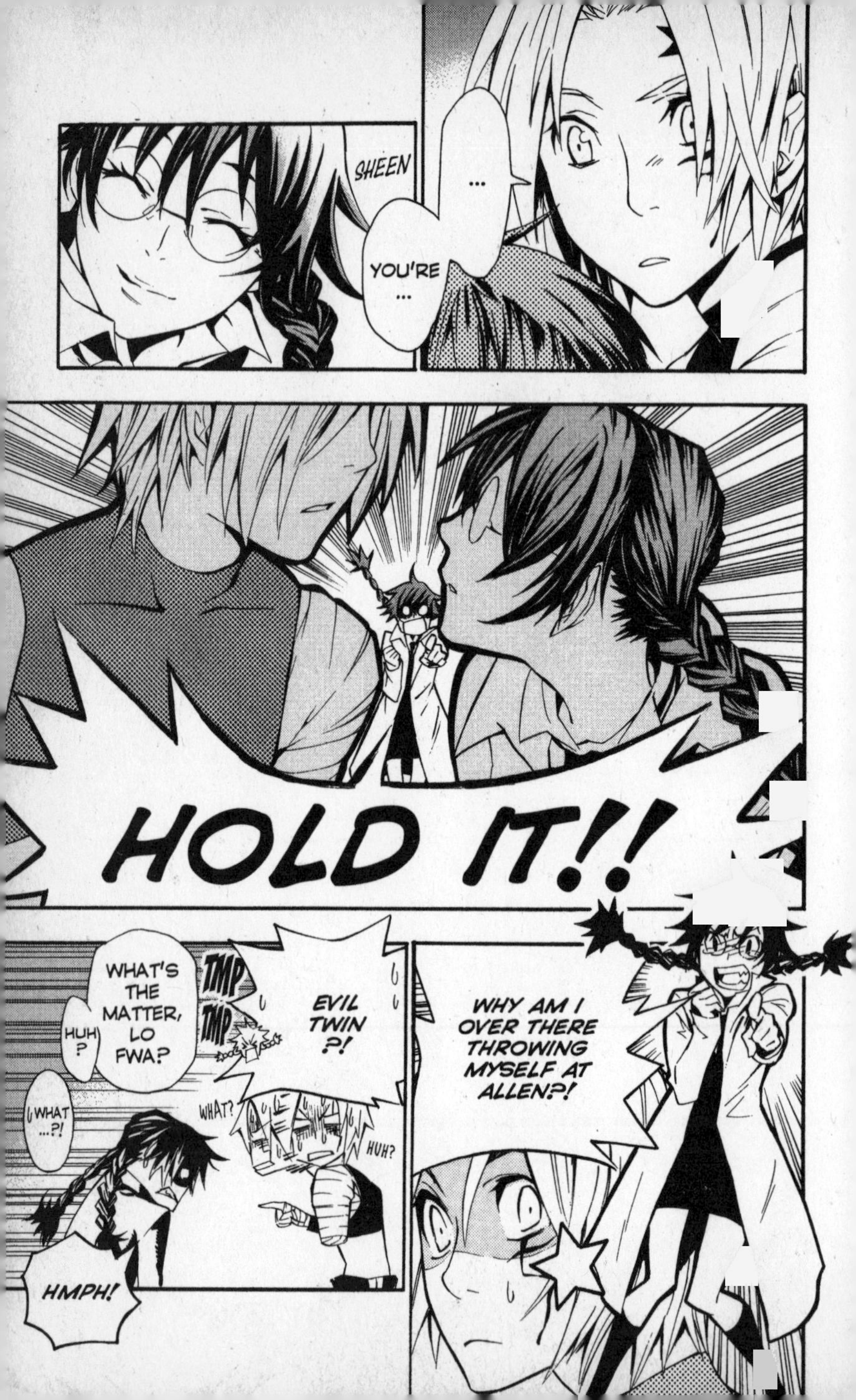
...
SHEEN
YOU'RE ...
HOLD IT!!
WHY AM I OVER THERE THROWING MYSELF AT ALLEN?!
EVIL TWIN ?!
TMP TMP
WHAT'S THE MATTER, LO FWA?
HUH ?
HUH?
WHAT?
WHAT ...?!
HMPH!

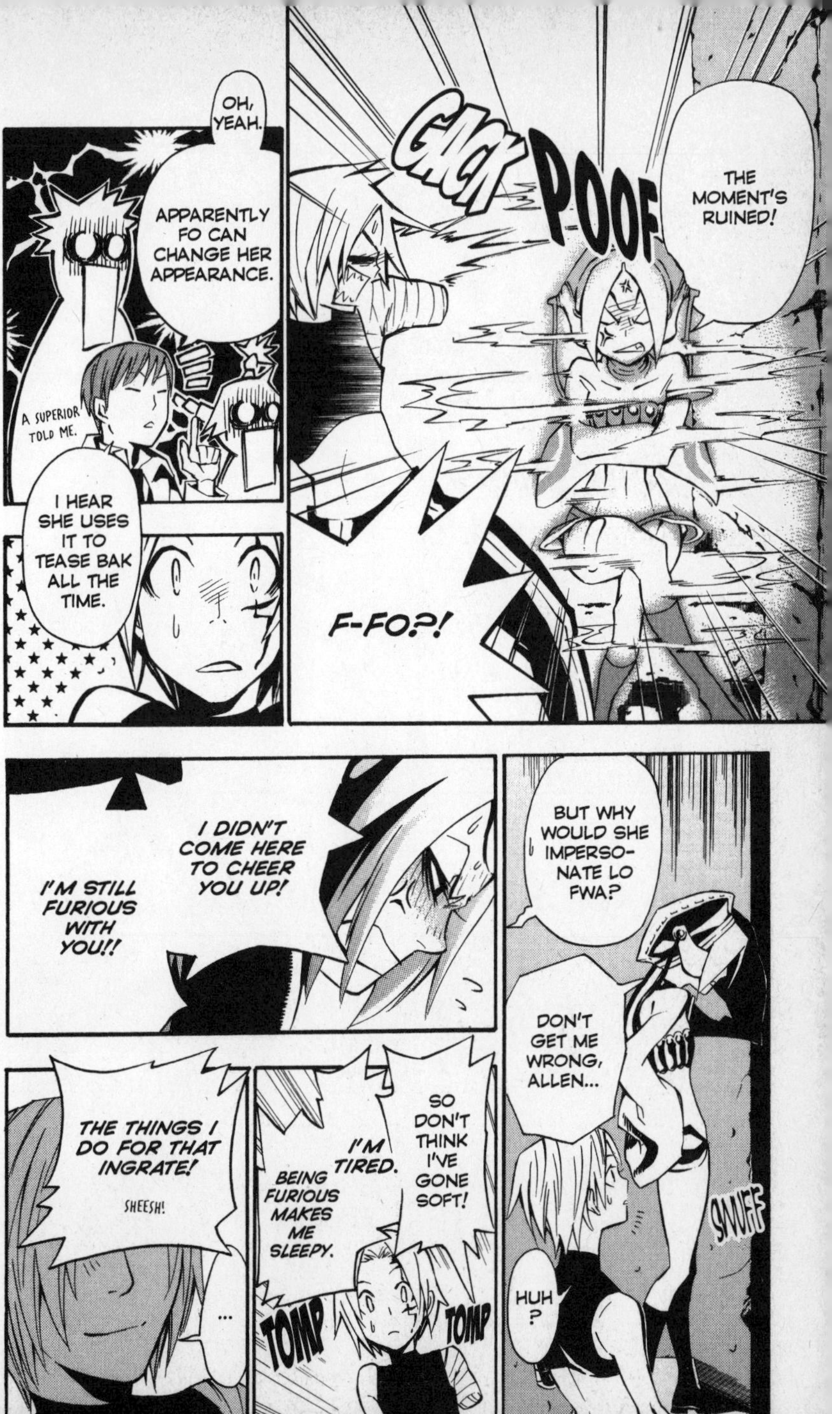
THE MOMENT'S RUINED!
POOF
GACK
F-FO?!
OH, YEAH.
APPARENTLY FO CAN CHANGE HER APPEARANCE.
A SUPERIOR TOLD ME.
I HEAR SHE USES IT TO TEASE BAK ALL THE TIME.
BUT WHY WOULD SHE IMPERSO-NATE LO FWA?
DON'T GET ME WRONG, ALLEN...
SNUFF
HUH?
I DIDN'T COME HERE TO CHEER YOU UP!
I'M STILL FURIOUS WITH YOU!!
SO DON'T THINK I'VE GONE SOFT!
I'M TIRED.
BEING FURIOUS MAKES ME SLEEPY.
TOMP
TOMP
THE THINGS I DO FOR THAT INGRATE!
SHEESH!
...

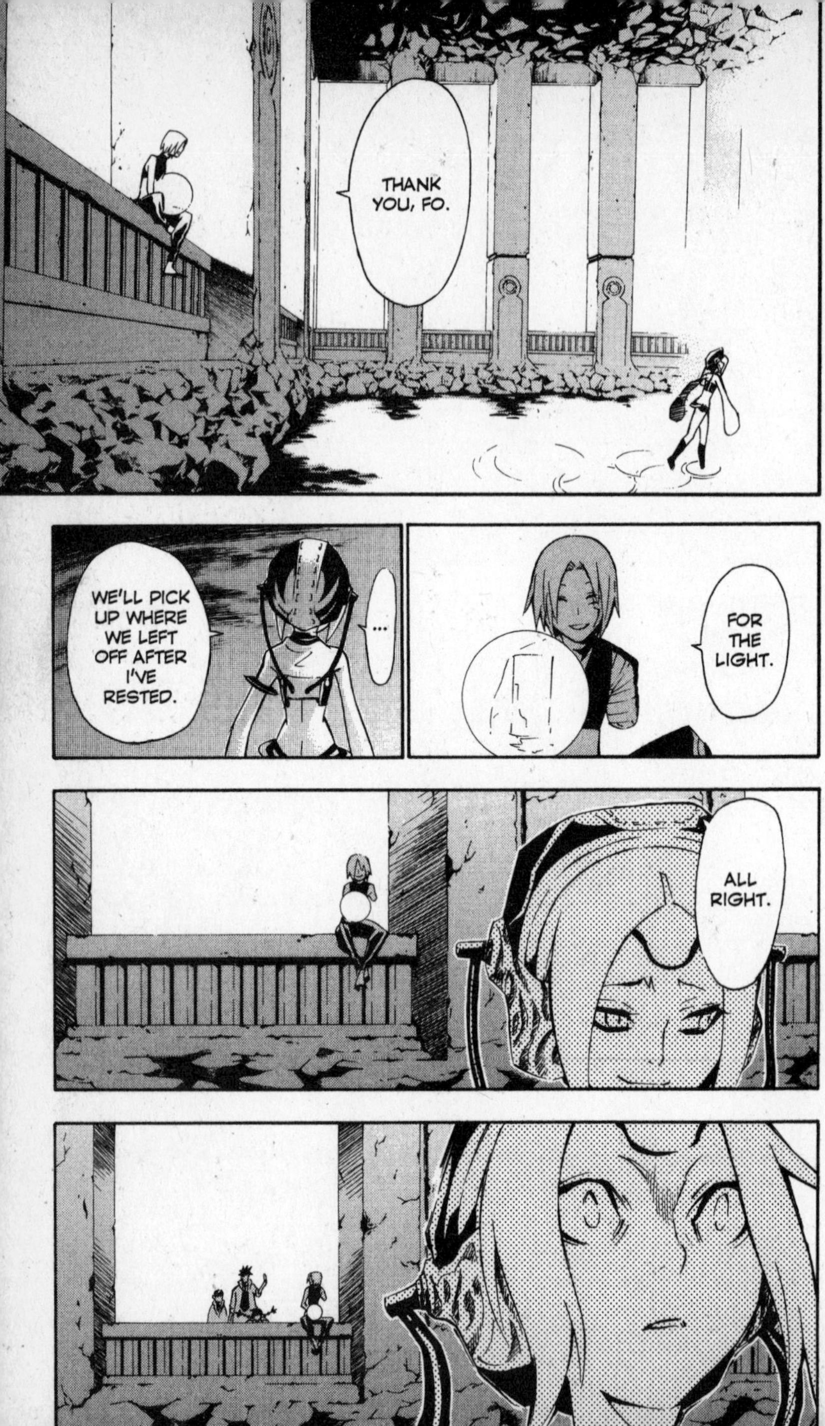
THANK YOU, FO.
FOR THE LIGHT.
...
WE'LL PICK UP WHERE WE LEFT OFF AFTER I'VE RESTED.
ALL RIGHT.

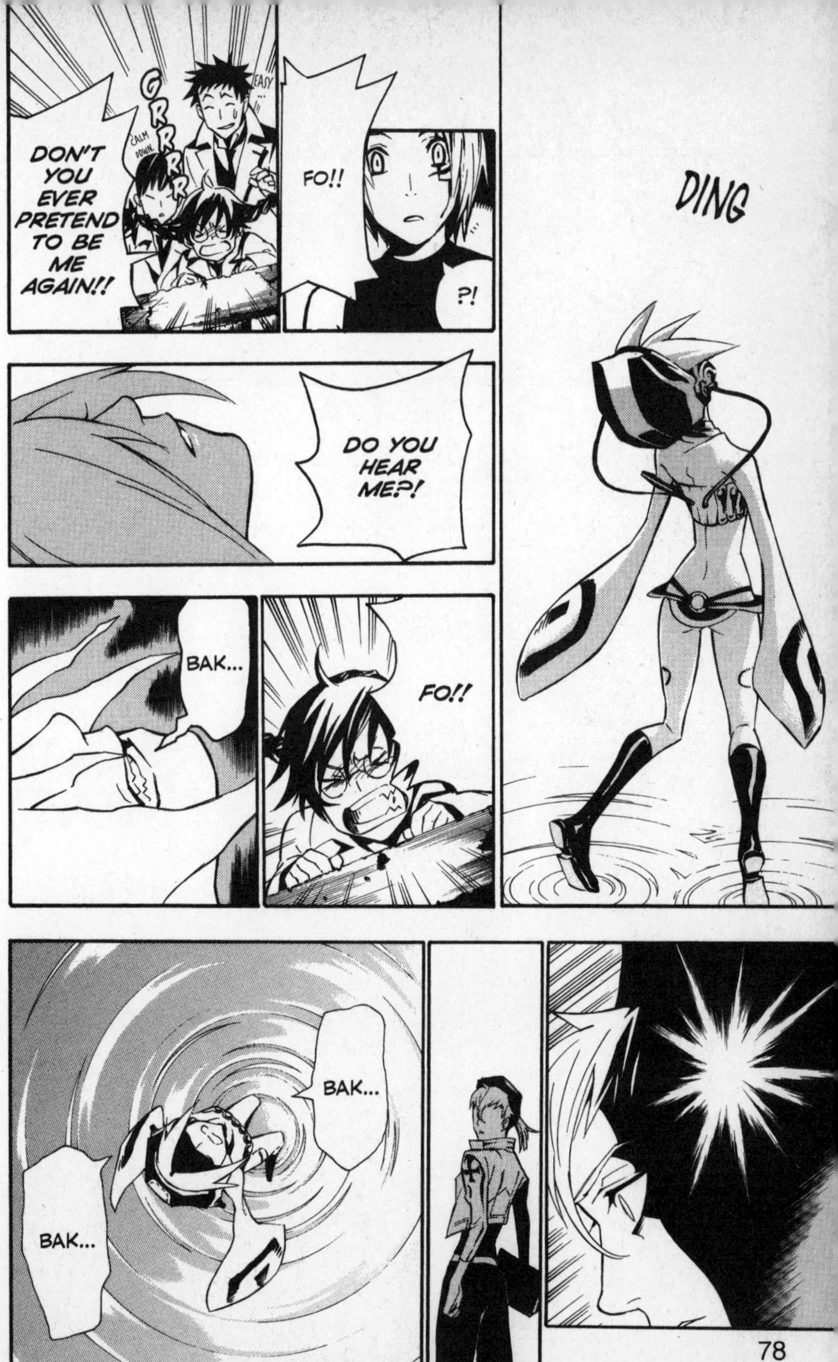
DING
FO!!
?!
DON'T YOU EVER PRETEND TO BE ME AGAIN!!
GRRRR
CALM DOWN.
EASY...!!
DO YOU HEAR ME?!
FO!!
BAK...
BAK...
BAK...

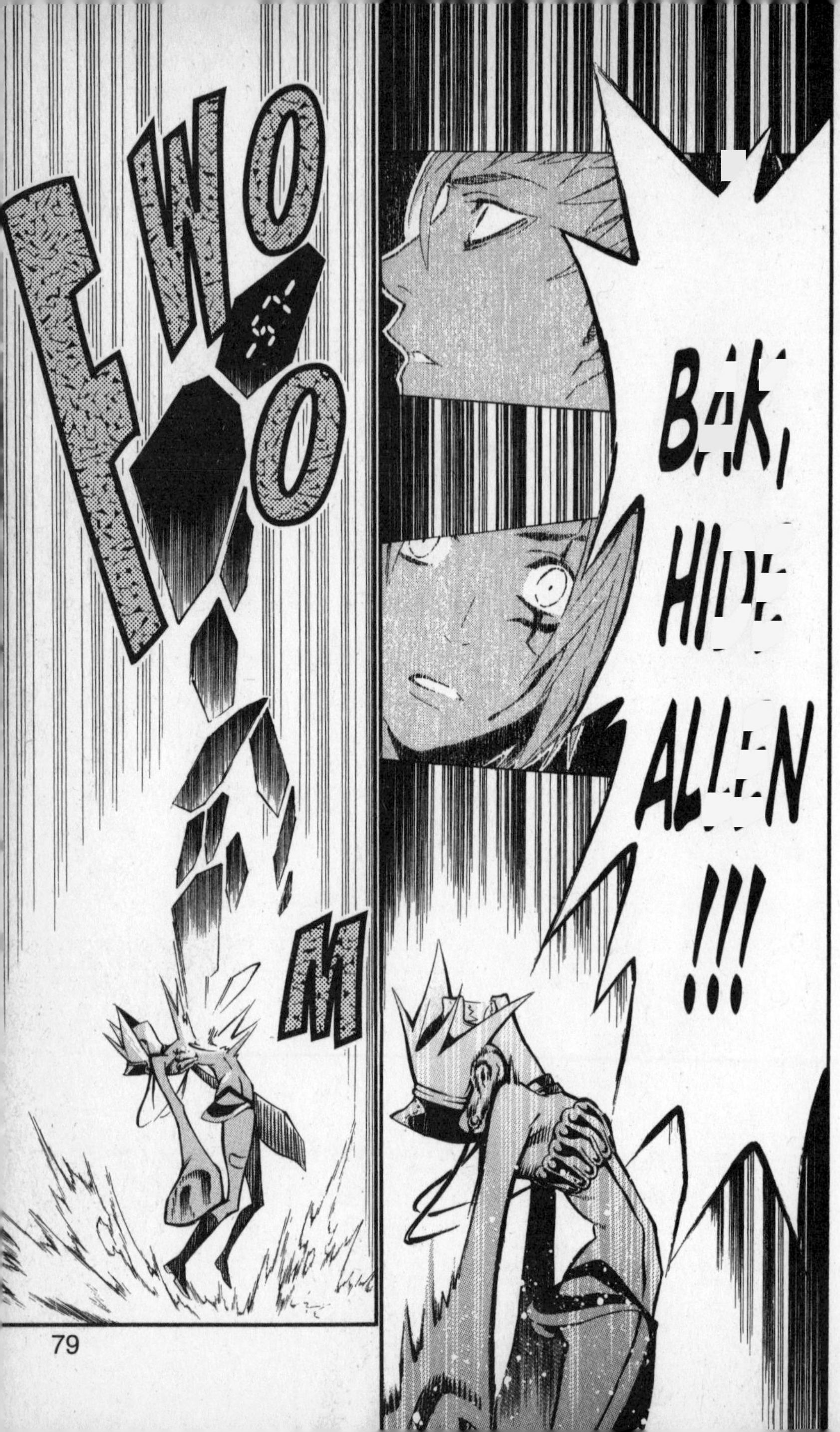
BAK, HIDE ALLEN!!!
FWOOM

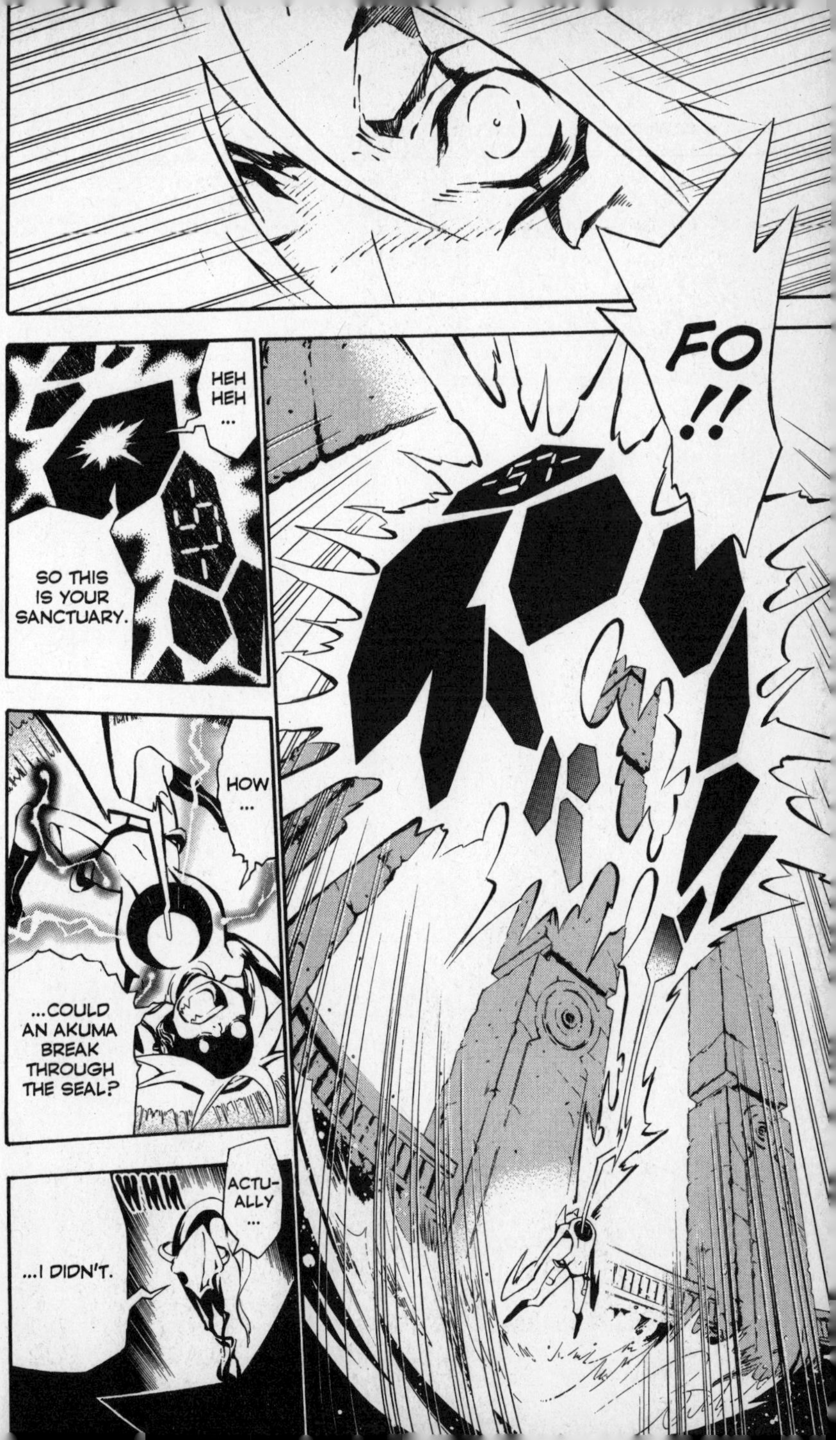
FO!!
HEH HEH ...
SO THIS IS YOUR SANCTUARY.
HOW ...
...COULD AN AKUMA BREAK THROUGH THE SEAL?
ACTU-ALLY ...
...I DIDN'T.
WMM

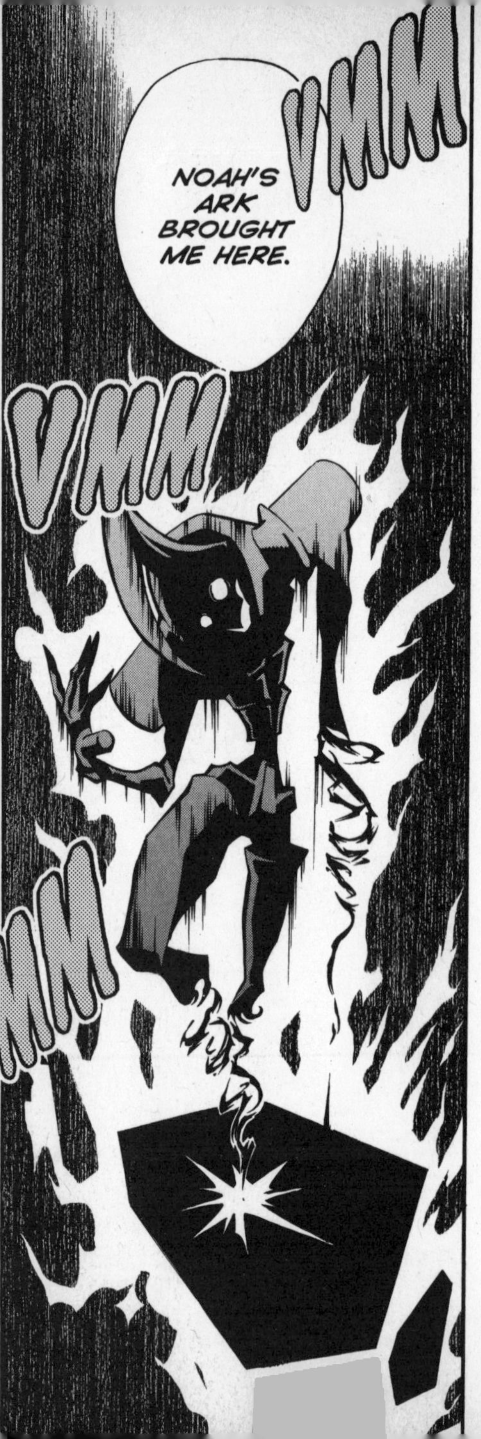
VMMM
NOAH'S ARK BROUGHT ME HERE.
VMMM
VMMM

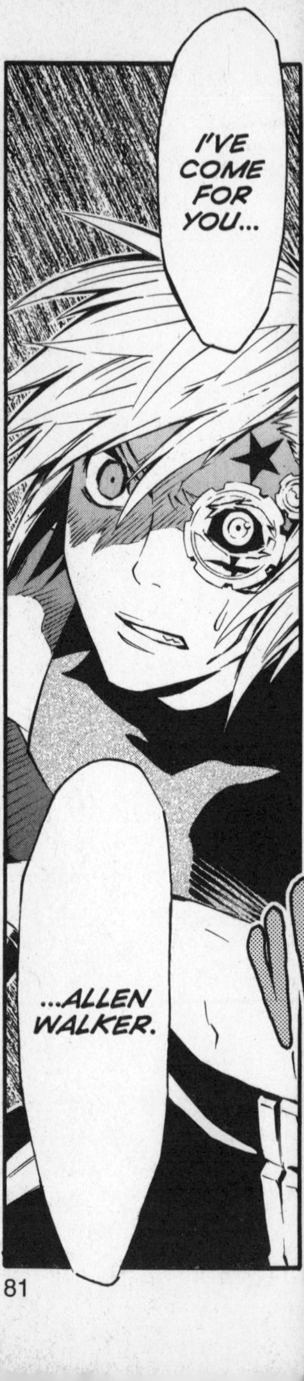
I'VE COME FOR YOU...
...ALLEN WALKER.

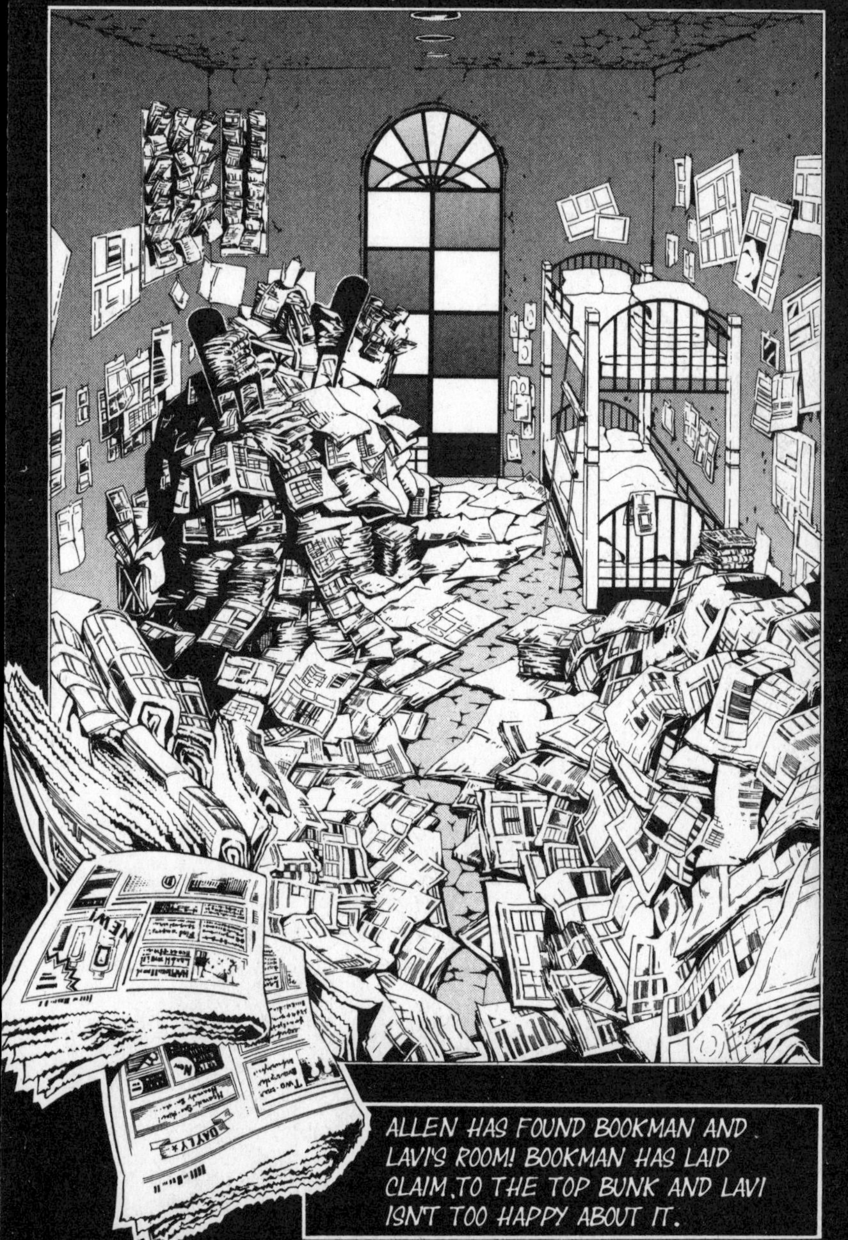
ALLEN HAS FOUND BOOKMAN AND LAVI'S ROOM! BOOKMAN HAS LAID CLAIM TO THE TOP BUNK AND LAVI ISN'T TOO HAPPY ABOUT IT.

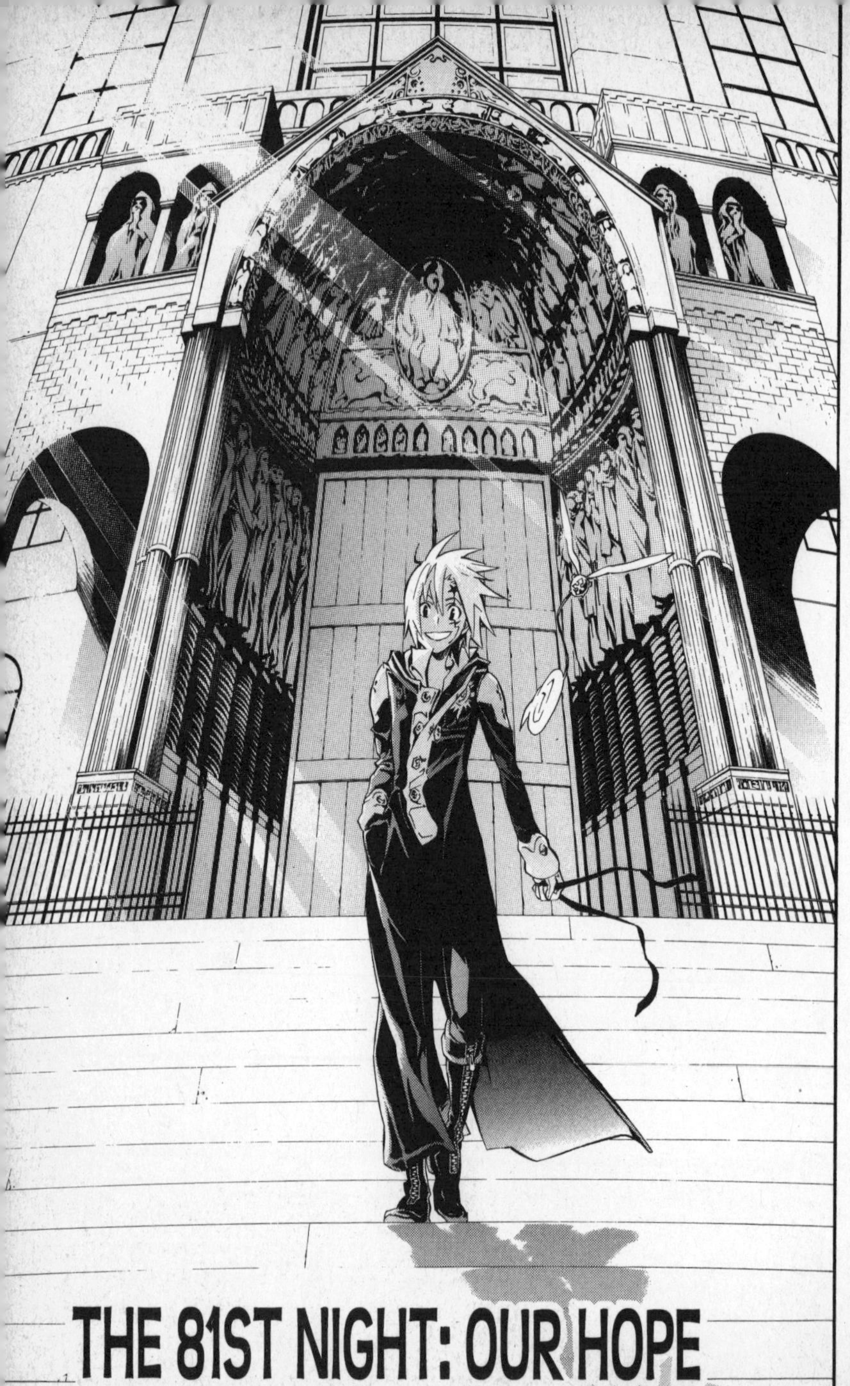

THE 81ST NIGHT: OUR HOPE

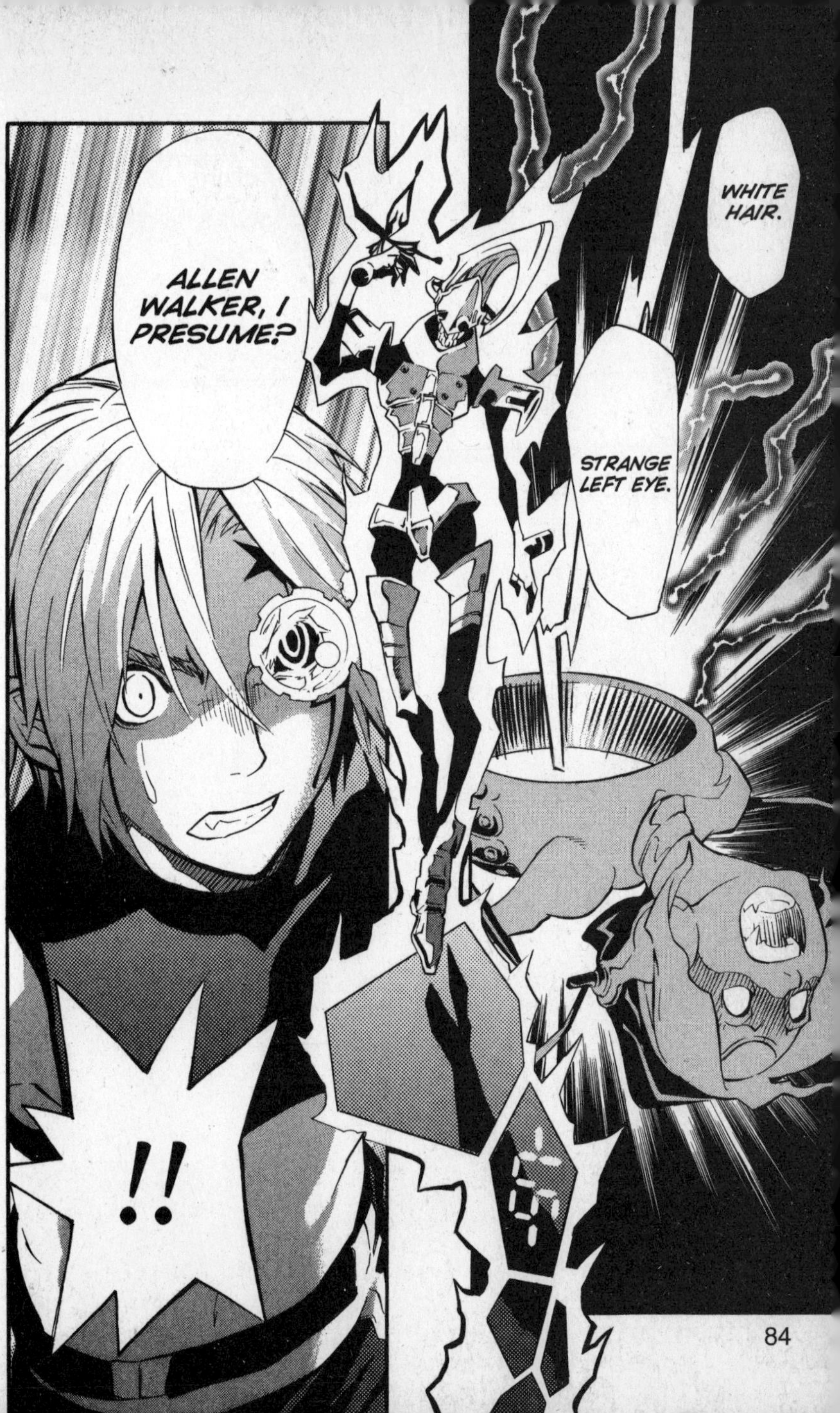
WHITE HAIR.
STRANGE LEFT EYE.
ALLEN WALKER, I PRESUME?
!!

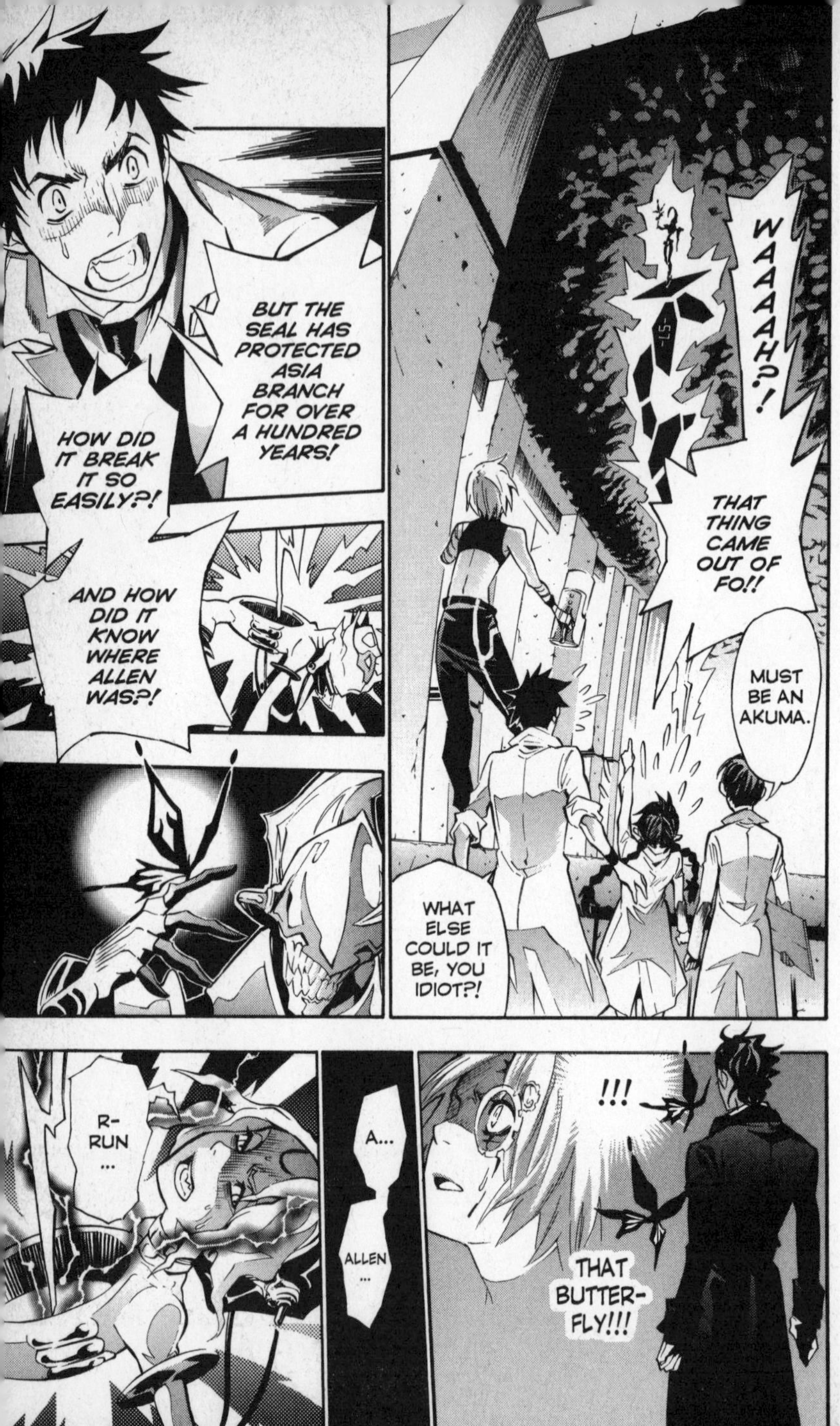
WAAAAAH?!
THAT THING CAME OUT OF FO!!
MUST BE AN AKUMA.
WHAT ELSE COULD IT BE, YOU IDIOT?!
BUT THE SEAL HAS PROTECTED ASIA BRANCH FOR OVER A HUNDRED YEARS!
HOW DID IT BREAK IT SO EASILY?!
AND HOW DID IT KNOW WHERE ALLEN WAS?!
!!!
THAT BUTTER-FLY!!!
A...
ALLEN ...
R-RUN ...

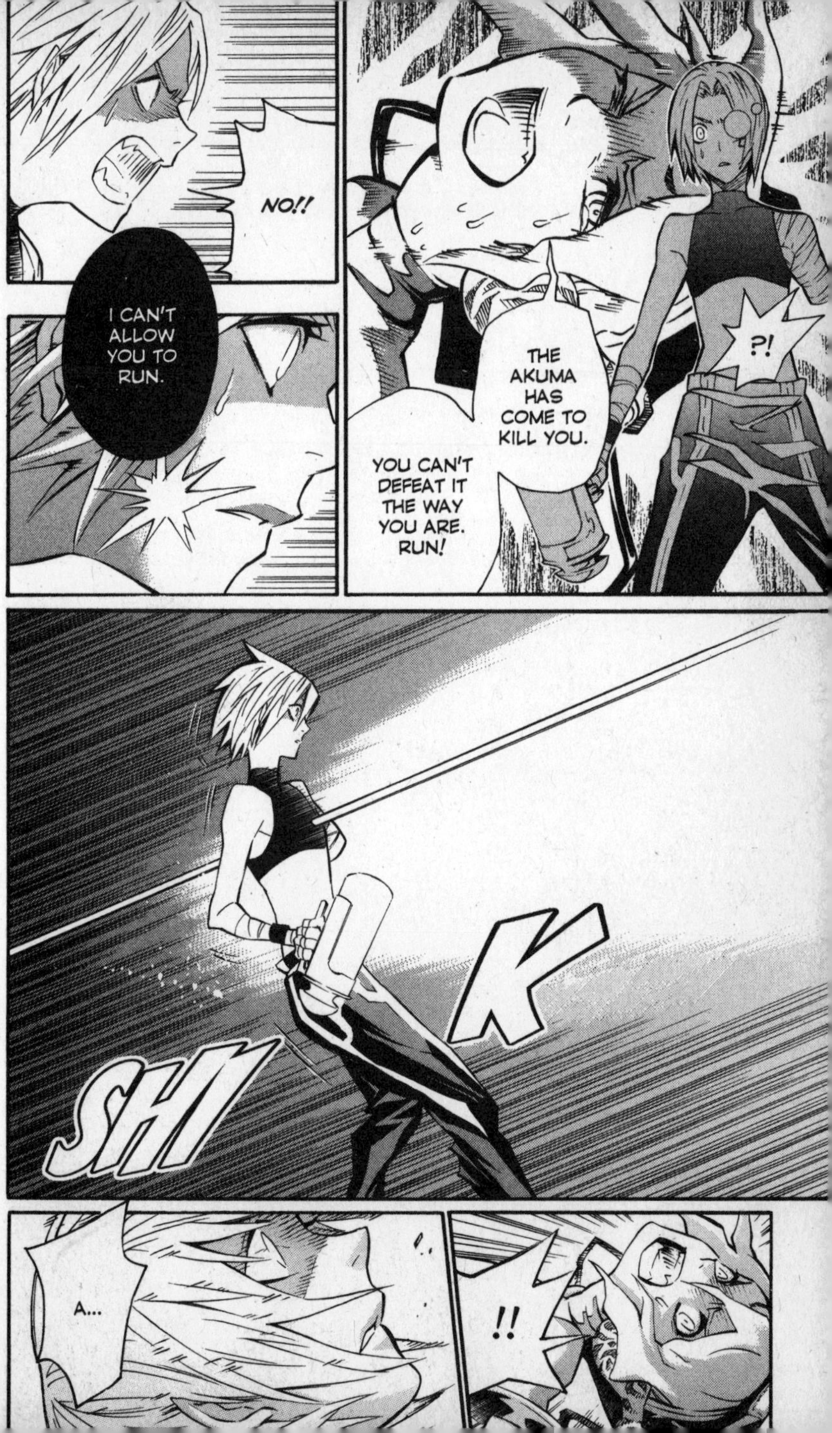
THE AKUMA HAS COME TO KILL YOU.
YOU CAN'T DEFEAT IT THE WAY YOU ARE. RUN!
?!
NO!!
I CAN'T ALLOW YOU TO RUN.
SHI
K
!!
A...

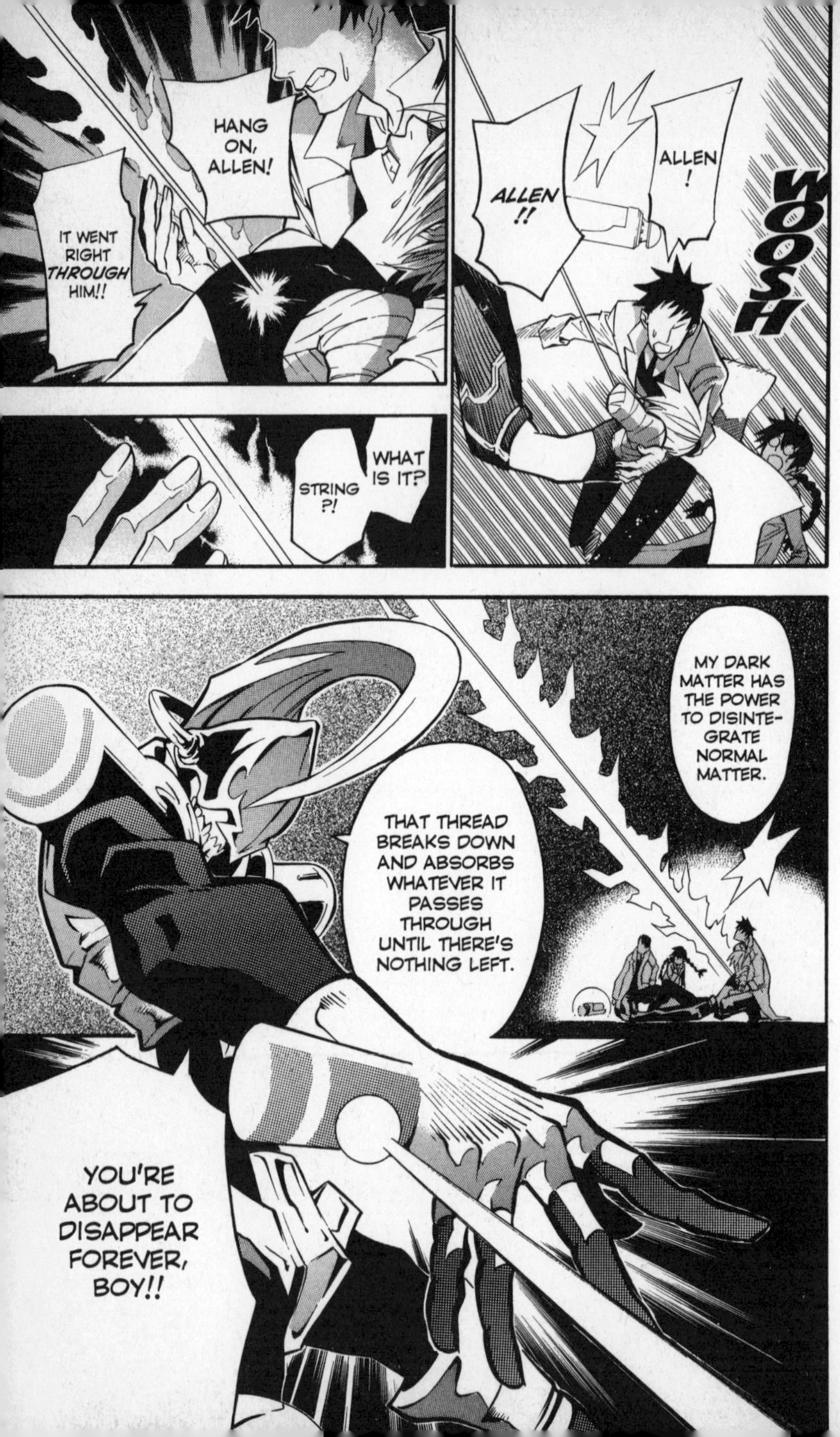
ALLEN!
ALLEN!!
WOOSH
HANG ON, ALLEN!
IT WENT RIGHT THROUGH HIM!!
WHAT IS IT?
STRING?!
MY DARK MATTER HAS THE POWER TO DISINTEGRATE NORMAL MATTER.
THAT THREAD BREAKS DOWN AND ABSORBS WHATEVER IT PASSES THROUGH UNTIL THERE'S NOTHING LEFT.
YOU'RE ABOUT TO DISAPPEAR FOREVER, BOY!!

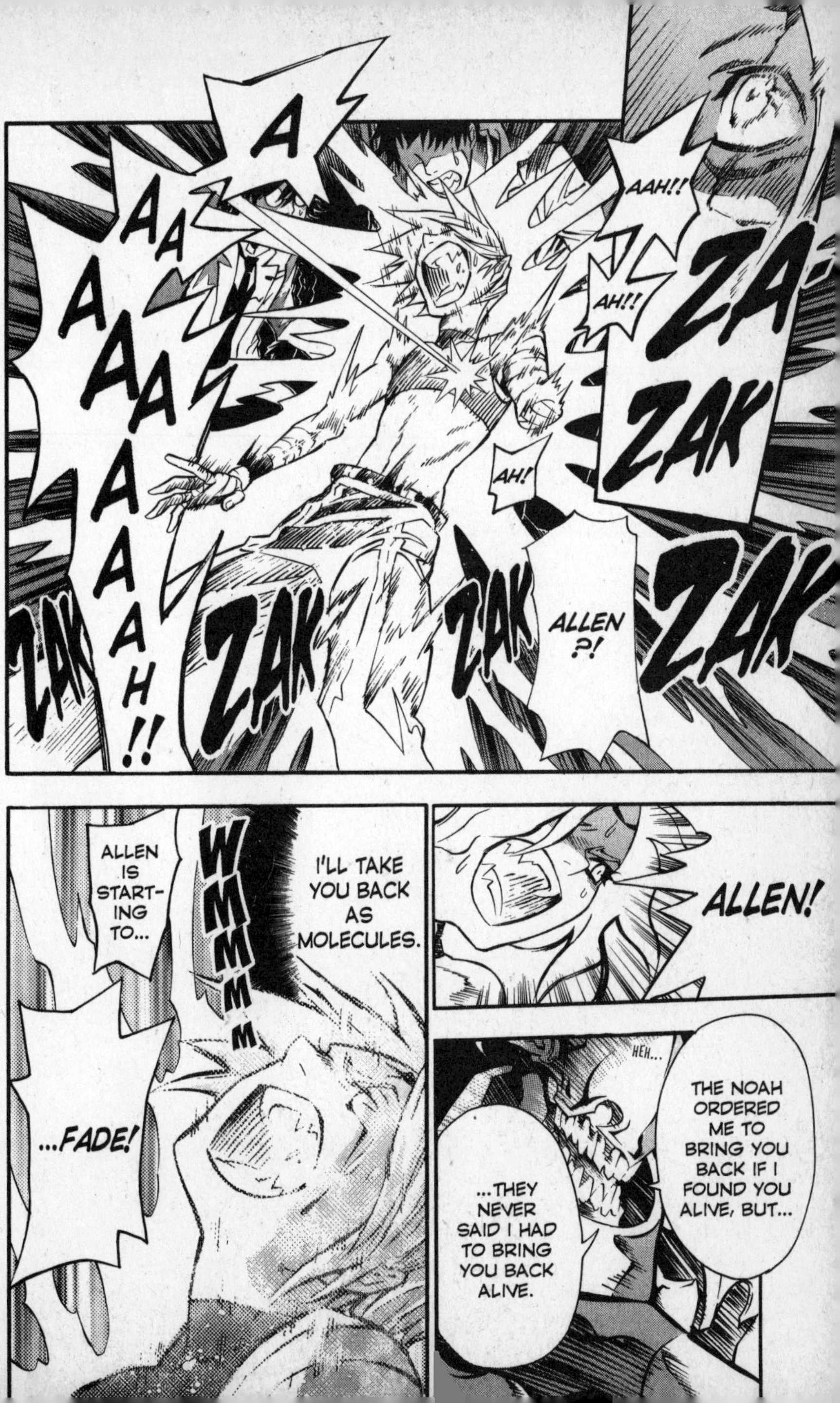
AAH!!
ZA-
ZAK
AH!!
A
AAAAAAAAAAH!!
AH!
ALLEN ?!
ZAK
ZAK
ZAK
ZAK
ALLEN!
HEH...
THE NOAH ORDERED ME TO BRING YOU BACK IF I FOUND YOU ALIVE, BUT...
...THEY NEVER SAID I HAD TO BRING YOU BACK ALIVE.
I'LL TAKE YOU BACK AS MOLECULES.
WMMMMM
ALLEN IS START-ING TO...
...FADE!

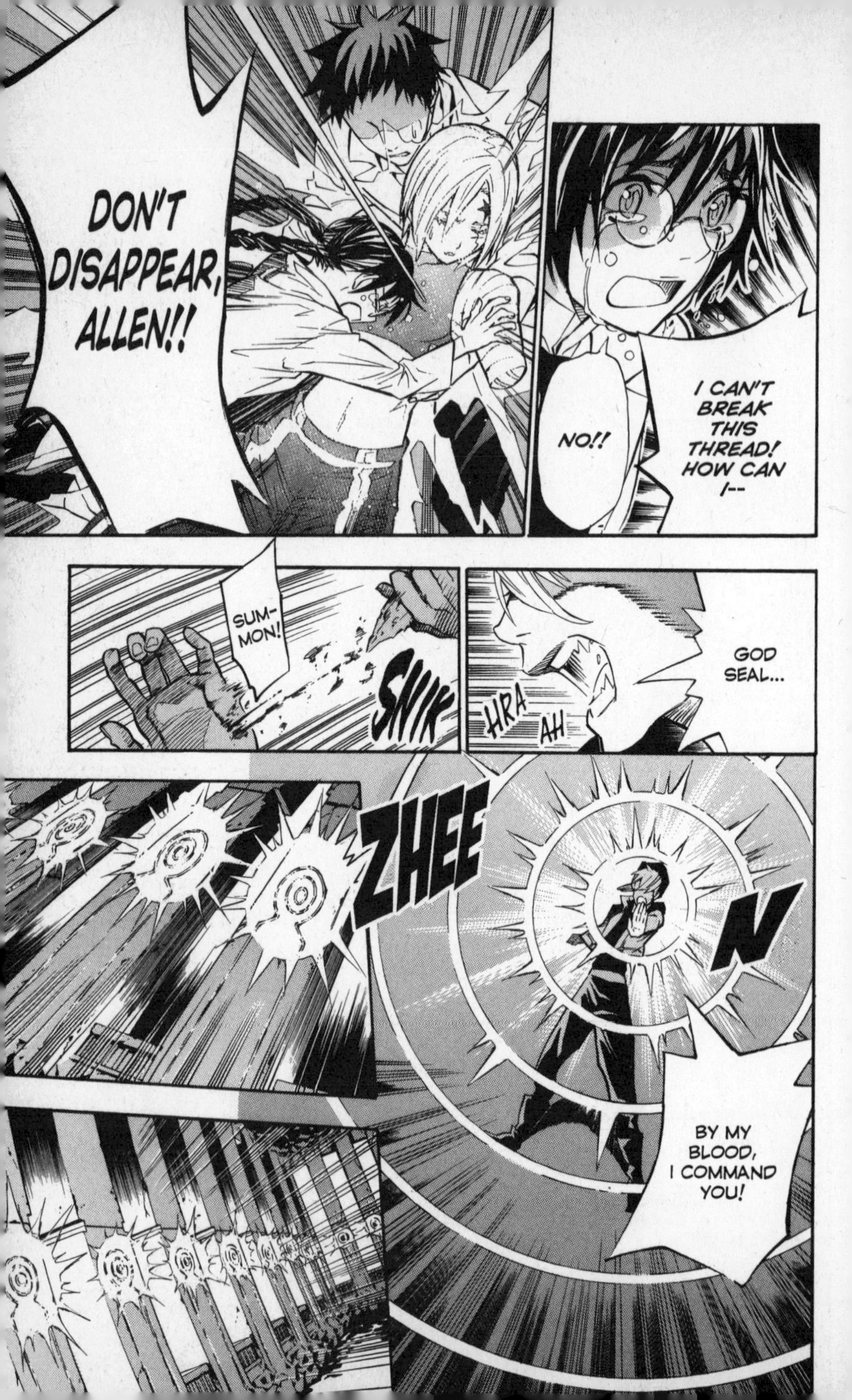
I CAN'T BREAK THIS THREAD! HOW CAN I--
NO!!
DON'T DISAPPEAR, ALLEN!!
GOD SEAL...
HRA AH
SUM-MON!
SNIK
ZHEE N
BY MY BLOOD, I COMMAND YOU!

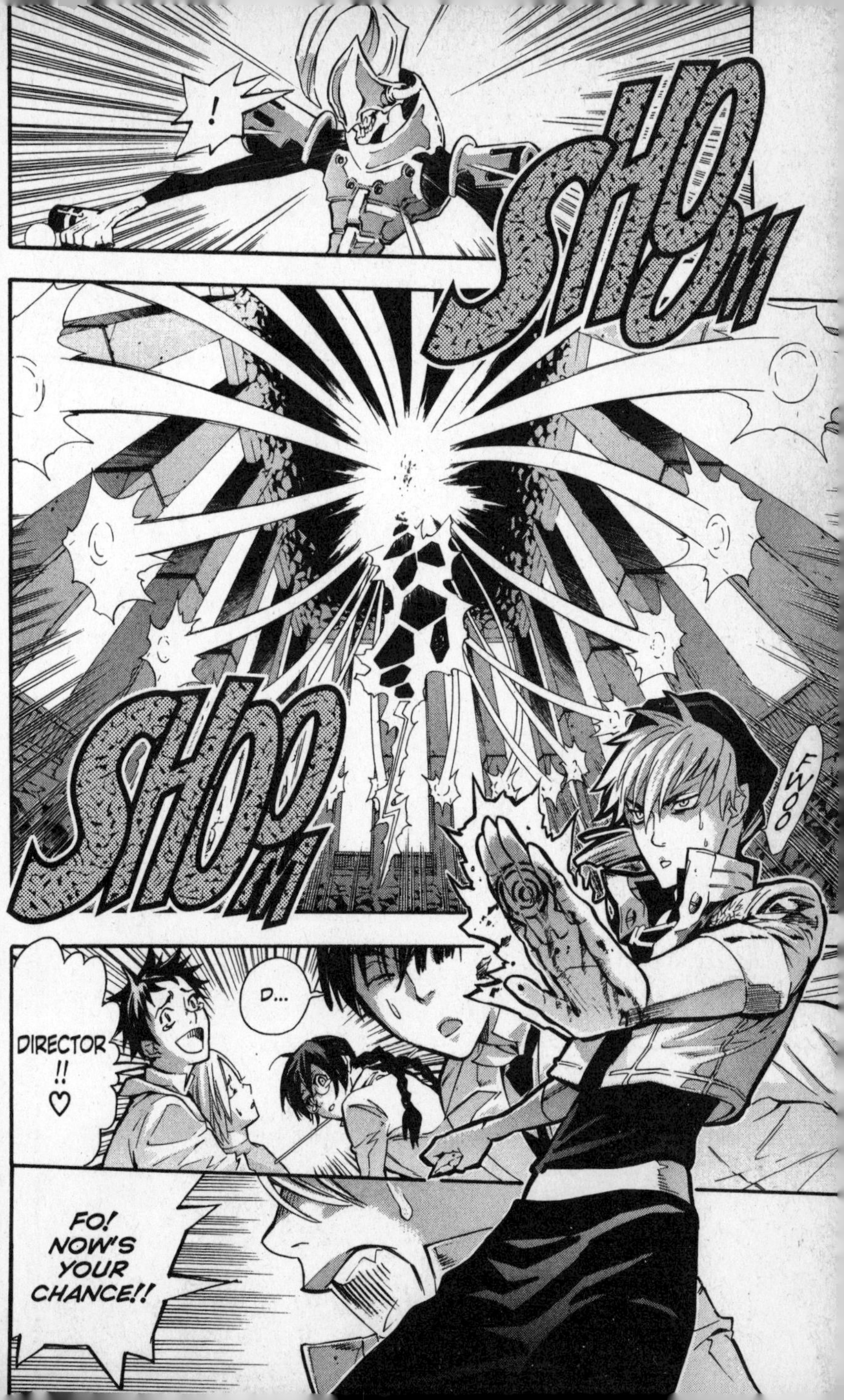
!
SHOOM
SHOOM
FWOO
D...
DIRECTOR !! ♡
FO! NOW'S YOUR CHANCE!!

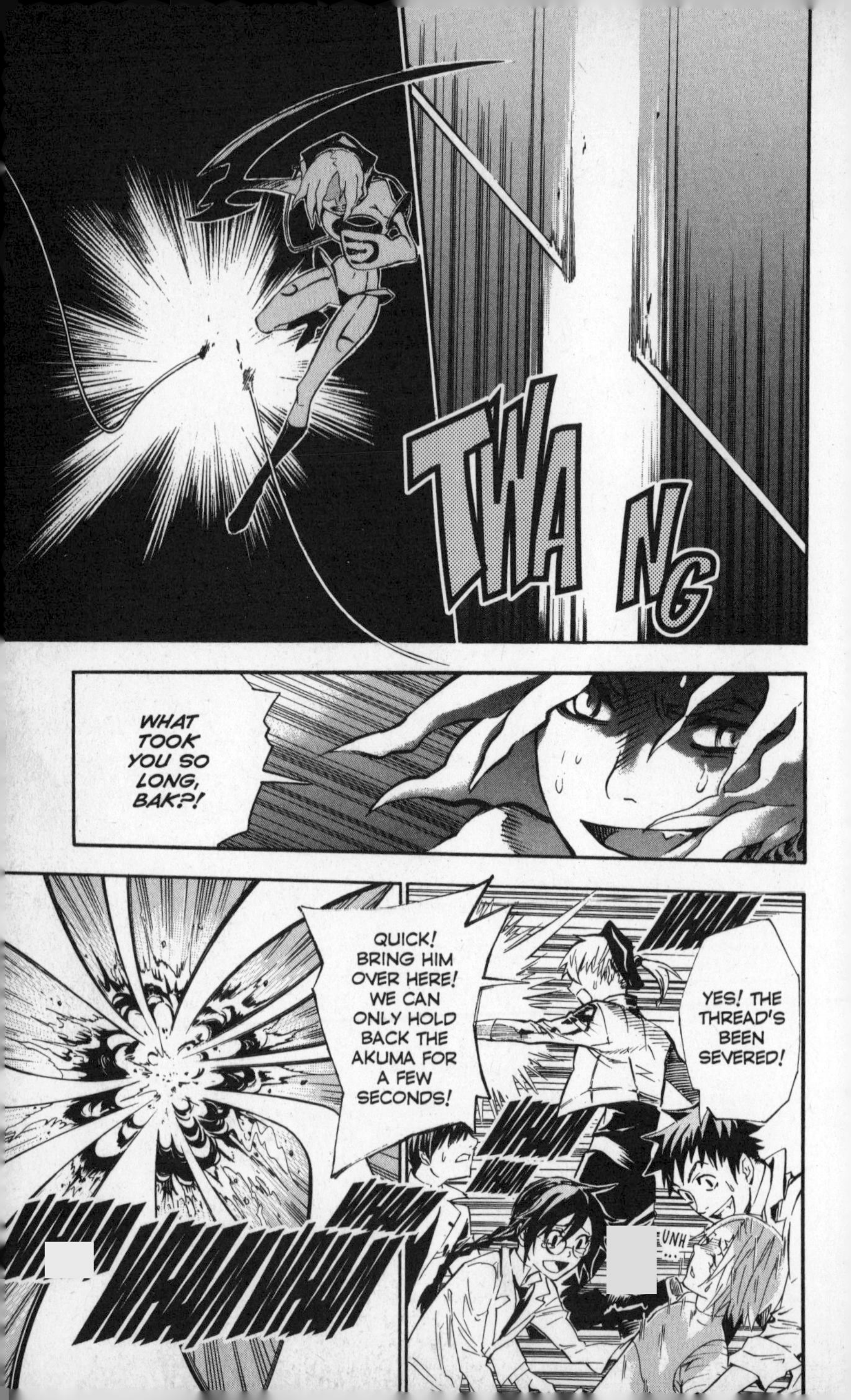
TWANG
WHAT TOOK YOU SO LONG, BAK?!
YES! THE THREAD'S BEEN SEVERED!
QUICK! BRING HIM OVER HERE! WE CAN ONLY HOLD BACK THE AKUMA FOR A FEW SECONDS!
UNH...

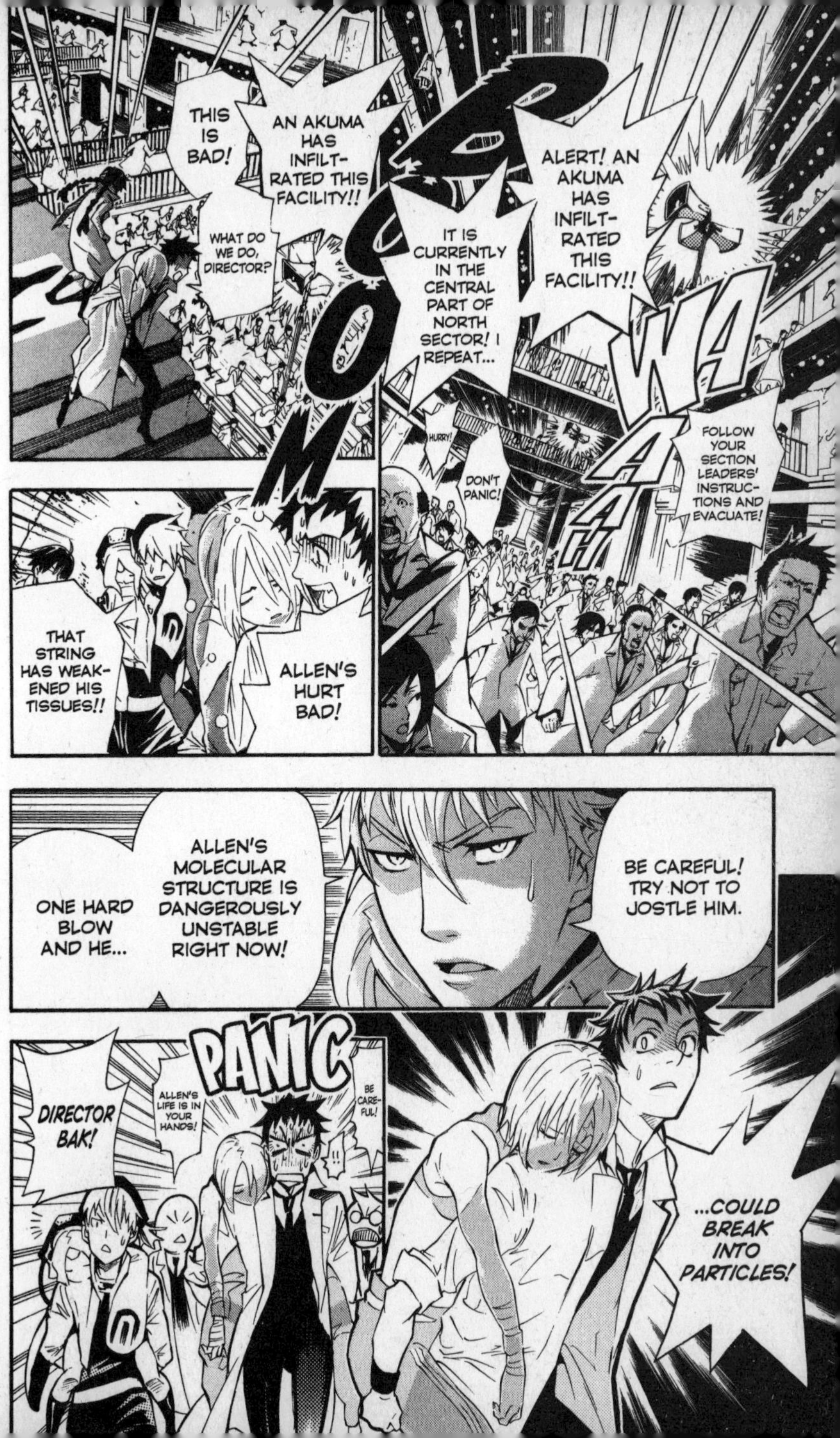
ALERT! AN AKUMA HAS INFILTRATED THIS FACILITY!!
IT IS CURRENTLY IN THE CENTRAL PART OF NORTH SECTOR! I REPEAT...
WAAAH
AN AKUMA HAS INFILTRATED THIS FACILITY!!
THIS IS BAD!
WHAT DO WE DO, DIRECTOR?
FOLLOW YOUR SECTION LEADERS' INSTRUCTIONS AND EVACUATE!
HURRY!
DON'T PANIC!
ALLEN'S HURT BAD!
THAT STRING HAS WEAKENED HIS TISSUES!!
BE CAREFUL! TRY NOT TO JOSTLE HIM.
ALLEN'S MOLECULAR STRUCTURE IS DANGEROUSLY UNSTABLE RIGHT NOW!
ONE HARD BLOW AND HE...
...COULD BREAK INTO PARTICLES!
PANIC
BE CAREFUL!
ALLEN'S LIFE IS IN YOUR HANDS!
DIRECTOR BAK!

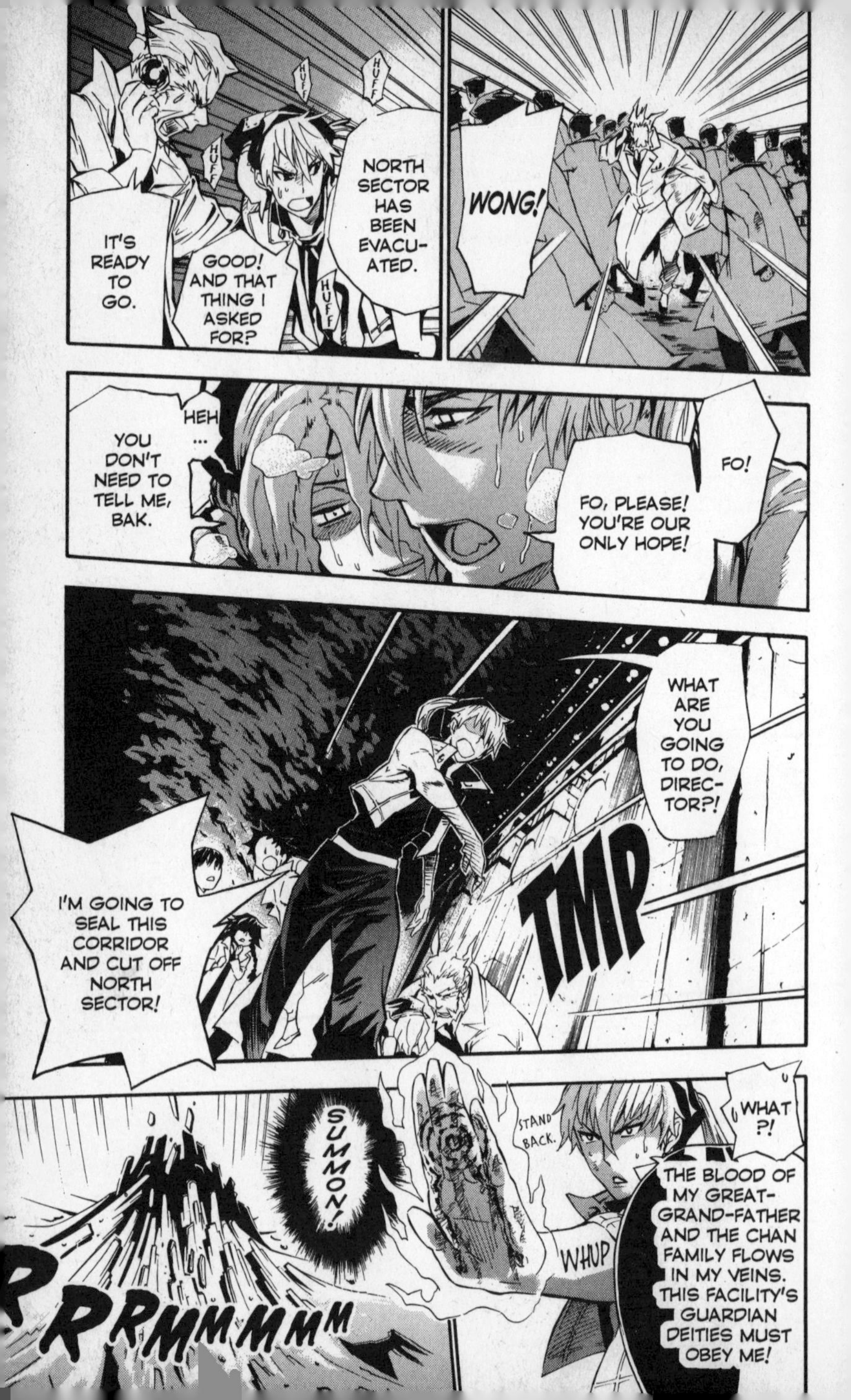
WONG!
NORTH SECTOR HAS BEEN EVACUATED.
HUFF
HUFF
HUFF
HUFF
GOOD! AND THAT THING I ASKED FOR?
IT'S READY TO GO.
FO!
FO, PLEASE! YOU'RE OUR ONLY HOPE!
HEH...
YOU DON'T NEED TO TELL ME, BAK.
WHAT ARE YOU GOING TO DO, DIRECTOR?!
TMP
I'M GOING TO SEAL THIS CORRIDOR AND CUT OFF NORTH SECTOR!
WHAT?!
THE BLOOD OF MY GREAT-GRAND-FATHER AND THE CHAN FAMILY FLOWS IN MY VEINS. THIS FACILITY'S GUARDIAN DEITIES MUST OBEY ME!
STAND BACK.
WHUP
SUMMON!
RRRMMMMM

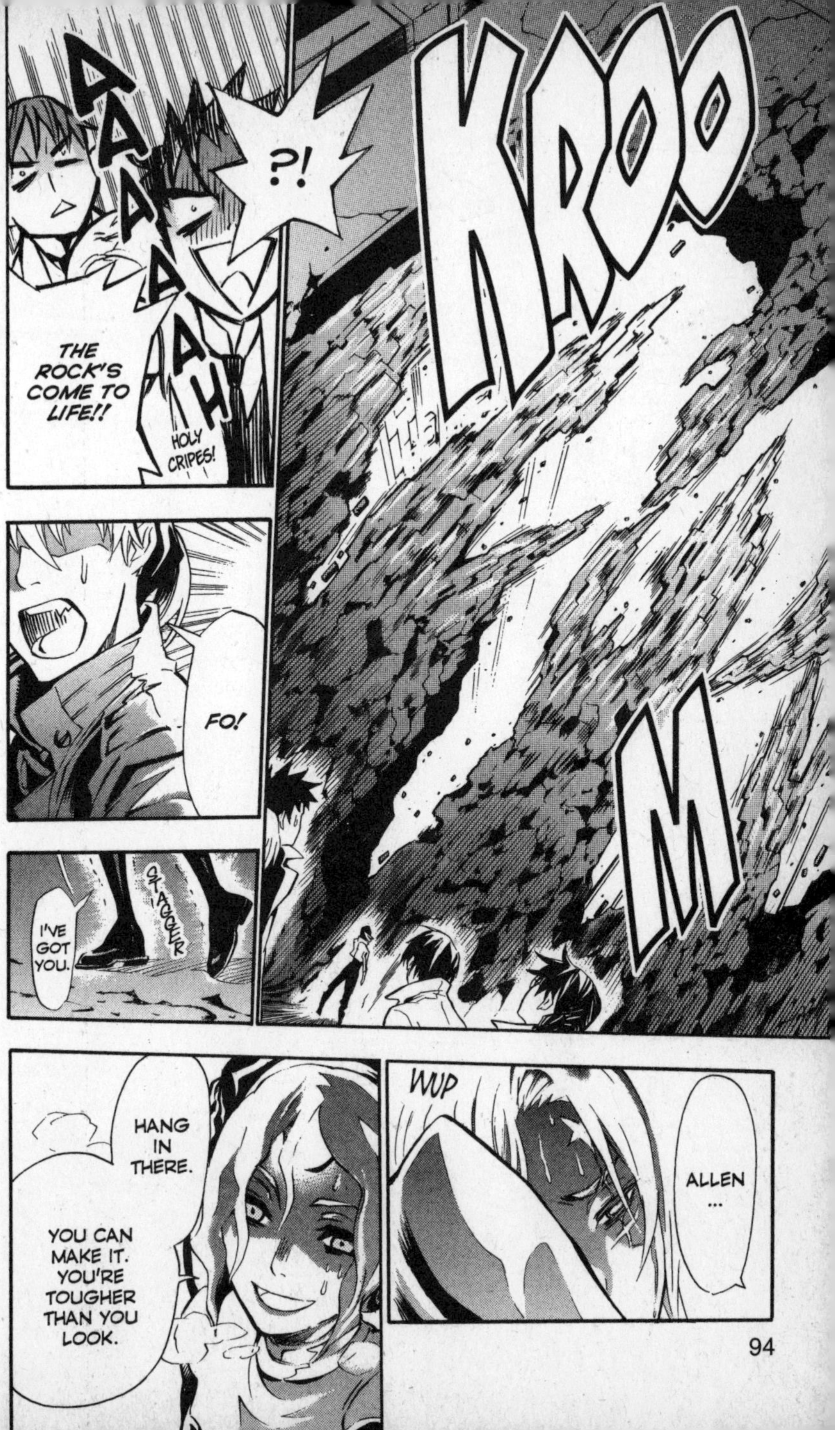
KROOOM
?!
AAAAAAH
THE ROCK'S COME TO LIFE!!
HOLY CRIPES!
FO!
STAGGER
I'VE GOT YOU.
WUP
ALLEN ...
HANG IN THERE.
YOU CAN MAKE IT. YOU'RE TOUGHER THAN YOU LOOK.

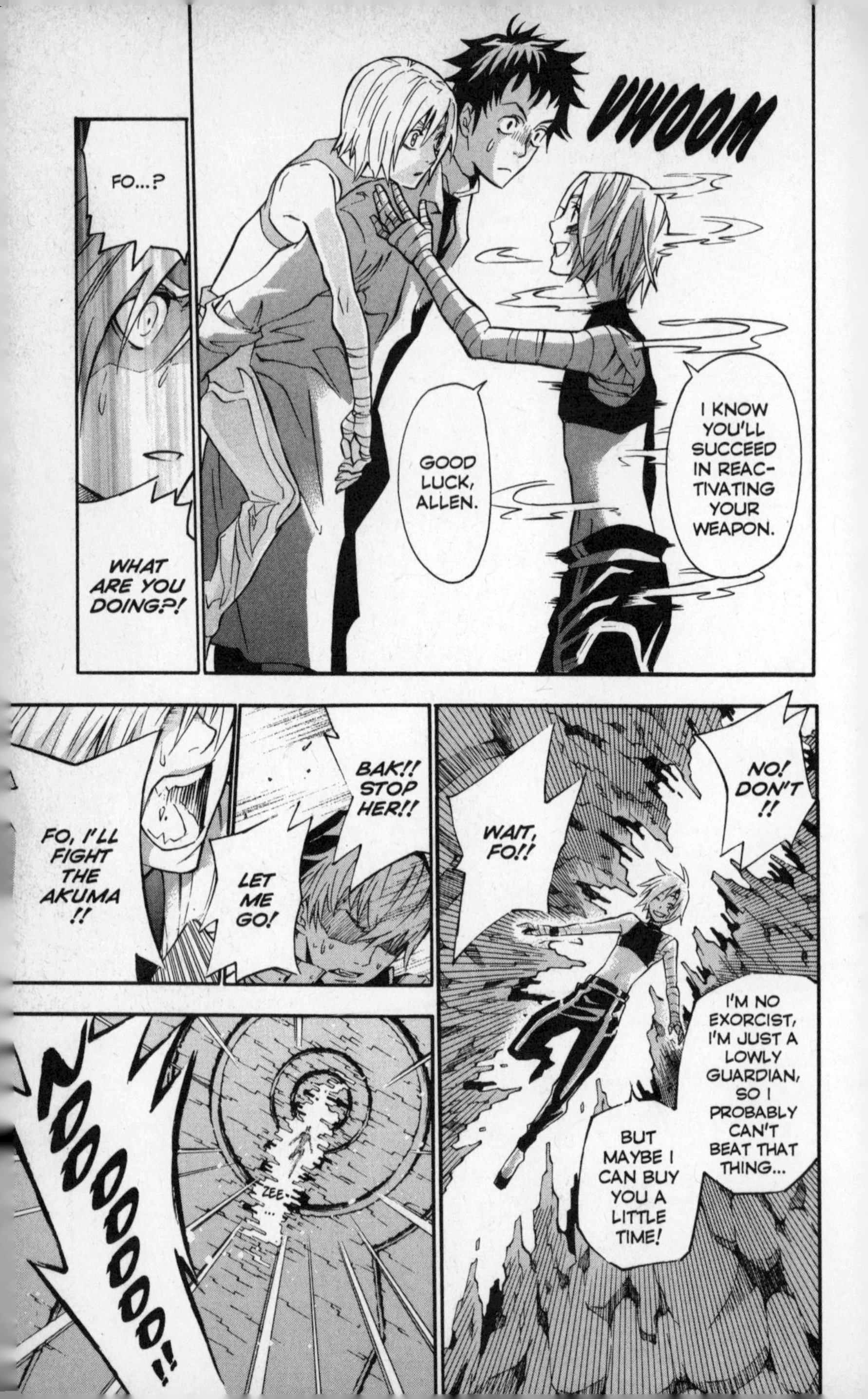
VWOOM
I KNOW YOU'LL SUCCEED IN REAC-TIVATING YOUR WEAPON.
GOOD LUCK, ALLEN.
FO...?
WHAT ARE YOU DOING?!
NO! DON'T !!
WAIT, FO!!
I'M NO EXORCIST, I'M JUST A LOWLY GUARDIAN, SO I PROBABLY CAN'T BEAT THAT THING...
BUT MAYBE I CAN BUY YOU A LITTLE TIME!
BAK!! STOP HER!!
LET ME GO!
FO, I'LL FIGHT THE AKUMA !!
ZOOOOOOM!!
ZEE...

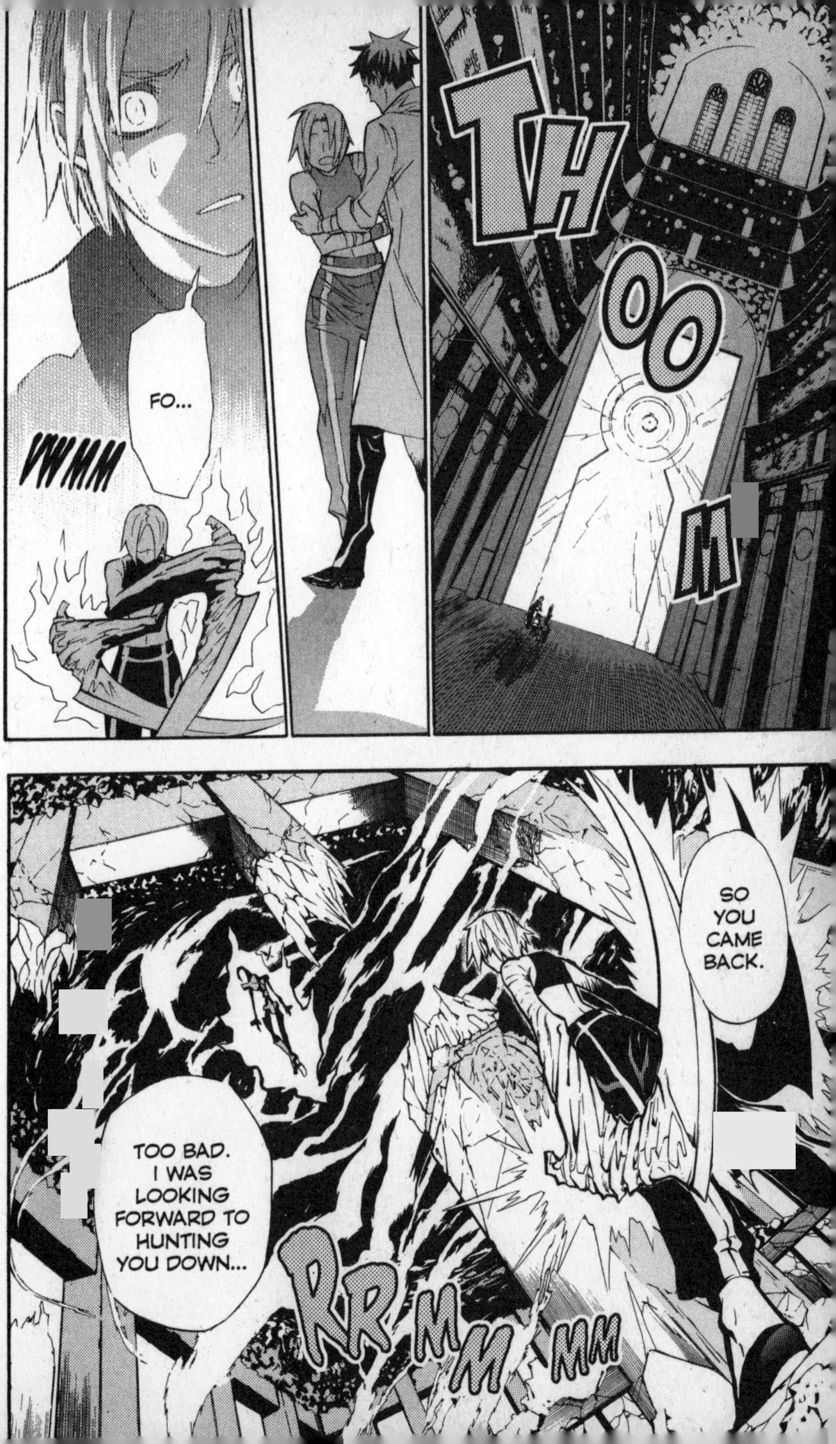

THOOM
FO...
VWMM
SO YOU CAME BACK.
TOO BAD. I WAS LOOKING FORWARD TO HUNTING YOU DOWN...
RRMMMM

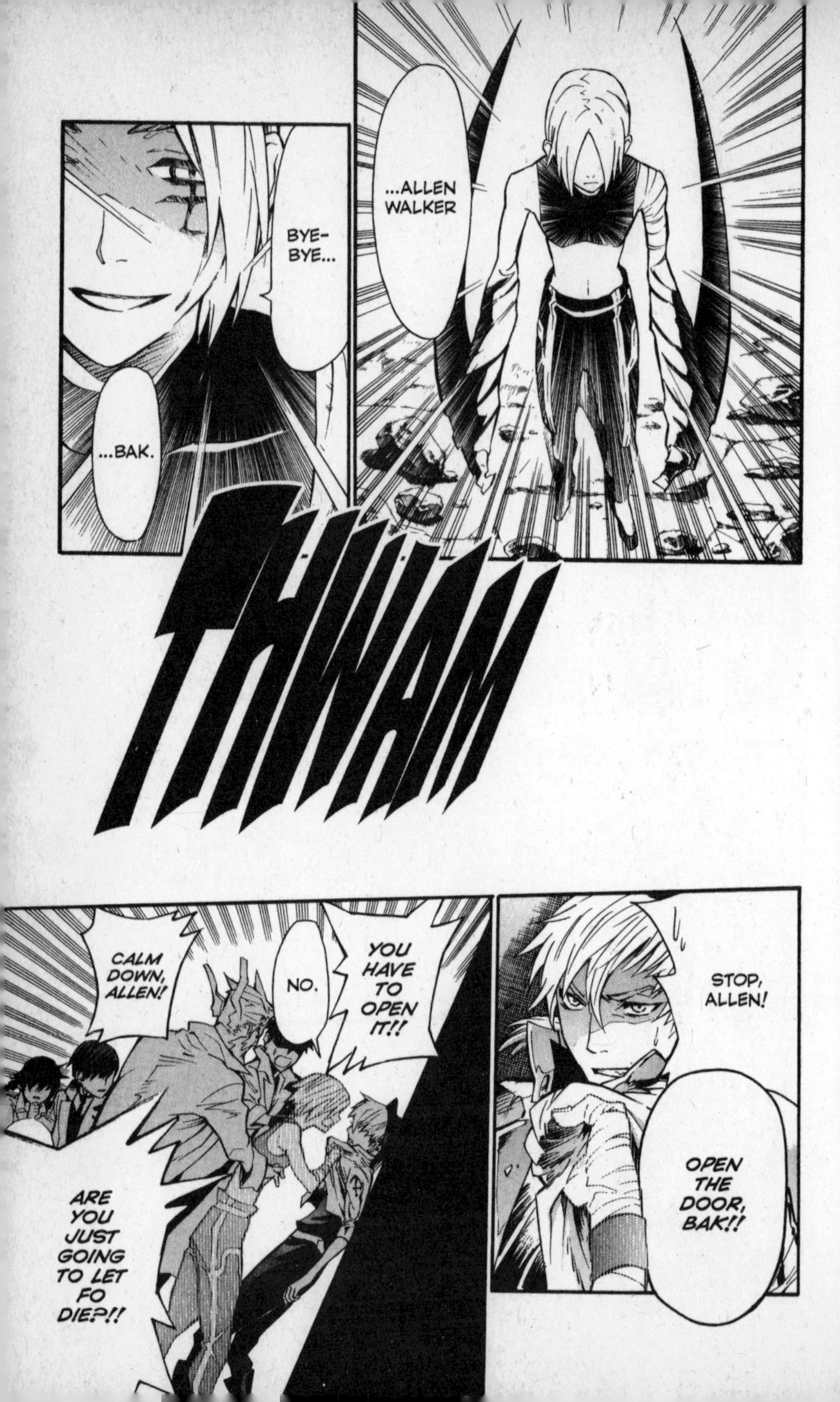
...ALLEN WALKER
BYE-BYE...
...BAK.
THWAM
STOP, ALLEN!
OPEN THE DOOR, BAK!!
YOU HAVE TO OPEN IT!!
NO.
CALM DOWN, ALLEN!
ARE YOU JUST GOING TO LET FO DIE?!!

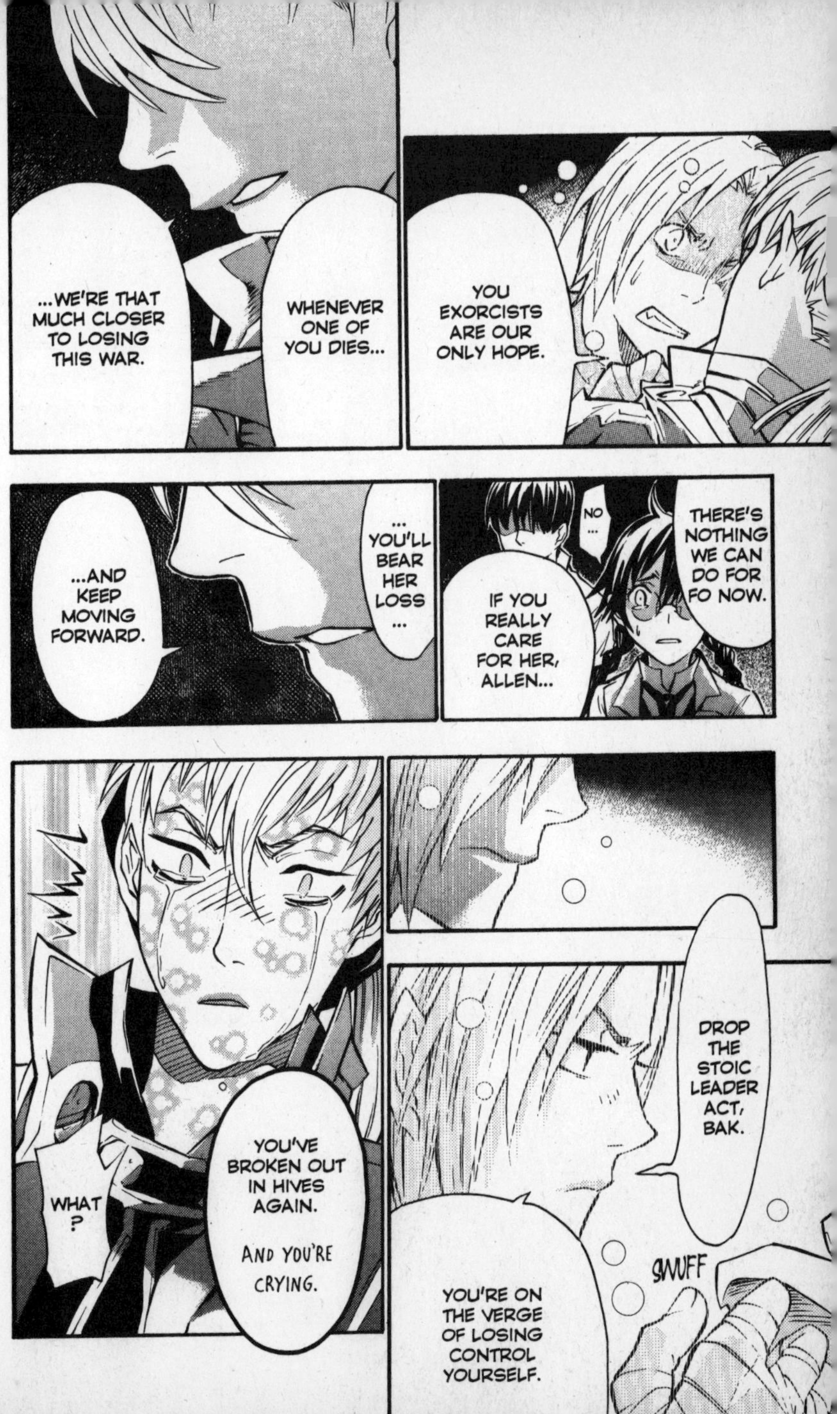
YOU EXORCISTS ARE OUR ONLY HOPE.
WHENEVER ONE OF YOU DIES...
...WE'RE THAT MUCH CLOSER TO LOSING THIS WAR.
THERE'S NOTHING WE CAN DO FOR FO NOW.
NO ...
IF YOU REALLY CARE FOR HER, ALLEN...
... YOU'LL BEAR HER LOSS ...
...AND KEEP MOVING FORWARD.
DROP THE STOIC LEADER ACT, BAK.
SNUFF
YOU'RE ON THE VERGE OF LOSING CONTROL YOURSELF.
YOU'VE BROKEN OUT IN HIVES AGAIN.
AND YOU'RE CRYING.
WHAT ?

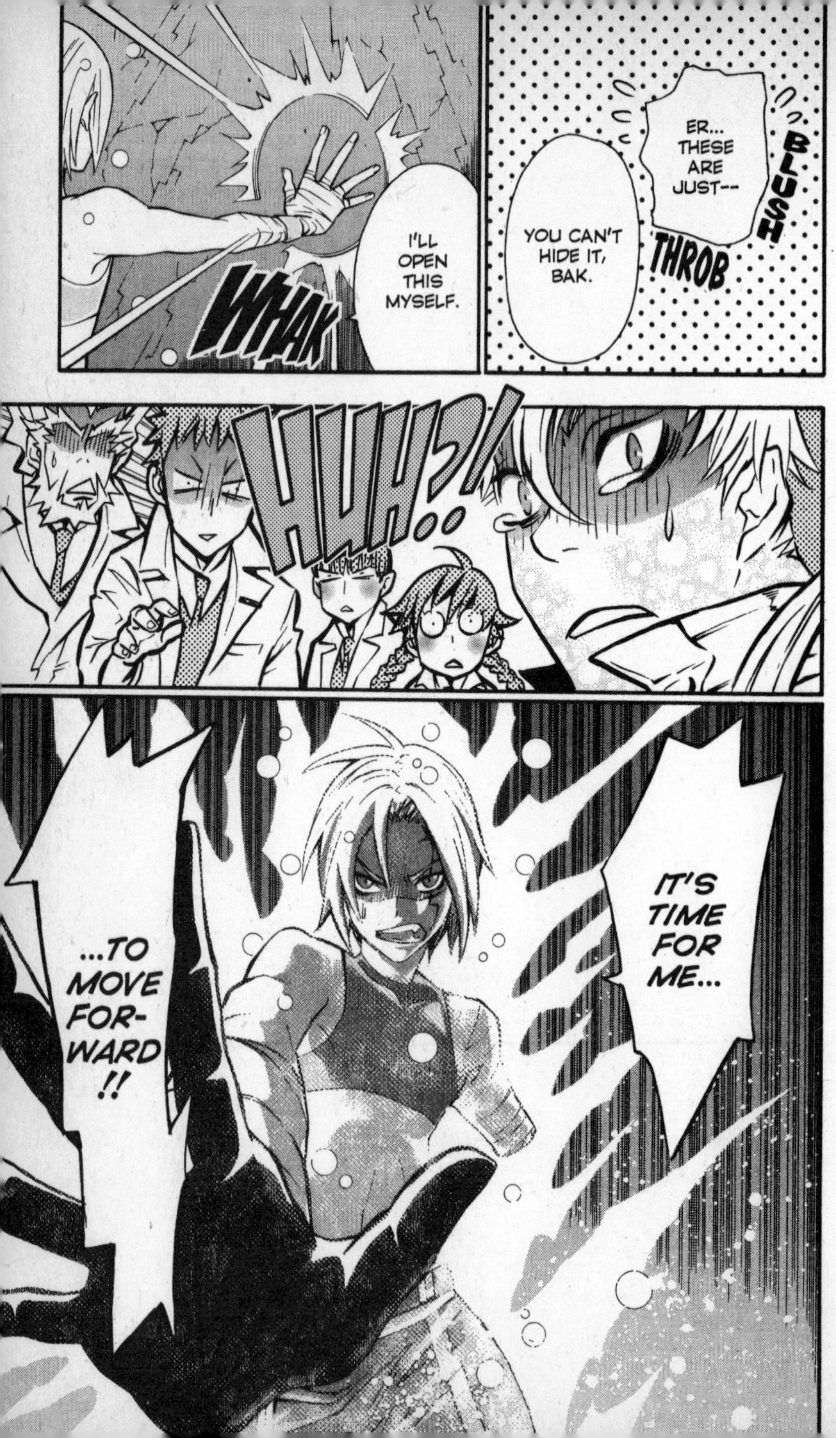
ER... THESE ARE JUST--
BLUSH
THROB
YOU CAN'T HIDE IT, BAK.
I'LL OPEN THIS MYSELF.
WHAK
HUH?!..
IT'S TIME FOR ME...
...TO MOVE FOR-WARD!!

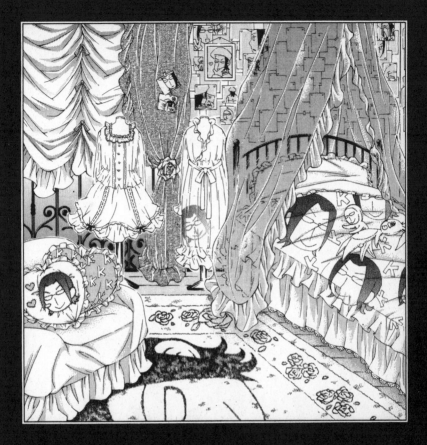

ALLEN STUMBLED ONTO THIS
DECORATOR'S NIGHTMARE!

KOMUI DESIGNED AND DECORATED THIS ROOM
FOR LENALEE, BUT THERE'S NO SIGN OF
HER HERE. IN FACT, IT SEEMS TO BE
UNINHABITED, THOUGH ACCORDING TO LAVI,
KOMUI SNEAKS AWAY FROM HIS WORK ONCE
A WEEK TO CLEAN THIS ABOMINATION.

THE 82ND NIGHT: AND THEN ALLEN WALKED ON

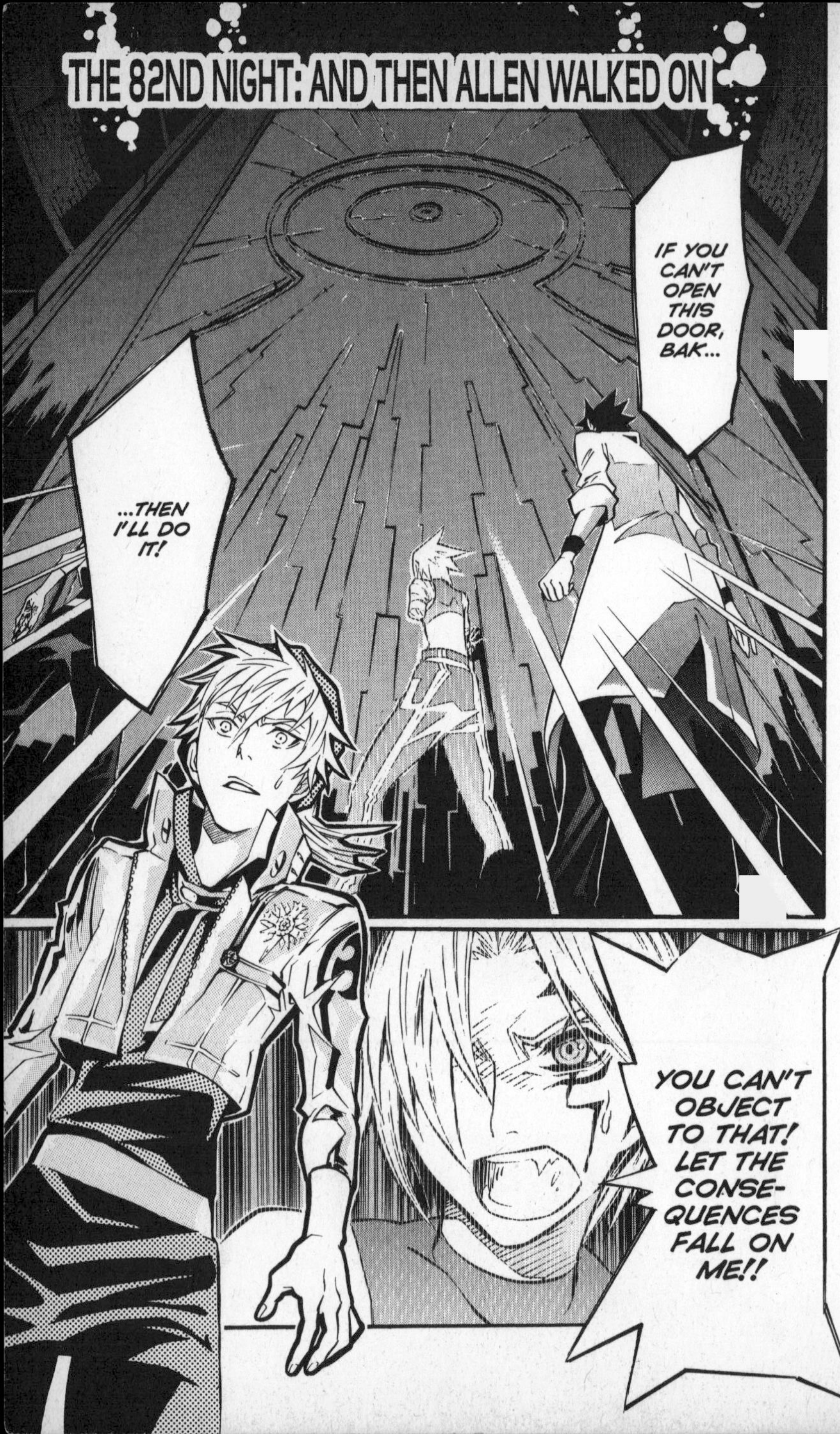
IF YOU CAN'T OPEN THIS DOOR, BAK...
...THEN I'LL DO IT!
YOU CAN'T OBJECT TO THAT! LET THE CONSE-QUENCES FALL ON ME!!

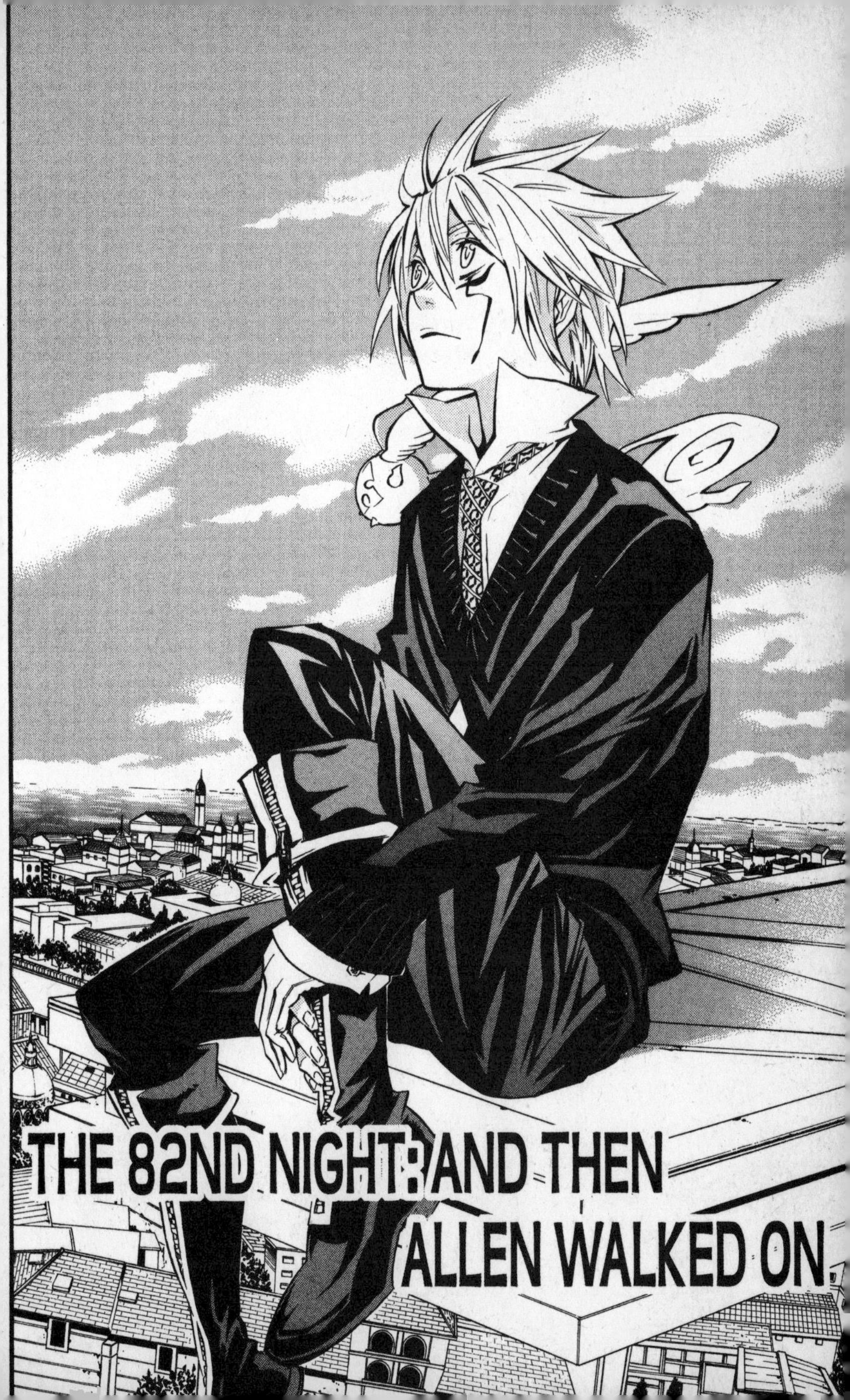
THE 82ND NIGHT: AND THEN ALLEN WALKED ON

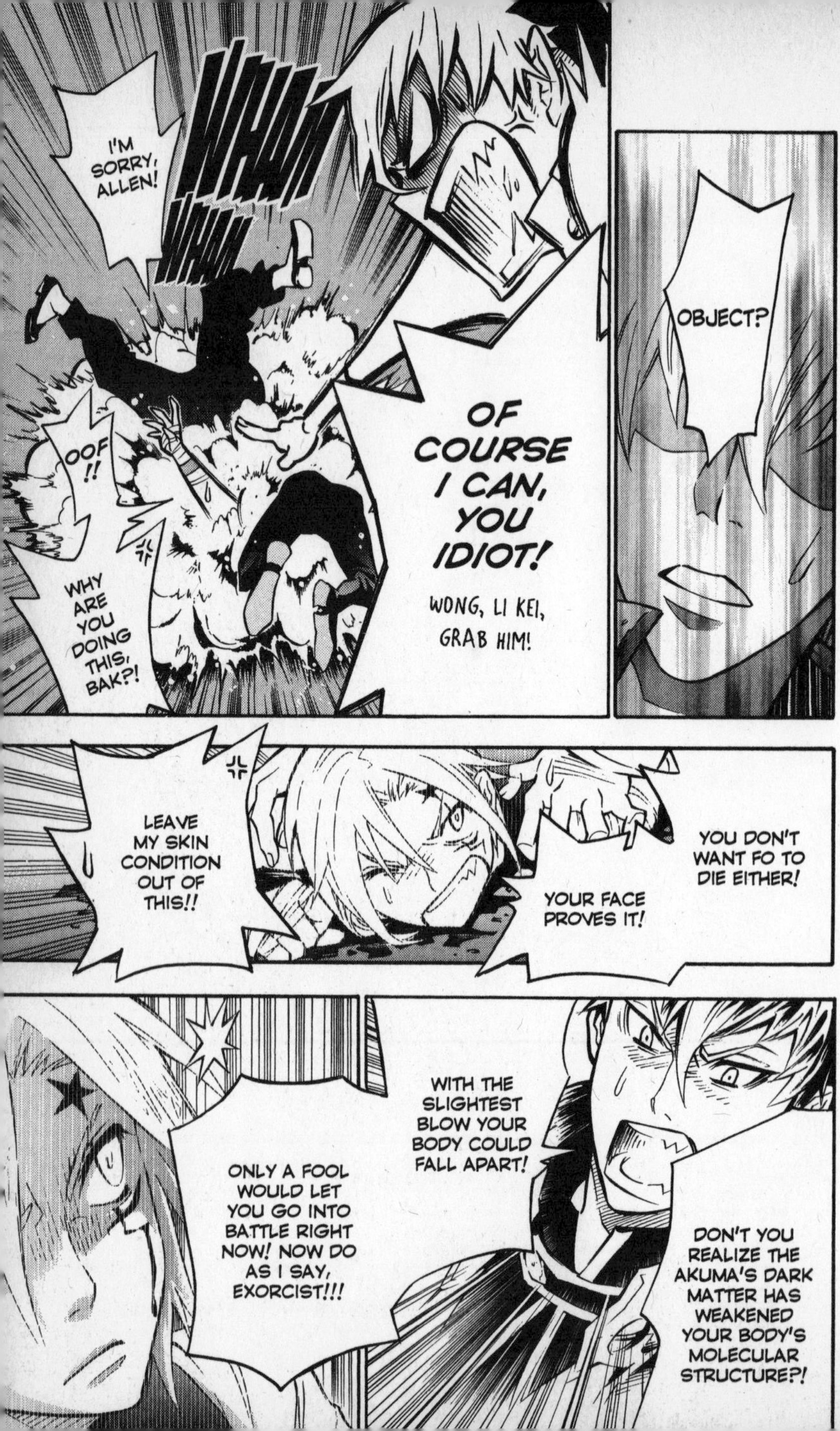
OBJECT?
OF COURSE I CAN, YOU IDIOT!
WONG, LI KEI, GRAB HIM!
I'M SORRY, ALLEN!
OOF!!
WHY ARE YOU DOING THIS, BAK?!
YOU DON'T WANT FO TO DIE EITHER!
YOUR FACE PROVES IT!
LEAVE MY SKIN CONDITION OUT OF THIS!!
DON'T YOU REALIZE THE AKUMA'S DARK MATTER HAS WEAKENED YOUR BODY'S MOLECULAR STRUCTURE?!
WITH THE SLIGHTEST BLOW YOUR BODY COULD FALL APART!
ONLY A FOOL WOULD LET YOU GO INTO BATTLE RIGHT NOW! NOW DO AS I SAY, EXORCIST!!!

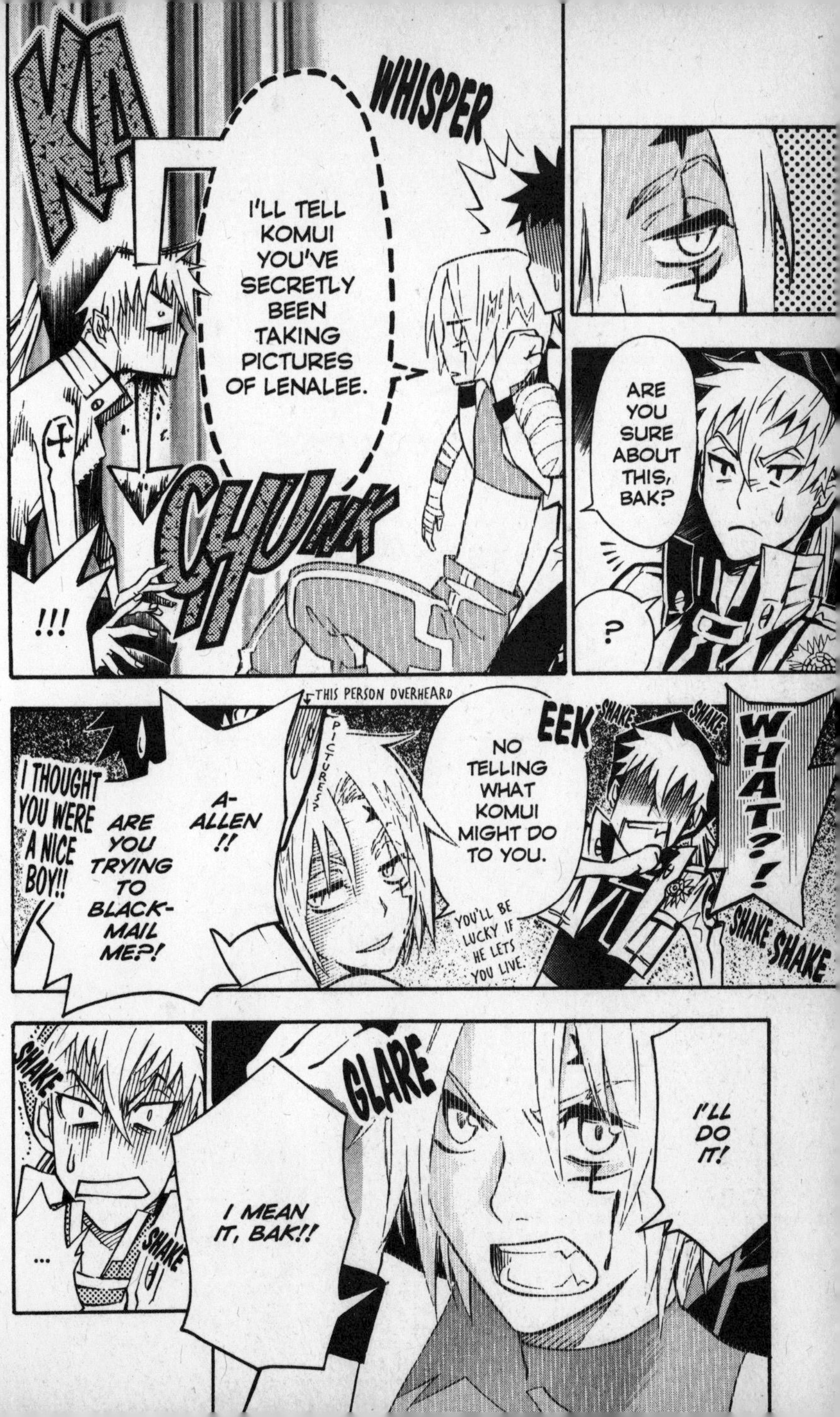
ARE YOU SURE ABOUT THIS, BAK?
?
WHISPER
I'LL TELL KOMUI YOU'VE SECRETLY BEEN TAKING PICTURES OF LENALEE.
KA
CHUNK
!!!
THIS PERSON OVERHEARD
WHAT?!
SHAKE SHAKE
SHAKE SHAKE
EEK
NO TELLING WHAT KOMUI MIGHT DO TO YOU.
YOU'LL BE LUCKY IF HE LETS YOU LIVE.
PICTURES?
A-ALLEN!!
ARE YOU TRYING TO BLACK-MAIL ME?!
I THOUGHT YOU WERE A NICE BOY!!
I'LL DO IT!
GLARE
I MEAN IT, BAK!!
SHAKE
SHAKE
...

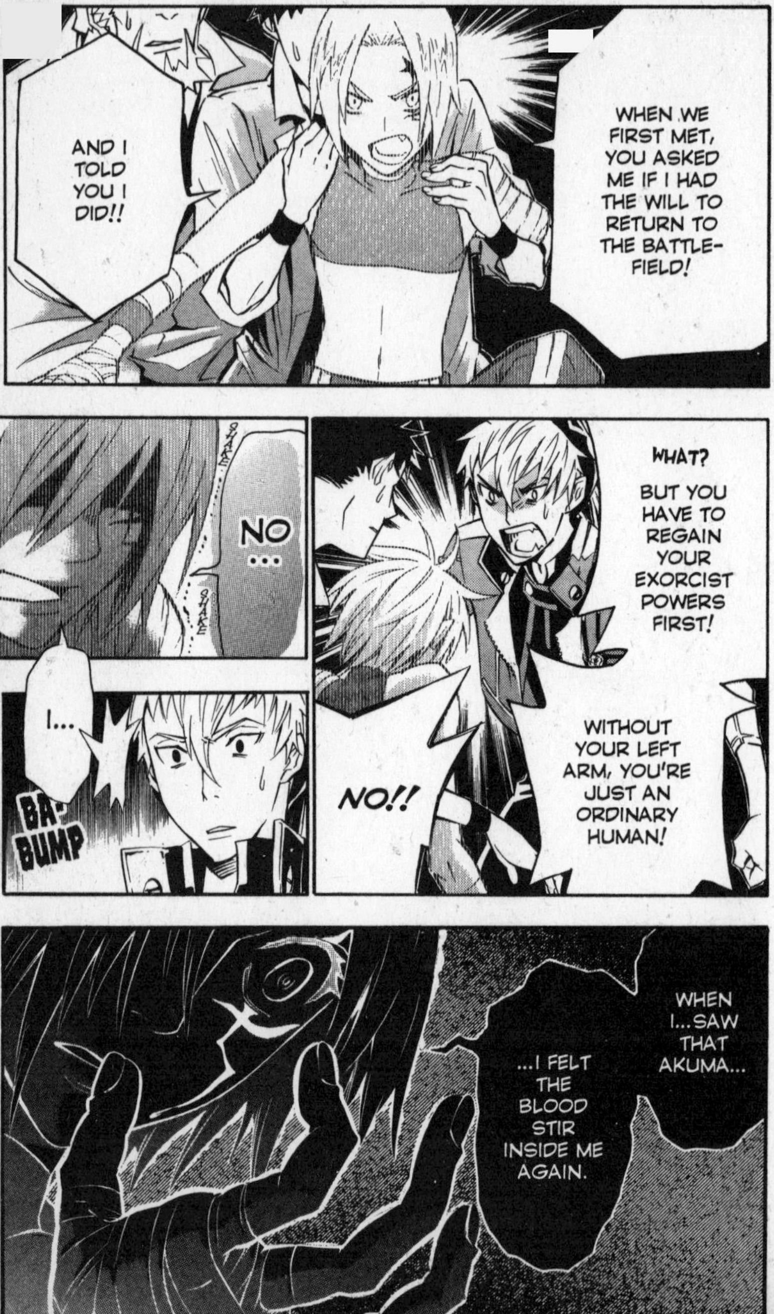
WHEN WE FIRST MET, YOU ASKED ME IF I HAD THE WILL TO RETURN TO THE BATTLE-FIELD!
AND I TOLD YOU I DID!!
WHAT?
BUT YOU HAVE TO REGAIN YOUR EXORCIST POWERS FIRST!
WITHOUT YOUR LEFT ARM, YOU'RE JUST AN ORDINARY HUMAN!
NO!!
SHAKE
NO...
SHAKE
I...
BA-BUMP
WHEN I...SAW THAT AKUMA...
...I FELT THE BLOOD STIR INSIDE ME AGAIN.

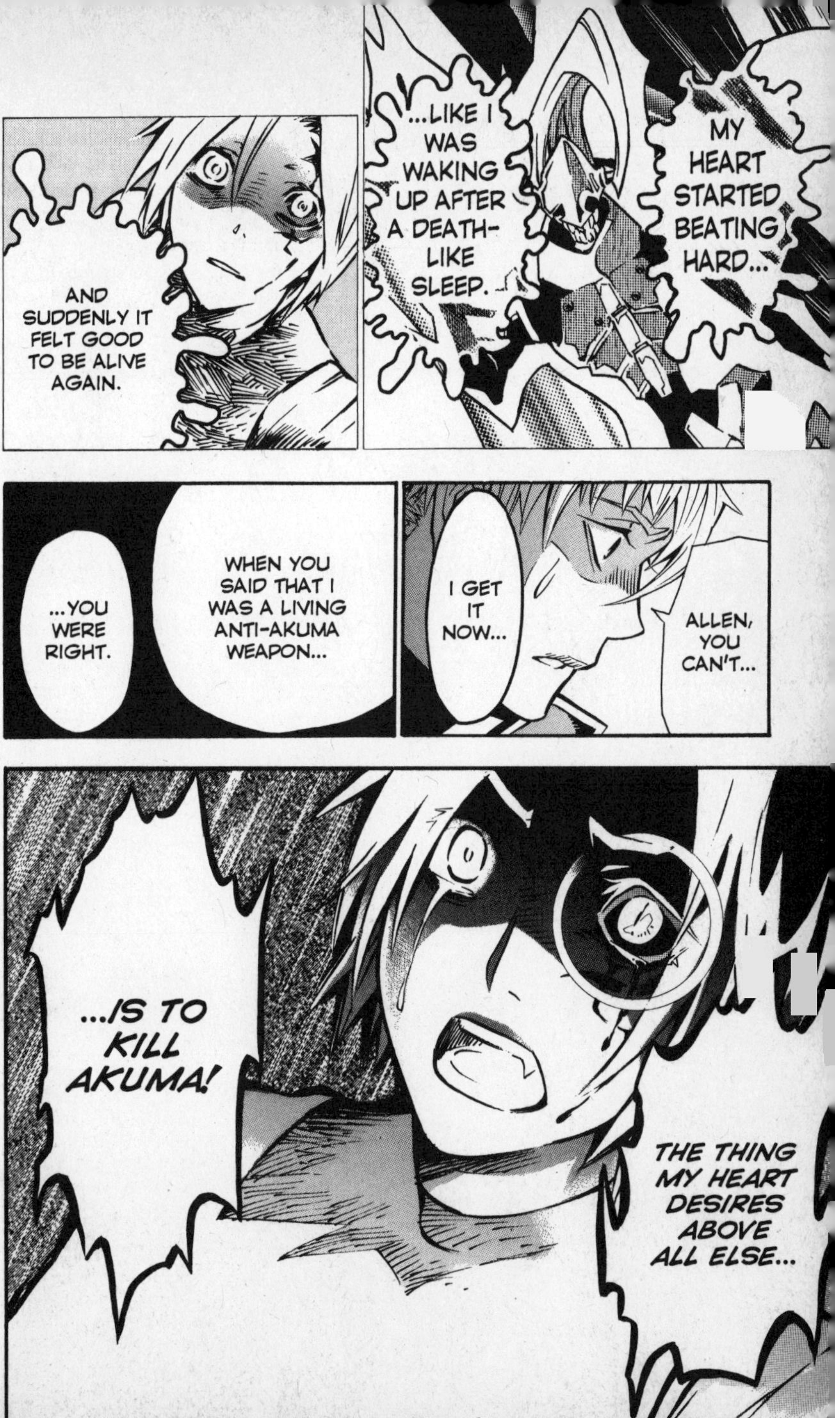
MY HEART STARTED BEATING HARD...
...LIKE I WAS WAKING UP AFTER A DEATH-LIKE SLEEP.
AND SUDDENLY IT FELT GOOD TO BE ALIVE AGAIN.
ALLEN, YOU CAN'T...
I GET IT NOW...
WHEN YOU SAID THAT I WAS A LIVING ANTI-AKUMA WEAPON...
...YOU WERE RIGHT.
THE THING MY HEART DESIRES ABOVE ALL ELSE...
...IS TO KILL AKUMA!

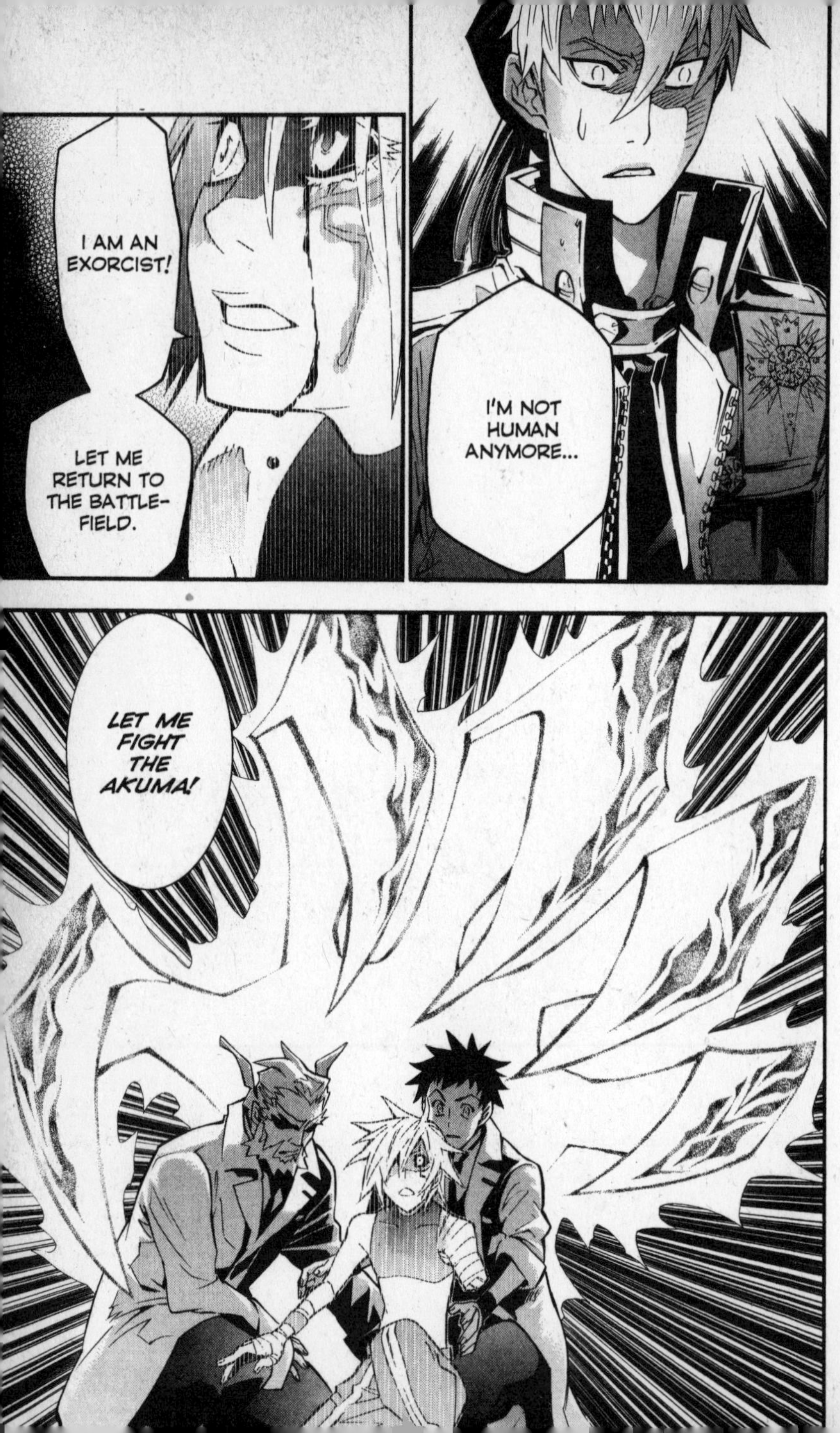
I'M NOT HUMAN ANYMORE...
I AM AN EXORCIST!
LET ME RETURN TO THE BATTLE-FIELD.
LET ME FIGHT THE AKUMA!

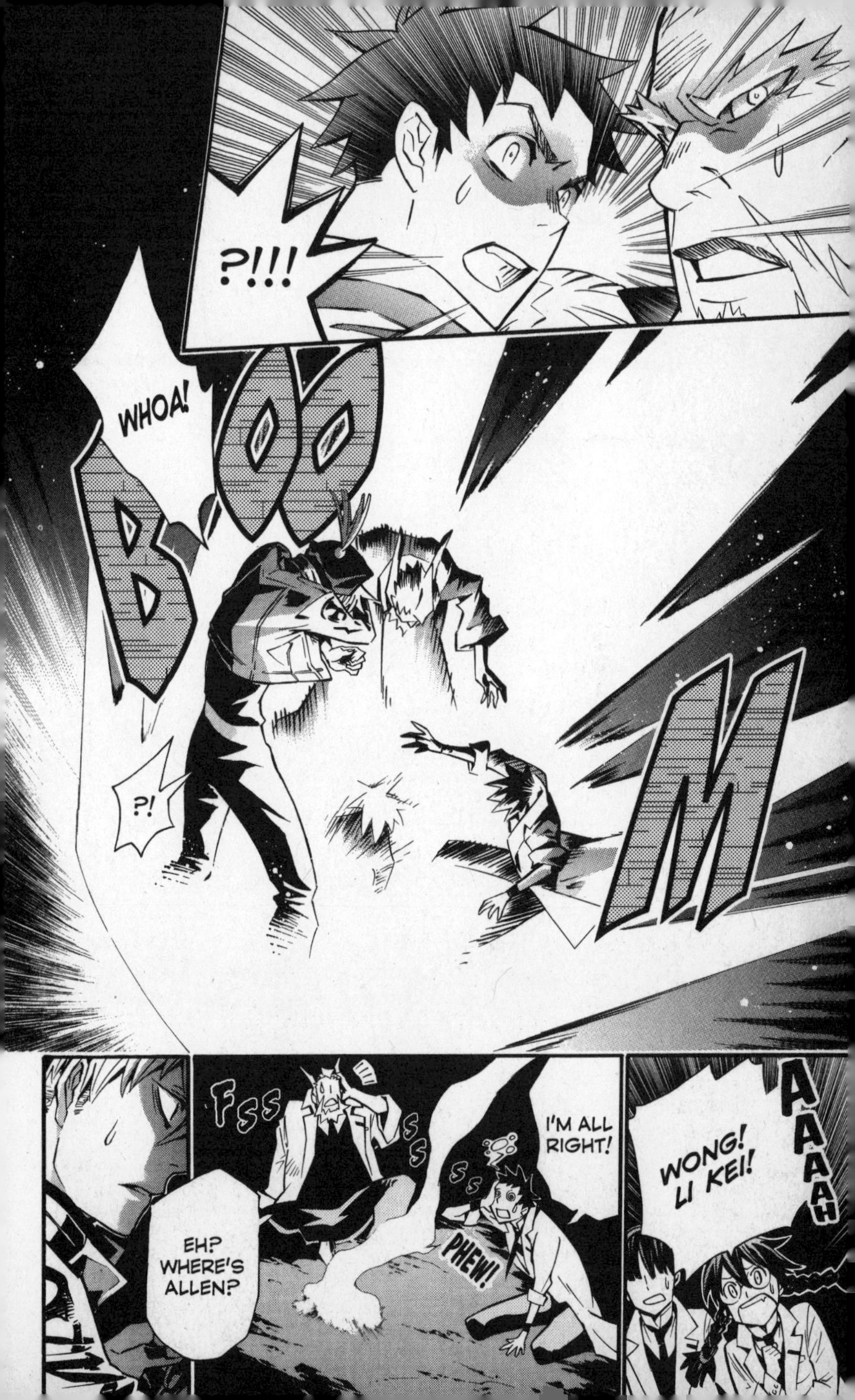
?!!!
BOOM
WHOA!
?!
AAAAAH
WONG! LI KEI!
I'M ALL RIGHT!
FSS
SSS
PHEW!
EH? WHERE'S ALLEN?

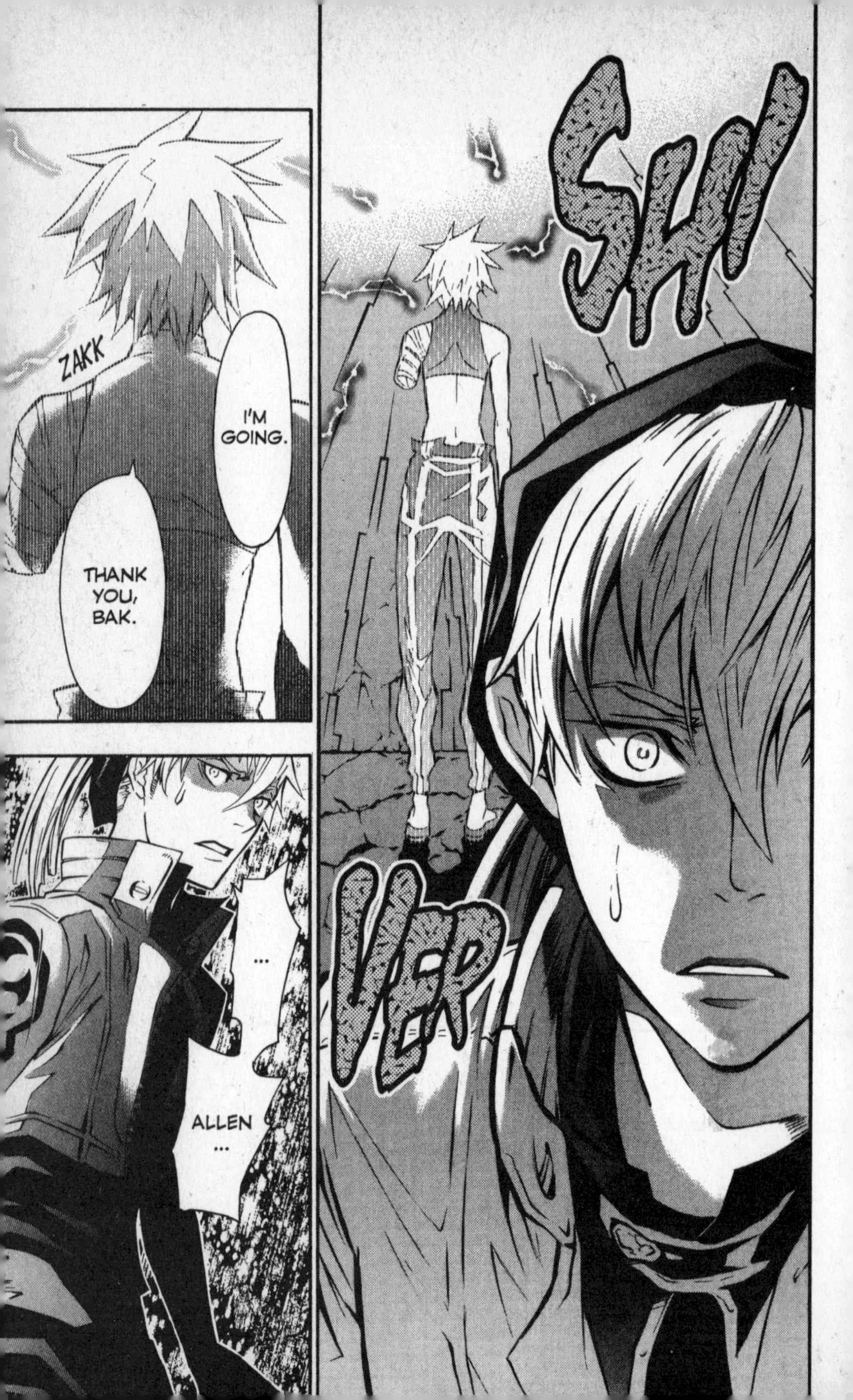
SHU
VER
I'M GOING.
ZAKK
THANK YOU, BAK.
...
ALLEN ...

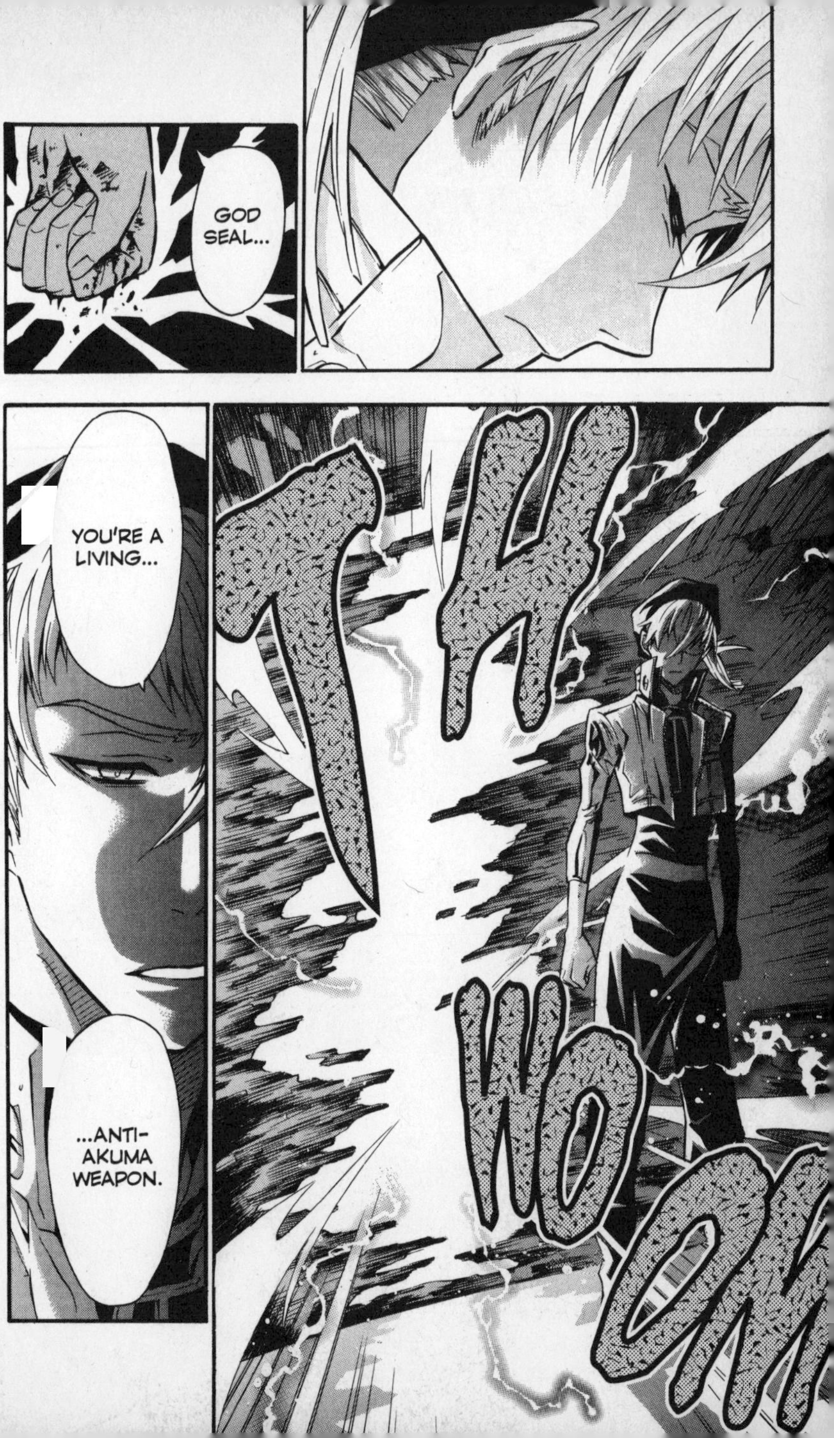
GOD SEAL...
THWOOM
YOU'RE A LIVING...
...ANTI-AKUMA WEAPON.

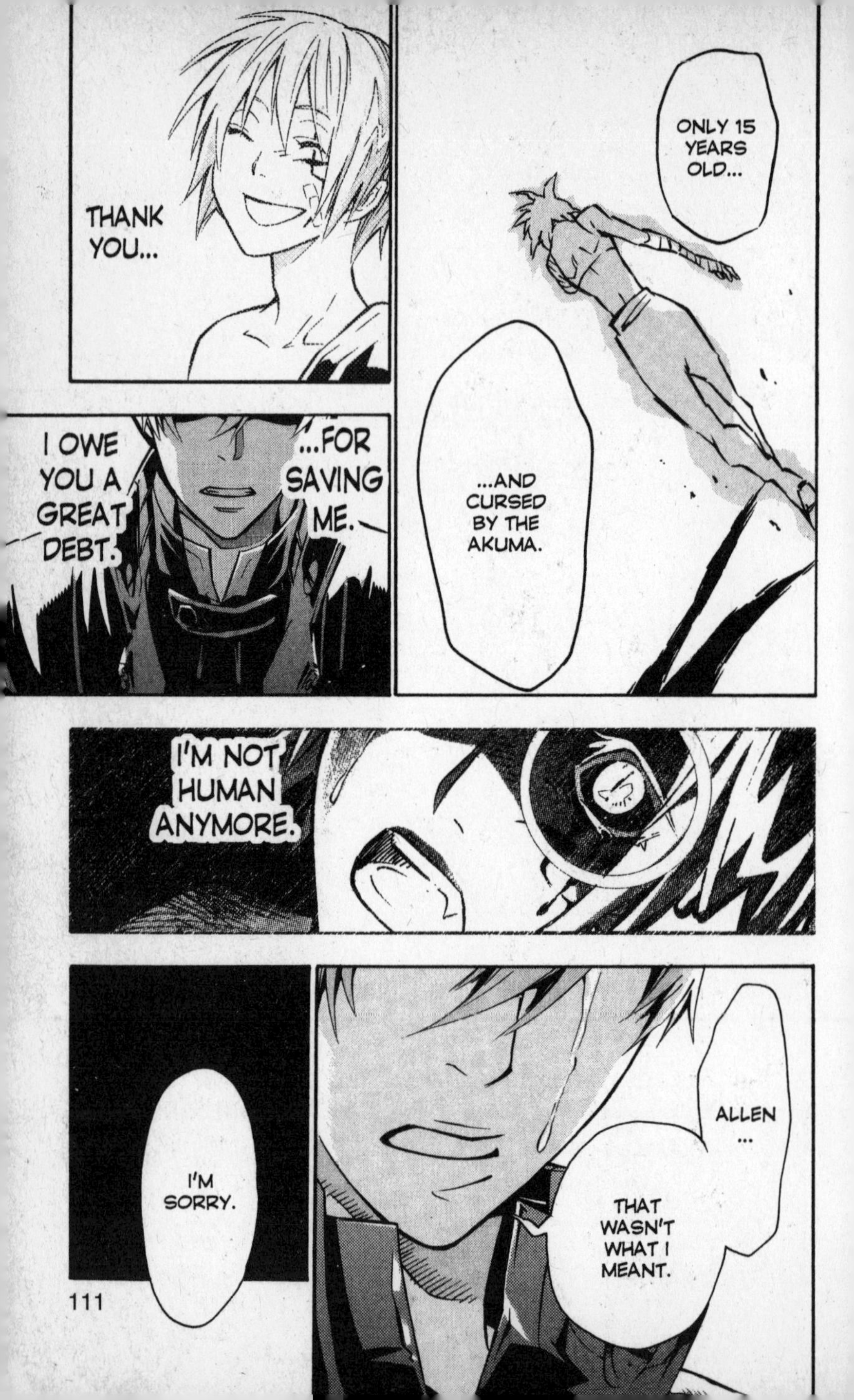
ONLY 15 YEARS OLD...
...AND CURSED BY THE AKUMA.
THANK YOU...
...FOR SAVING ME.
I OWE YOU A GREAT DEBT.
I'M NOT HUMAN ANYMORE.
ALLEN ...
THAT WASN'T WHAT I MEANT.
I'M SORRY.

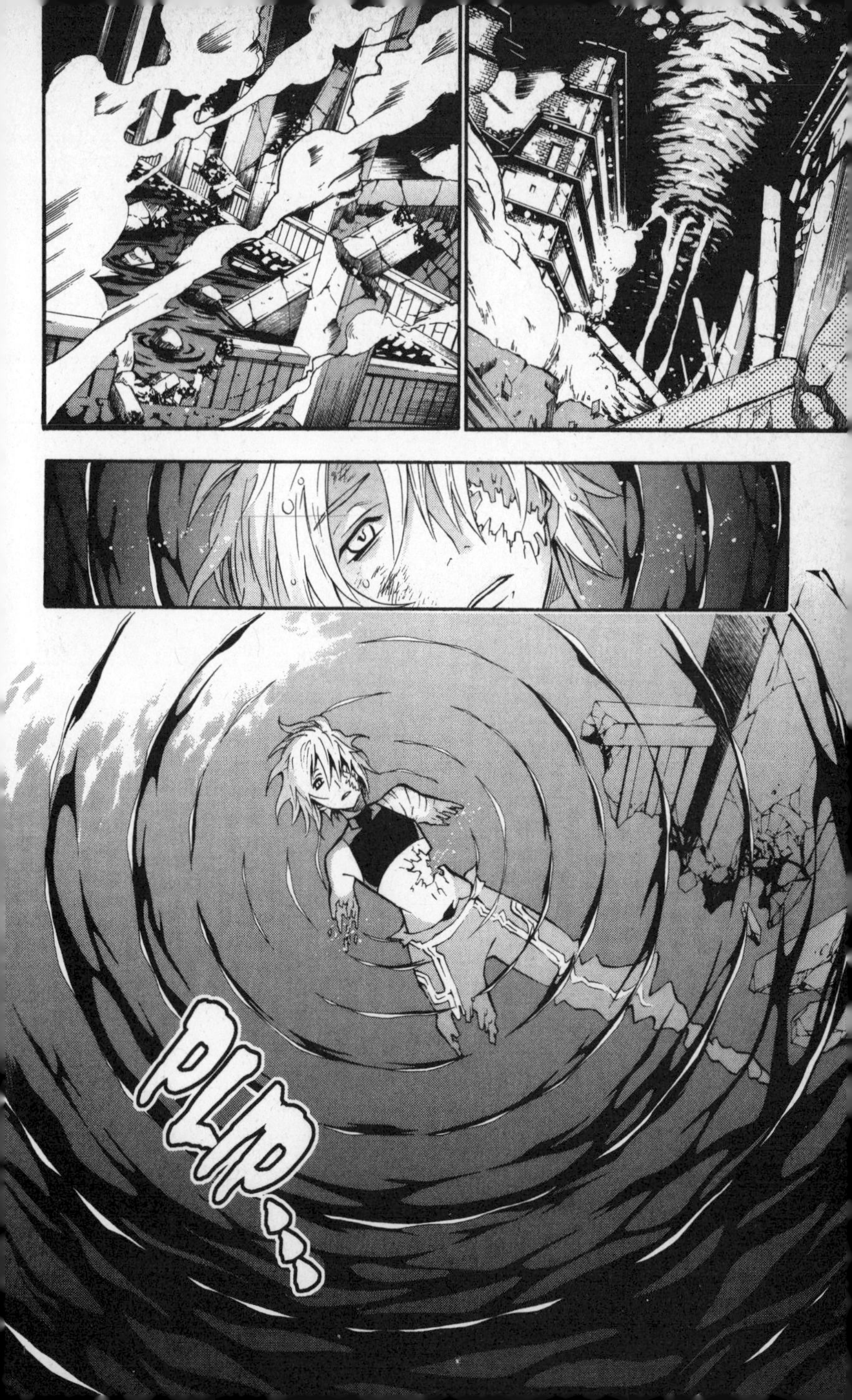
PLIP...

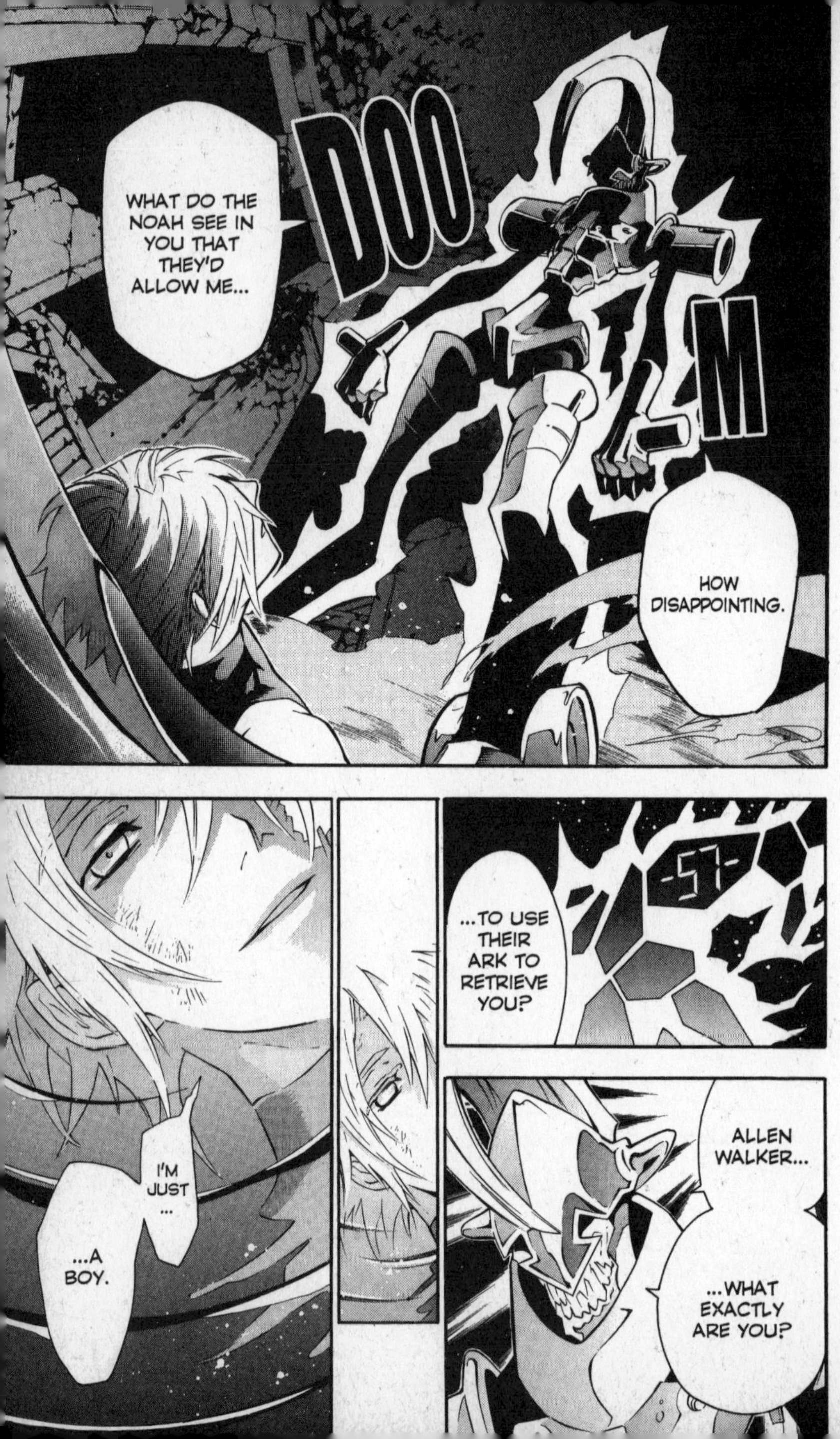
DOOM
HOW DISAPPOINTING.
WHAT DO THE NOAH SEE IN YOU THAT THEY'D ALLOW ME...
-57-
...TO USE THEIR ARK TO RETRIEVE YOU?
ALLEN WALKER...
...WHAT EXACTLY ARE YOU?
I'M JUST ...
...A BOY.

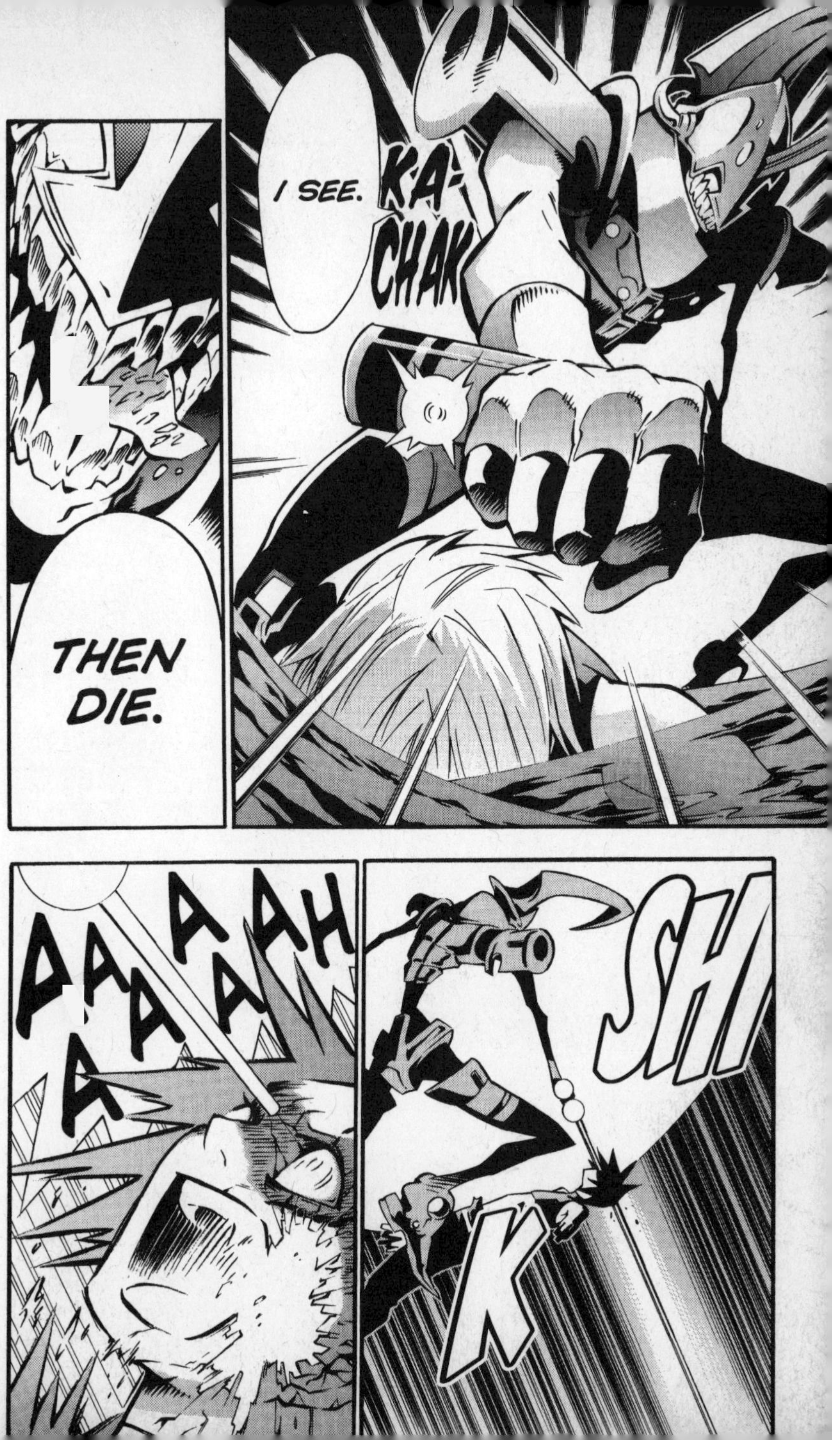

I SEE.
KA-CHAK
THEN DIE.
SH
K
AAAAAAAH

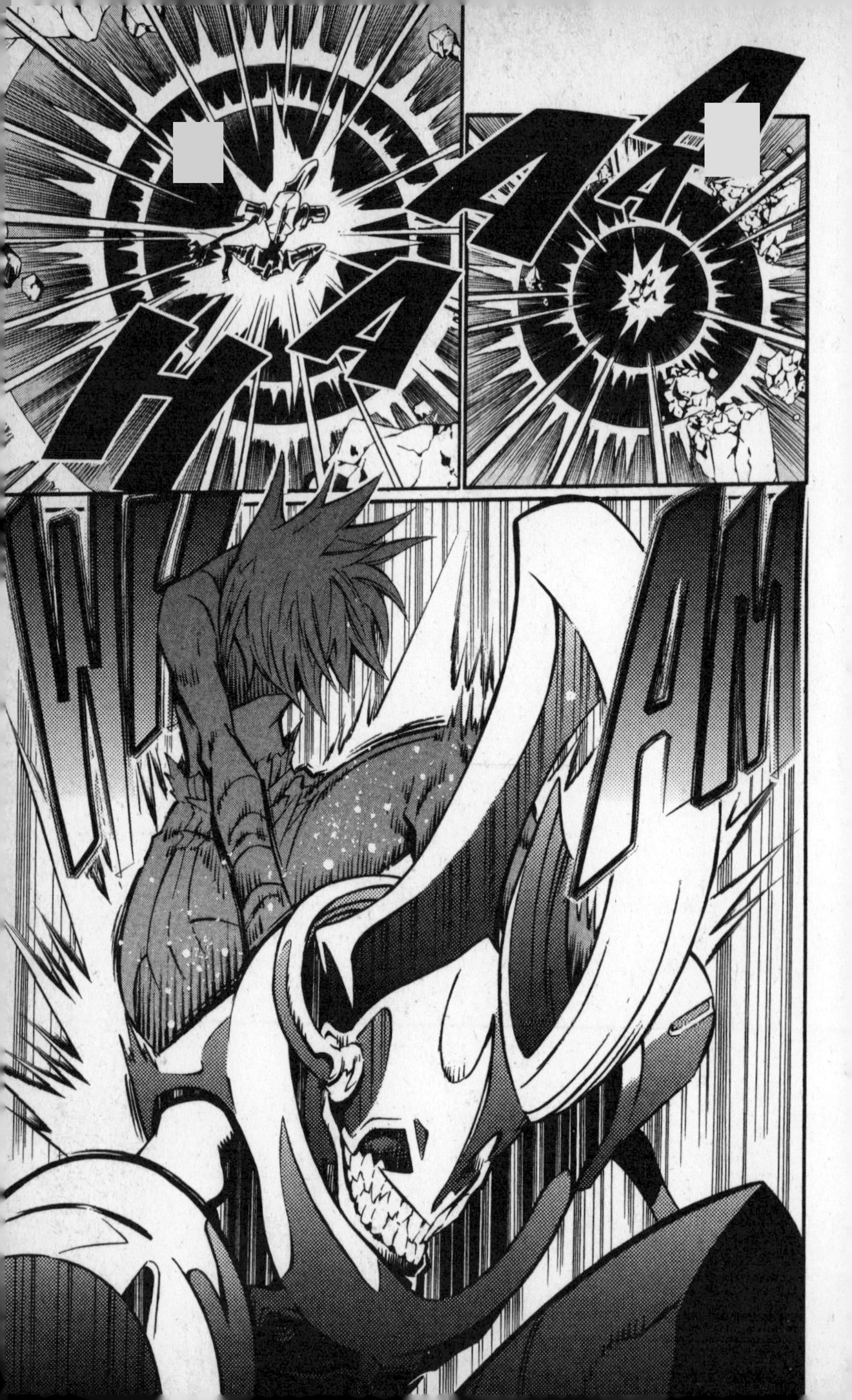

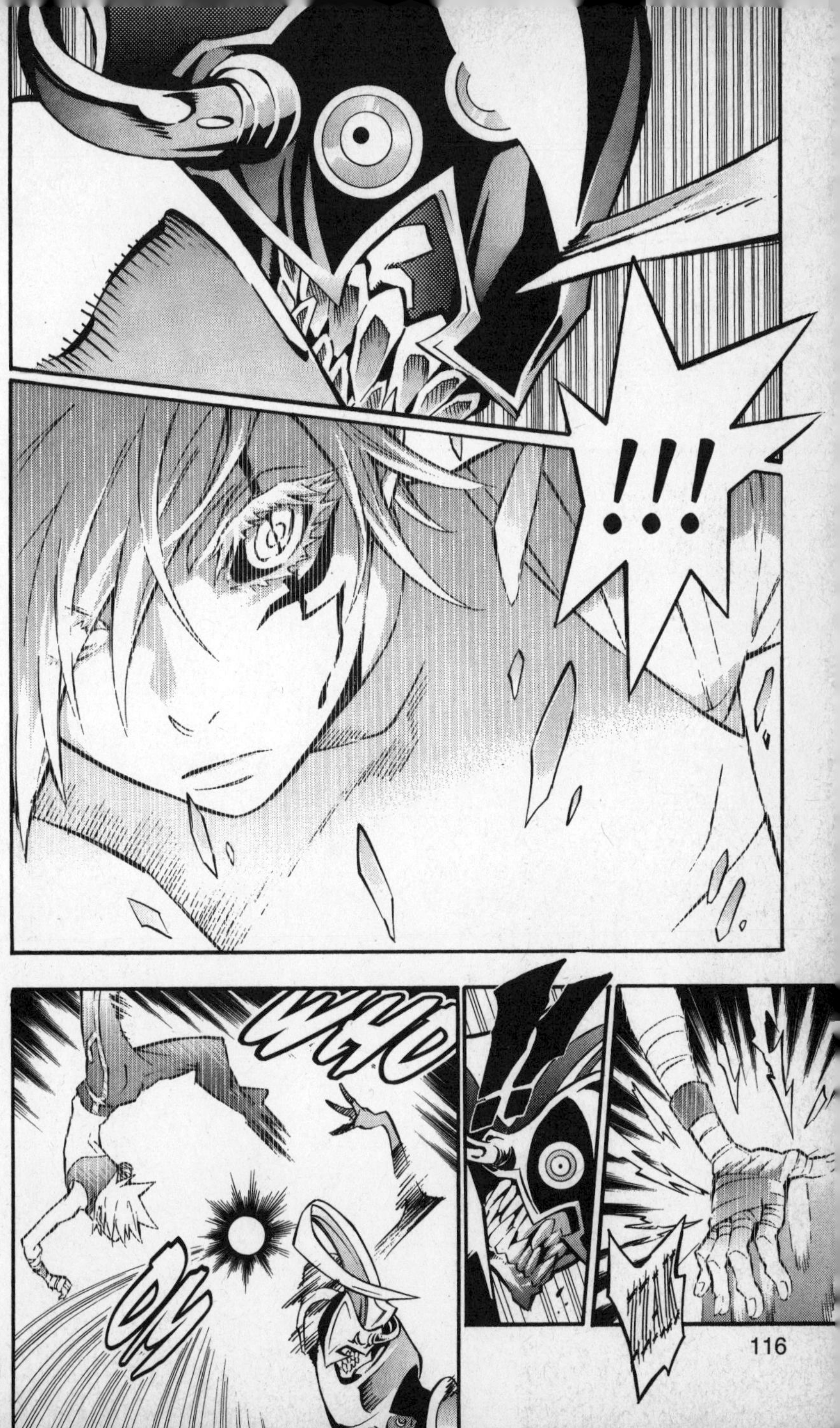
!!!

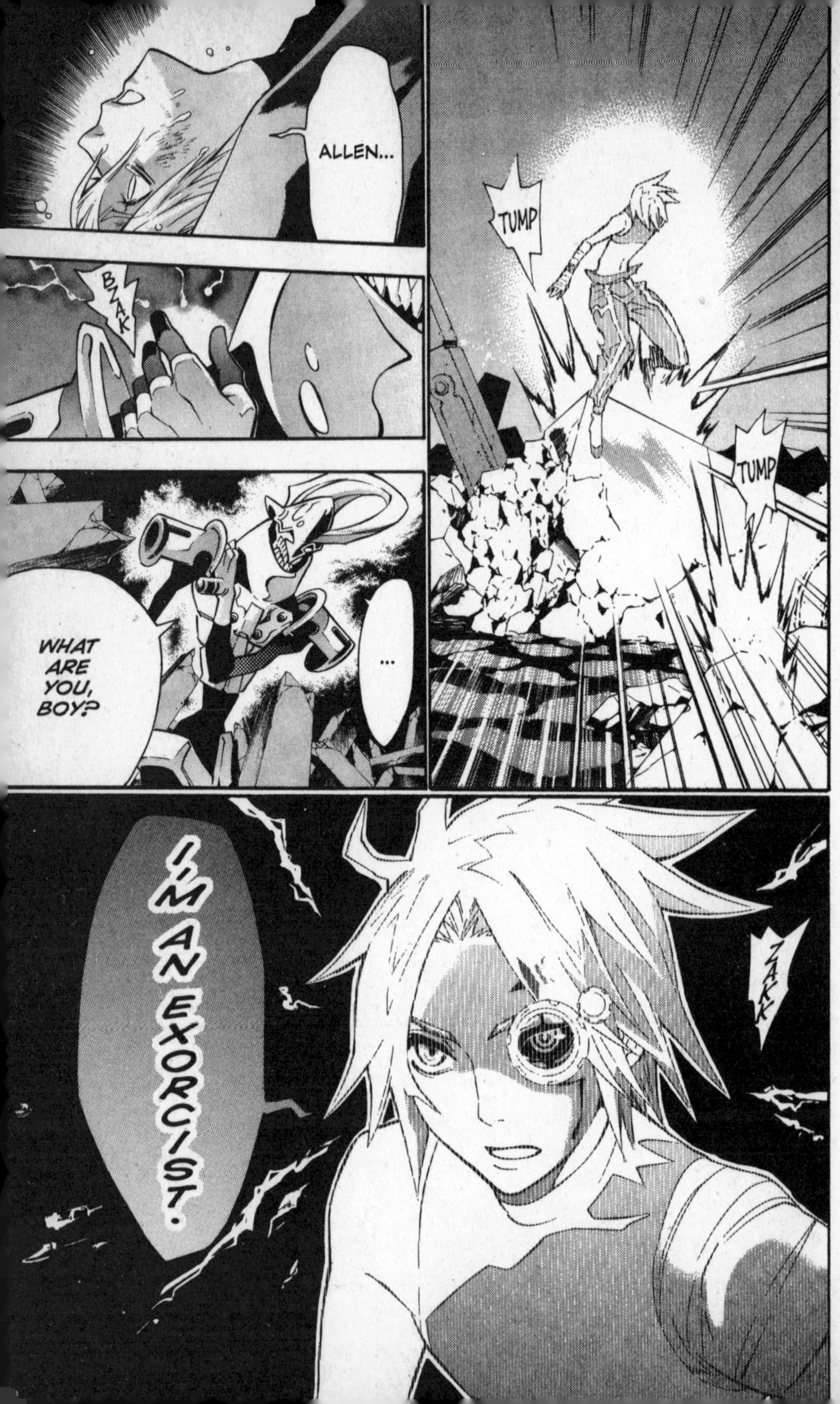
TUMP
TUMP
ALLEN...
BZAK
...
WHAT ARE YOU, BOY?
ZAKK
I'M AN EXORCIST.

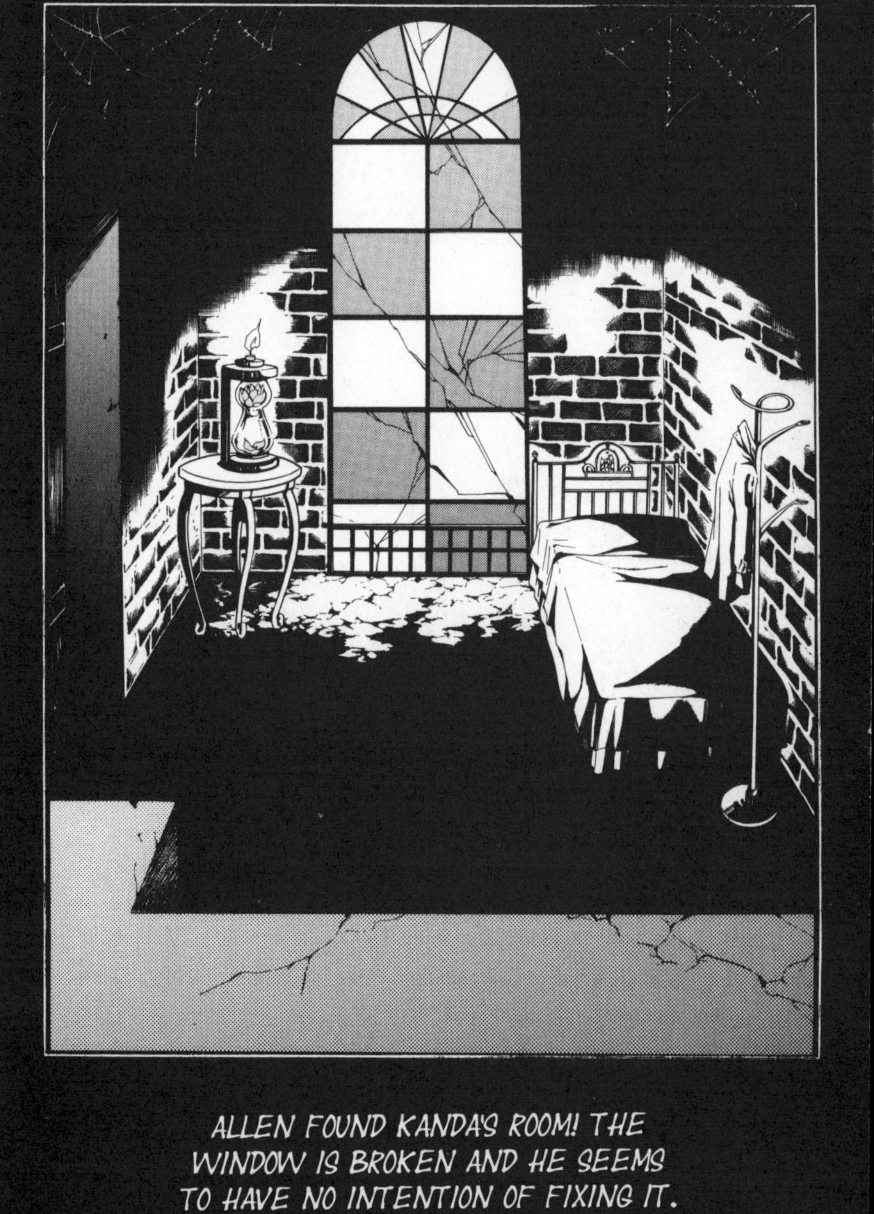

ALLEN FOUND KANDA'S ROOM! THE WINDOW IS BROKEN AND HE SEEMS TO HAVE NO INTENTION OF FIXING IT.

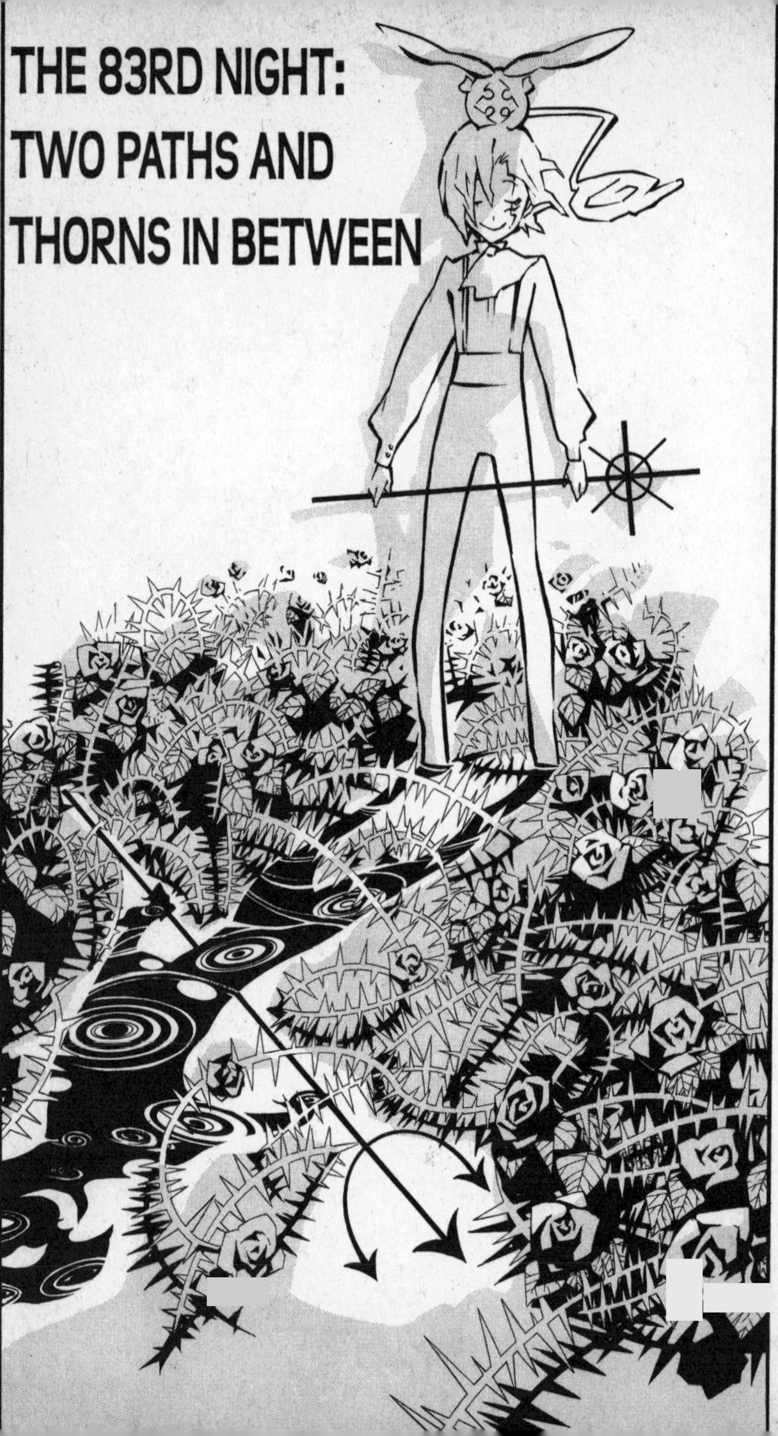
THE 83RD NIGHT:
TWO PATHS AND
THORNS IN BETWEEN

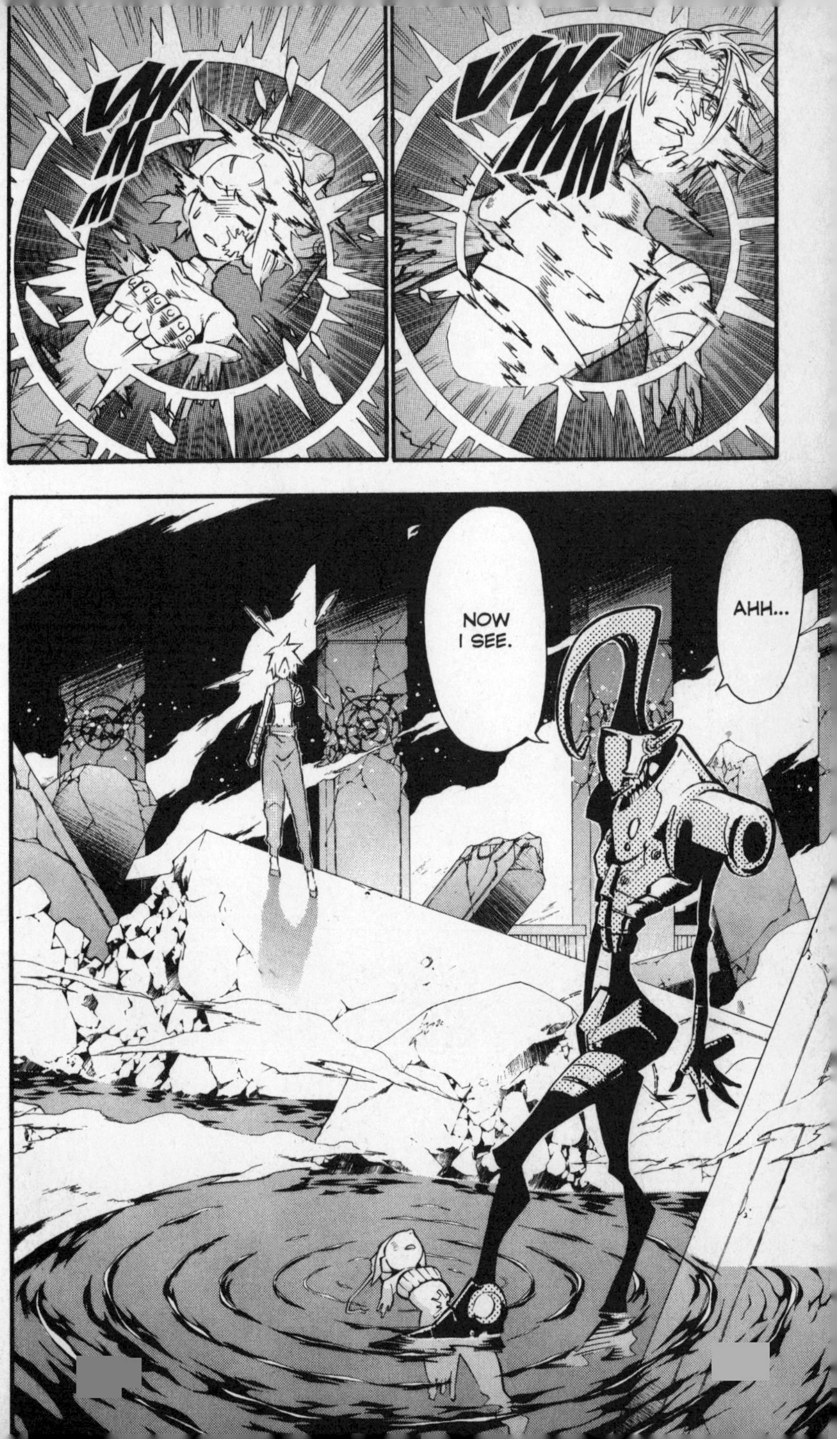
AHH...
NOW I SEE.

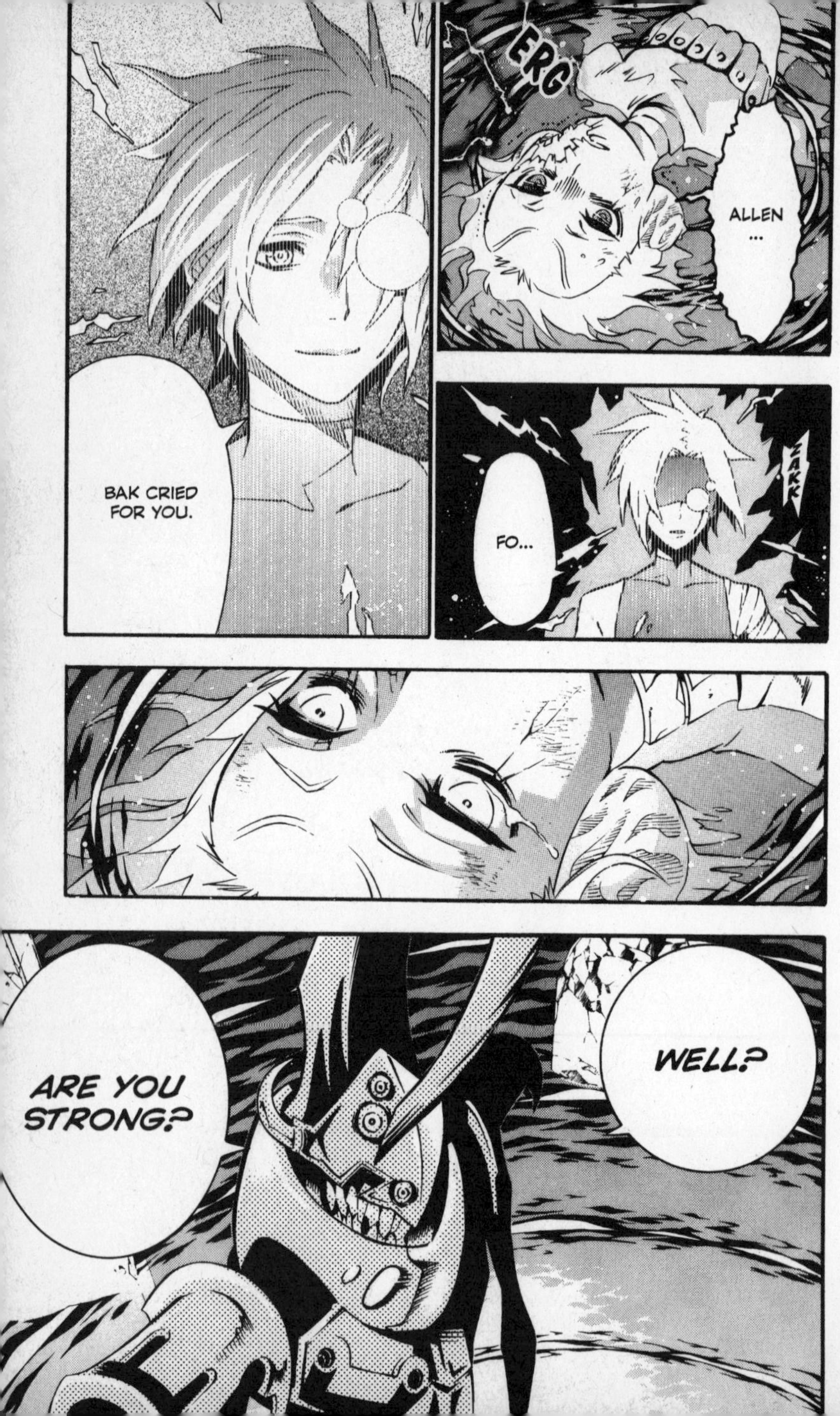
ERG
ALLEN ...
FO...
ZAKK
BAK CRIED FOR YOU.
WELL?
ARE YOU STRONG?

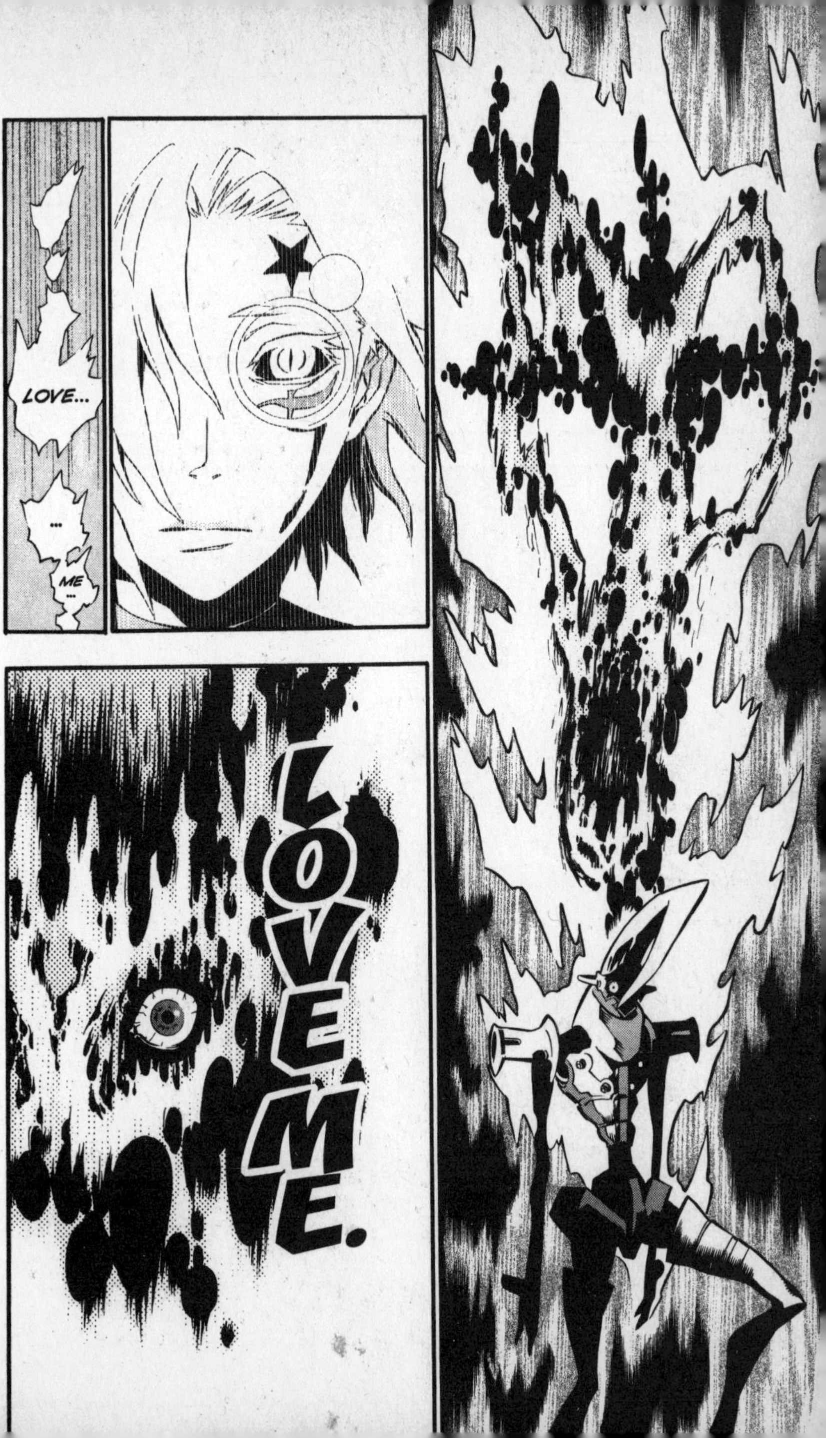
LOVE...
...
ME
...
LOVE ME.

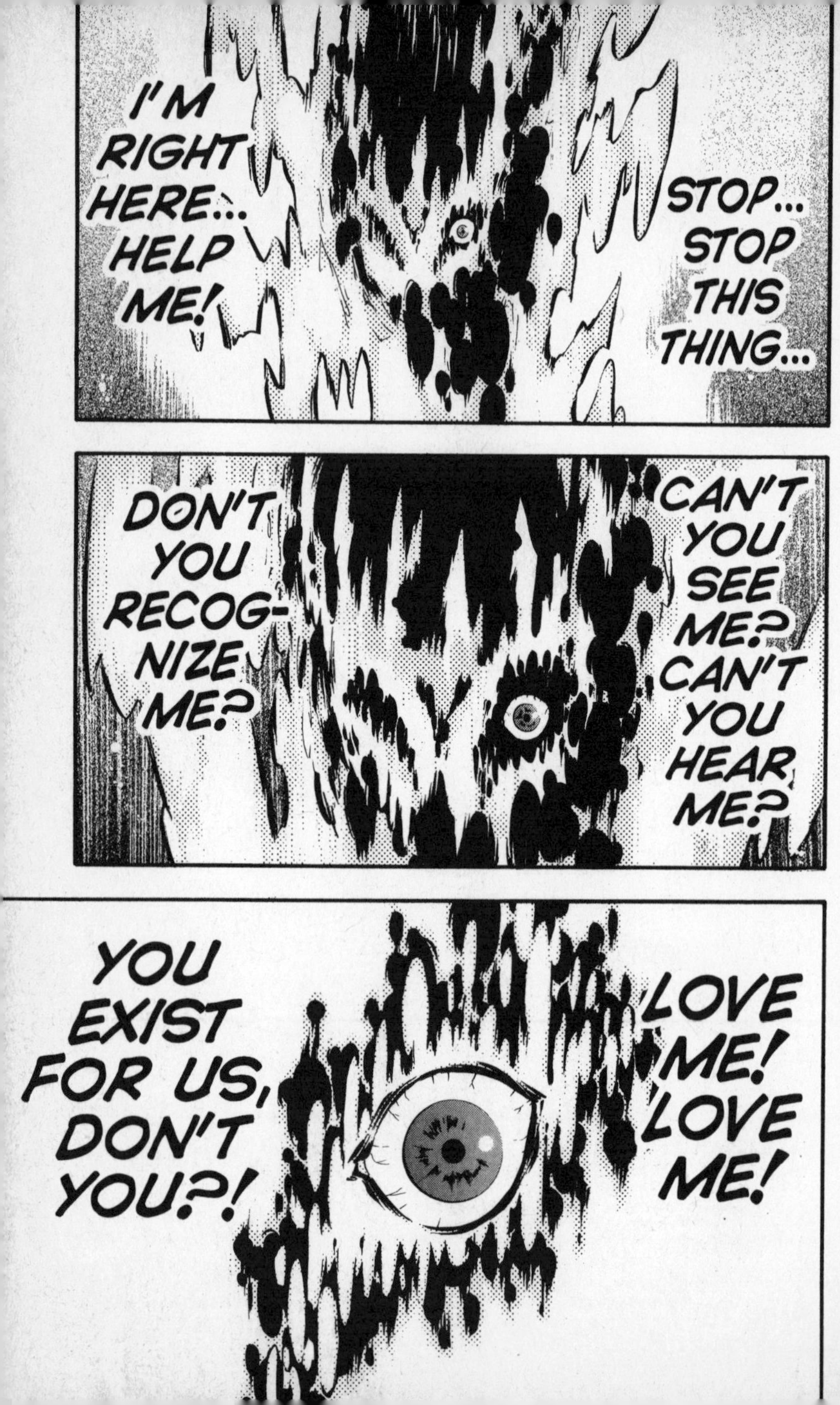
STOP... STOP THIS THING...
I'M RIGHT HERE... HELP ME!
CAN'T YOU SEE ME? CAN'T YOU HEAR ME?
DON'T YOU RECOGNIZE ME?
LOVE ME! LOVE ME!
YOU EXIST FOR US, DON'T YOU?!

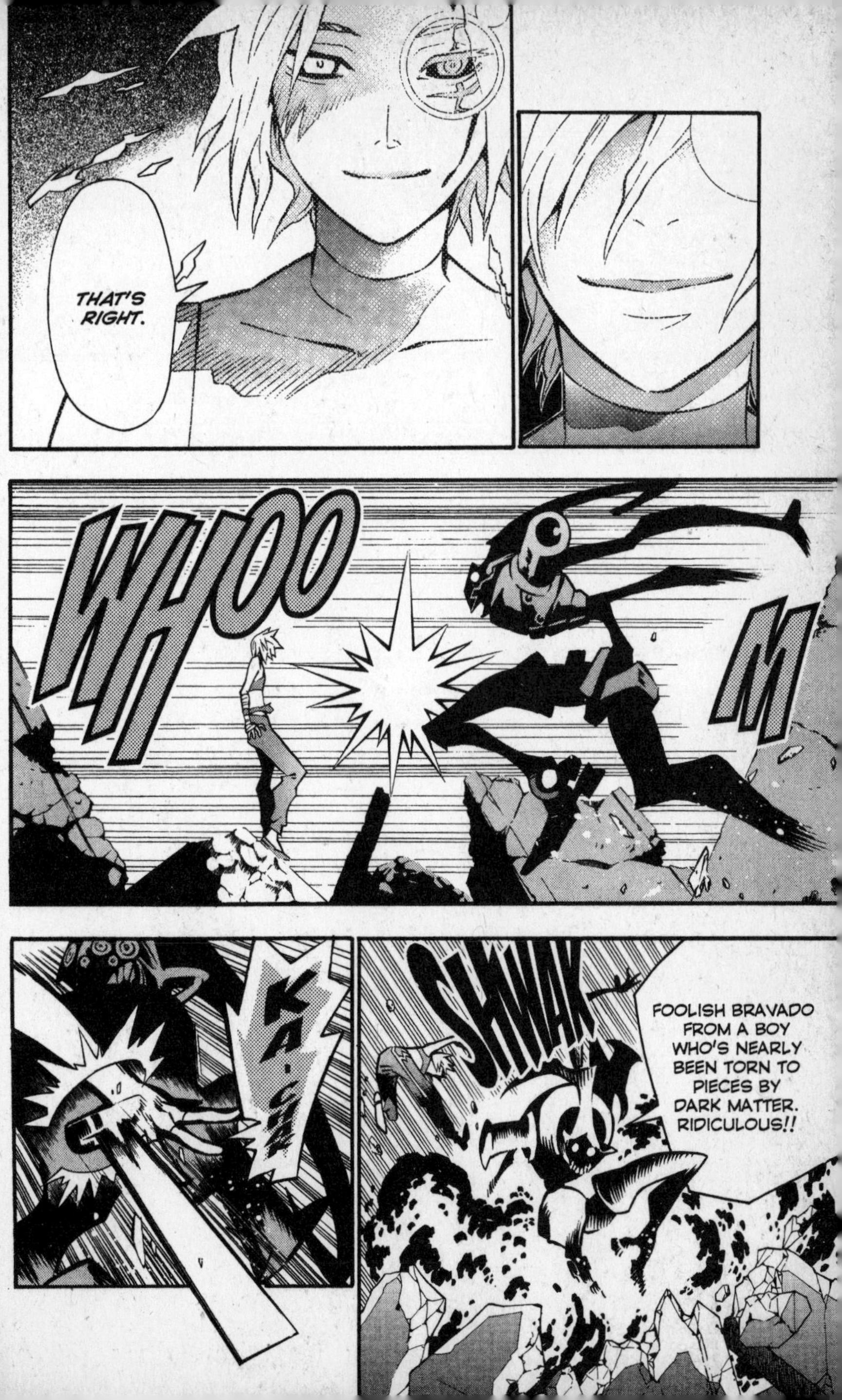
THAT'S RIGHT.
WHOOM
FOOLISH BRAVADO FROM A BOY WHO'S NEARLY BEEN TORN TO PIECES BY DARK MATTER. RIDICULOUS!!
SHWAK
KA-CHAK

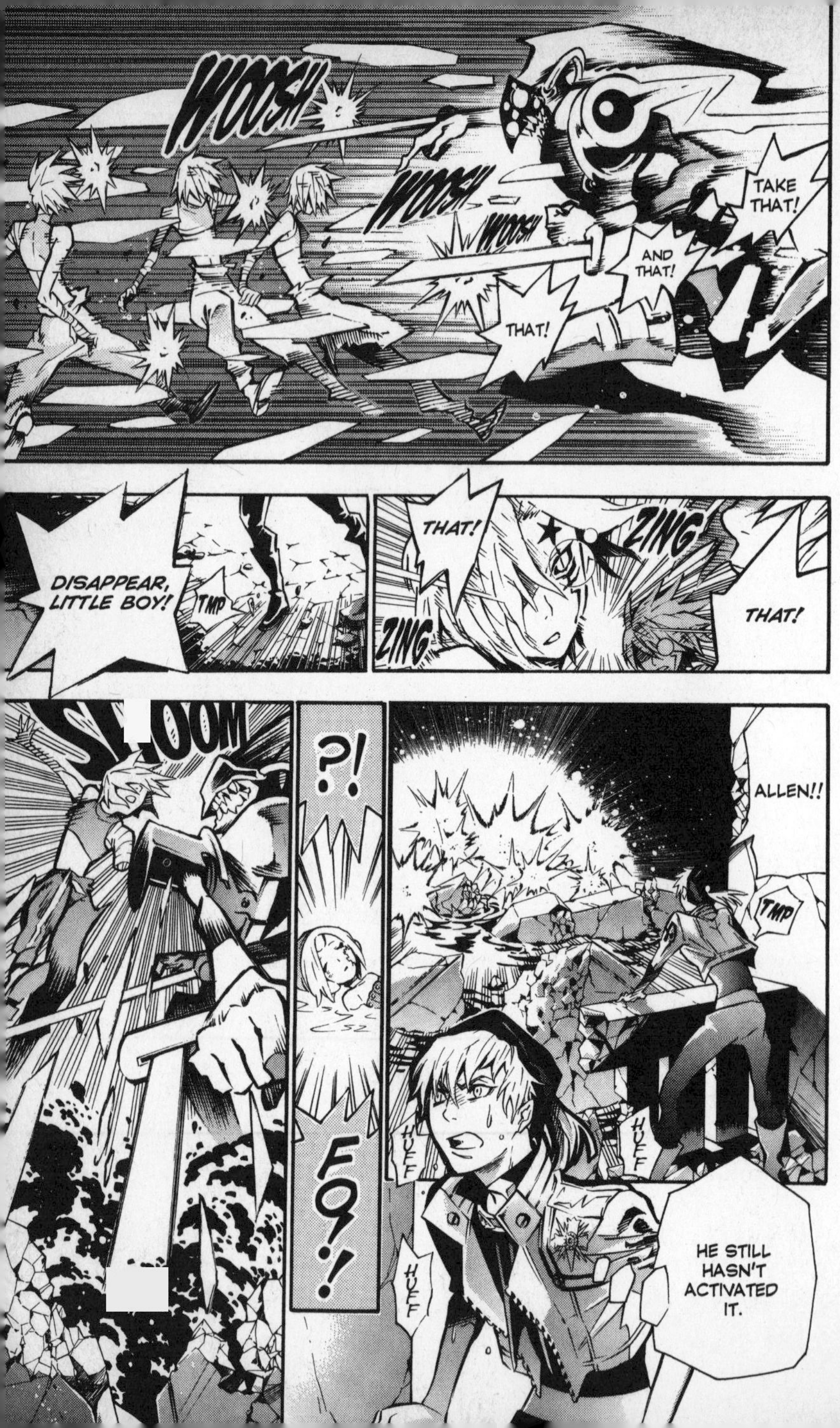
TAKE THAT!
AND THAT!
WOOSH
WOOSH
THAT!
WOOSH
THAT!
ZING
THAT!
ZING
DISAPPEAR, LITTLE BOY!
TMP
ALLEN!!
TMP
HUFF
HUFF
HE STILL HASN'T ACTIVATED IT.
HUFF
?!

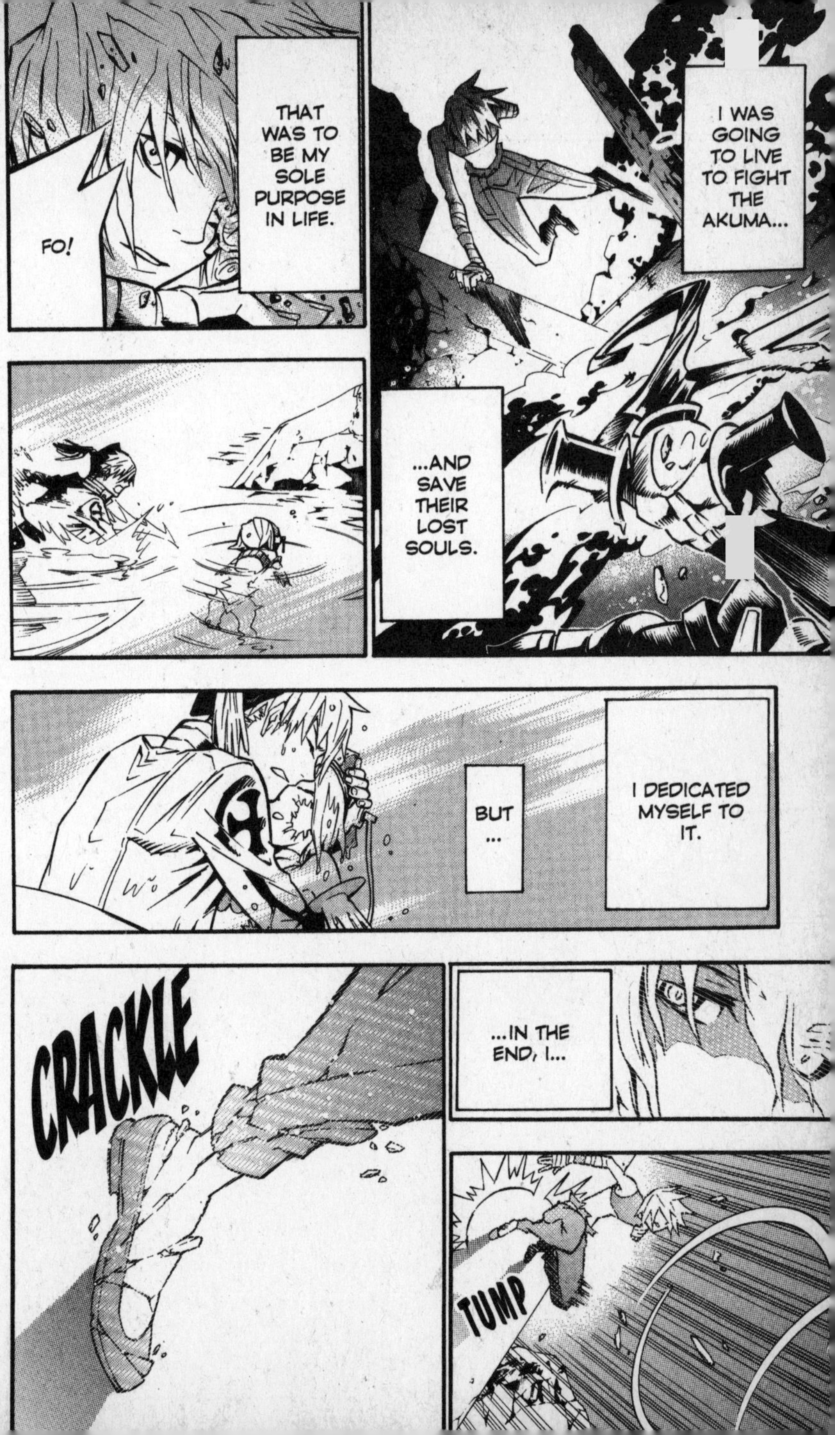
I WAS GOING TO LIVE TO FIGHT THE AKUMA...
...AND SAVE THEIR LOST SOULS.
THAT WAS TO BE MY SOLE PURPOSE IN LIFE.
FO!
I DEDICATED MYSELF TO IT.
BUT ...
...IN THE END, I...
TUMP
CRACKLE

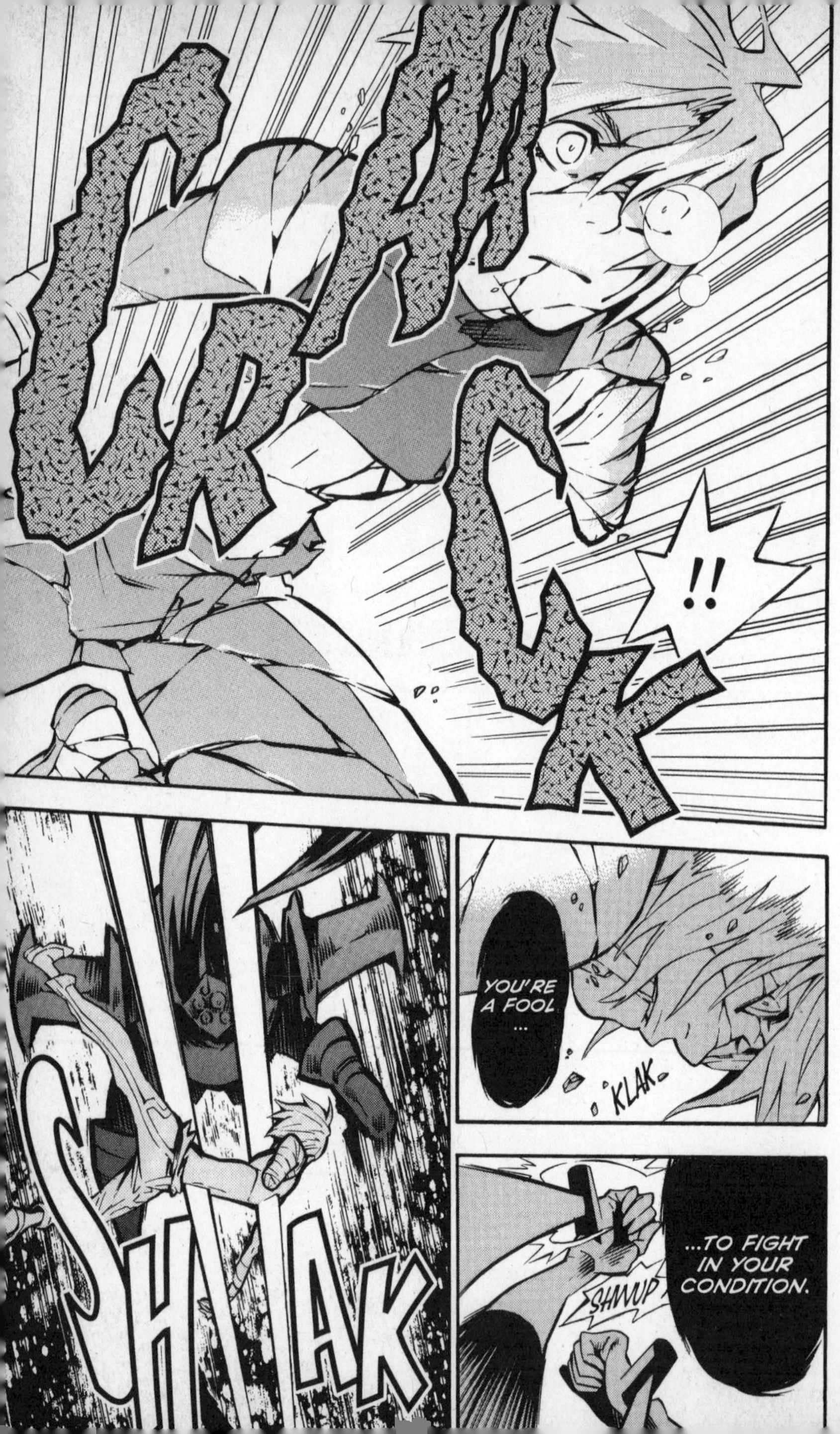
CRACK
!!
YOU'RE A FOOL ...
KLAK
...TO FIGHT IN YOUR CONDITION.
SHWUP
SHAK

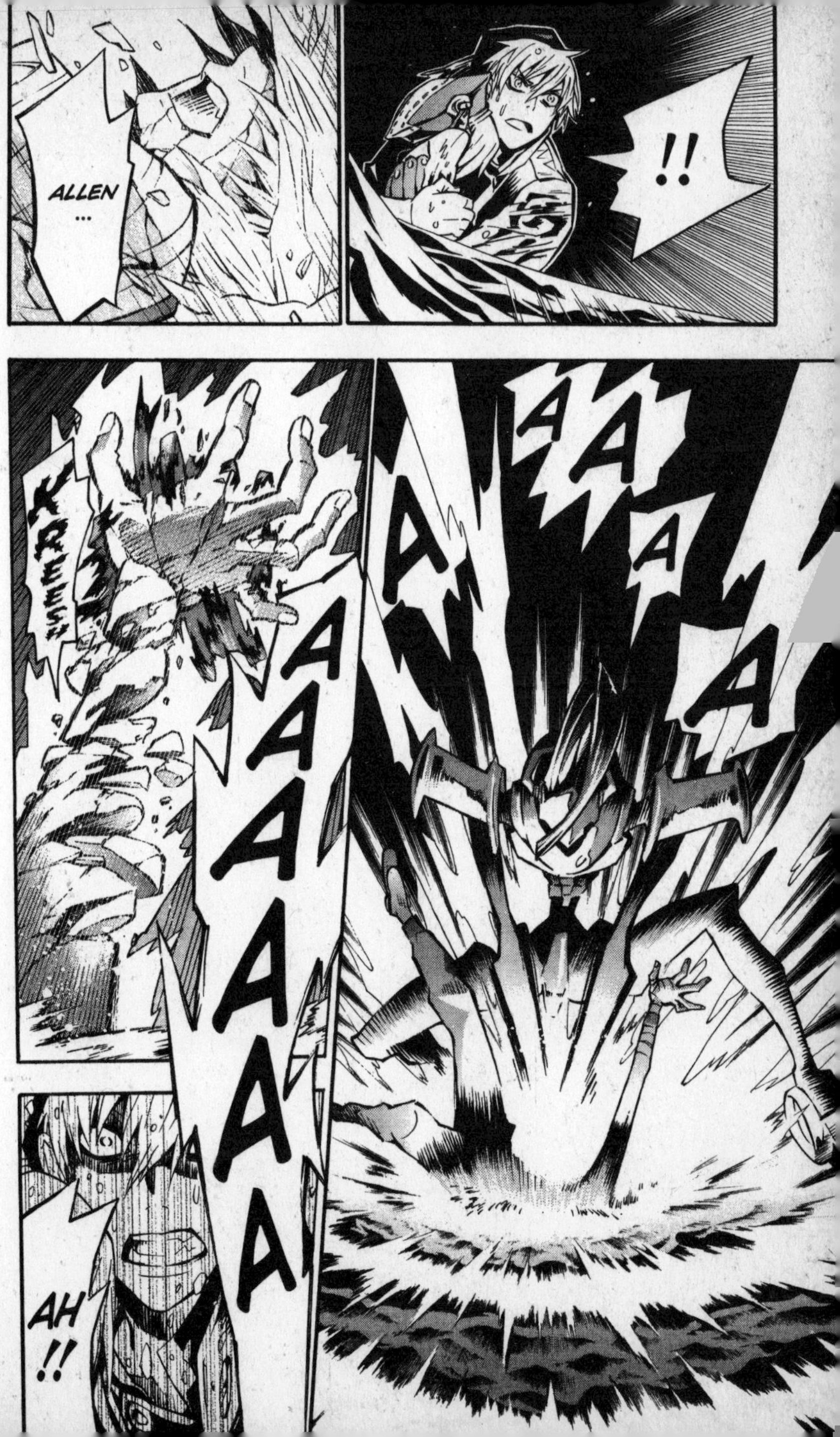
!!
ALLEN ...
AAAAAAAAAAAAAAAAAA
KREESH
AH !!

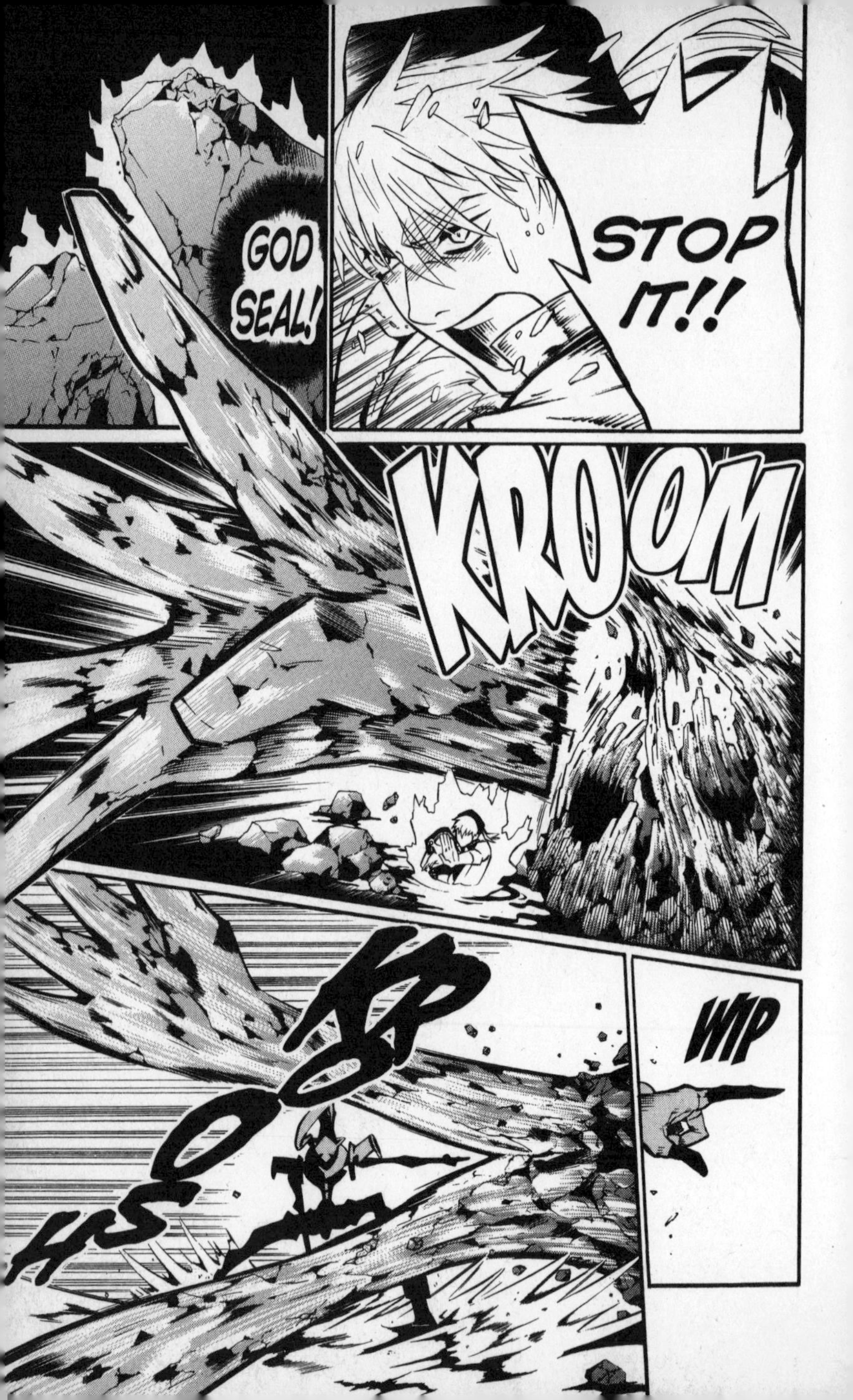
STOP IT!!
GOD SEAL!
KROOM
WIP

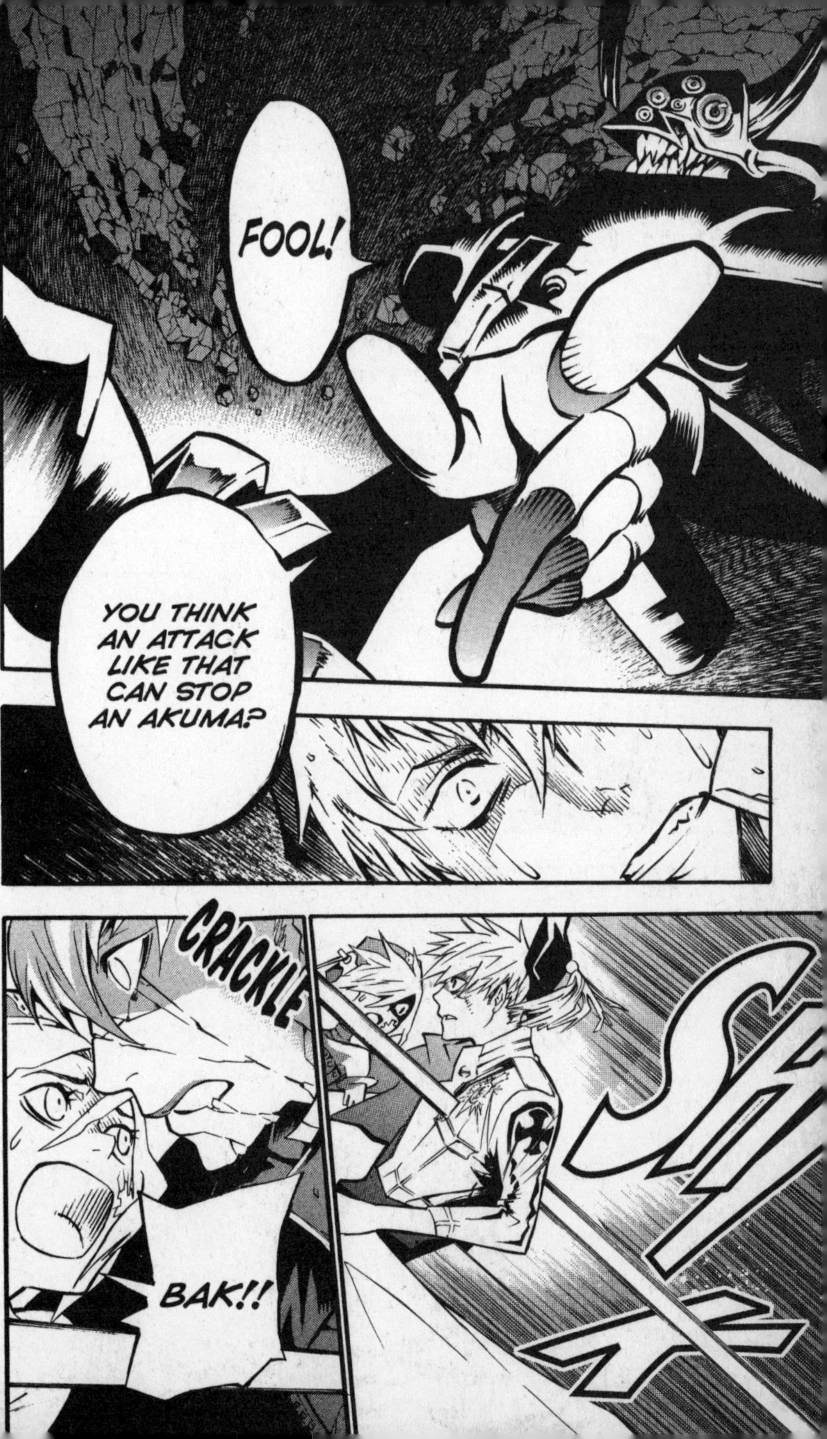
FOOL!
YOU THINK AN ATTACK LIKE THAT CAN STOP AN AKUMA?
CRACKLE
BAK!!

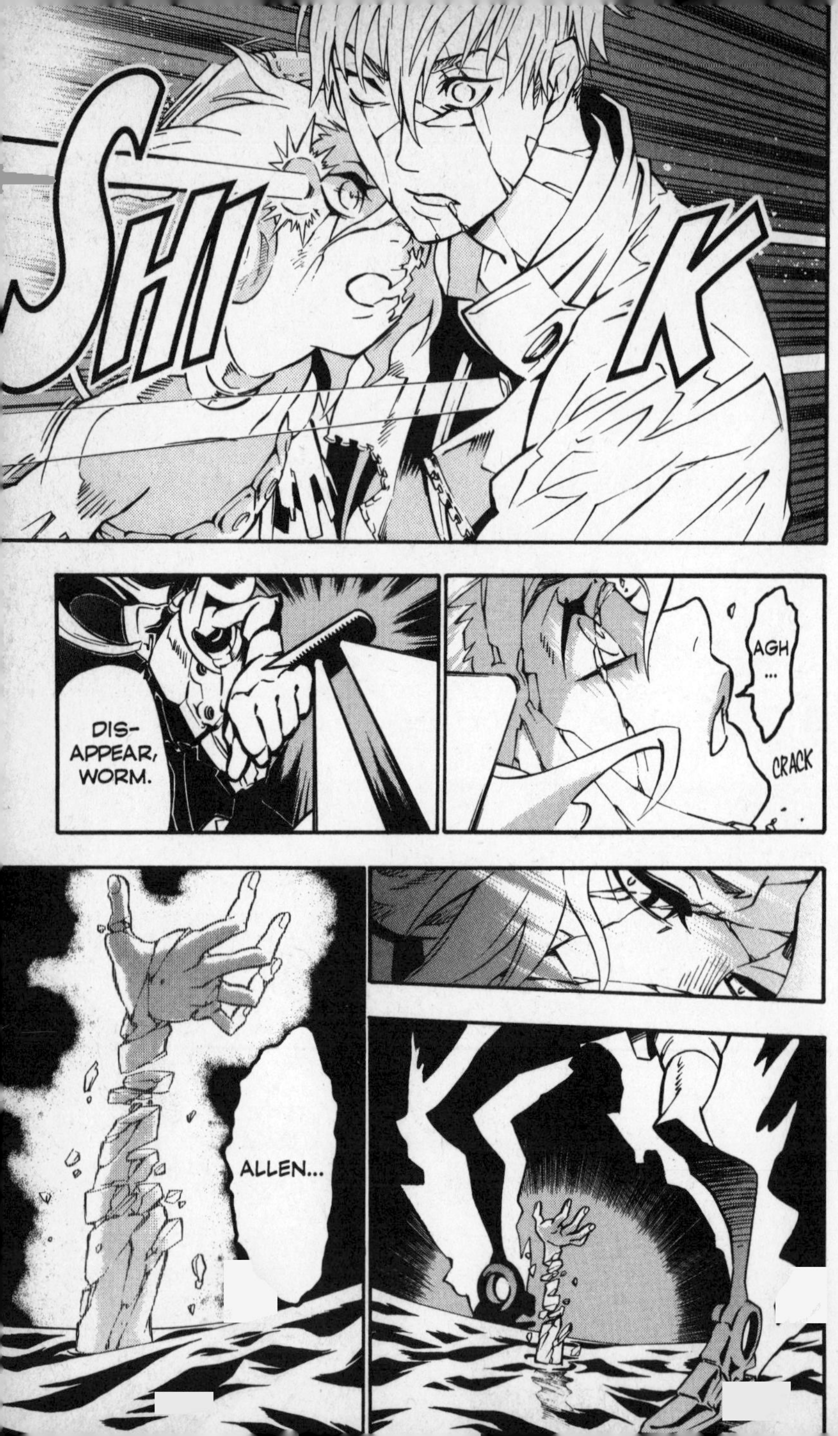
SHICK
AGH...
CRACK
DIS-APPEAR, WORM.
ALLEN...

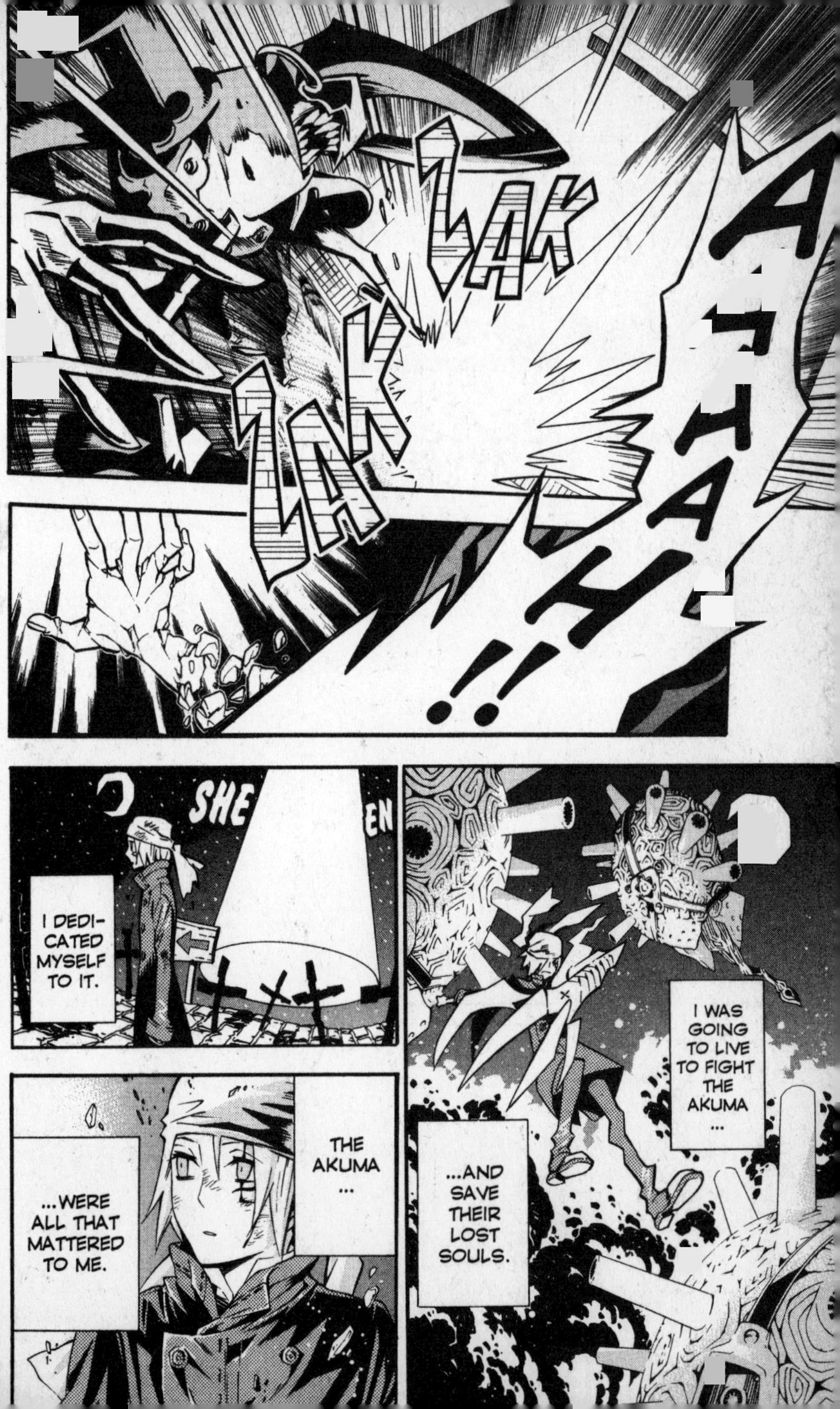
LAK
LAK
I WAS GOING TO LIVE TO FIGHT THE AKUMA...
...AND SAVE THEIR LOST SOULS.
SHE
EN
I DEDICATED MYSELF TO IT.
THE AKUMA...
...WERE ALL THAT MATTERED TO ME.

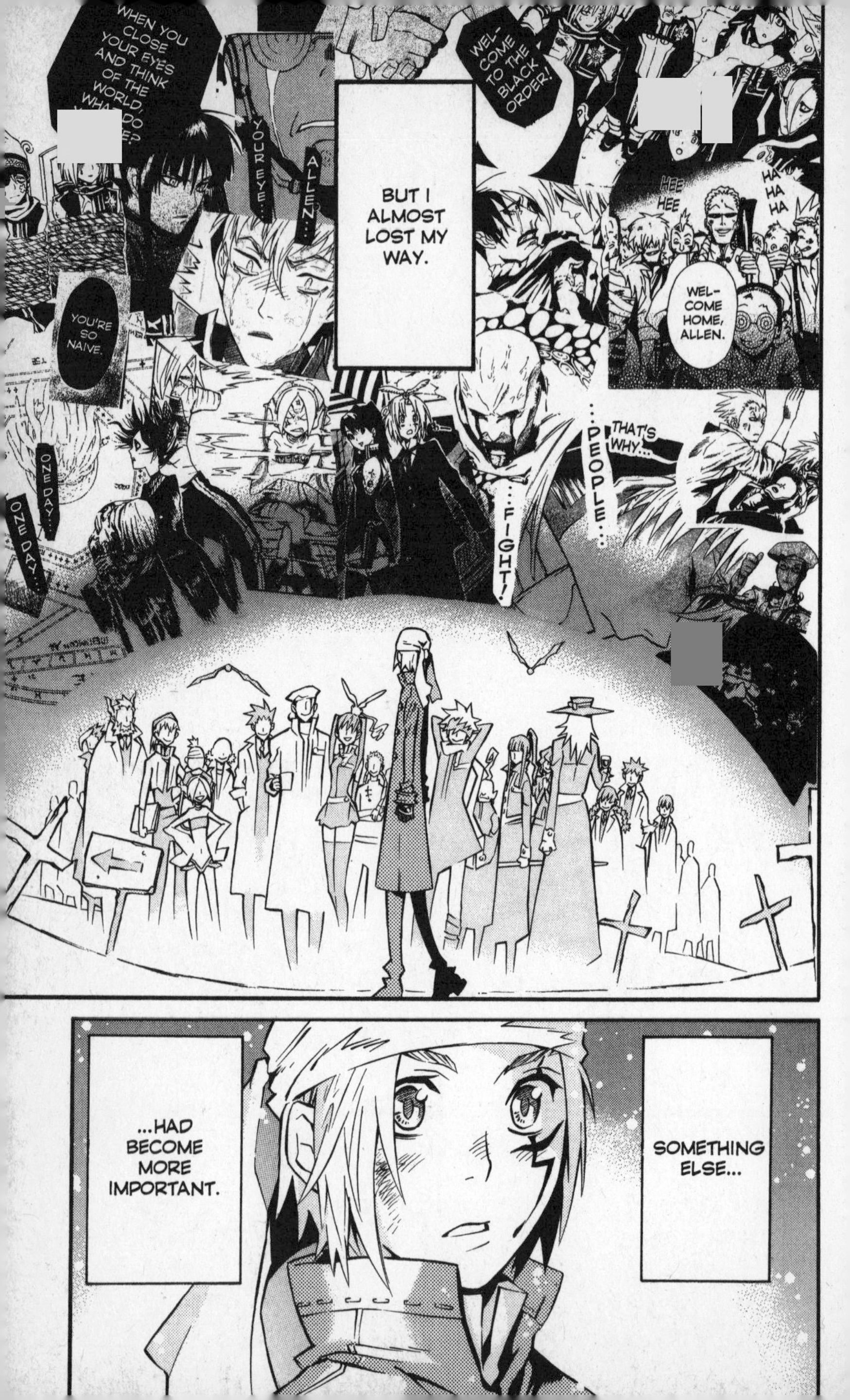
HA HA HA
HEE HEE
WEL-COME HOME, ALLEN.
WEL-COME TO THE BLACK ORDER!
BUT I ALMOST LOST MY WAY.
ALLEN...
YOUR EYE...
WHEN YOU CLOSE YOUR EYES AND THINK OF THE WORLD, WHAT DO
YOU'RE SO NAIVE.
THAT'S WHY...
...PEOPLE...
...FIGHT!
ONE DAY...
ONE DAY...
SOMETHING ELSE...
...HAD BECOME MORE IMPORTANT.

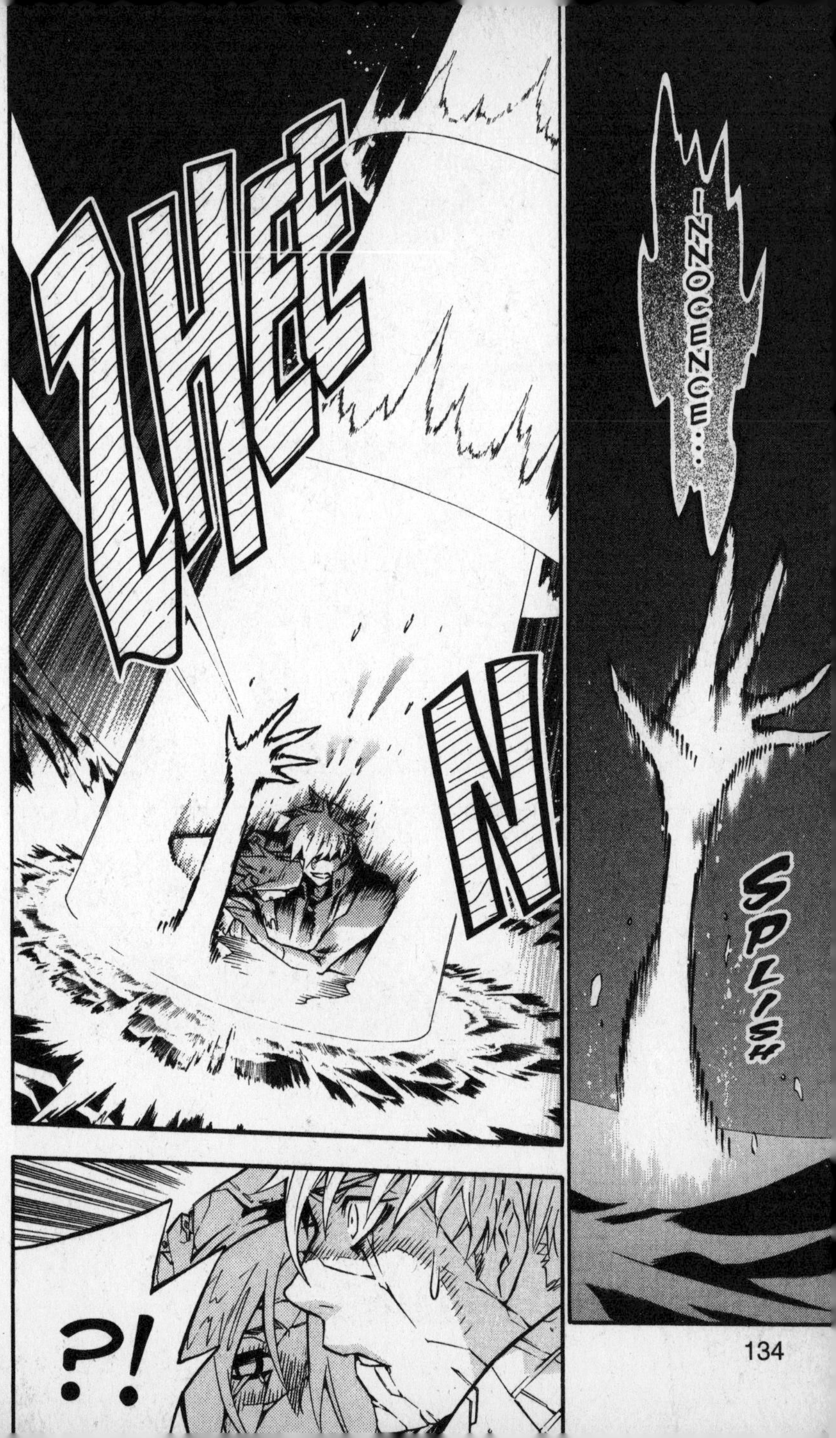
INNOCENCE...
SPLISH
ZHEEN
?!

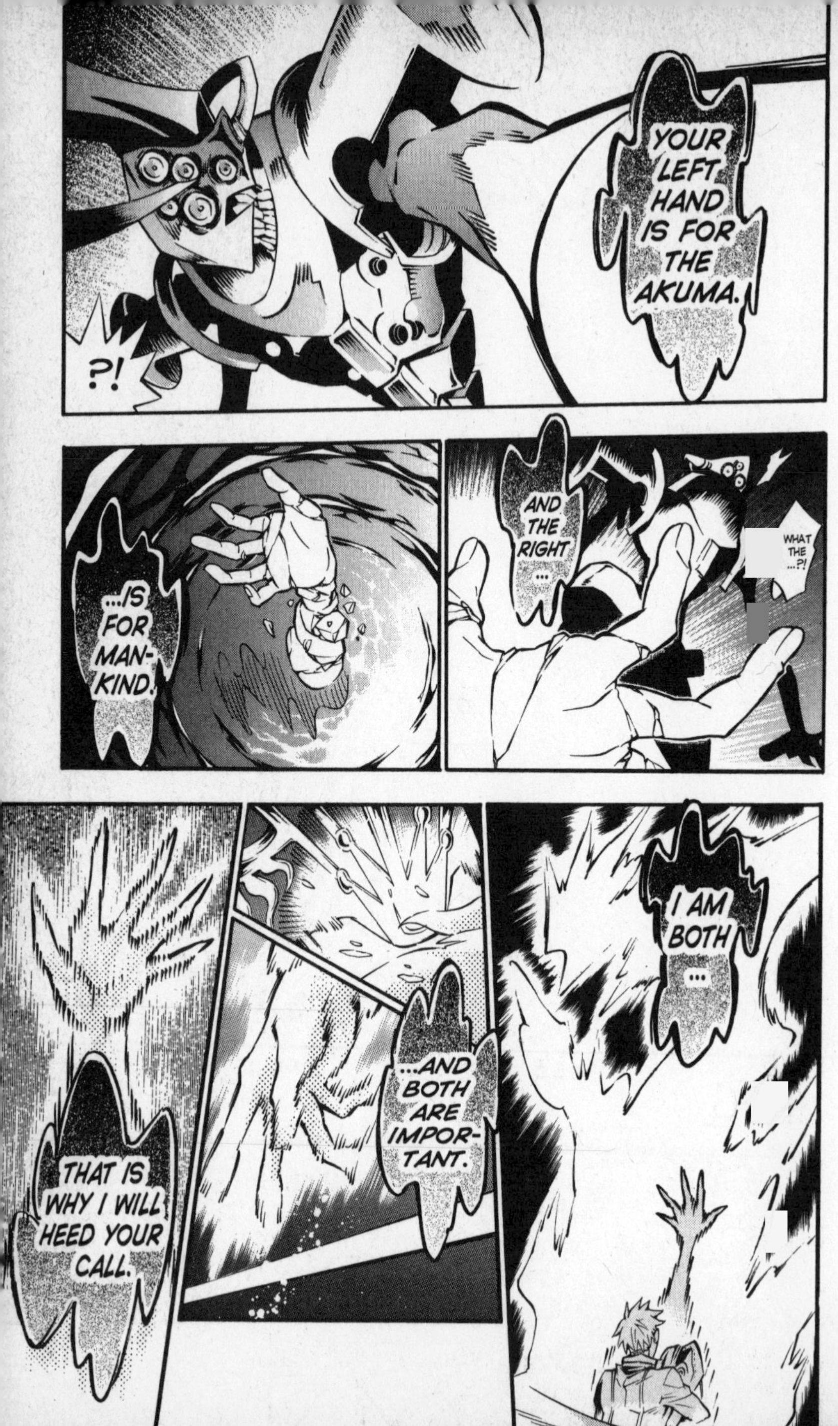
YOUR LEFT HAND IS FOR THE AKUMA.
?!
AND THE RIGHT ...
WHAT THE ...?!
...IS FOR MAN-KIND.
I AM BOTH ...
...AND BOTH ARE IMPOR-TANT.
THAT IS WHY I WILL HEED YOUR CALL.

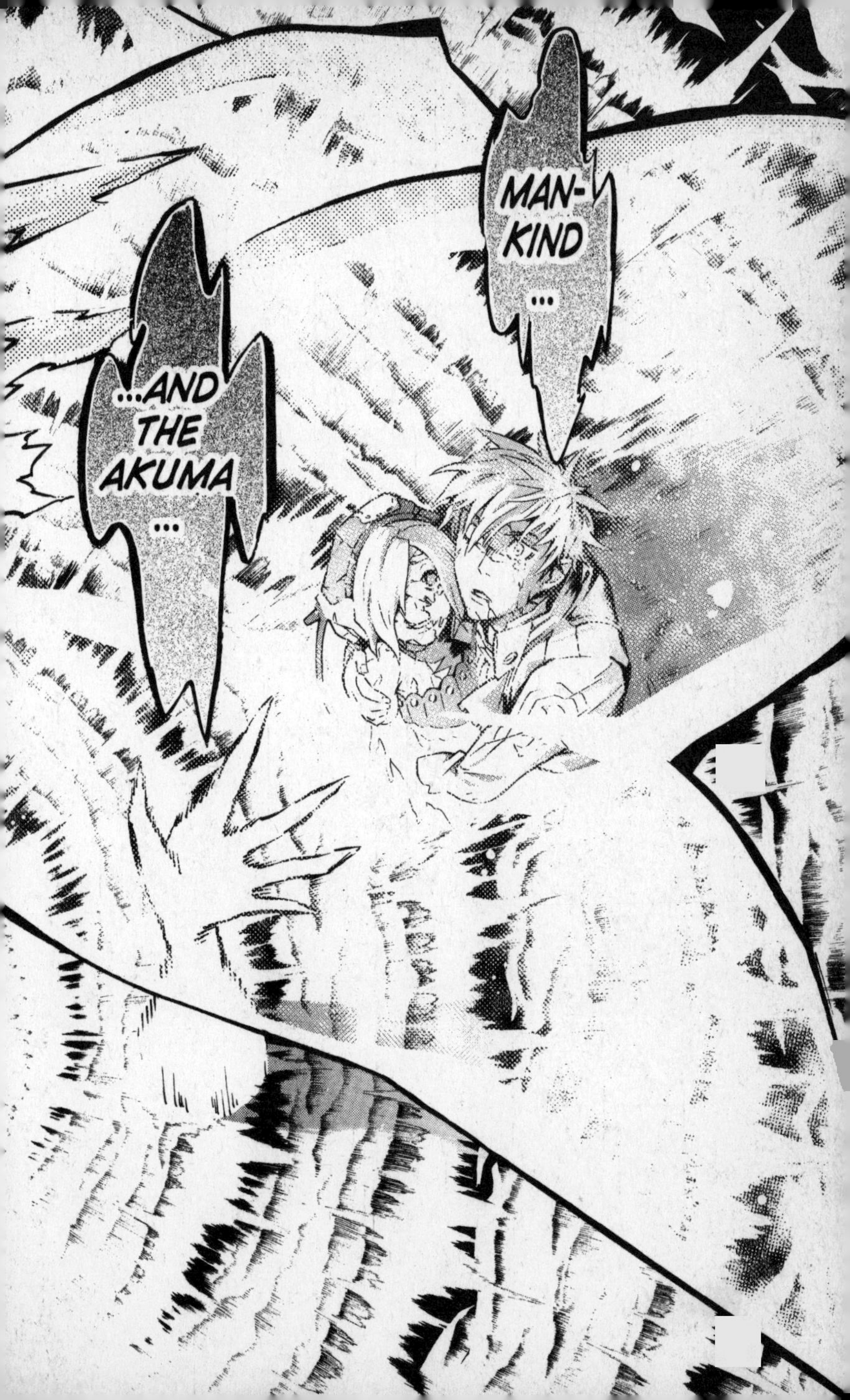
MAN-KIND ...
...AND THE AKUMA ...

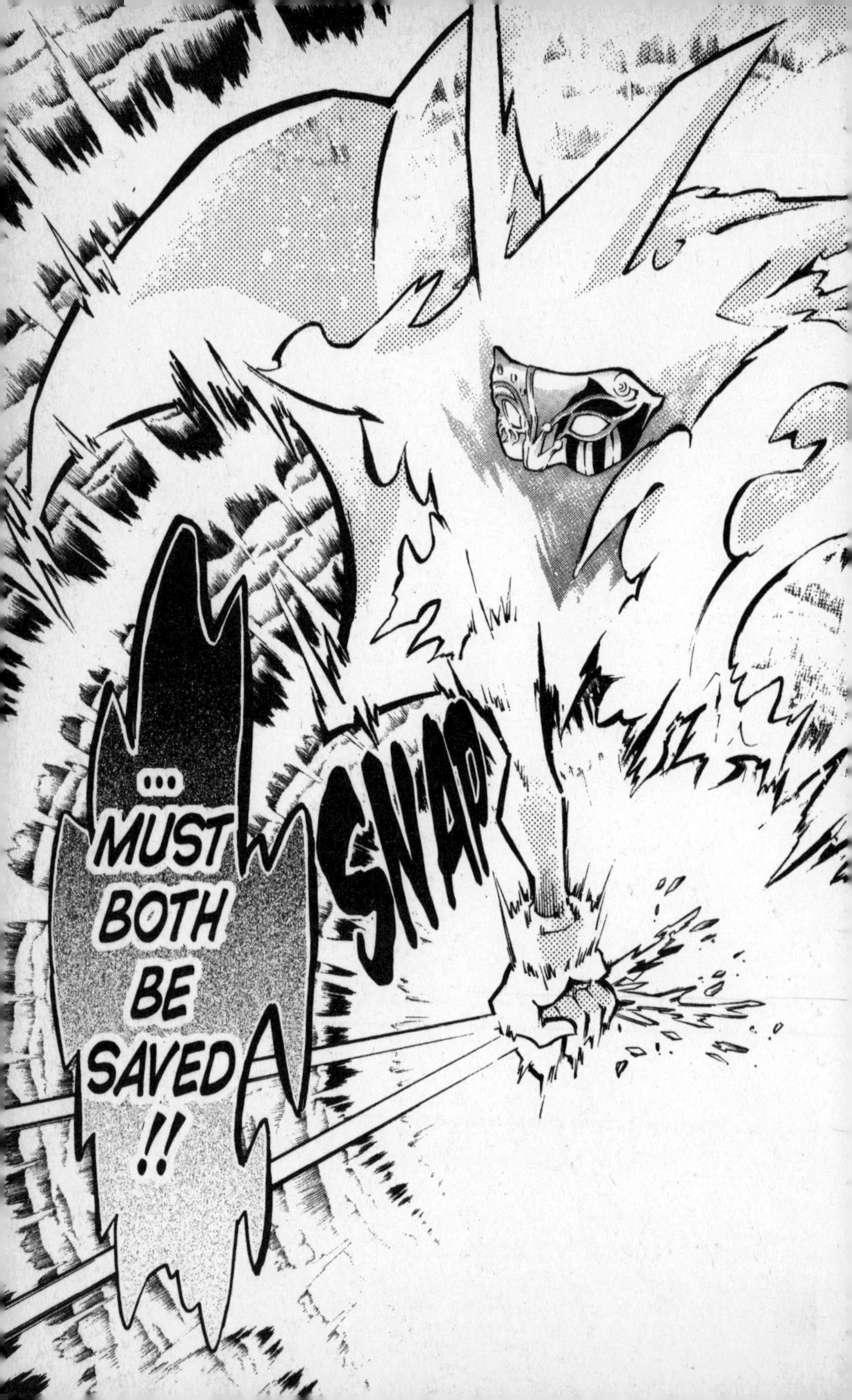
...MUST BOTH BE SAVED!!
SNAP!

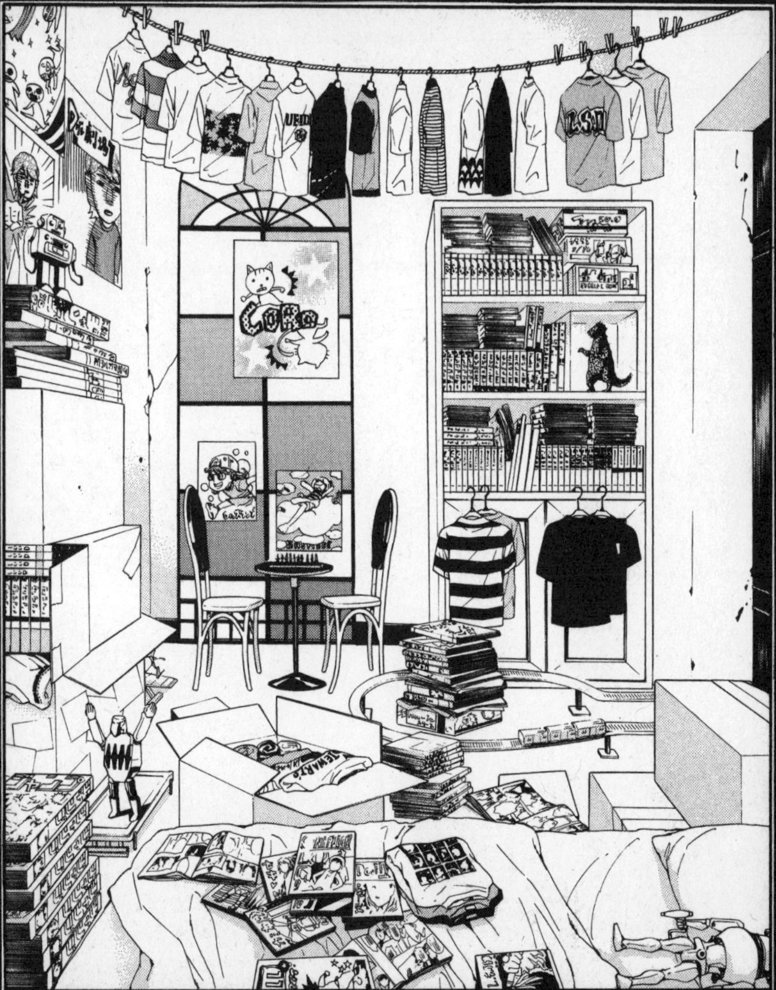

THIS IS THE ROOM OF JOHNNY GILL OF THE SCIENCE DIVISION.
IT APPEARS HE HASN'T COME BACK TO HIS ROOM YET TODAY.
ACCORDING TO LAVI, HE WAS GETTING A GARLIC INJECTION IN
THE INFIRMARY AND SUFFERING A NOSEBLEED.

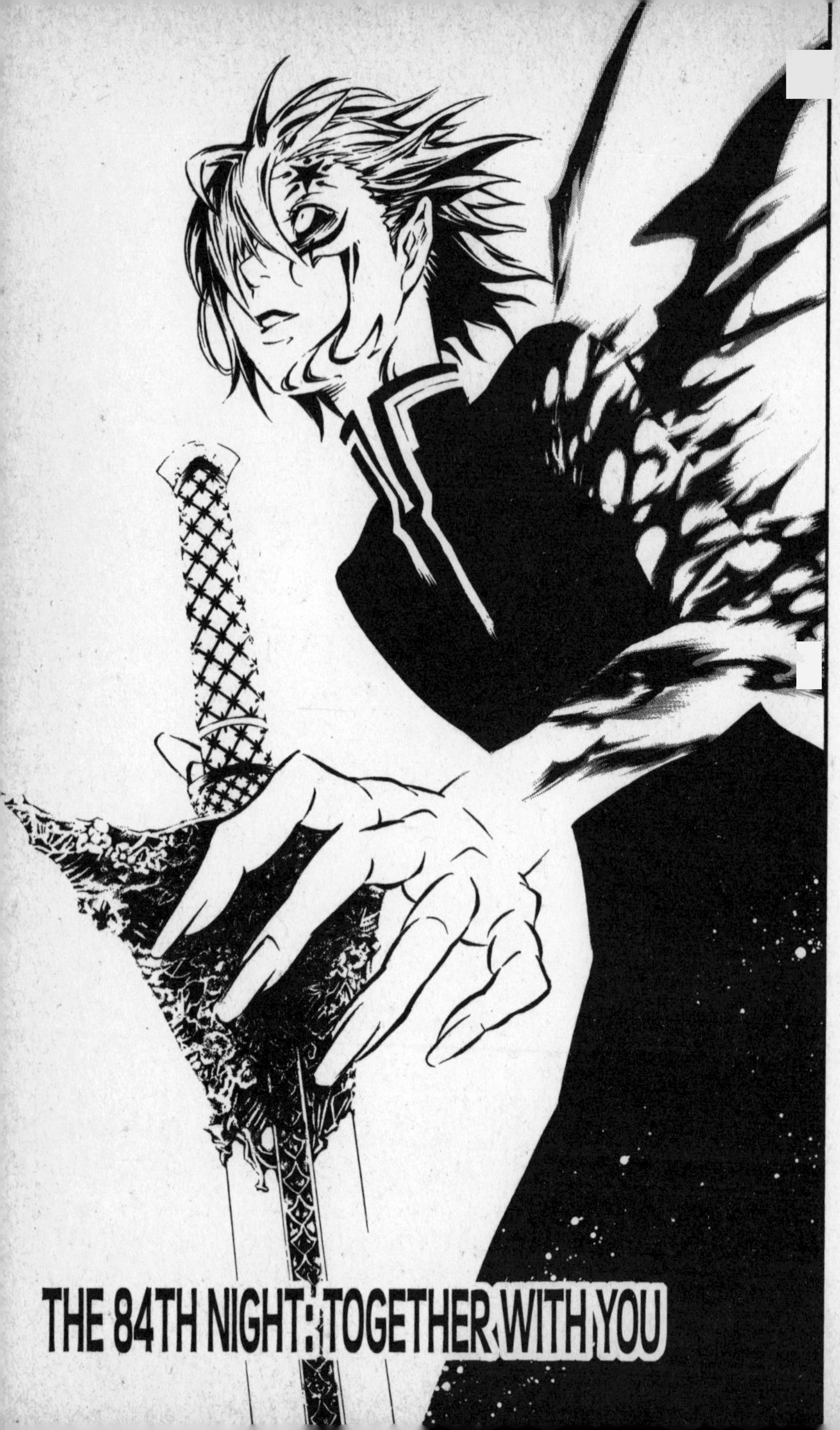

THE 84TH NIGHT: TOGETHER WITH YOU

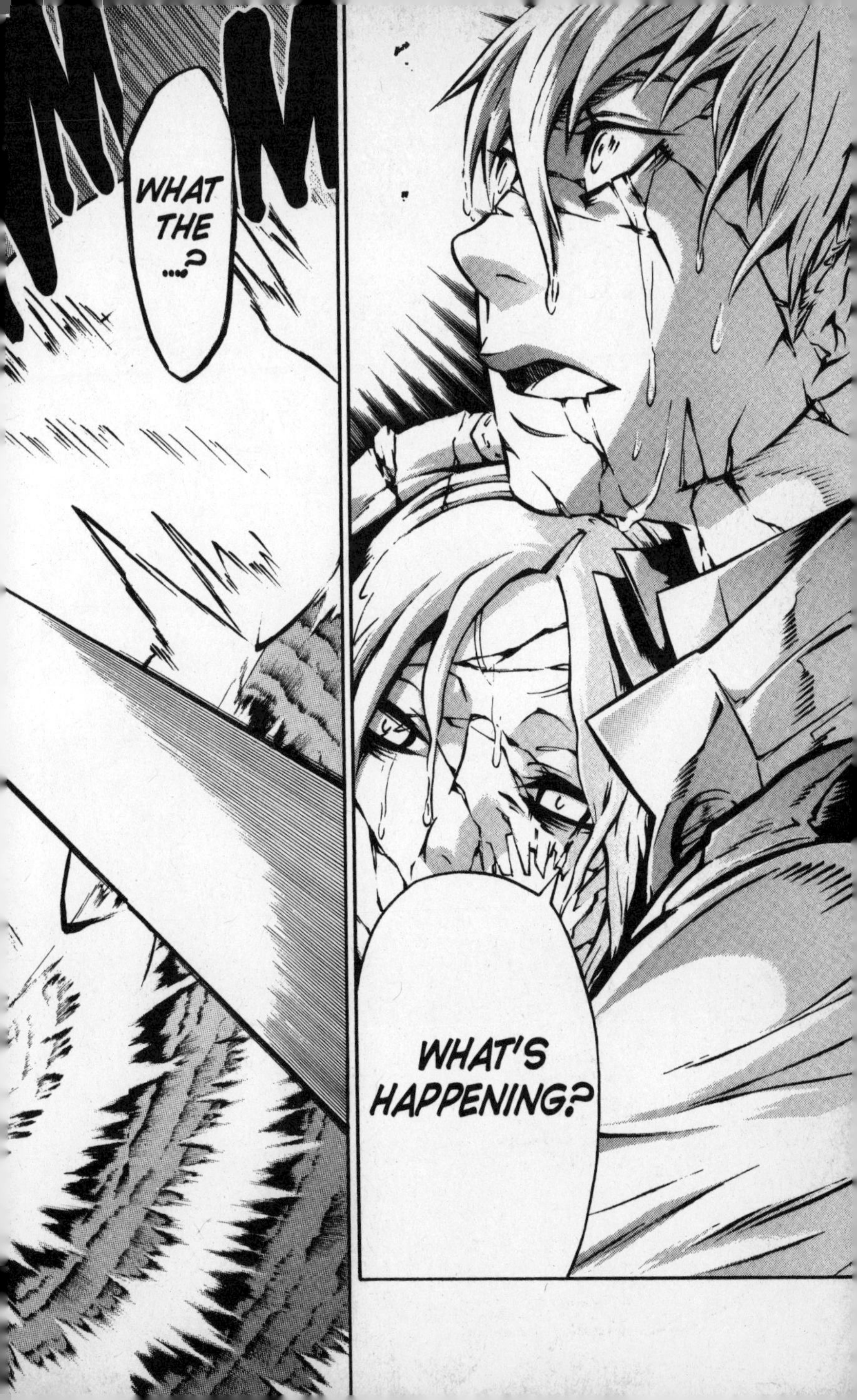
WHAT'S HAPPENING?
WHAT THE ...?

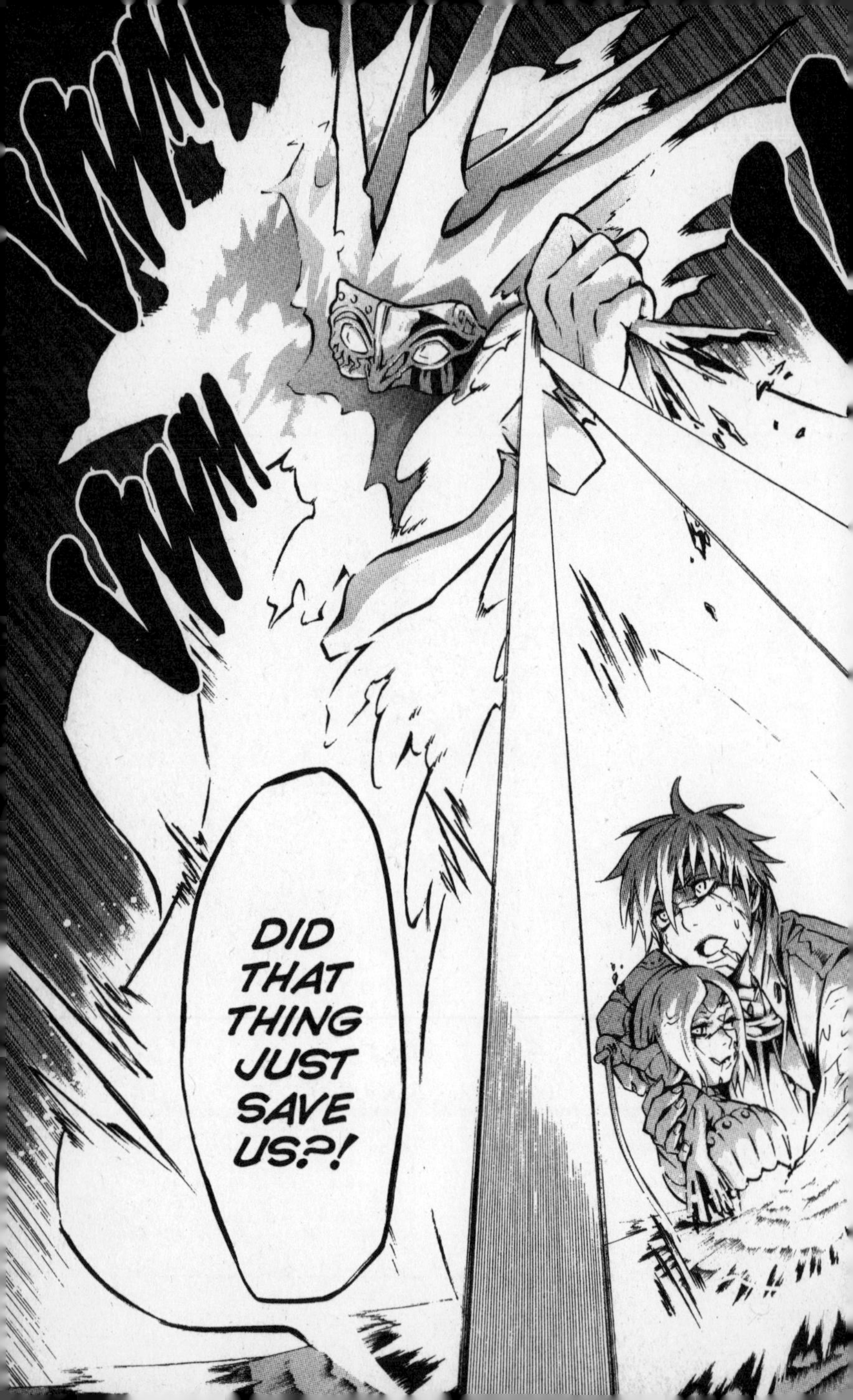
DID THAT THING JUST SAVE US?!

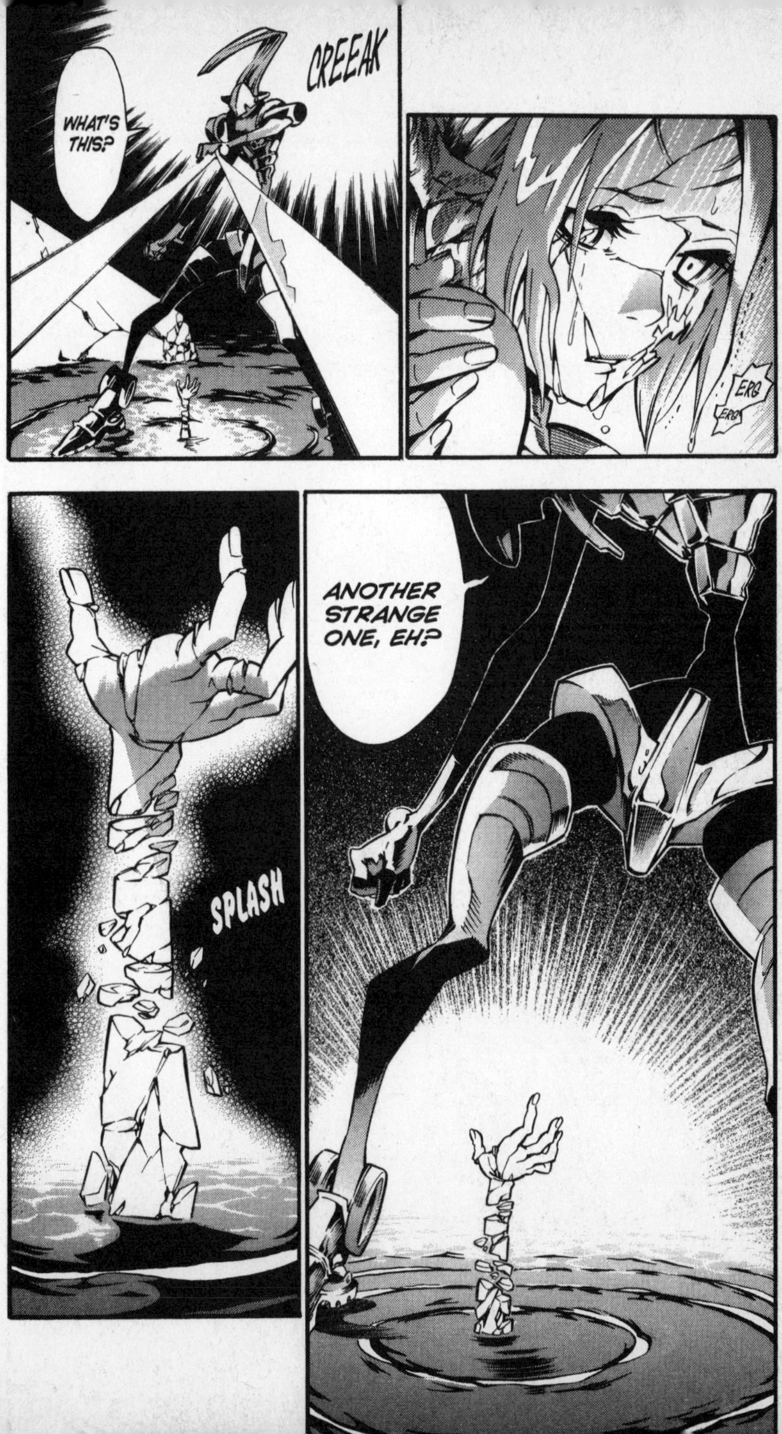
ERG
ERG
CREEAK
WHAT'S THIS?
ANOTHER STRANGE ONE, EH?
SPLASH

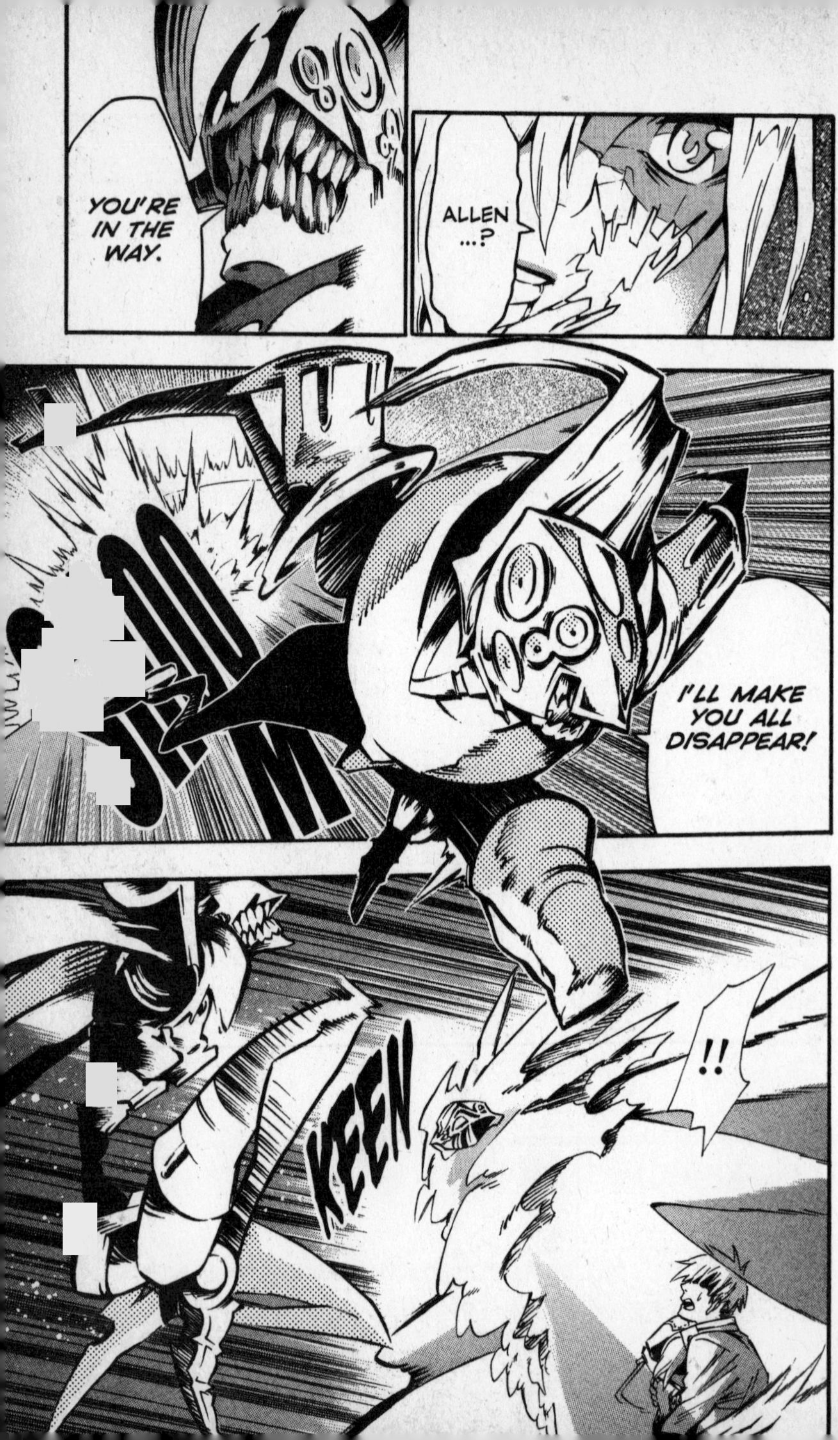
ALLEN ...?
YOU'RE IN THE WAY.
I'LL MAKE YOU ALL DISAPPEAR!
DOOM
!!
KEEN

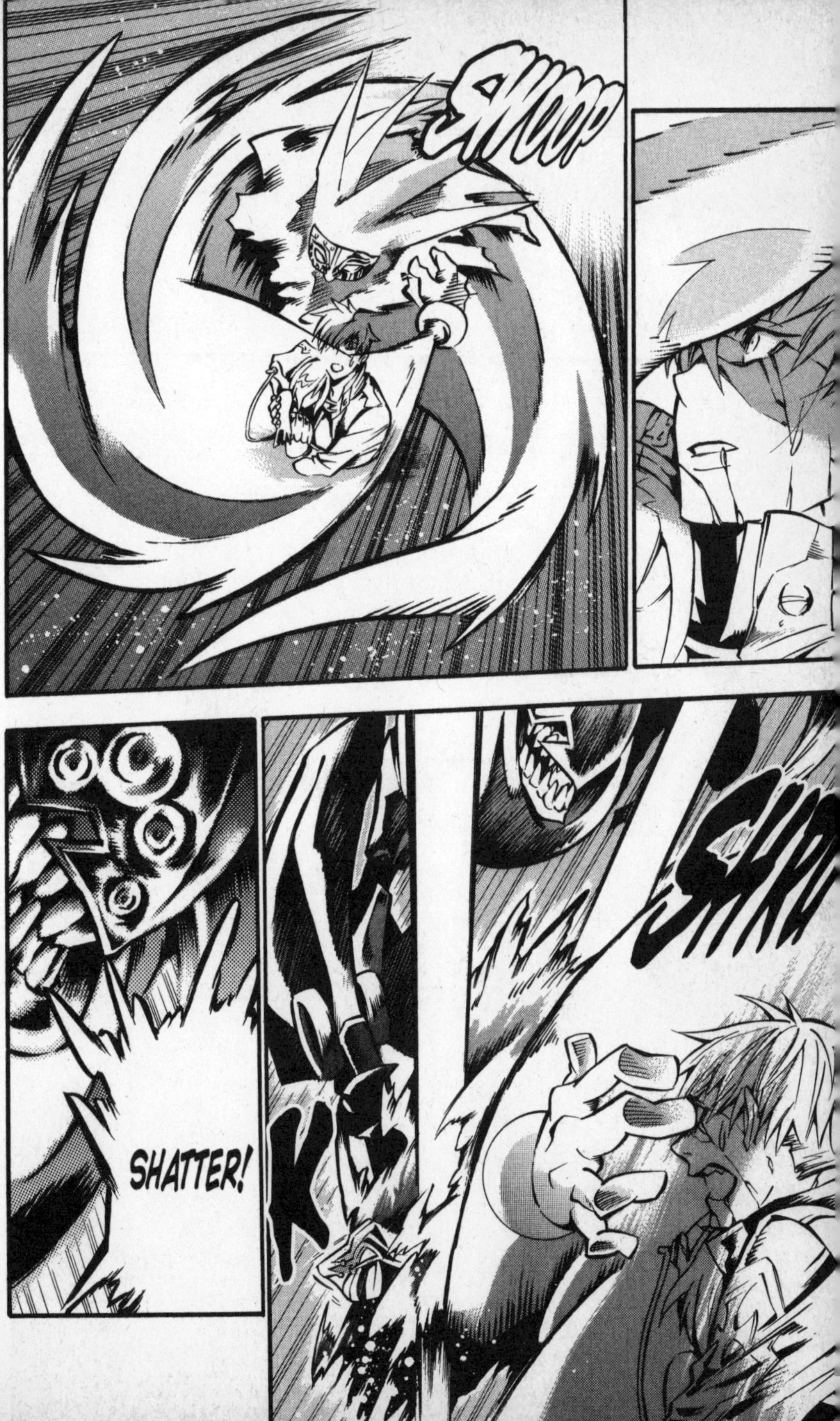
SHOOP
SHATTER!

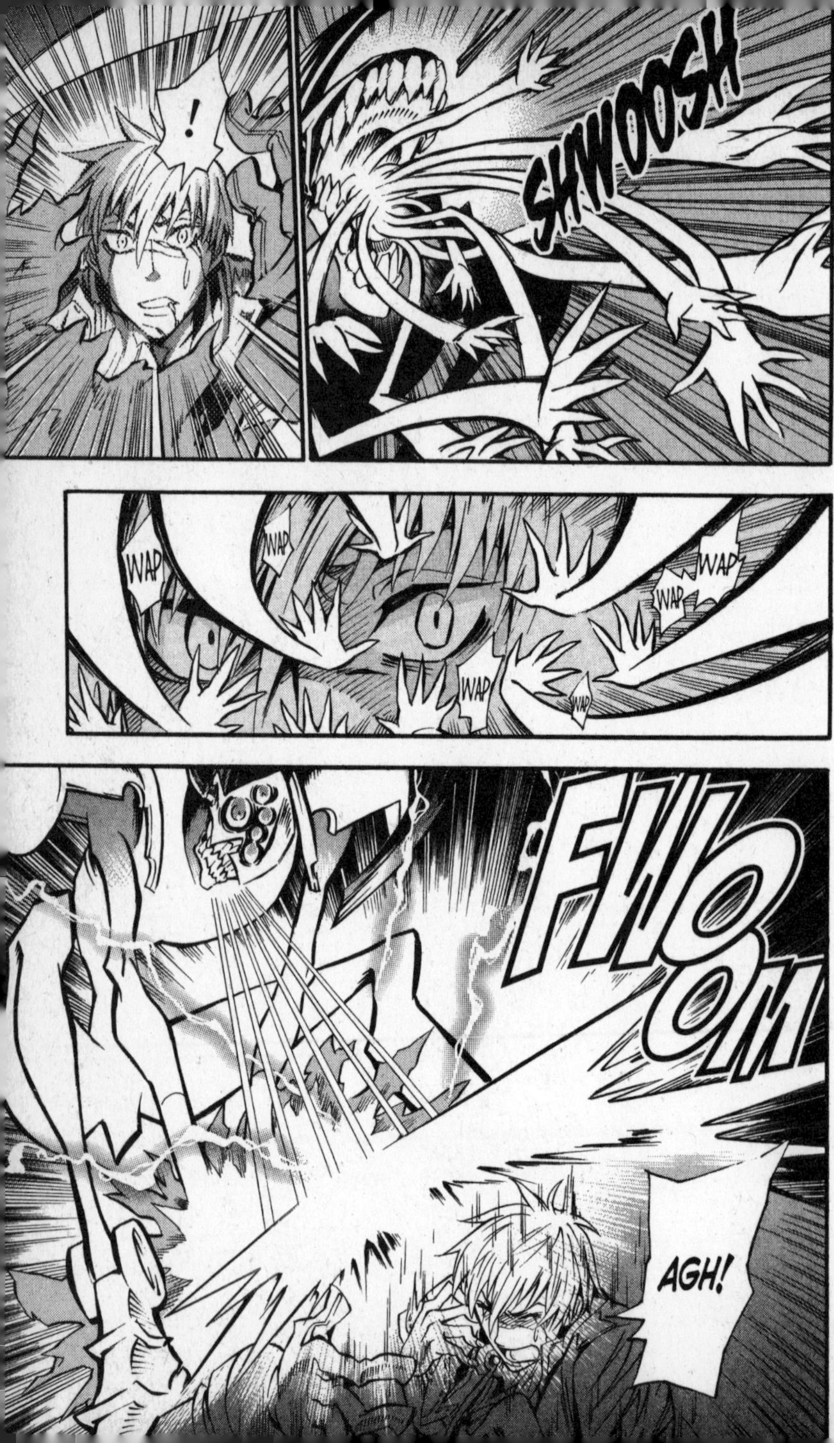
SHWOOSH
!
WAP
WAP
WAP
WAP
WAP
WAP
AGH!

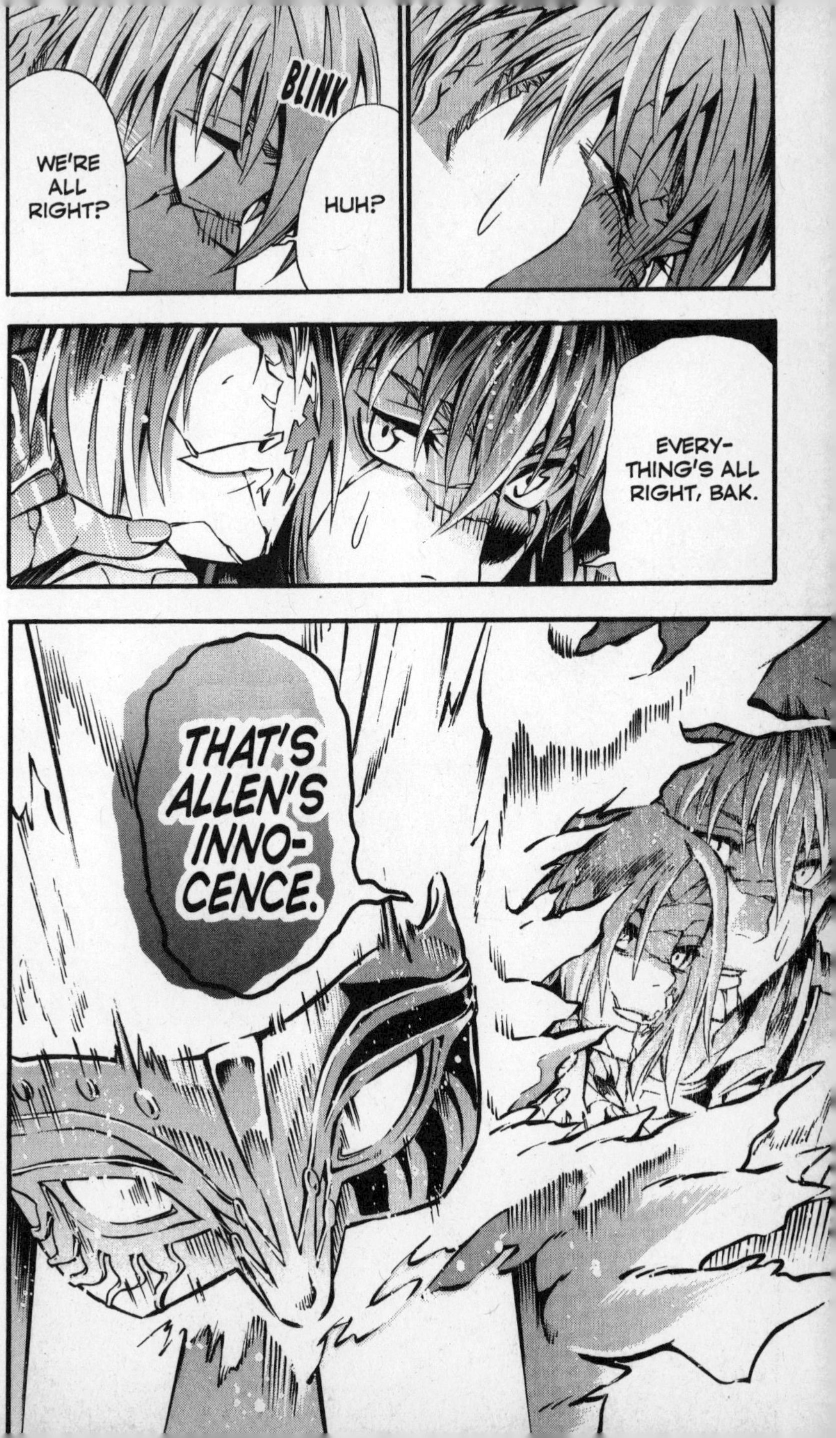
BLINK
HUH?
WE'RE ALL RIGHT?
EVERY-THING'S ALL RIGHT, BAK.
THAT'S ALLEN'S INNO-CENCE.

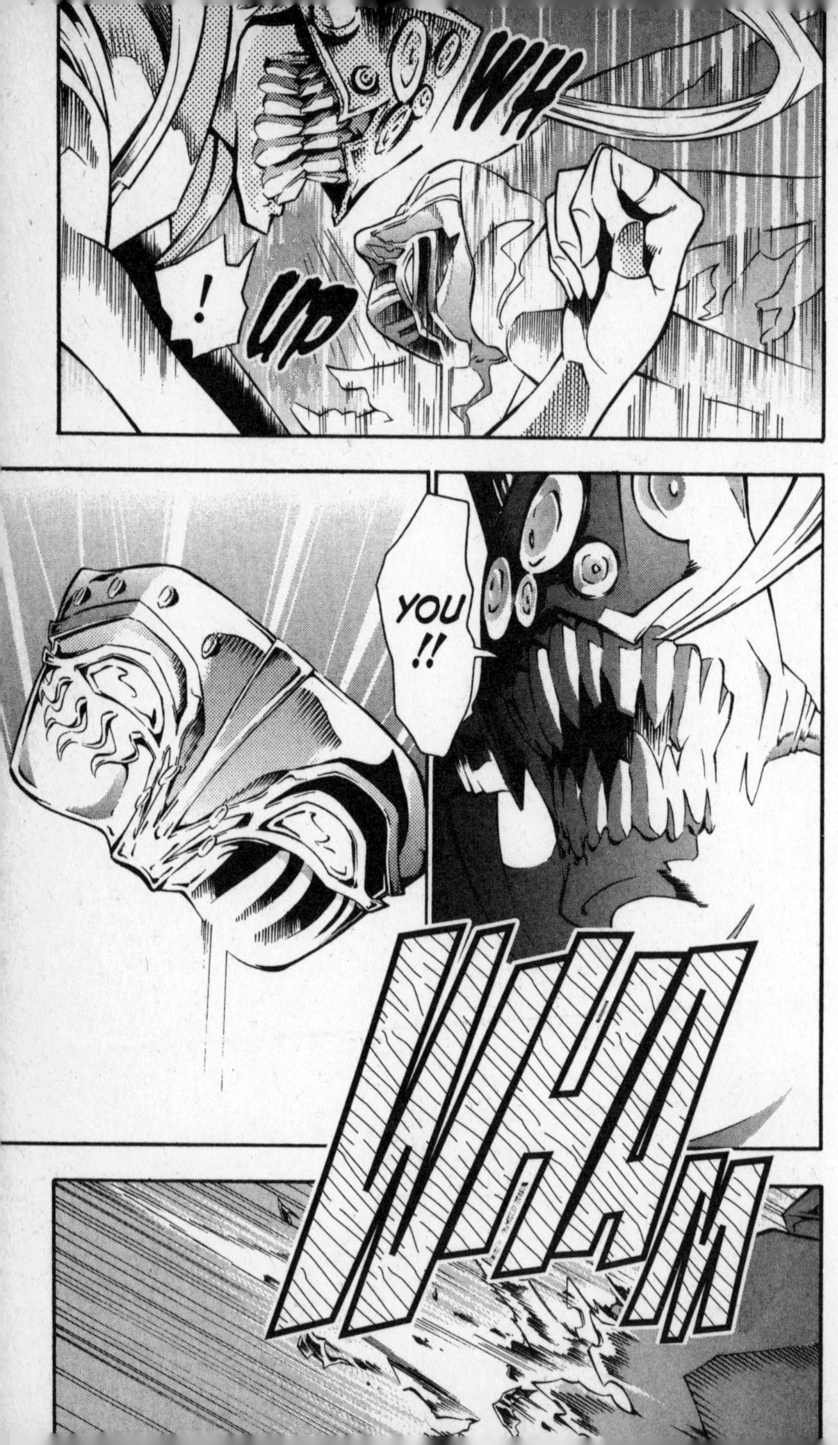
WH
UP
!
YOU !!
WHAM

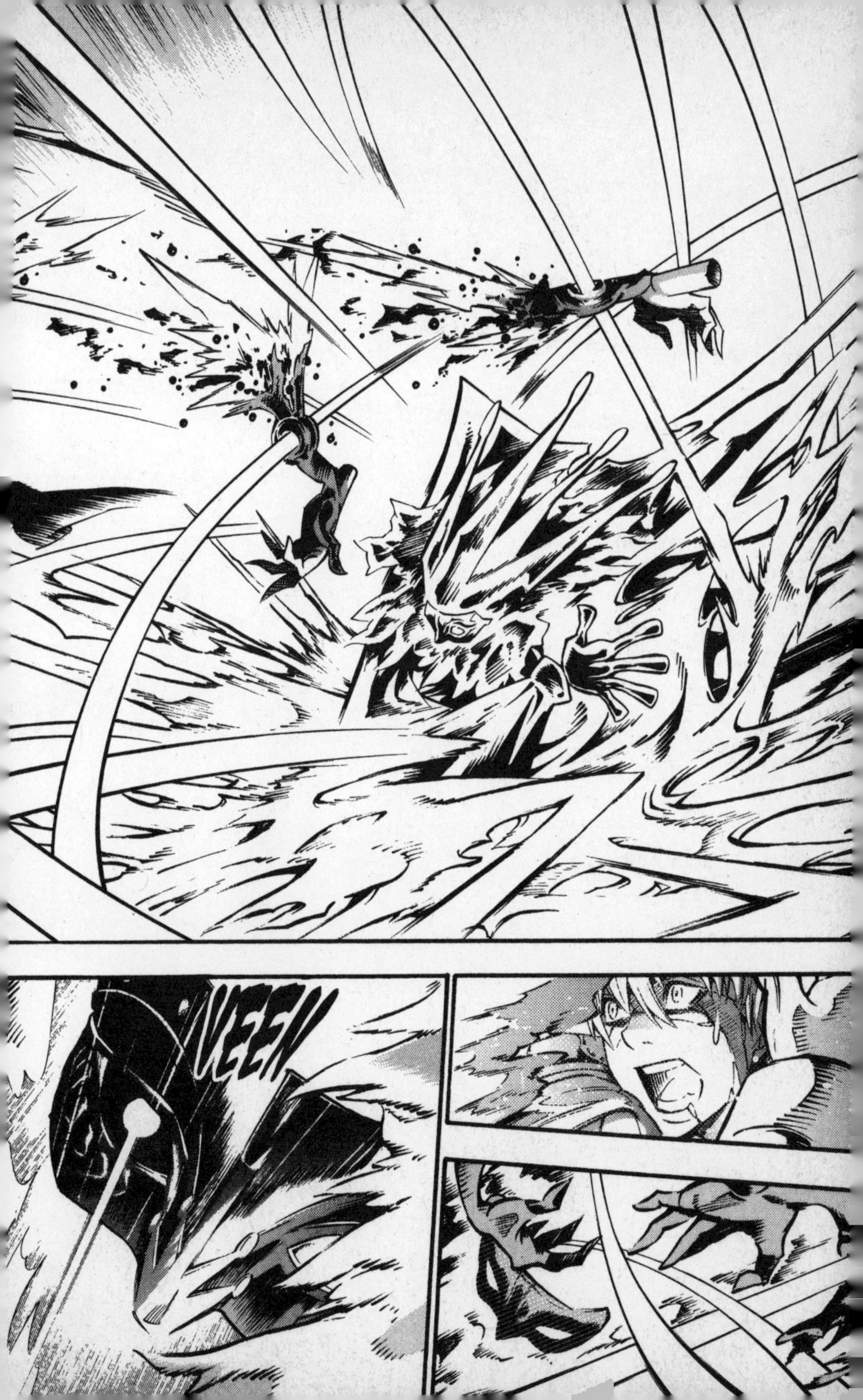
VEEN

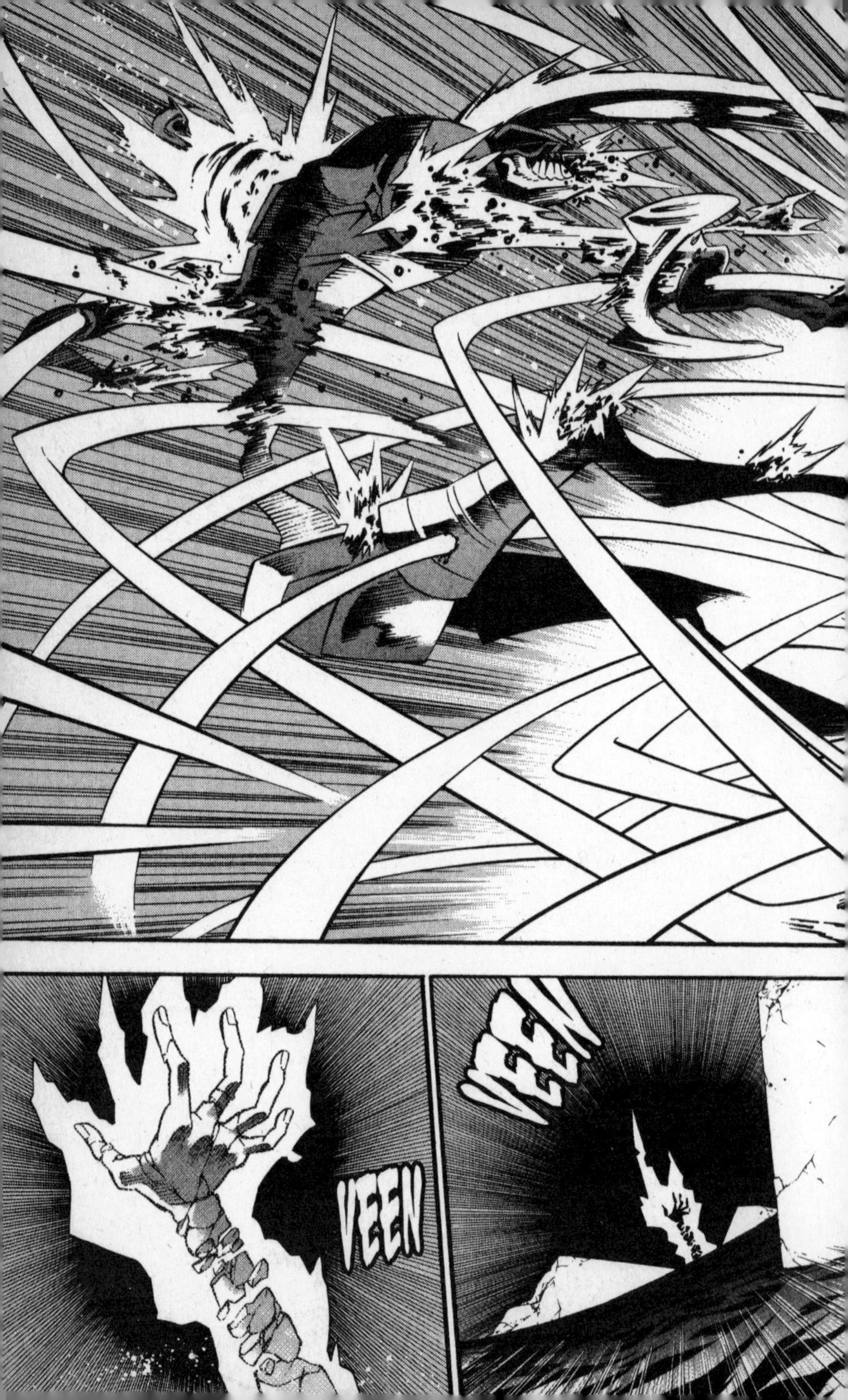
VEEN
VEEN

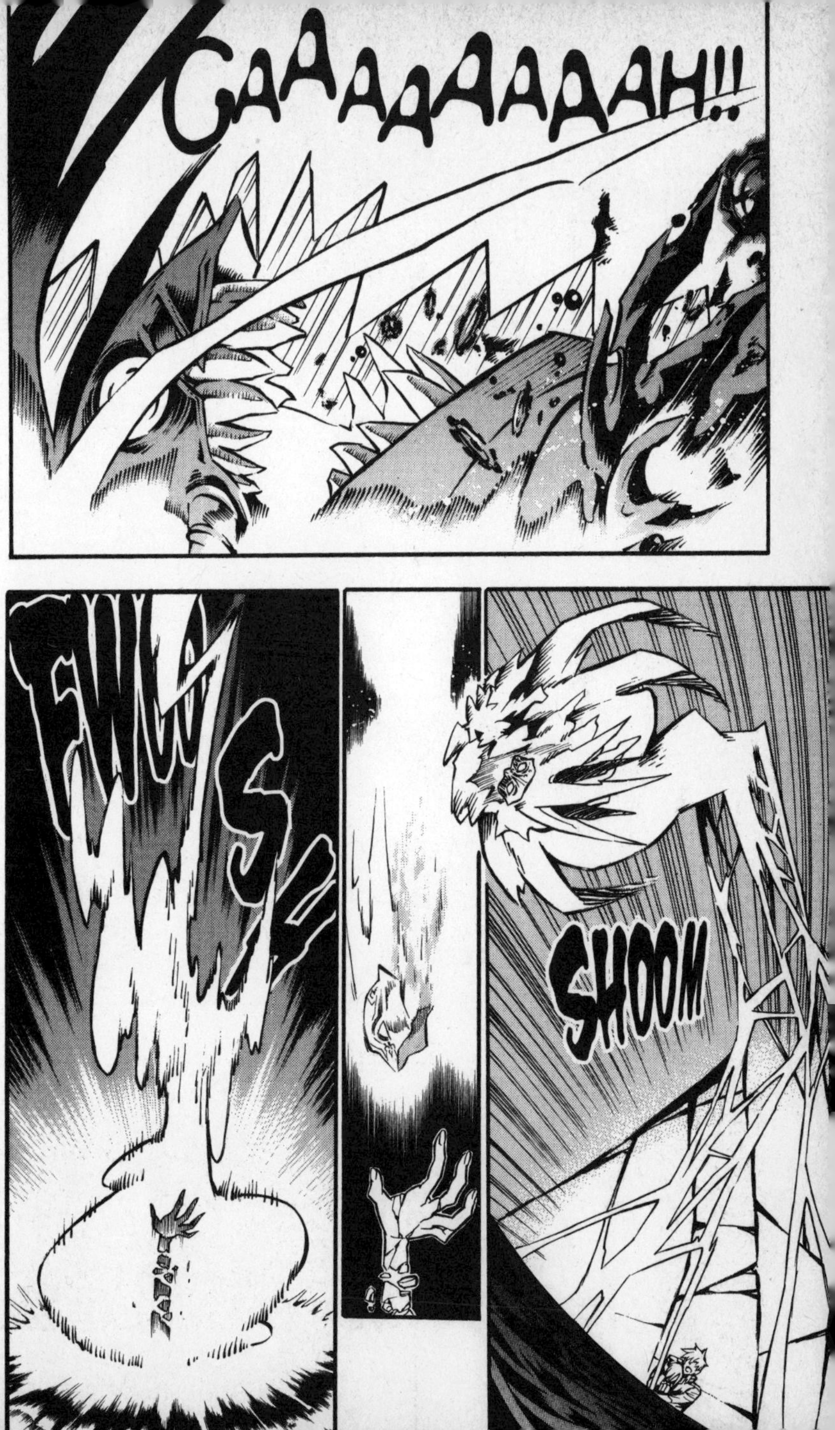
GAAAAAAAAH!!
SHOOM
FWOOSH

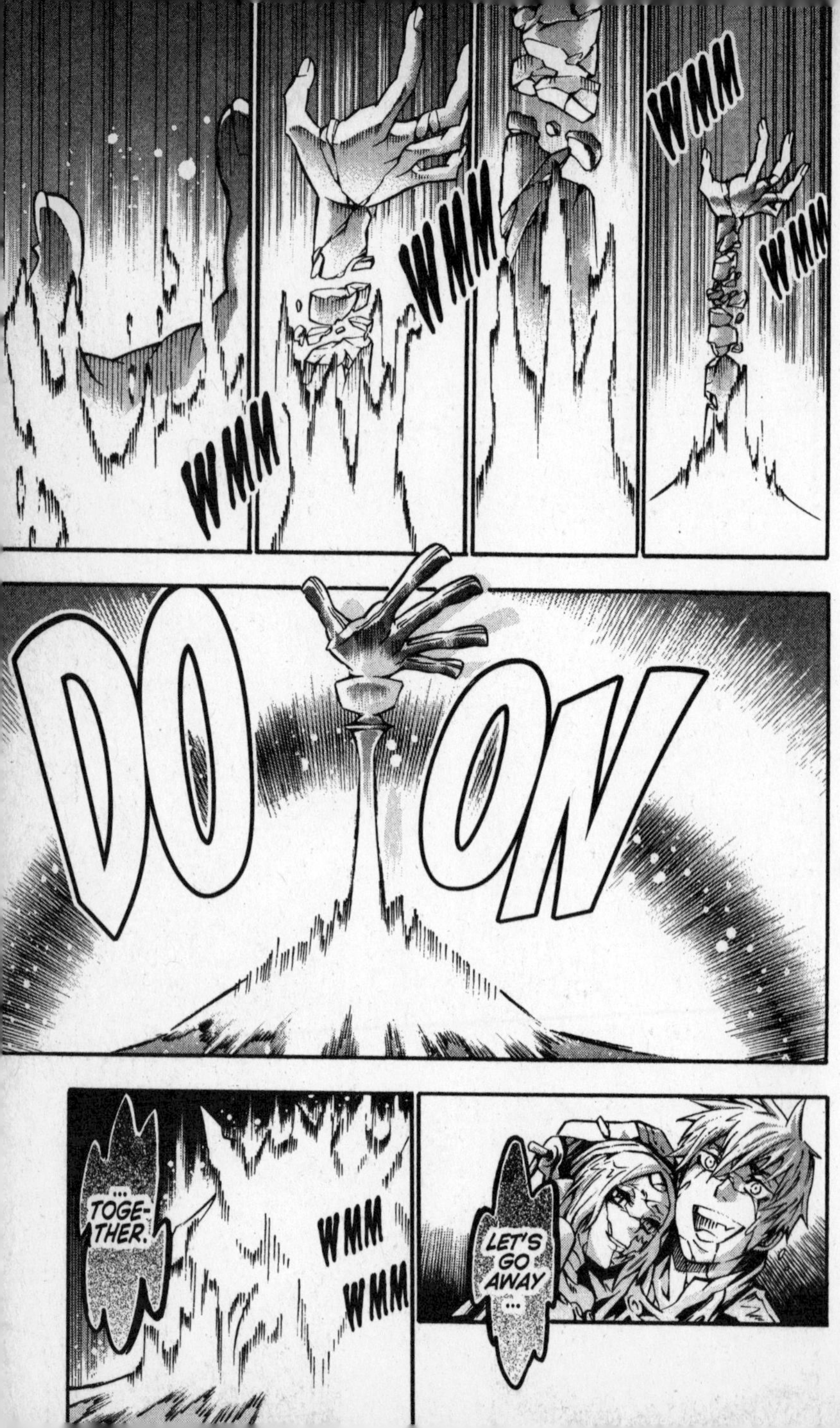
WMM
WMM
WMM
WMM
WMM
DOON
LET'S GO AWAY ...
WMM
WMM
... TOGE-THER.

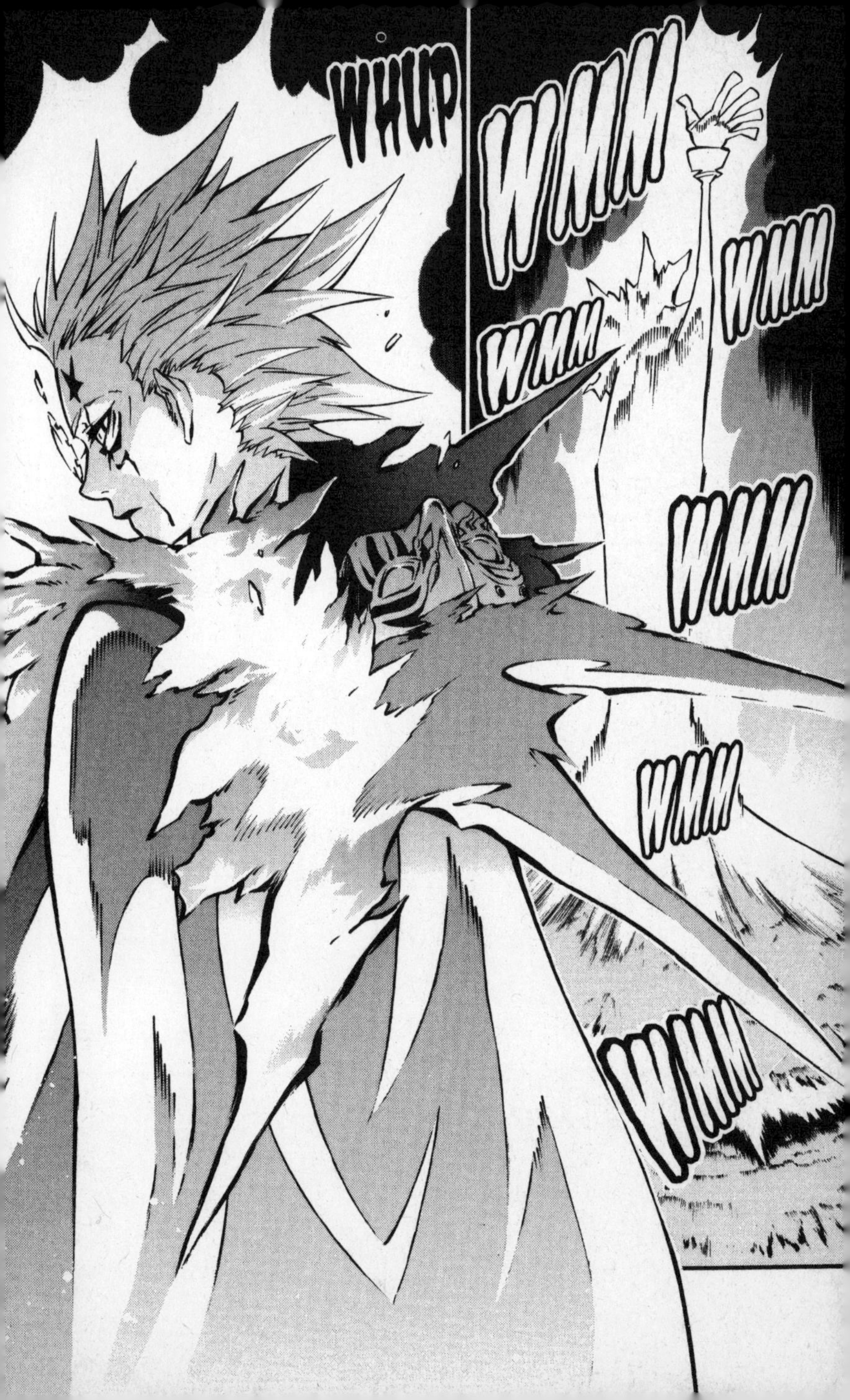
WMMM
WMMM
WMMM
WMMM
WMMM
WMMM
WHUP

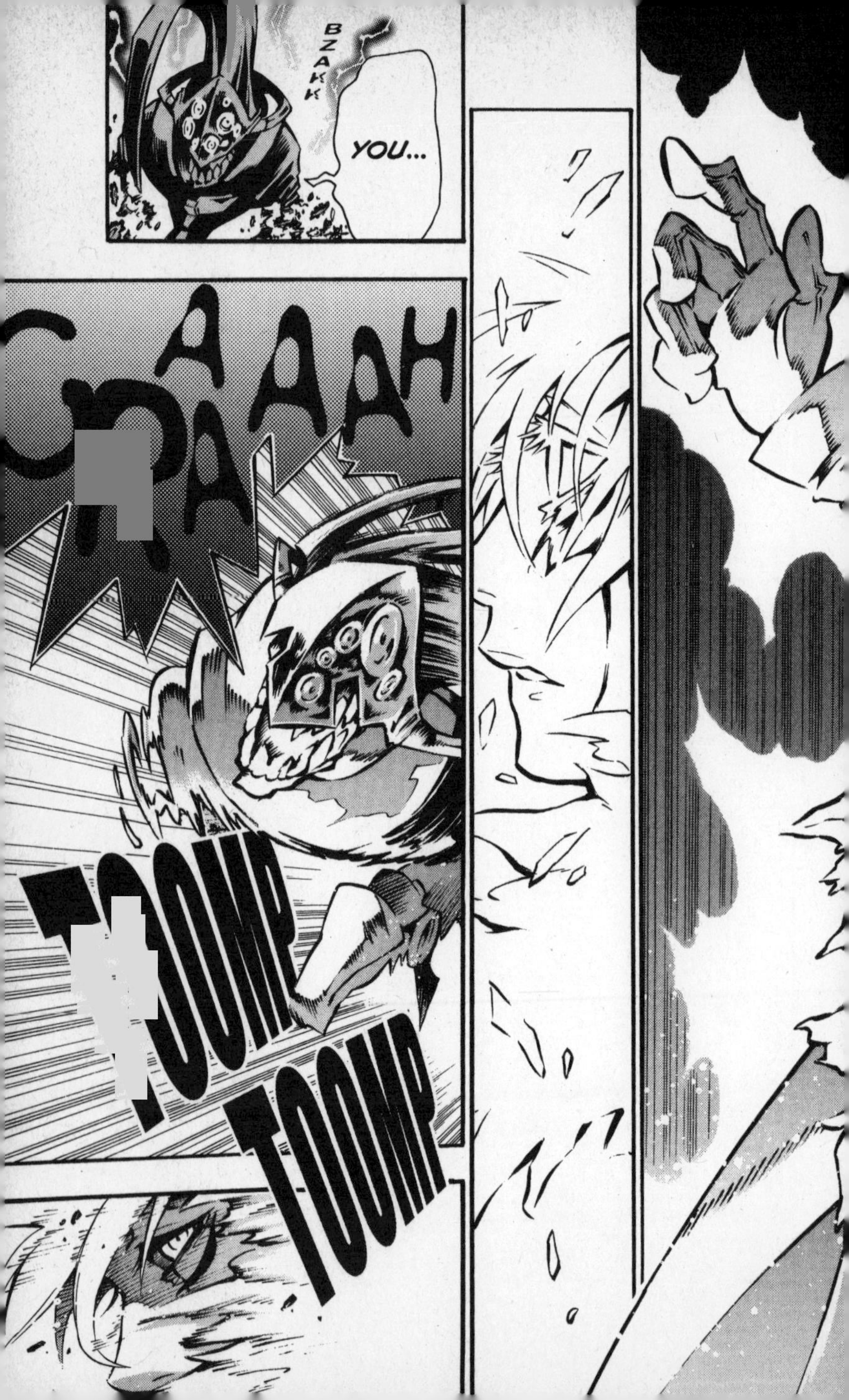
BZAKK
YOU...
AAAAH
TOOMP
TOOMP

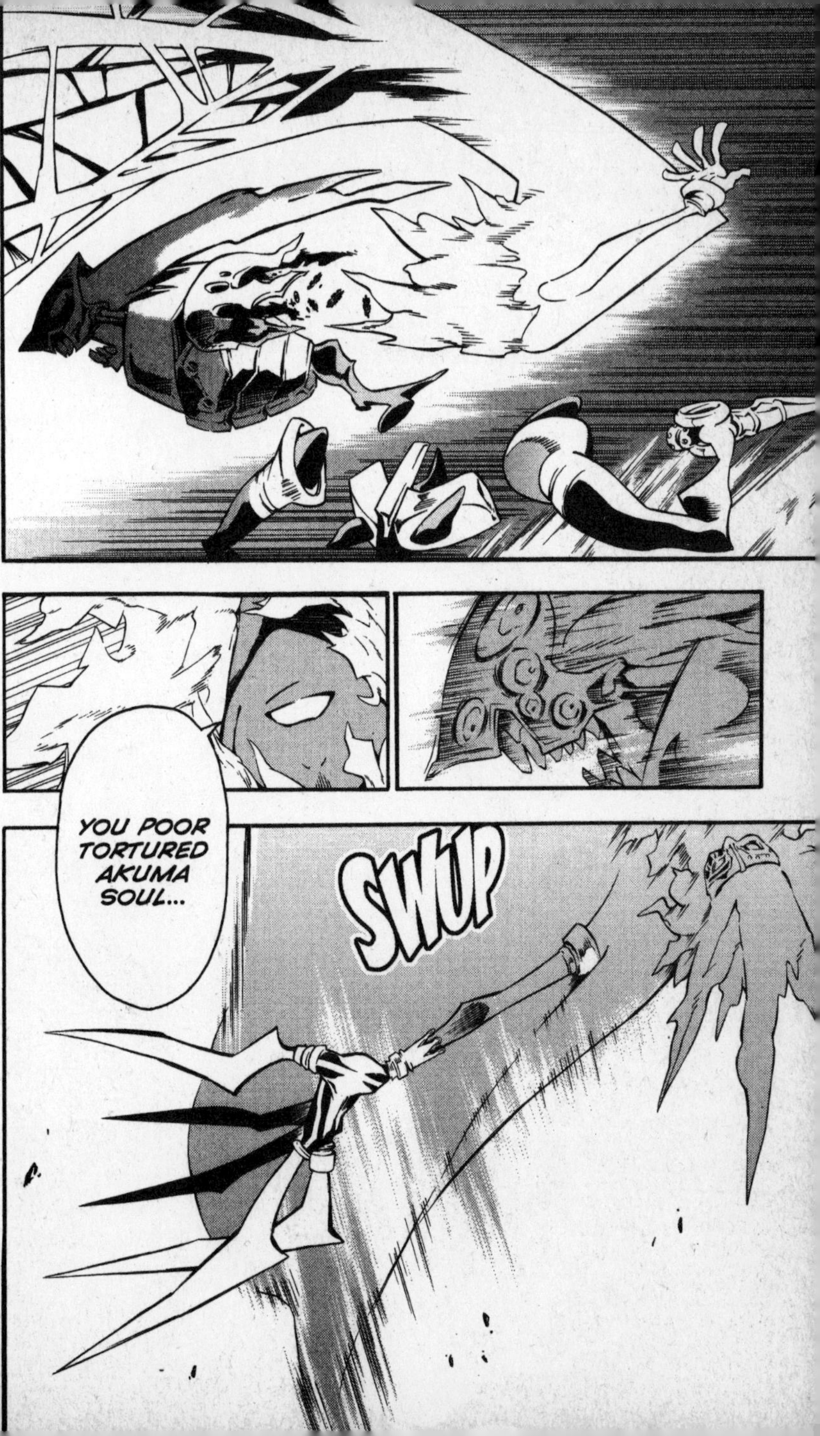
YOU POOR TORTURED AKUMA SOUL...
SWUP

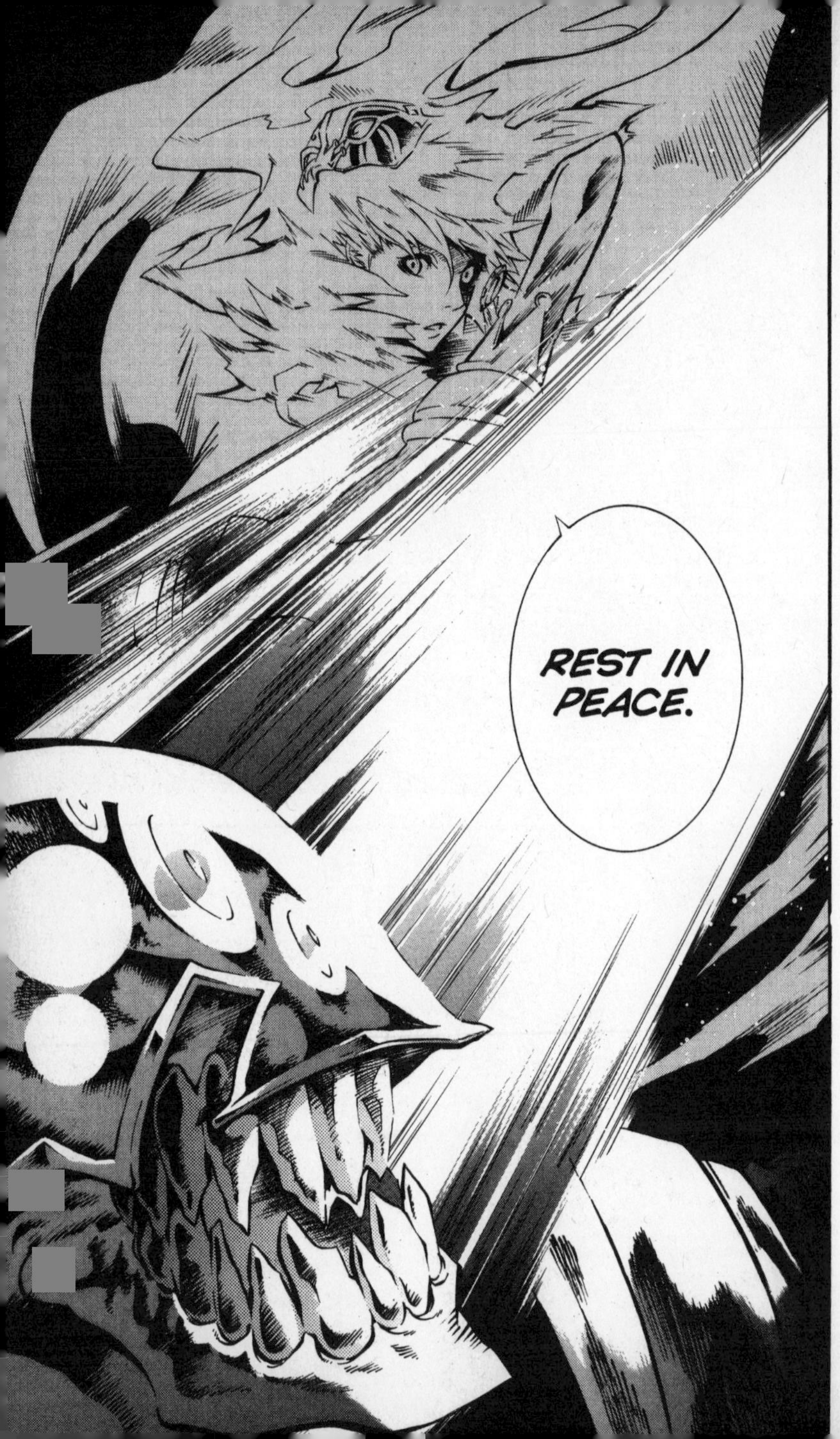
REST IN PEACE.

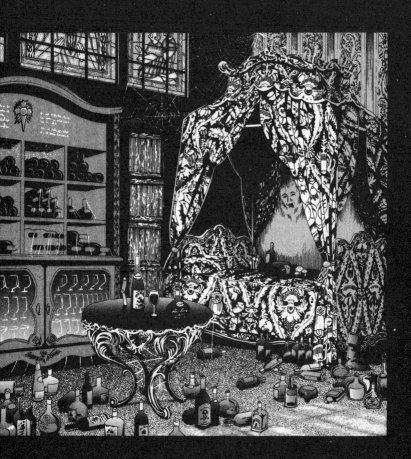

ALLEN FOUND A ROOM FILLED WITH OLD
EMPTY LIQUOR BOTTLES AND COBWEBS! IT
APPEARS TO HAVE BEEN UNINHABITED
FOR MANY YEARS. ALLEN SUDDENLY FELT
SICK SO HE CLOSED THE DOOR AND LEFT.

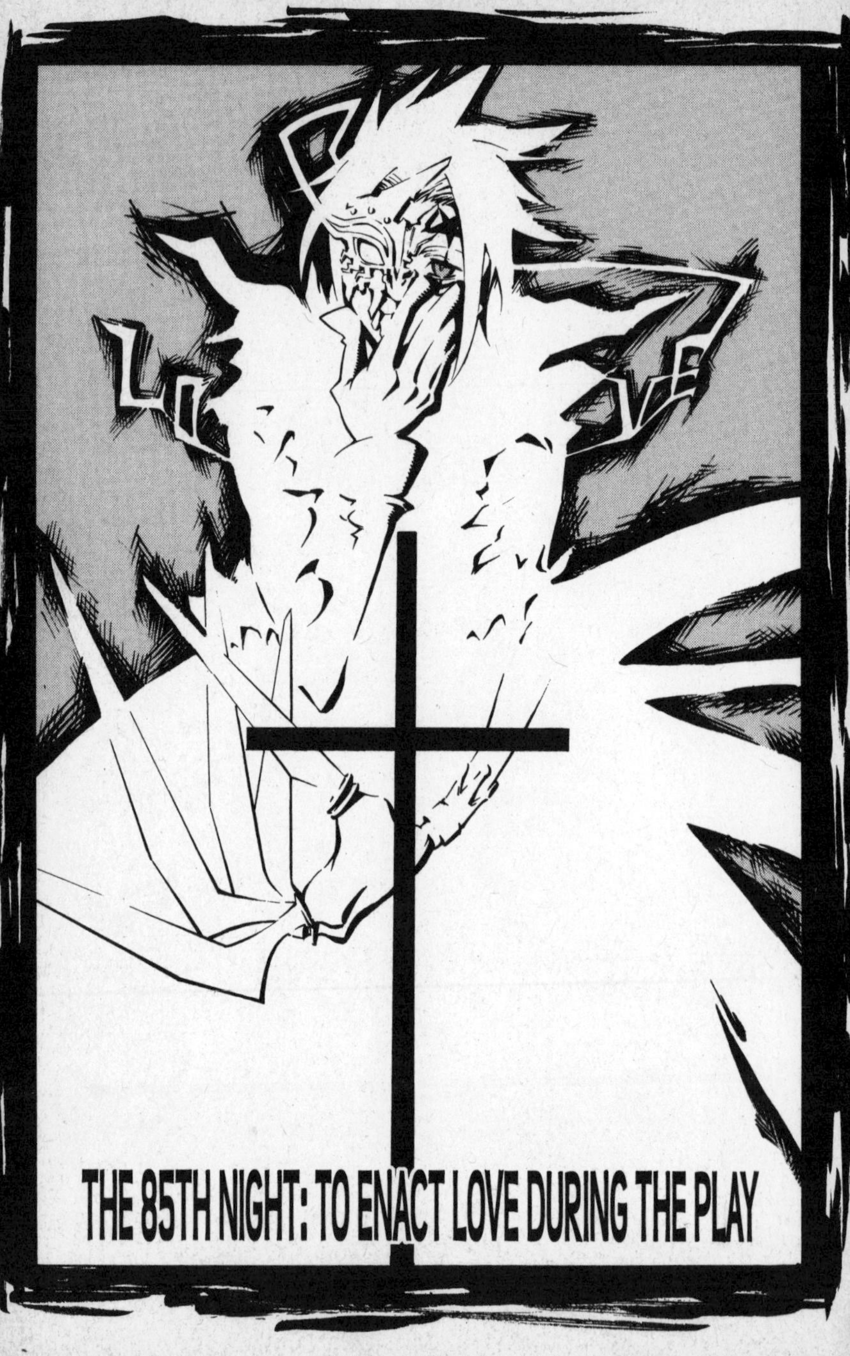

THE 85TH NIGHT: TO ENACT LOVE DURING THE PLAY

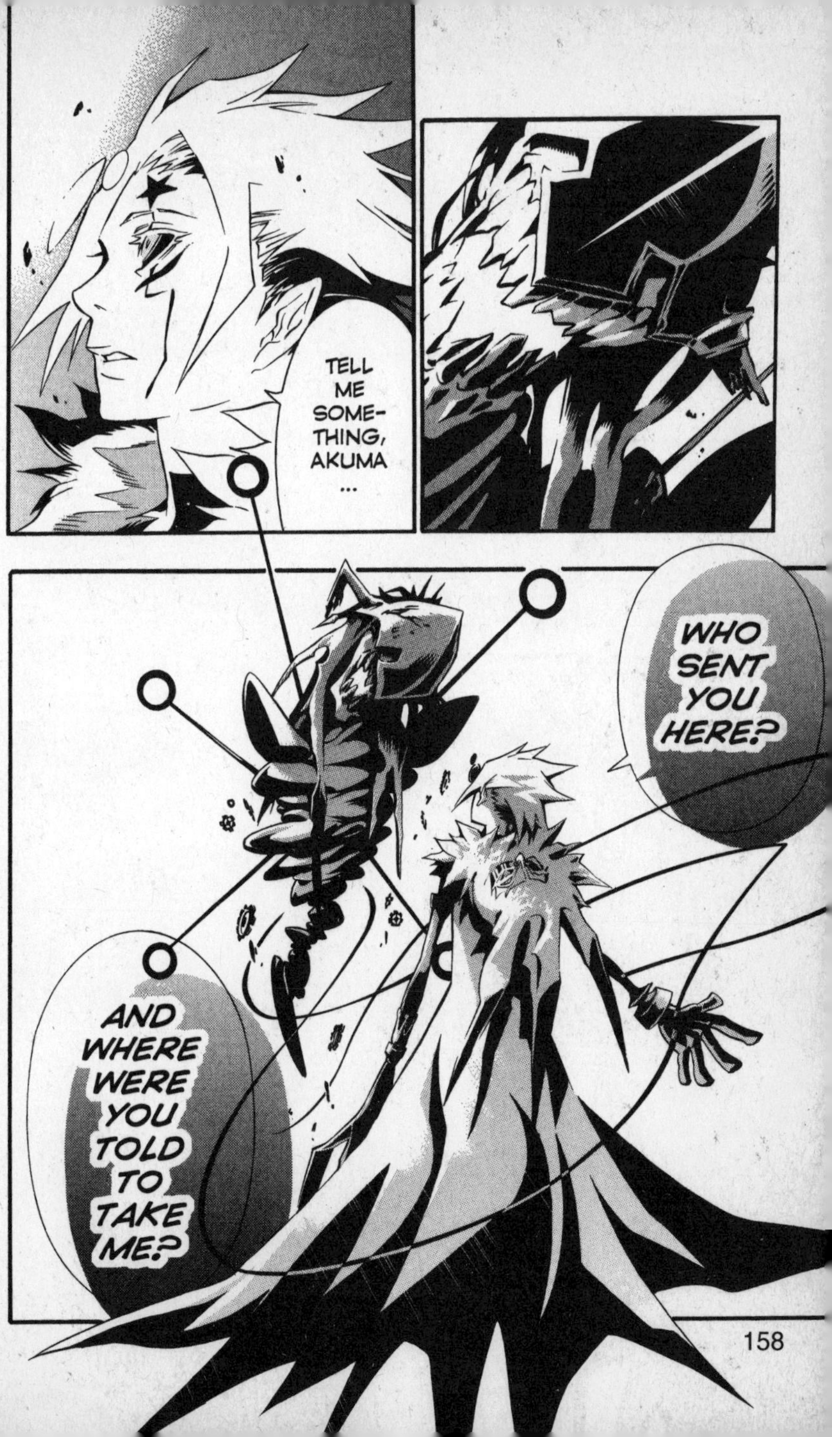
TELL ME SOME-THING, AKUMA ...
WHO SENT YOU HERE?
AND WHERE WERE YOU TOLD TO TAKE ME?

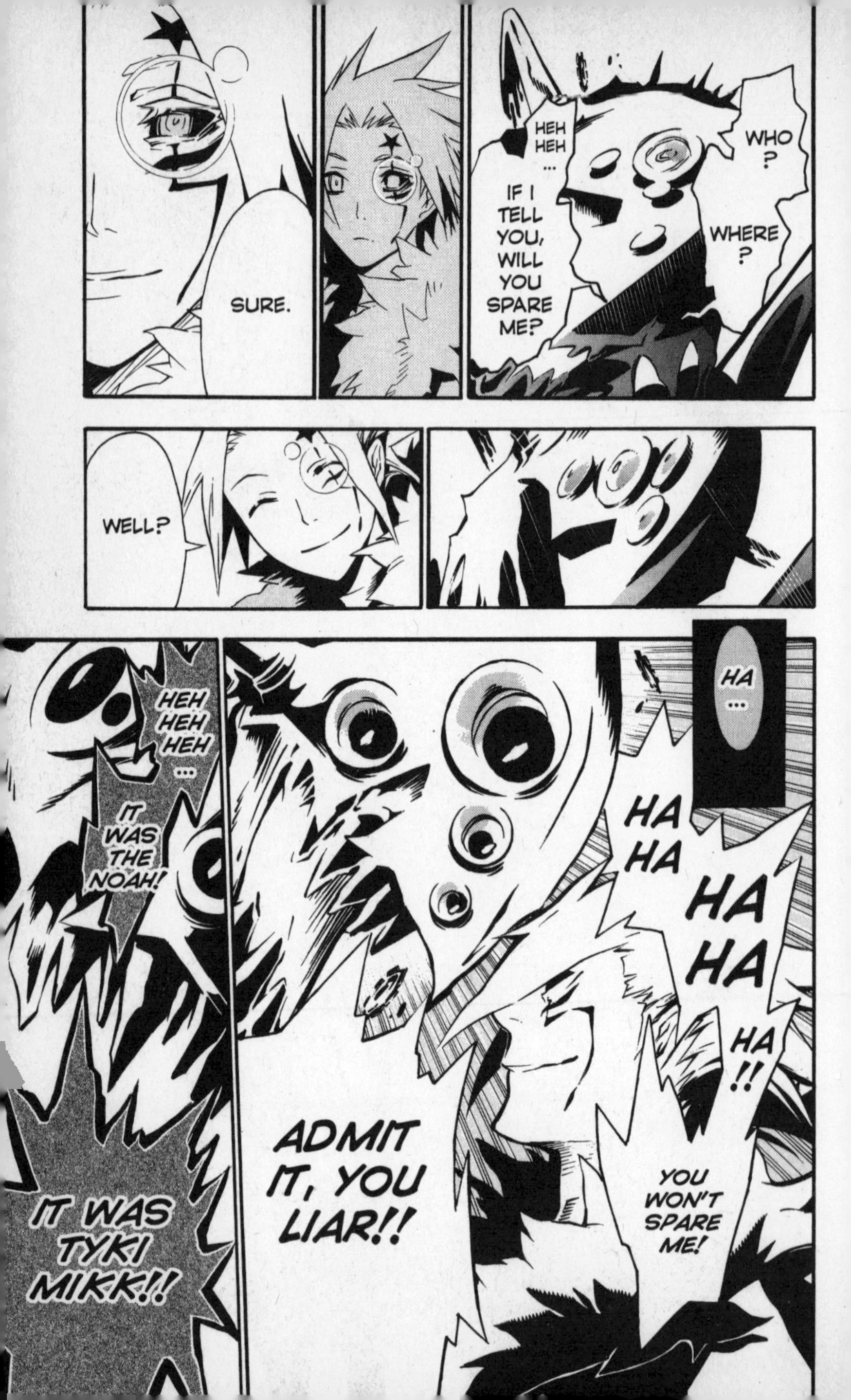
WHO?
WHERE?
HEH HEH ...
IF I TELL YOU, WILL YOU SPARE ME?
SURE.
WELL?
HA ...
HA HA HA HA HA!!
YOU WON'T SPARE ME!
ADMIT IT, YOU LIAR!!
HEH HEH HEH ...
IT WAS THE NOAH!
IT WAS TYKI MIKK!!

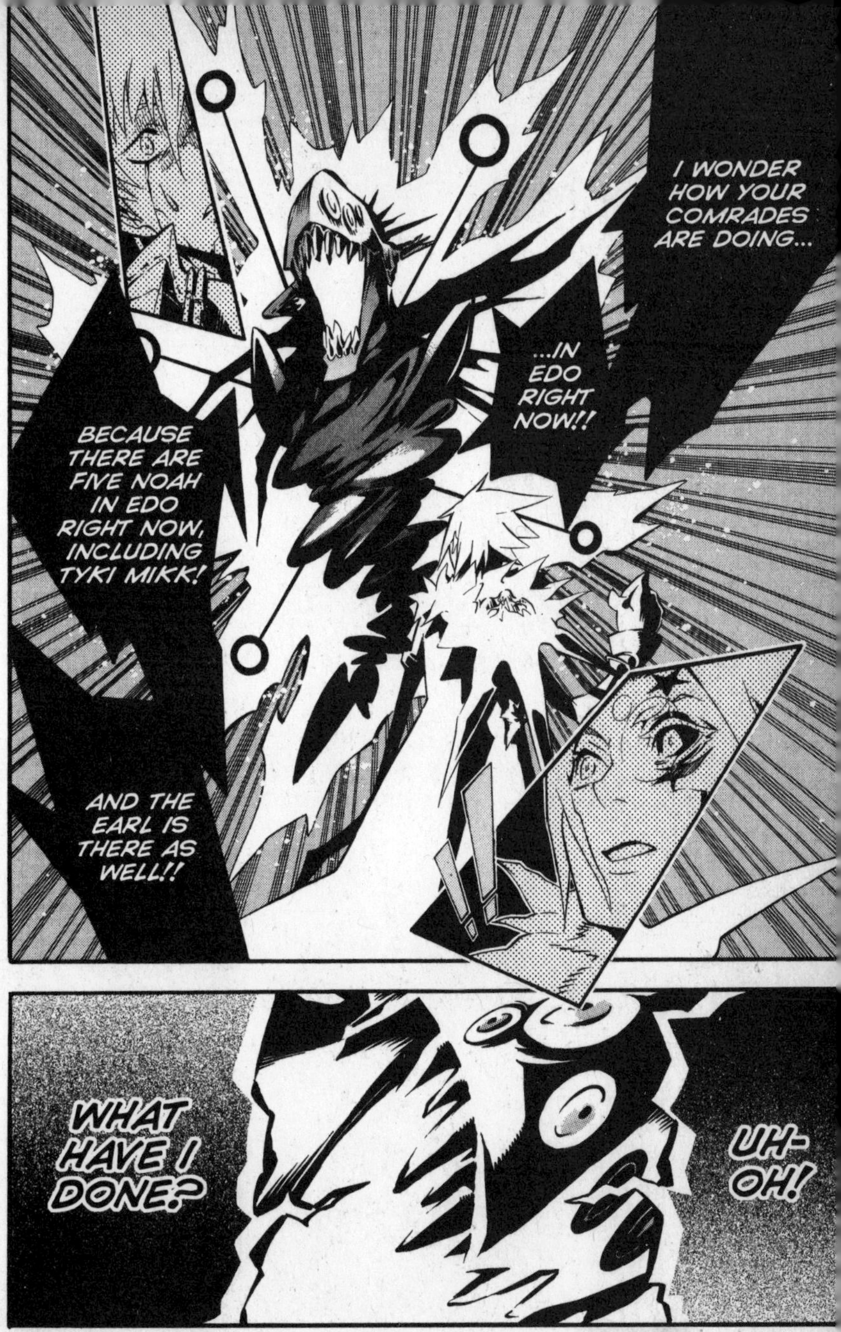
I WONDER HOW YOUR COMRADES ARE DOING...
...IN EDO RIGHT NOW!!
BECAUSE THERE ARE FIVE NOAH IN EDO RIGHT NOW, INCLUDING TYKI MIKK!
AND THE EARL IS THERE AS WELL!!
UH-OH!
WHAT HAVE I DONE?

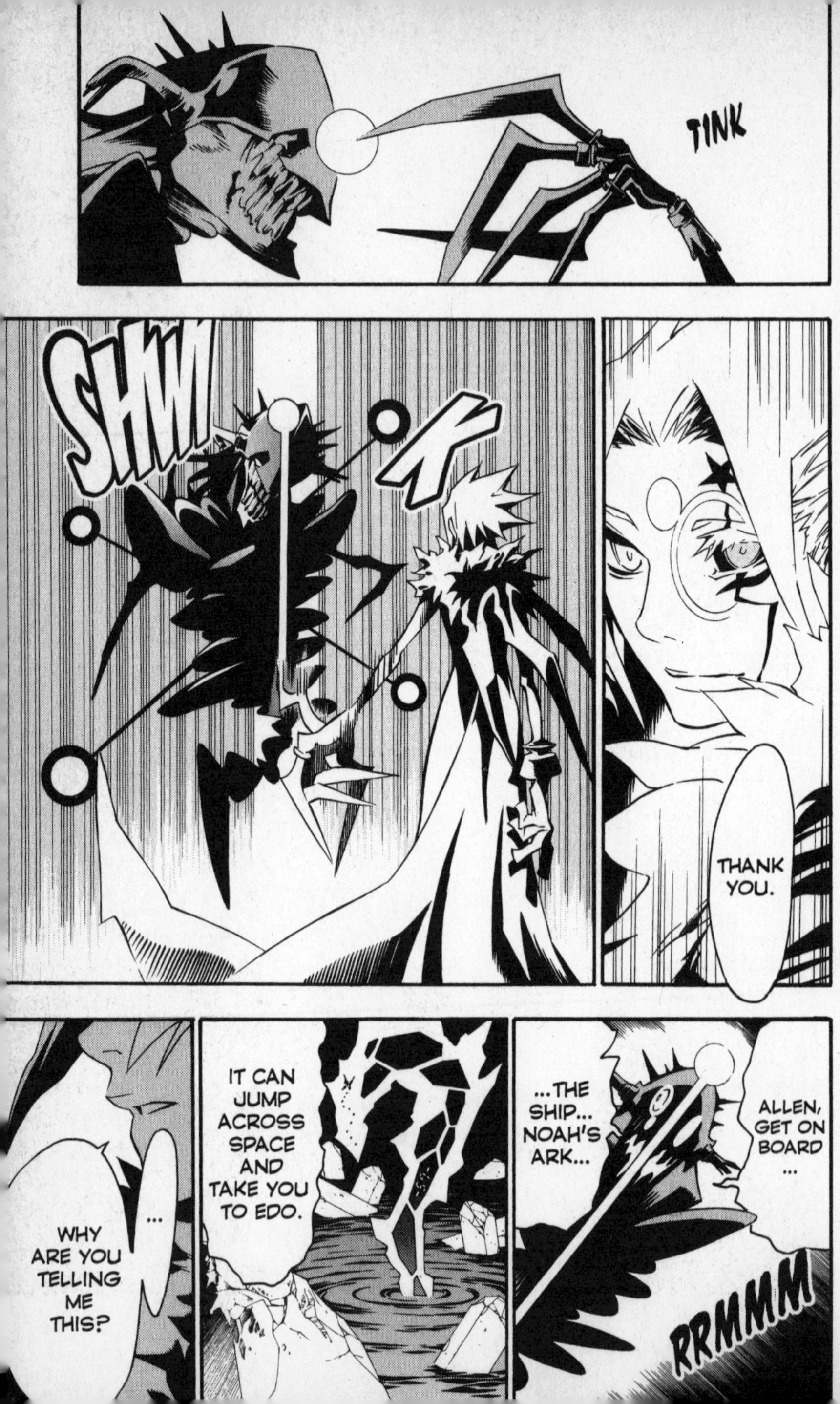
TINK
THANK YOU.
SHIN
ALLEN, GET ON BOARD ...
...THE SHIP... NOAH'S ARK...
RRMMM
IT CAN JUMP ACROSS SPACE AND TAKE YOU TO EDO.
...
WHY ARE YOU TELLING ME THIS?

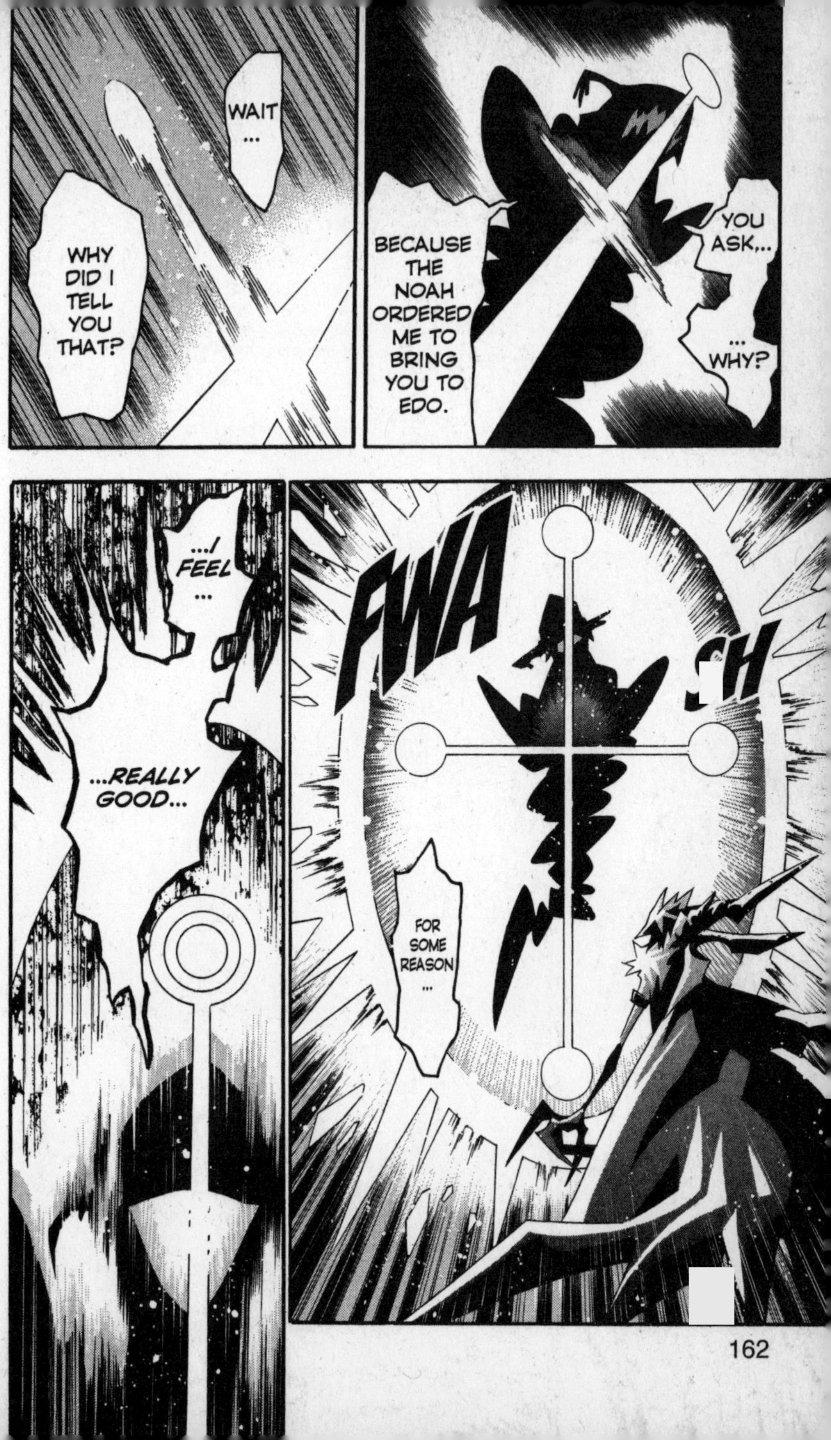
YOU ASK...
...WHY?
BECAUSE THE NOAH ORDERED ME TO BRING YOU TO EDO.
WAIT...
WHY DID I TELL YOU THAT?
FWA
SH
FOR SOME REASON...
...I FEEL...
...REALLY GOOD...

READ THIS WAY

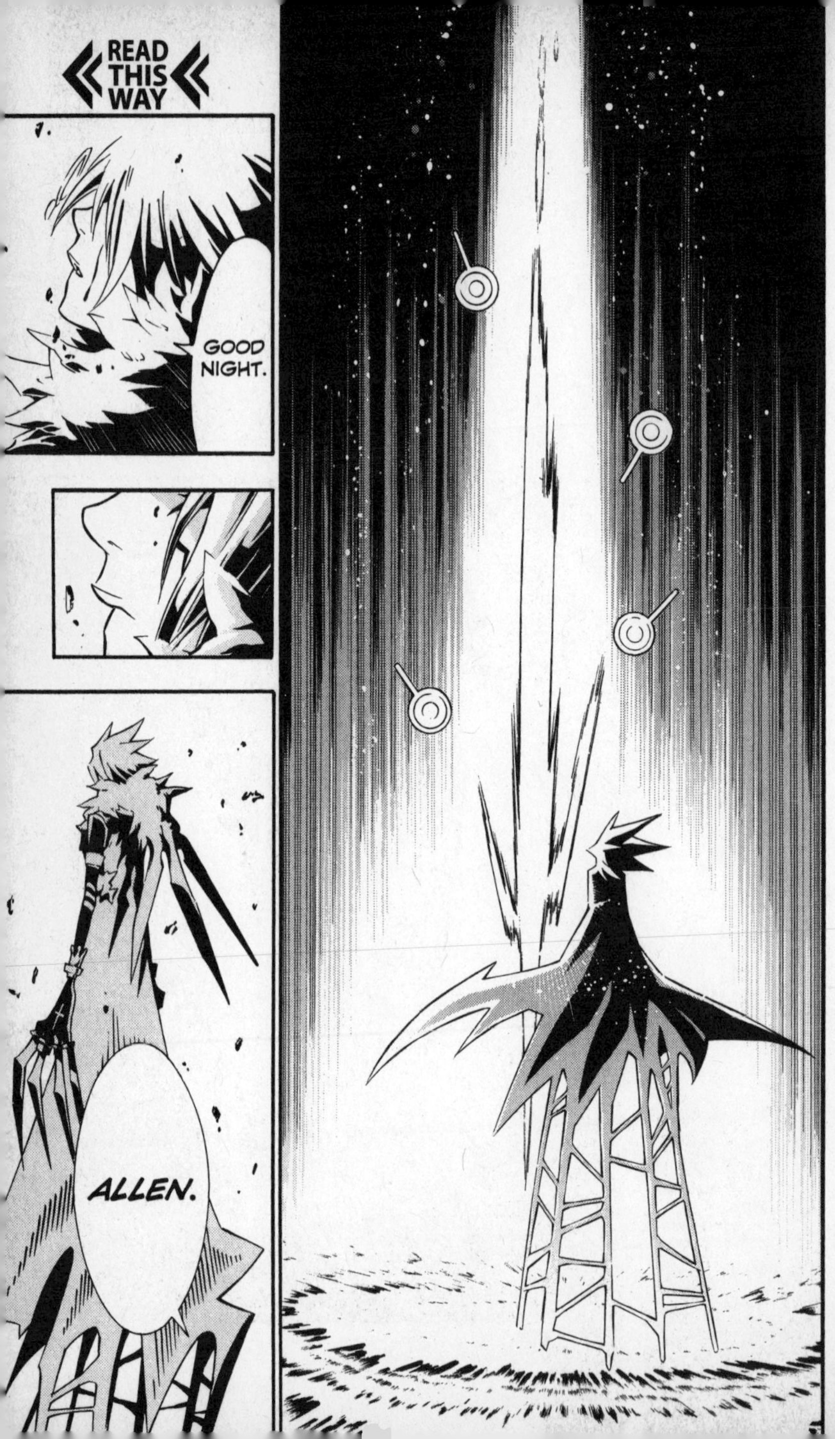
GOOD NIGHT.
ALLEN.

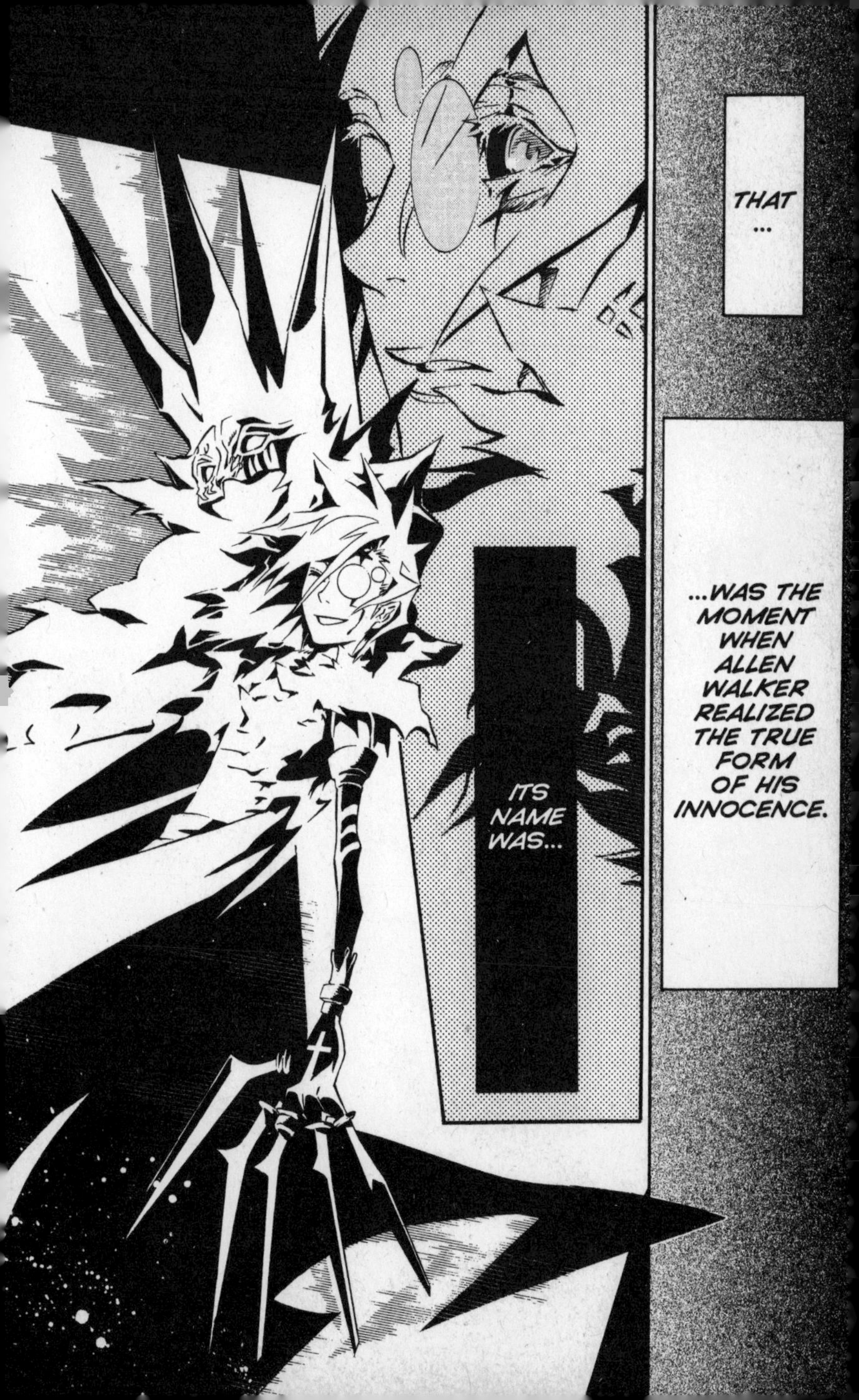
THAT ...
...WAS THE MOMENT WHEN ALLEN WALKER REALIZED THE TRUE FORM OF HIS INNOCENCE.
ITS NAME WAS...

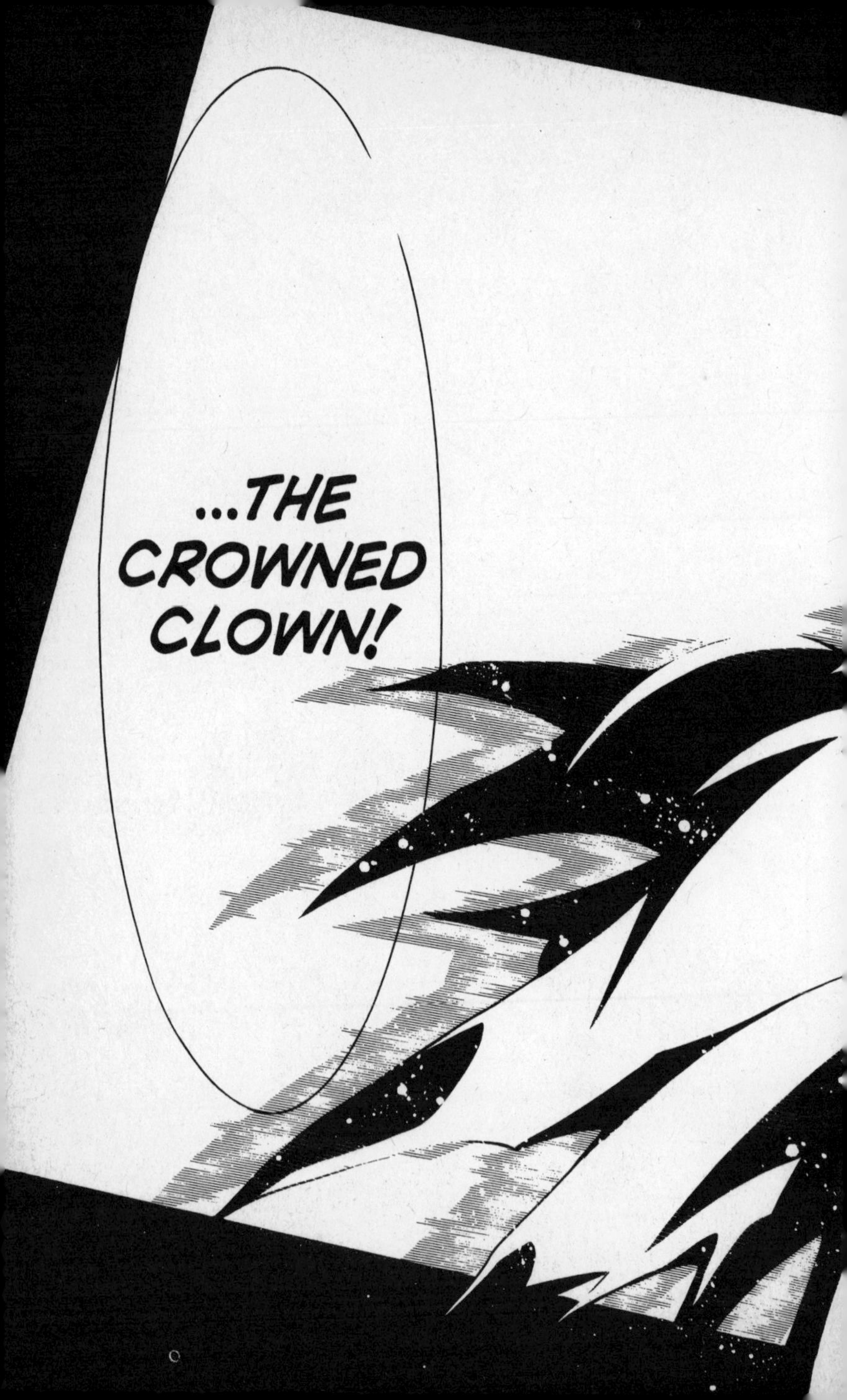
...THE CROWNED CLOWN!

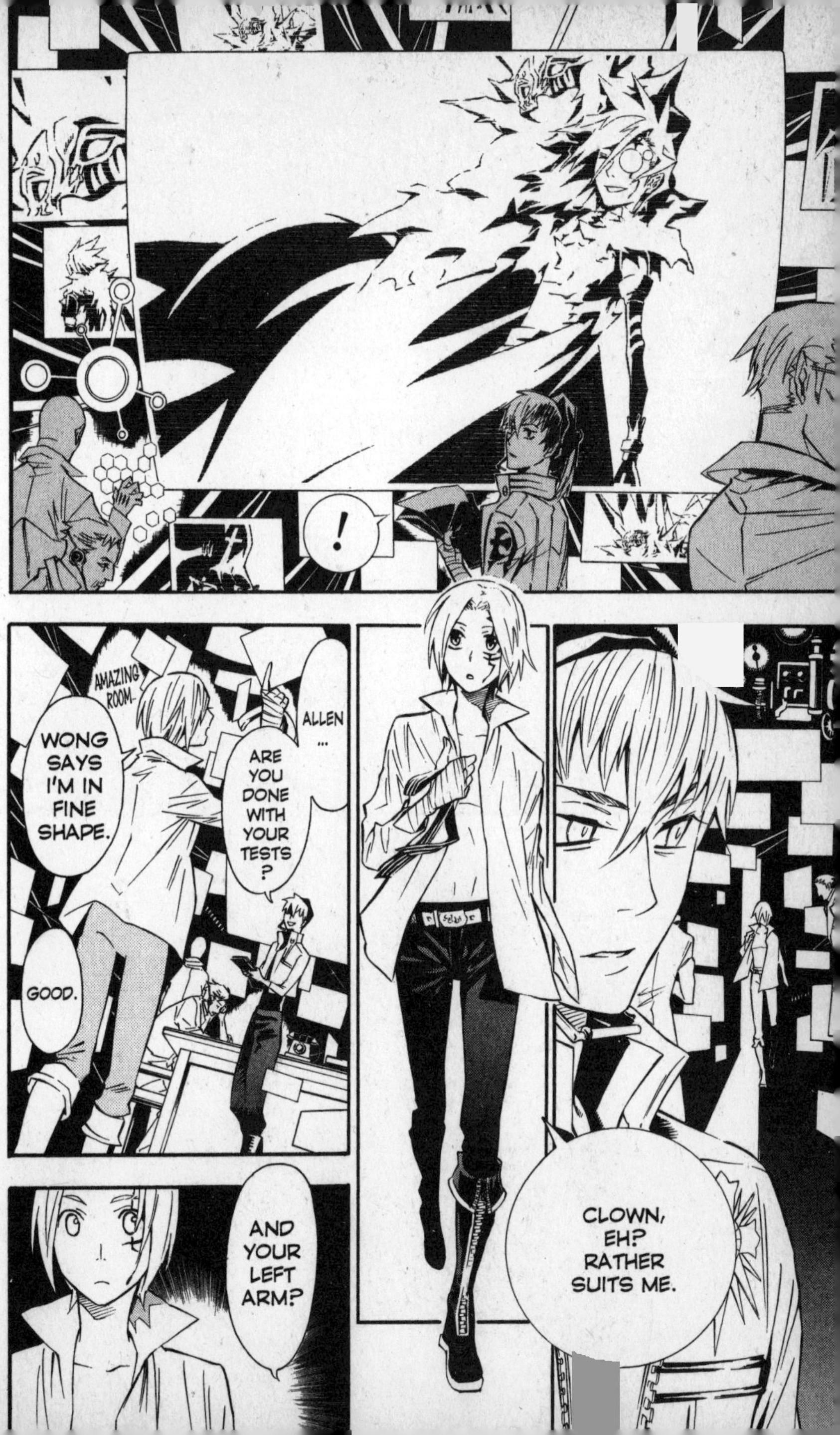
!
CLOWN, EH? RATHER SUITS ME.
ALLEN ...
ARE YOU DONE WITH YOUR TESTS?
AMAZING ROOM...
WONG SAYS I'M IN FINE SHAPE.
GOOD.
AND YOUR LEFT ARM?

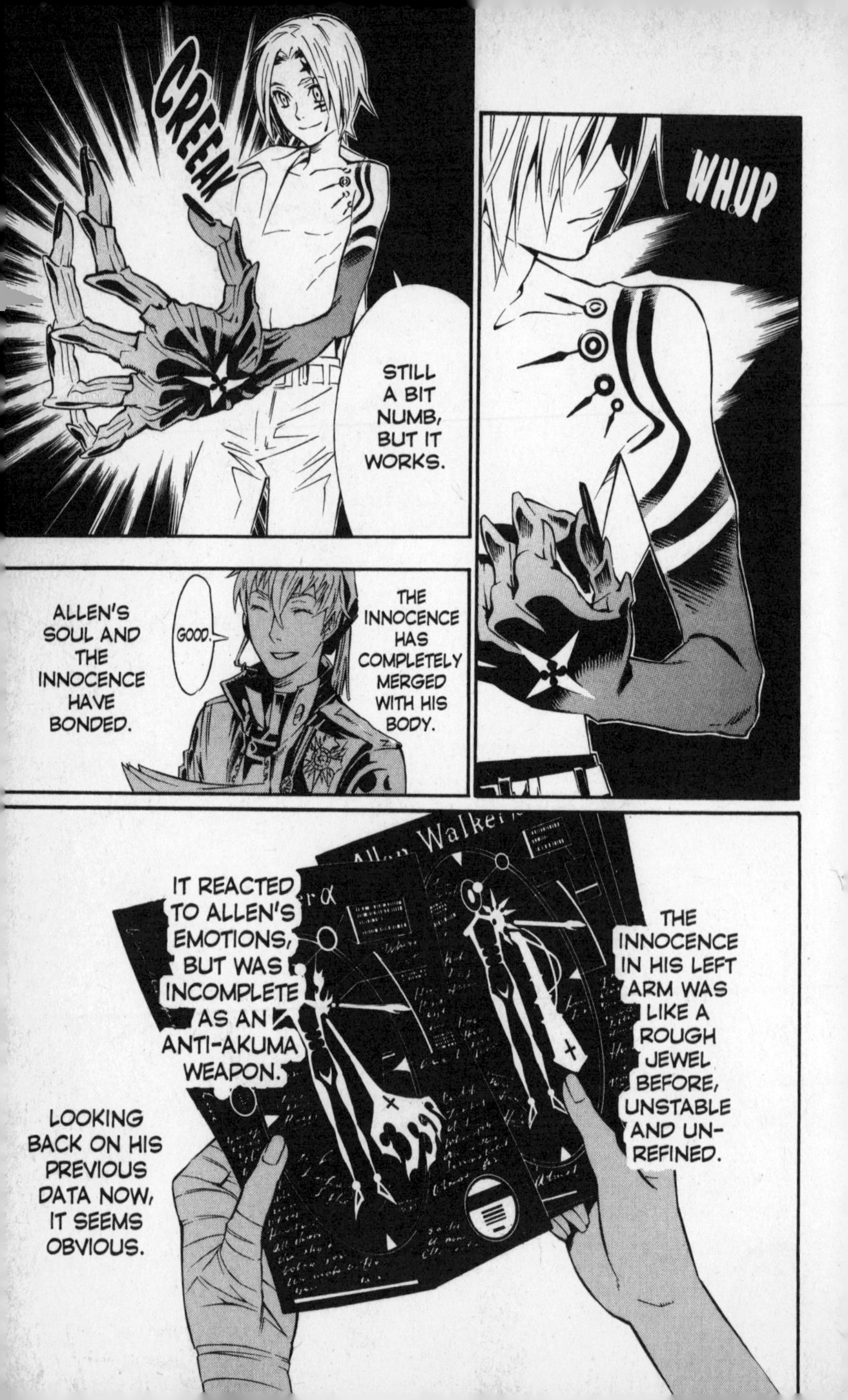
WHUP
CREEAK
STILL A BIT NUMB, BUT IT WORKS.
THE INNOCENCE HAS COMPLETELY MERGED WITH HIS BODY.
GOOD.
ALLEN'S SOUL AND THE INNOCENCE HAVE BONDED.
THE INNOCENCE IN HIS LEFT ARM WAS LIKE A ROUGH JEWEL BEFORE, UNSTABLE AND UN-REFINED.
IT REACTED TO ALLEN'S EMOTIONS, BUT WAS INCOMPLETE AS AN ANTI-AKUMA WEAPON.
LOOKING BACK ON HIS PREVIOUS DATA NOW, IT SEEMS OBVIOUS.

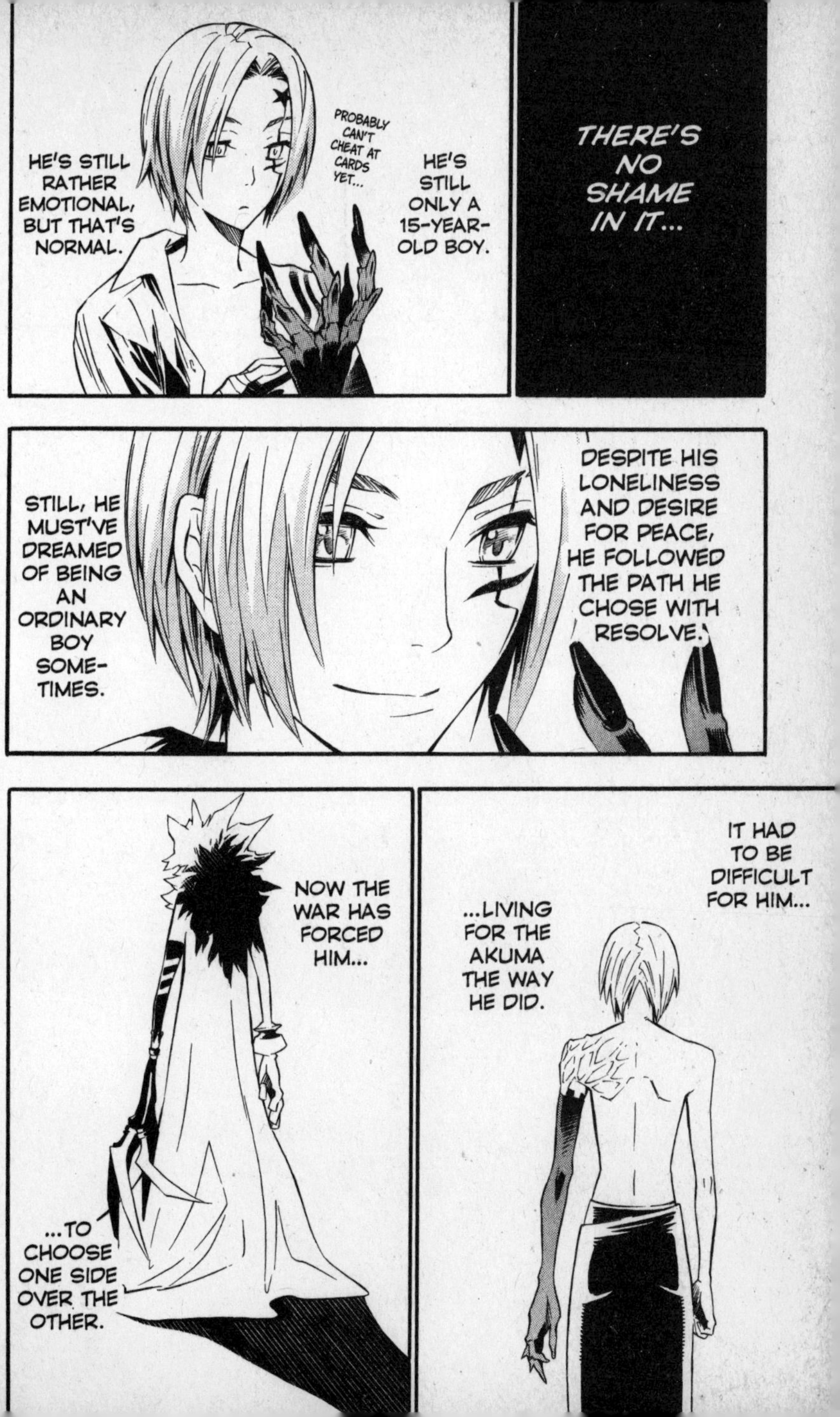
THERE'S NO SHAME IN IT...
HE'S STILL ONLY A 15-YEAR-OLD BOY.
PROBABLY CAN'T CHEAT AT CARDS YET...
HE'S STILL RATHER EMOTIONAL, BUT THAT'S NORMAL.
DESPITE HIS LONELINESS AND DESIRE FOR PEACE, HE FOLLOWED THE PATH HE CHOSE WITH RESOLVE.
STILL, HE MUST'VE DREAMED OF BEING AN ORDINARY BOY SOME-TIMES.
IT HAD TO BE DIFFICULT FOR HIM...
...LIVING FOR THE AKUMA THE WAY HE DID.
NOW THE WAR HAS FORCED HIM...
...TO CHOOSE ONE SIDE OVER THE OTHER.

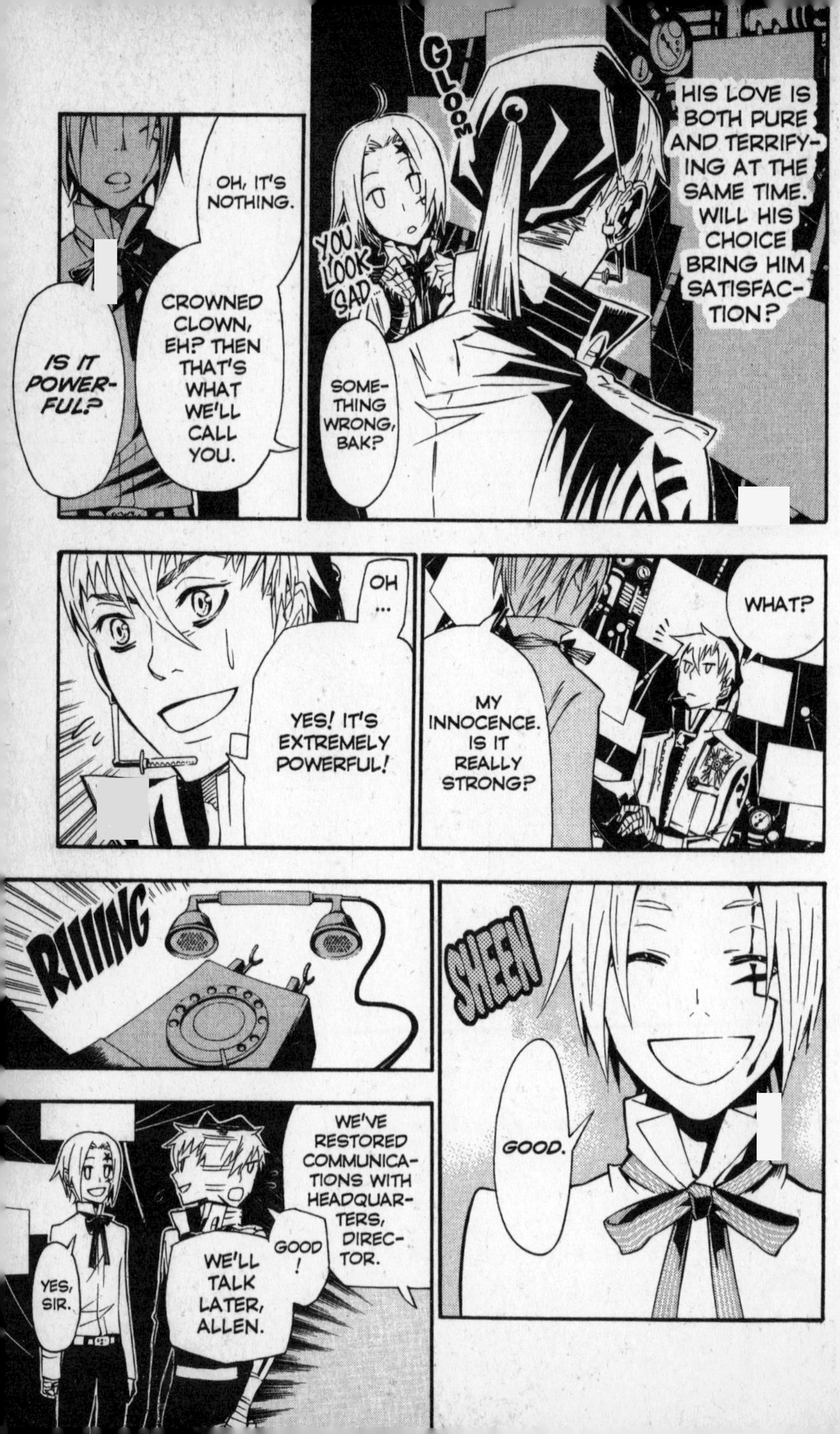
HIS LOVE IS BOTH PURE AND TERRIFYING AT THE SAME TIME. WILL HIS CHOICE BRING HIM SATISFACTION?
GLOOM
YOU LOOK SAD...
SOMETHING WRONG, BAK?
OH, IT'S NOTHING.
CROWNED CLOWN, EH? THEN THAT'S WHAT WE'LL CALL YOU.
IS IT POWERFUL?
WHAT?
MY INNOCENCE. IS IT REALLY STRONG?
OH ...
YES! IT'S EXTREMELY POWERFUL!
SHEEN
GOOD.
RIIIING
WE'VE RESTORED COMMUNICATIONS WITH HEADQUARTERS, DIRECTOR.
GOOD!
WE'LL TALK LATER, ALLEN.
YES, SIR.

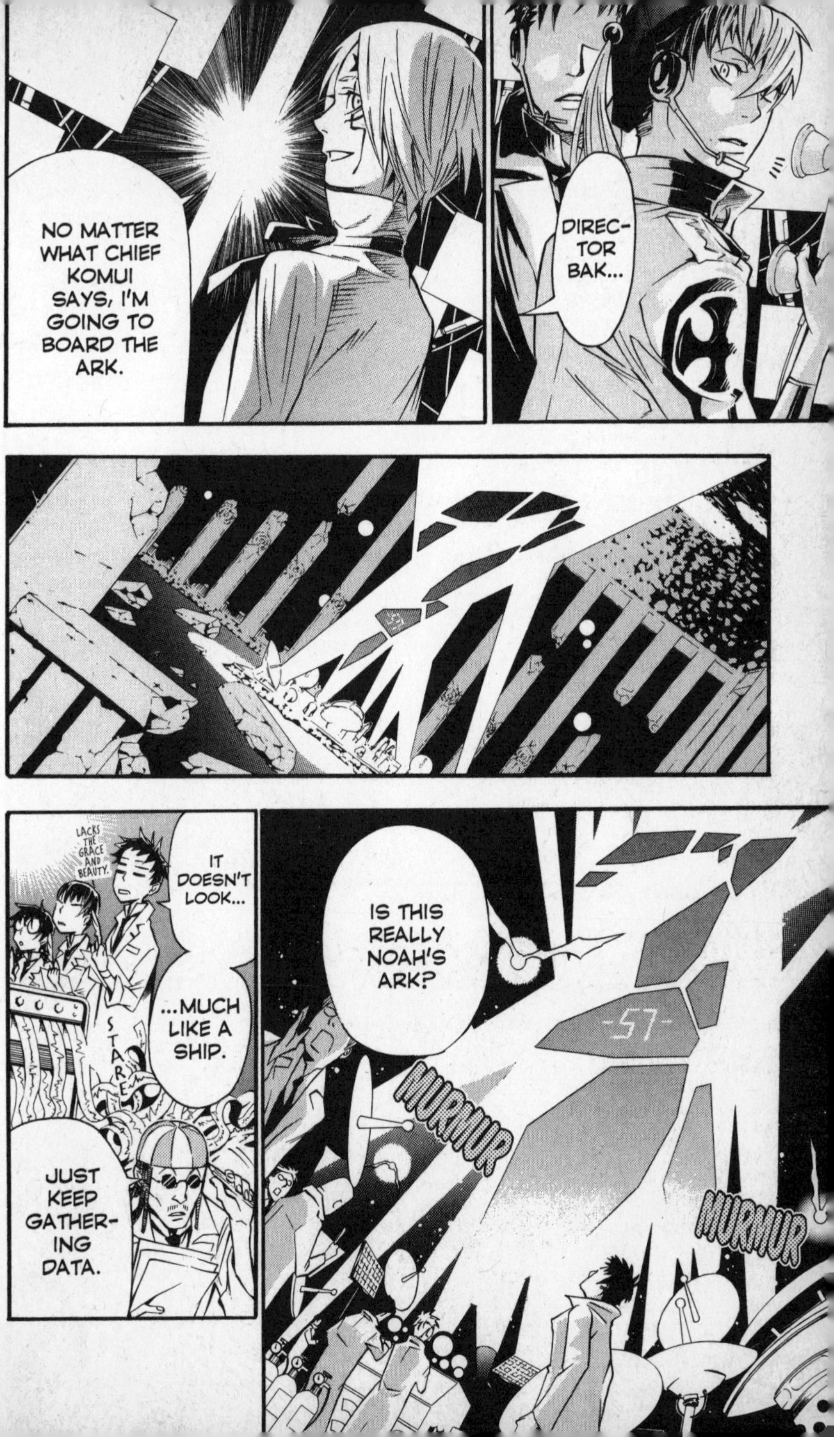
DIRECTOR BAK...
NO MATTER WHAT CHIEF KOMUI SAYS, I'M GOING TO BOARD THE ARK.
IS THIS REALLY NOAH'S ARK?
MURMUR
MURMUR
IT DOESN'T LOOK...
...MUCH LIKE A SHIP.
LACKS THE GRACE AND BEAUTY.
STARE
JUST KEEP GATHERING DATA.

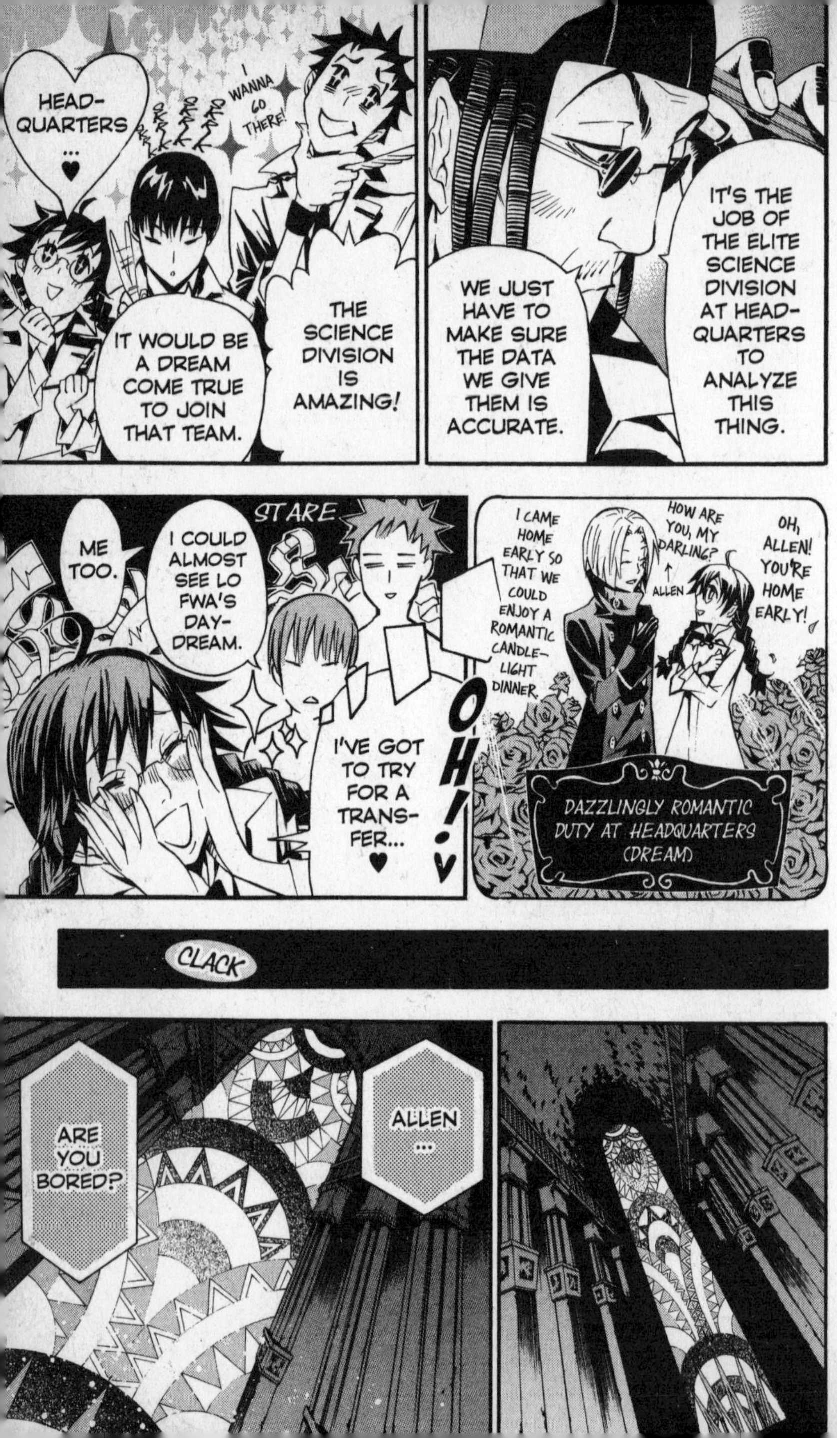
IT'S THE JOB OF THE ELITE SCIENCE DIVISION AT HEAD-QUARTERS TO ANALYZE THIS THING.
WE JUST HAVE TO MAKE SURE THE DATA WE GIVE THEM IS ACCURATE.
I WANNA GO THERE!
HEAD-QUARTERS ... ♥
THE SCIENCE DIVISION IS AMAZING!
IT WOULD BE A DREAM COME TRUE TO JOIN THAT TEAM.
OH, ALLEN! YOU'RE HOME EARLY!
HOW ARE YOU, MY DARLING?
ALLEN
I CAME HOME EARLY SO THAT WE COULD ENJOY A ROMANTIC CANDLE-LIGHT DINNER.
DAZZLINGLY ROMANTIC DUTY AT HEADQUARTERS (DREAM)
OH!♥
I'VE GOT TO TRY FOR A TRANS-FER... ♥
STARE
I COULD ALMOST SEE LO FWA'S DAY-DREAM.
ME TOO.
CLACK
ALLEN ...
ARE YOU BORED?

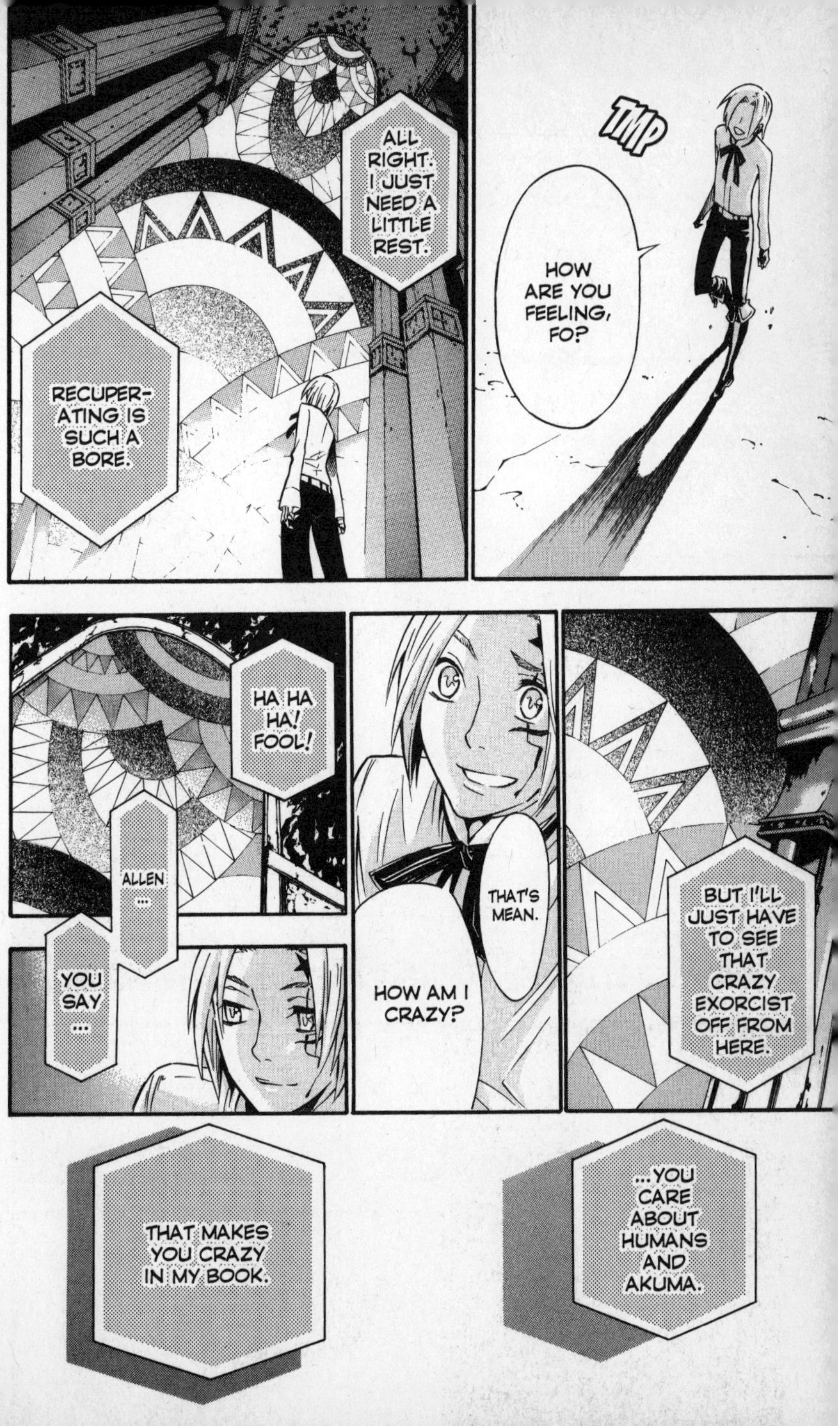
TMP
HOW ARE YOU FEELING, FO?
ALL RIGHT. I JUST NEED A LITTLE REST.
RECUPER-ATING IS SUCH A BORE.
BUT I'LL JUST HAVE TO SEE THAT CRAZY EXORCIST OFF FROM HERE.
THAT'S MEAN.
HOW AM I CRAZY?
HA HA HA! FOOL!
ALLEN ...
YOU SAY ...
...YOU CARE ABOUT HUMANS AND AKUMA.
THAT MAKES YOU CRAZY IN MY BOOK.

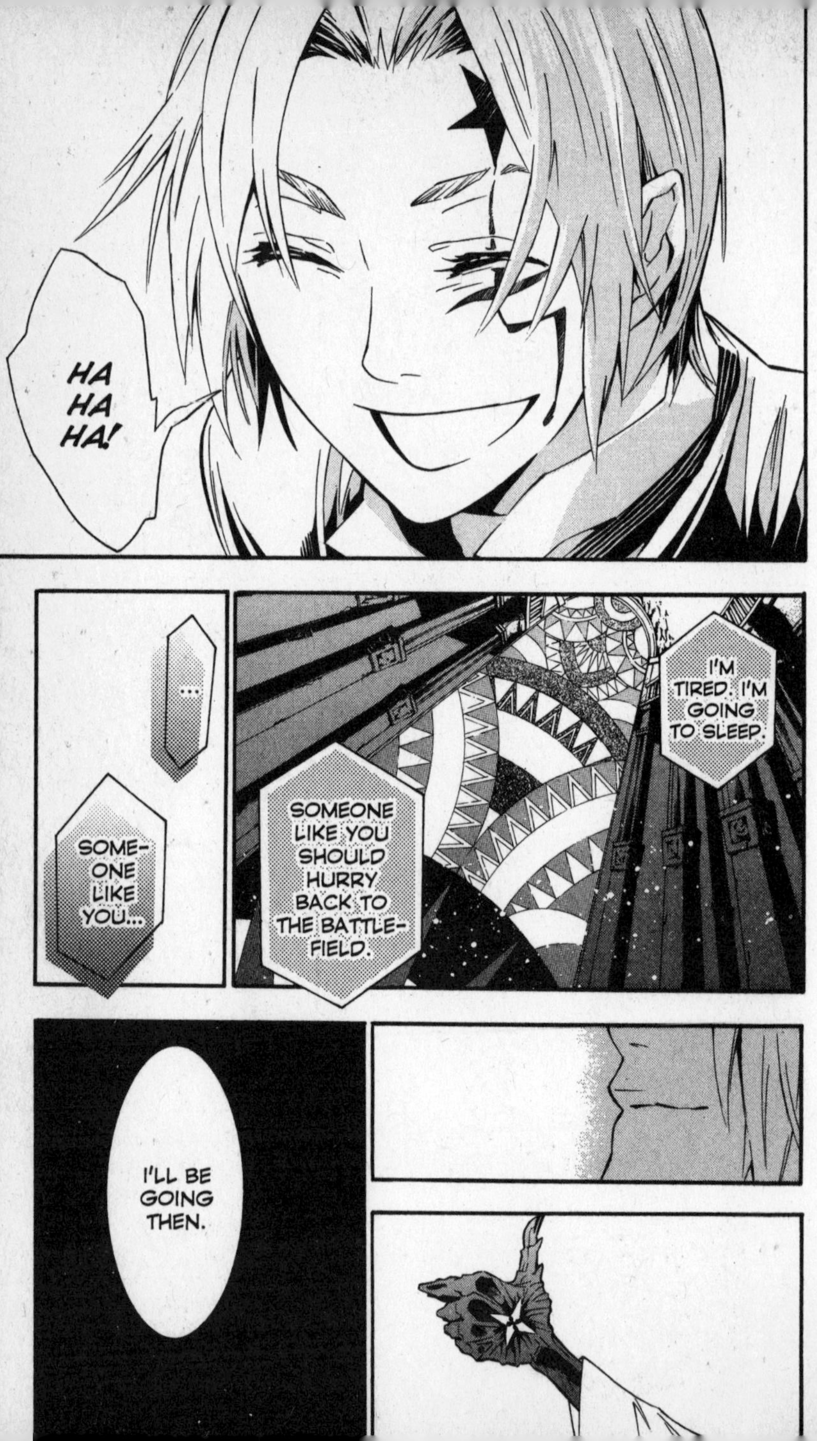
HA HA HA!
I'M TIRED. I'M GOING TO SLEEP.
SOMEONE LIKE YOU SHOULD HURRY BACK TO THE BATTLE-FIELD.
...
SOME-ONE LIKE YOU...
I'LL BE GOING THEN.

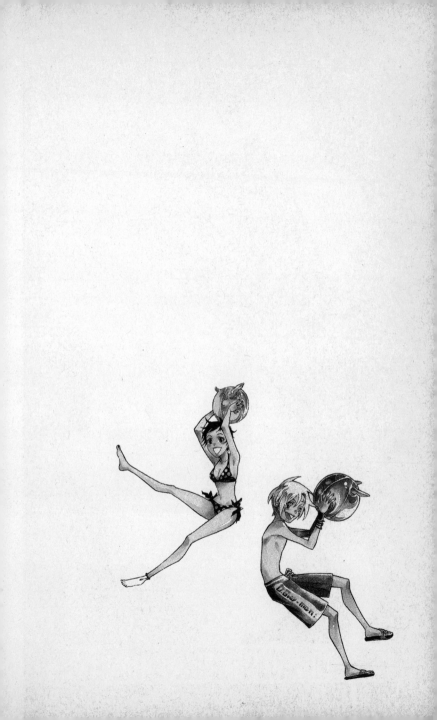

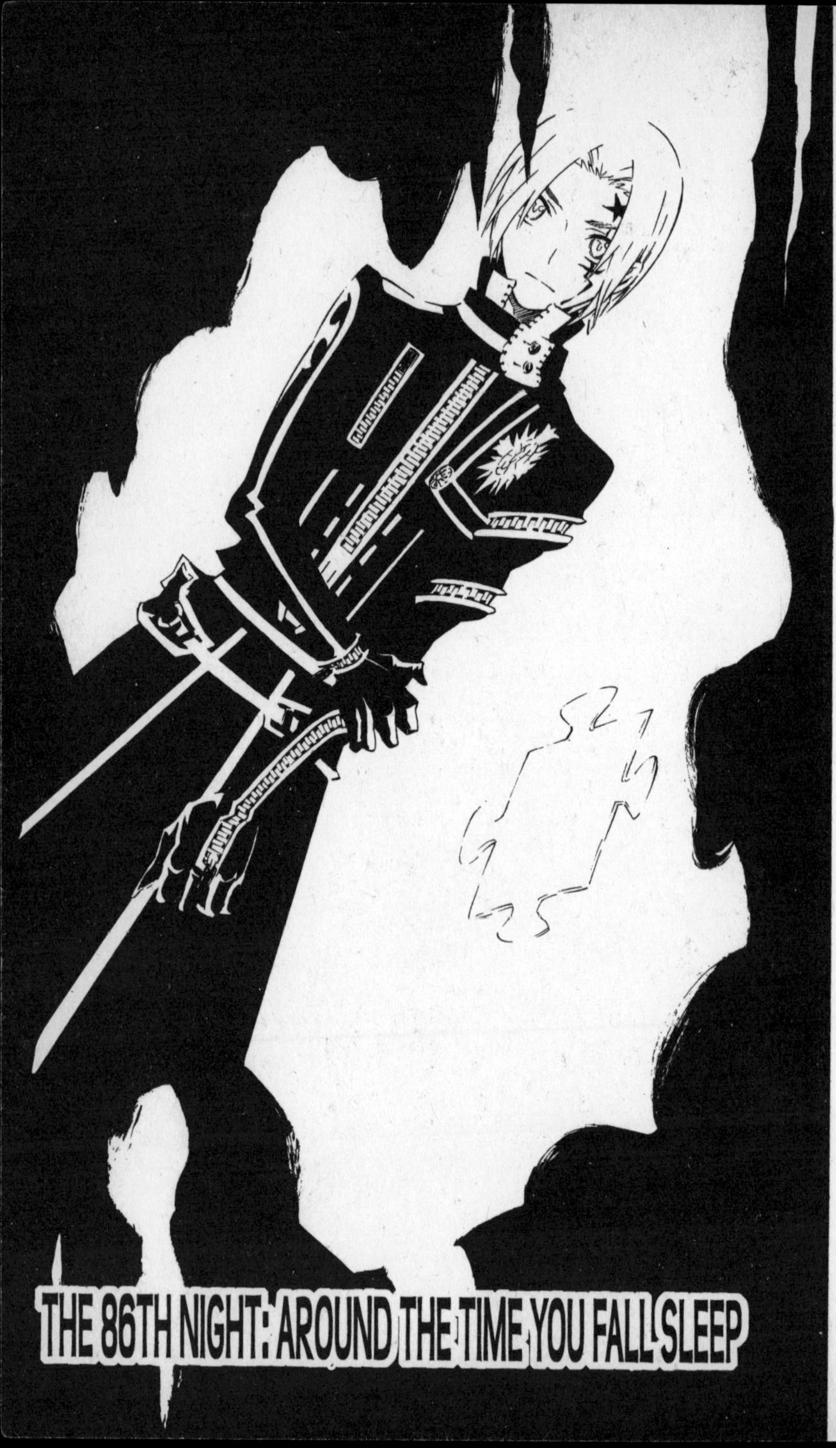
THE 86TH NIGHT: AROUND THE TIME YOU FALL SLEEP

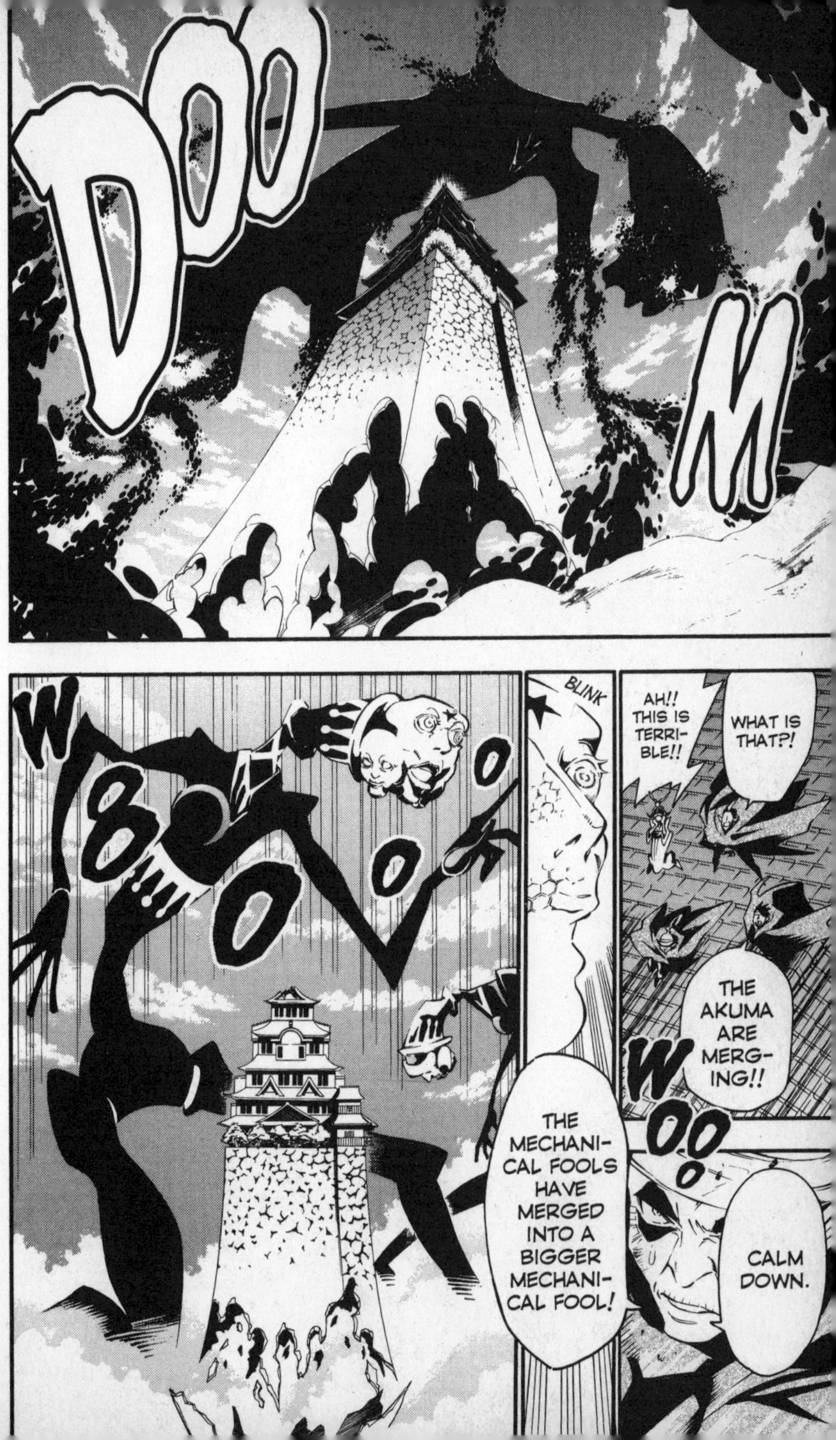
DOOOM
WHAT IS THAT?!
AH!! THIS IS TERRI-BLE!!
THE AKUMA ARE MERG-ING!!
WOOO
CALM DOWN.
THE MECHANI-CAL FOOLS HAVE MERGED INTO A BIGGER MECHANI-CAL FOOL!
BLINK
WBOOOO

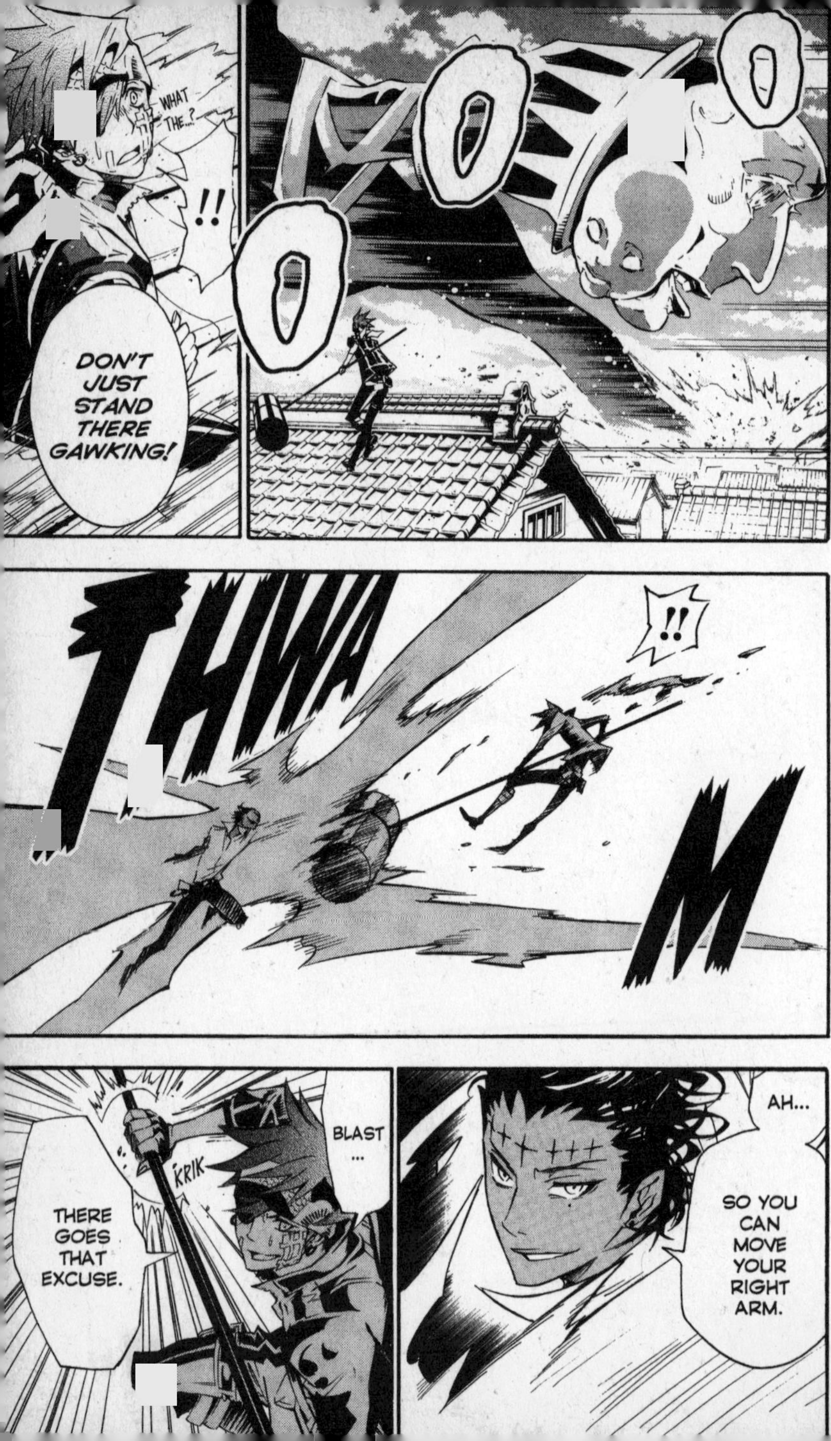
WHAT THE..?
!!
DON'T JUST STAND THERE GAWKING!
!!
THWAM
AH...
SO YOU CAN MOVE YOUR RIGHT ARM.
BLAST...
KRIK
THERE GOES THAT EXCUSE.

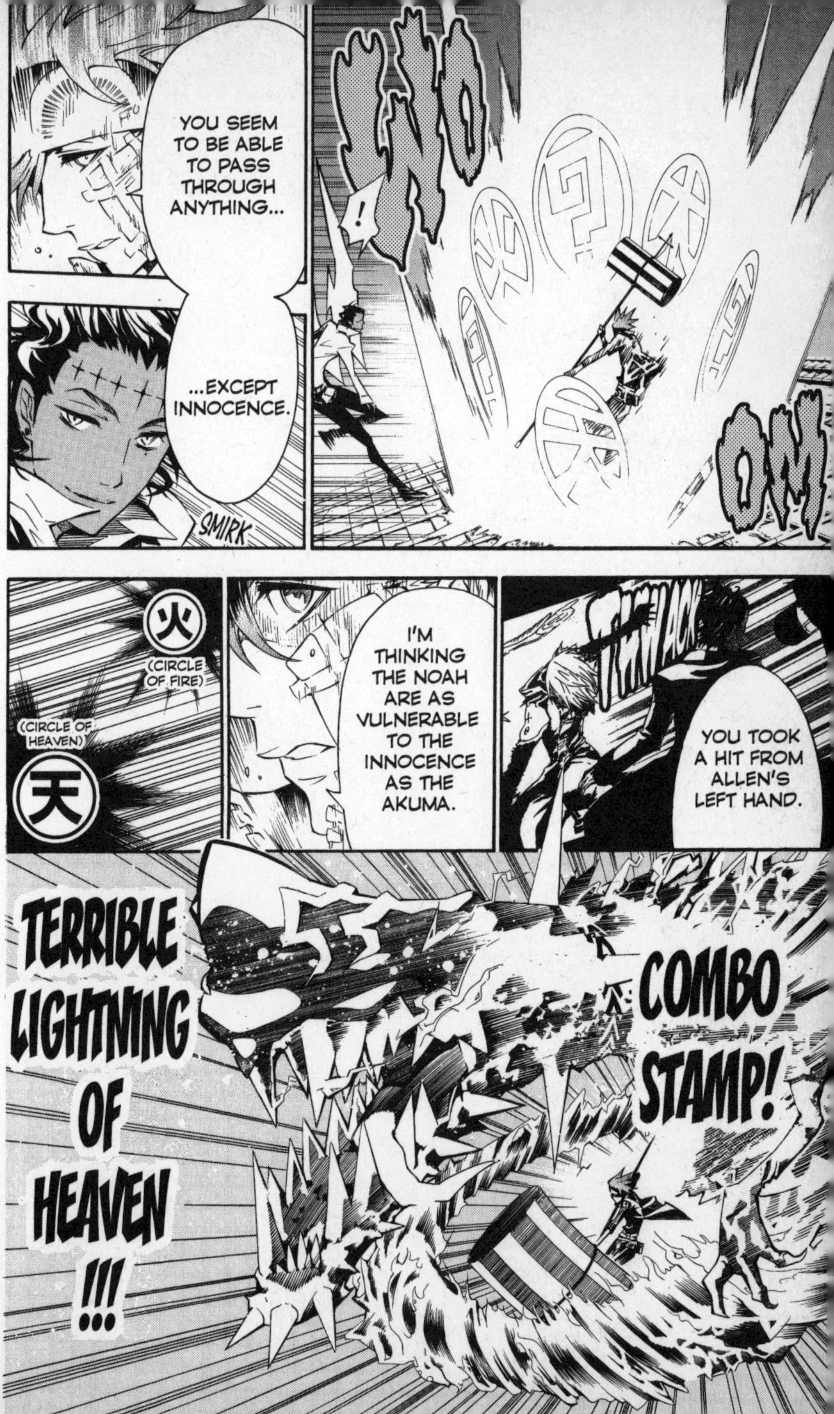
!
YOU SEEM TO BE ABLE TO PASS THROUGH ANYTHING...
...EXCEPT INNOCENCE.
SMIRK
YOU TOOK A HIT FROM ALLEN'S LEFT HAND.
I'M THINKING THE NOAH ARE AS VULNERABLE TO THE INNOCENCE AS THE AKUMA.
火
(CIRCLE OF FIRE)
(CIRCLE OF HEAVEN)
天
COMBO STAMP!
TERRIBLE LIGHTNING OF HEAVEN!!!

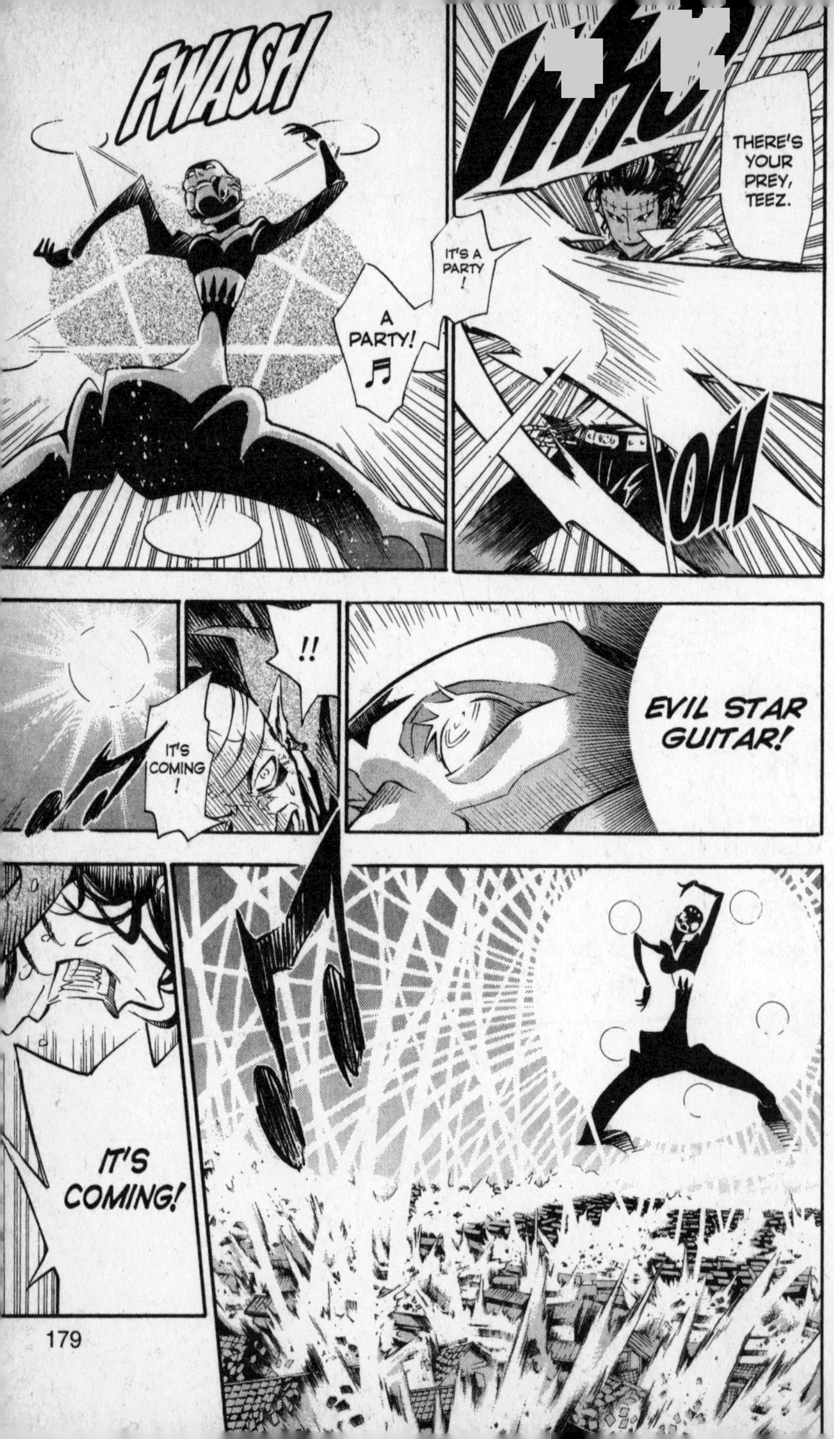

THERE'S YOUR PREY, TEEZ.
IT'S A PARTY!
A PARTY! ♬
OM
FWASH
EVIL STAR GUITAR!
!!
IT'S COMING!
IT'S COMING!

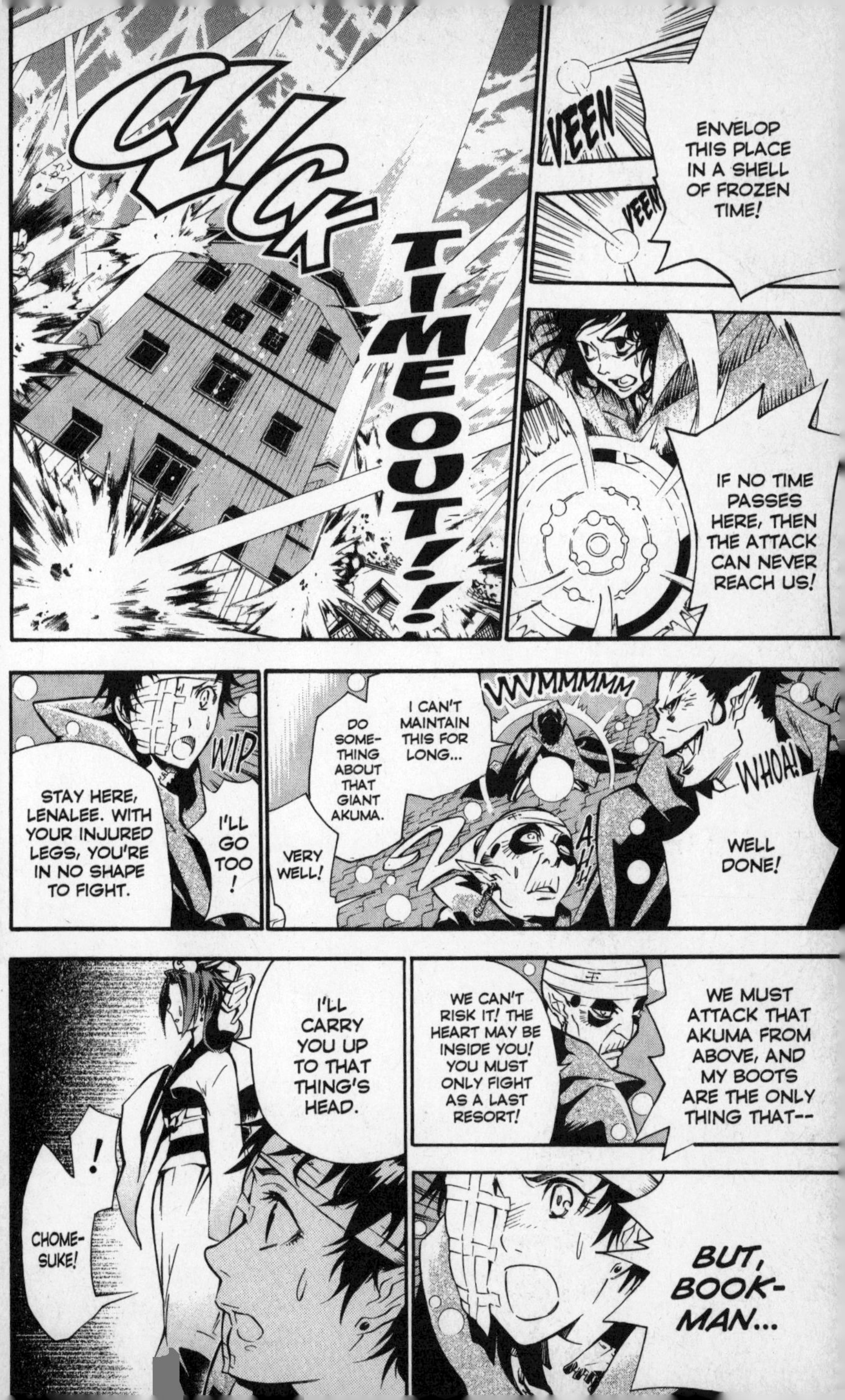
VEEN
ENVELOP THIS PLACE IN A SHELL OF FROZEN TIME!
VEEN
IF NO TIME PASSES HERE, THEN THE ATTACK CAN NEVER REACH US!
CLICK
TIME OUT!!
WVMMMMM
WHOA!
I CAN'T MAINTAIN THIS FOR LONG...
DO SOMETHING ABOUT THAT GIANT AKUMA.
WELL DONE!
AAH
VERY WELL!
WIP
I'LL GO TOO!
STAY HERE, LENALEE. WITH YOUR INJURED LEGS, YOU'RE IN NO SHAPE TO FIGHT.
WE MUST ATTACK THAT AKUMA FROM ABOVE, AND MY BOOTS ARE THE ONLY THING THAT--
WE CAN'T RISK IT! THE HEART MAY BE INSIDE YOU! YOU MUST ONLY FIGHT AS A LAST RESORT!
BUT, BOOKMAN...
I'LL CARRY YOU UP TO THAT THING'S HEAD.
!
CHOME-SUKE!

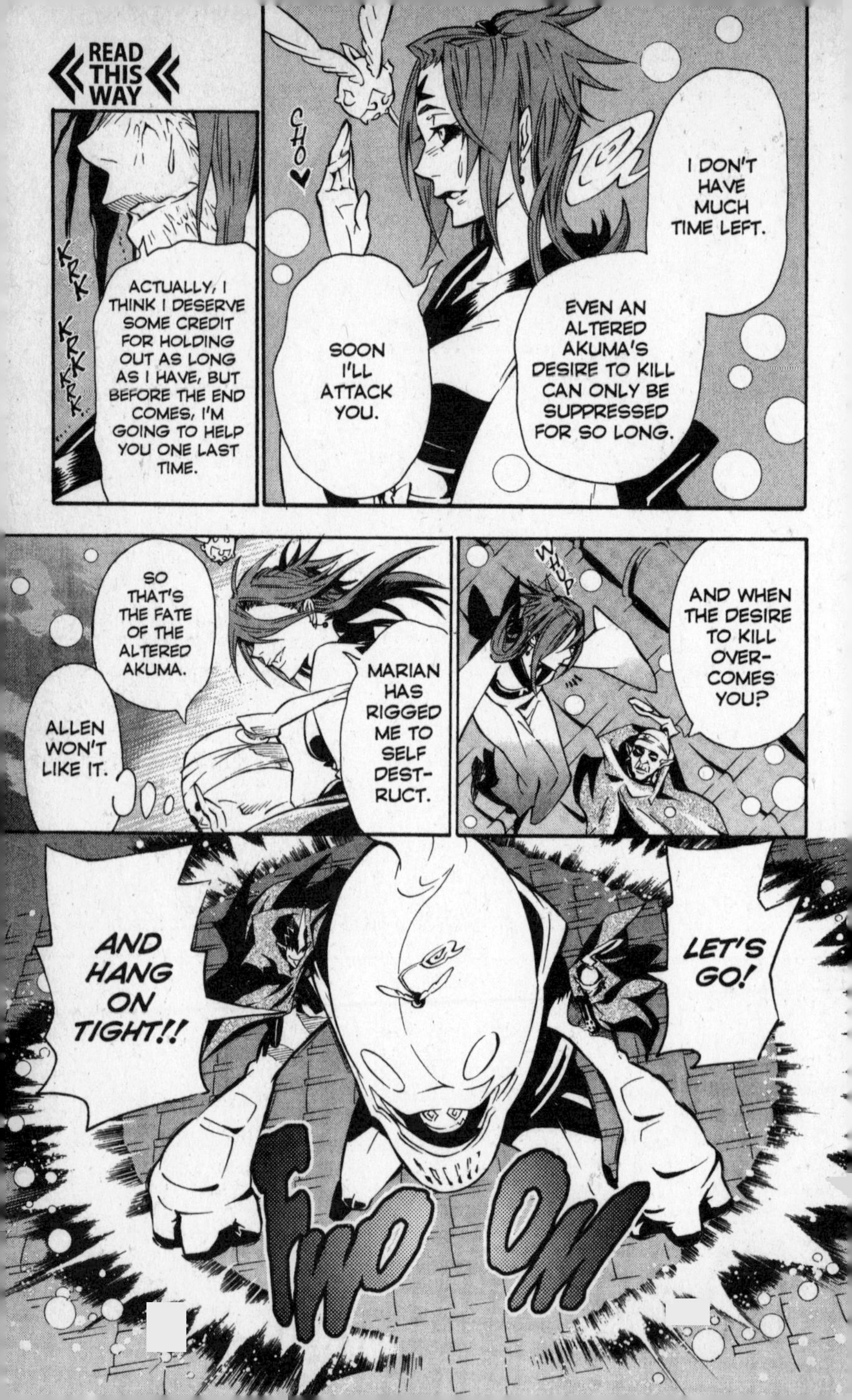
READ THIS WAY
I DON'T HAVE MUCH TIME LEFT.
EVEN AN ALTERED AKUMA'S DESIRE TO KILL CAN ONLY BE SUPPRESSED FOR SO LONG.
CHO♥
SOON I'LL ATTACK YOU.
KRK KRK KRK
ACTUALLY, I THINK I DESERVE SOME CREDIT FOR HOLDING OUT AS LONG AS I HAVE, BUT BEFORE THE END COMES, I'M GOING TO HELP YOU ONE LAST TIME.
WHUP
AND WHEN THE DESIRE TO KILL OVER-COMES YOU?
MARIAN HAS RIGGED ME TO SELF DEST-RUCT.
SO THAT'S THE FATE OF THE ALTERED AKUMA.
ALLEN WON'T LIKE IT.
LET'S GO!
AND HANG ON TIGHT!!
FWOOM

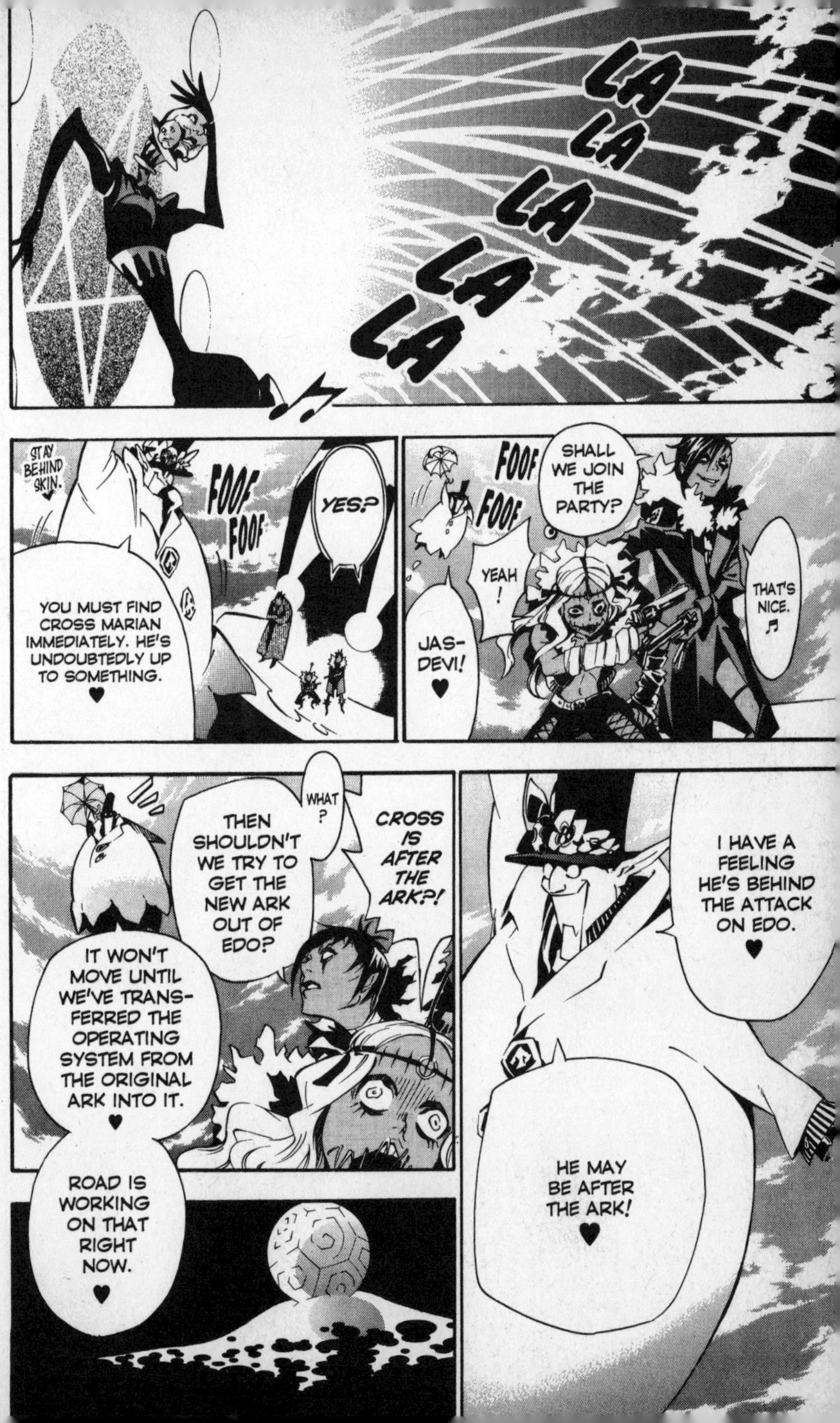
LA LA LA LA LA
SHALL WE JOIN THE PARTY?
FOOF FOOF
THAT'S NICE. ♪
YEAH!
JAS-DEVI! ♥
YES?
FOOF FOOF
STAY BEHIND SKIN. ♥
YOU MUST FIND CROSS MARIAN IMMEDIATELY. HE'S UNDOUBTEDLY UP TO SOMETHING. ♥
I HAVE A FEELING HE'S BEHIND THE ATTACK ON EDO. ♥
HE MAY BE AFTER THE ARK! ♥
CROSS IS AFTER THE ARK?!
WHAT?
THEN SHOULDN'T WE TRY TO GET THE NEW ARK OUT OF EDO?
IT WON'T MOVE UNTIL WE'VE TRANS-FERRED THE OPERATING SYSTEM FROM THE ORIGINAL ARK INTO IT. ♥
ROAD IS WORKING ON THAT RIGHT NOW. ♥

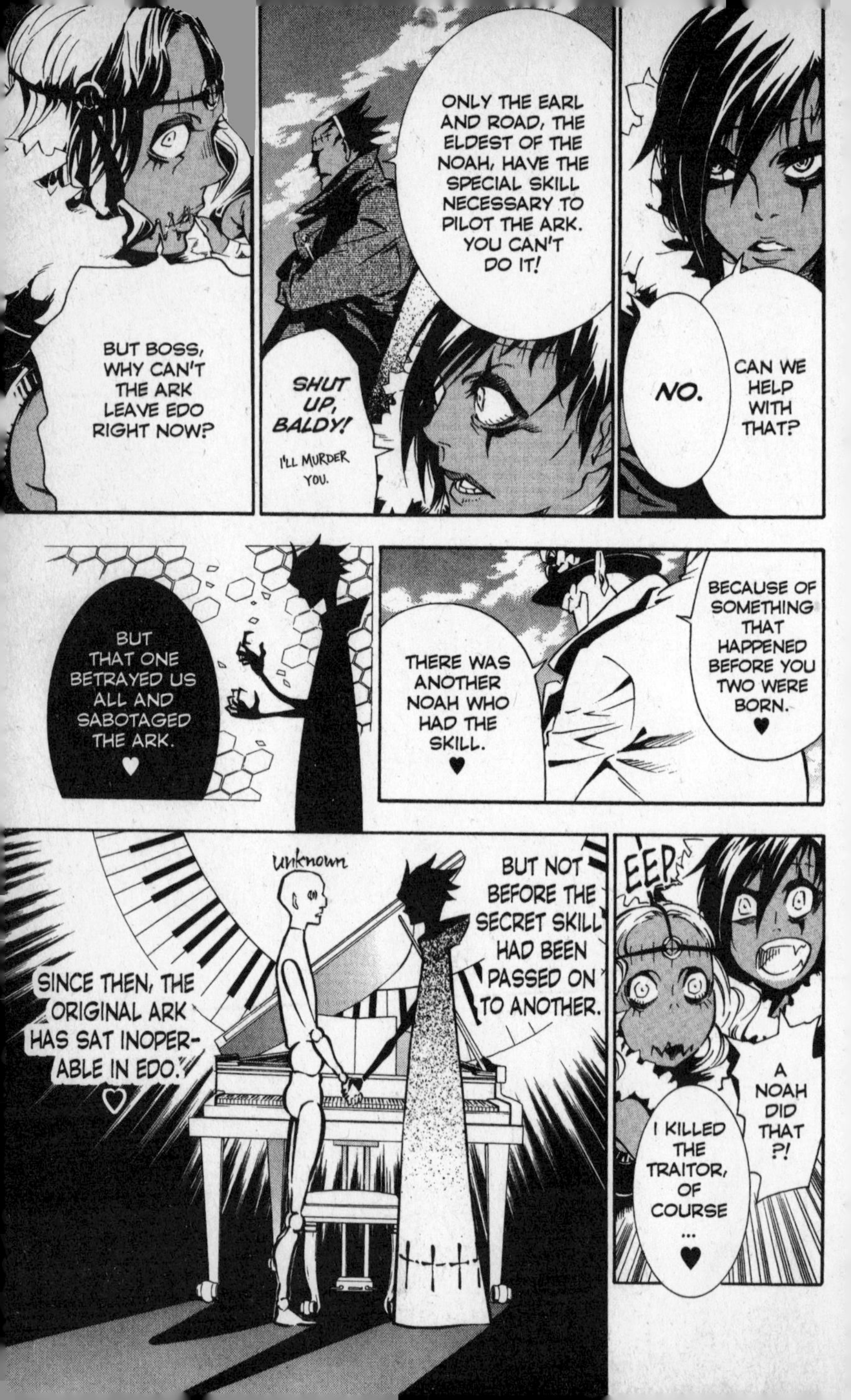
CAN WE HELP WITH THAT?
NO.
ONLY THE EARL AND ROAD, THE ELDEST OF THE NOAH, HAVE THE SPECIAL SKILL NECESSARY TO PILOT THE ARK. YOU CAN'T DO IT!
SHUT UP, BALDY!
I'LL MURDER YOU.
BUT BOSS, WHY CAN'T THE ARK LEAVE EDO RIGHT NOW?
BECAUSE OF SOMETHING THAT HAPPENED BEFORE YOU TWO WERE BORN. ♥
THERE WAS ANOTHER NOAH WHO HAD THE SKILL. ♥
BUT THAT ONE BETRAYED US ALL AND SABOTAGED THE ARK. ♥
EEP
A NOAH DID THAT?!
I KILLED THE TRAITOR, OF COURSE... ♥
BUT NOT BEFORE THE SECRET SKILL HAD BEEN PASSED ON TO ANOTHER.
unknown
SINCE THEN, THE ORIGINAL ARK HAS SAT INOPER-ABLE IN EDO. ♥

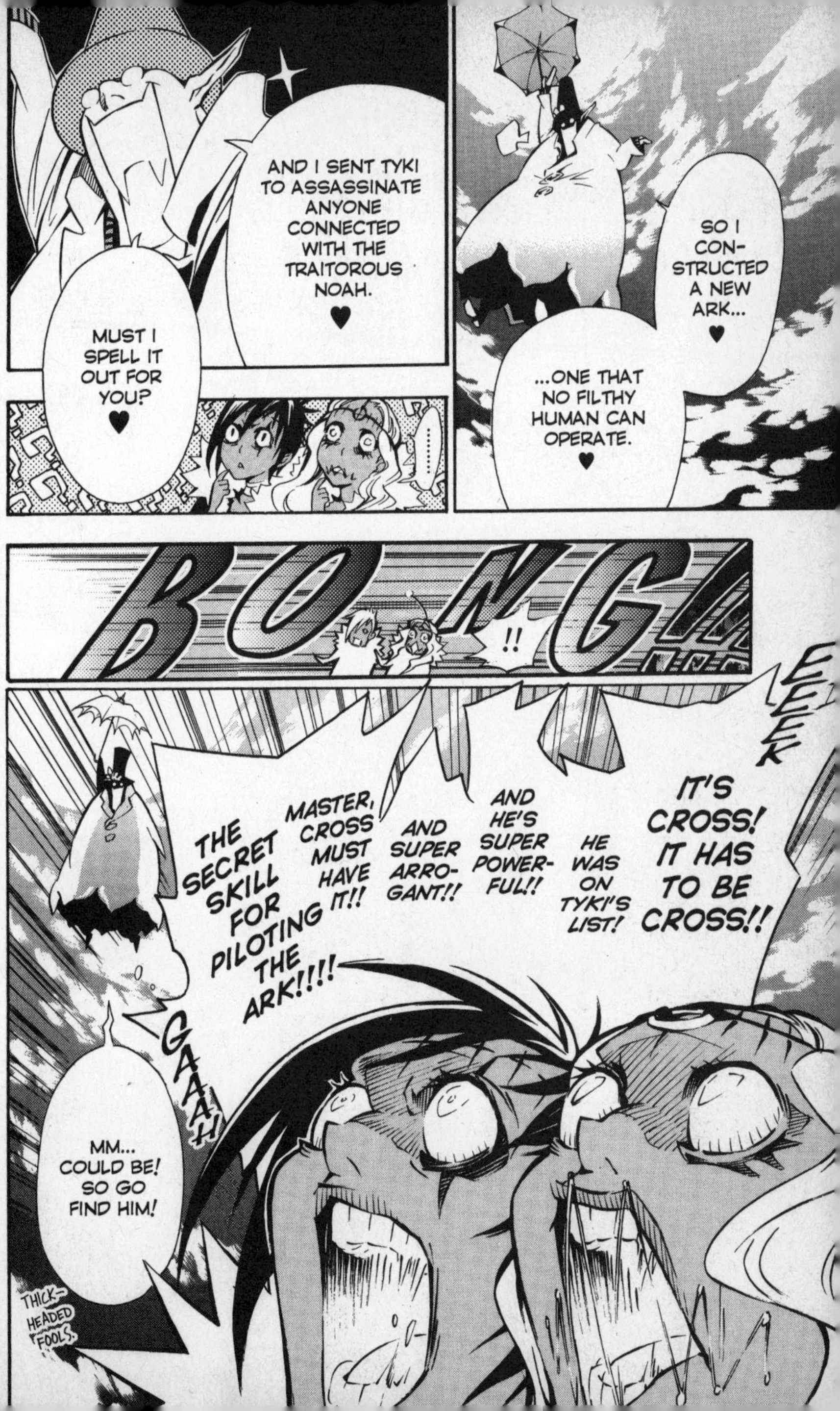
SO I CONSTRUCTED A NEW ARK... ♥
...ONE THAT NO FILTHY HUMAN CAN OPERATE. ♥
AND I SENT TYKI TO ASSASSINATE ANYONE CONNECTED WITH THE TRAITOROUS NOAH. ♥
MUST I SPELL IT OUT FOR YOU? ♥
......
BONG!
!!
EEEEEK
IT'S CROSS! IT HAS TO BE CROSS!!
HE WAS ON TYKI'S LIST!
AND HE'S SUPER POWERFUL!!
AND SUPER ARROGANT!!
MASTER, CROSS MUST HAVE IT!!
THE SECRET SKILL FOR PILOTING THE ARK!!!!
GAAAH
MM... COULD BE! SO GO FIND HIM!
THICK-HEADED FOOLS.

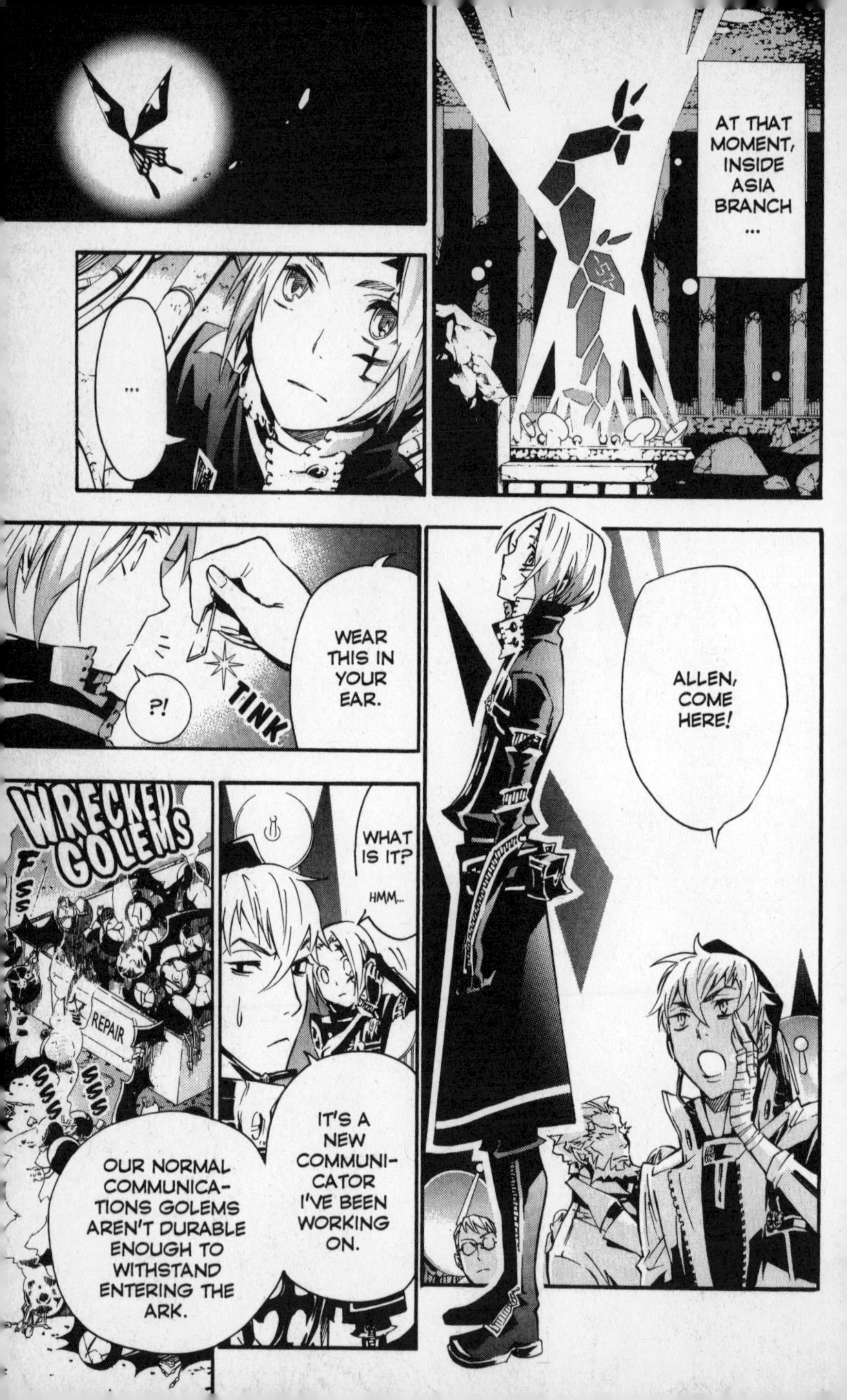
AT THAT MOMENT, INSIDE ASIA BRANCH ...
...
ALLEN, COME HERE!
WEAR THIS IN YOUR EAR.
TINK
?!
WHAT IS IT?
HMM...
IT'S A NEW COMMUNICATOR I'VE BEEN WORKING ON.
WRECKED GOLEMS
FSS
REPAIR
SSS
SSS
OUR NORMAL COMMUNICATIONS GOLEMS AREN'T DURABLE ENOUGH TO WITHSTAND ENTERING THE ARK.

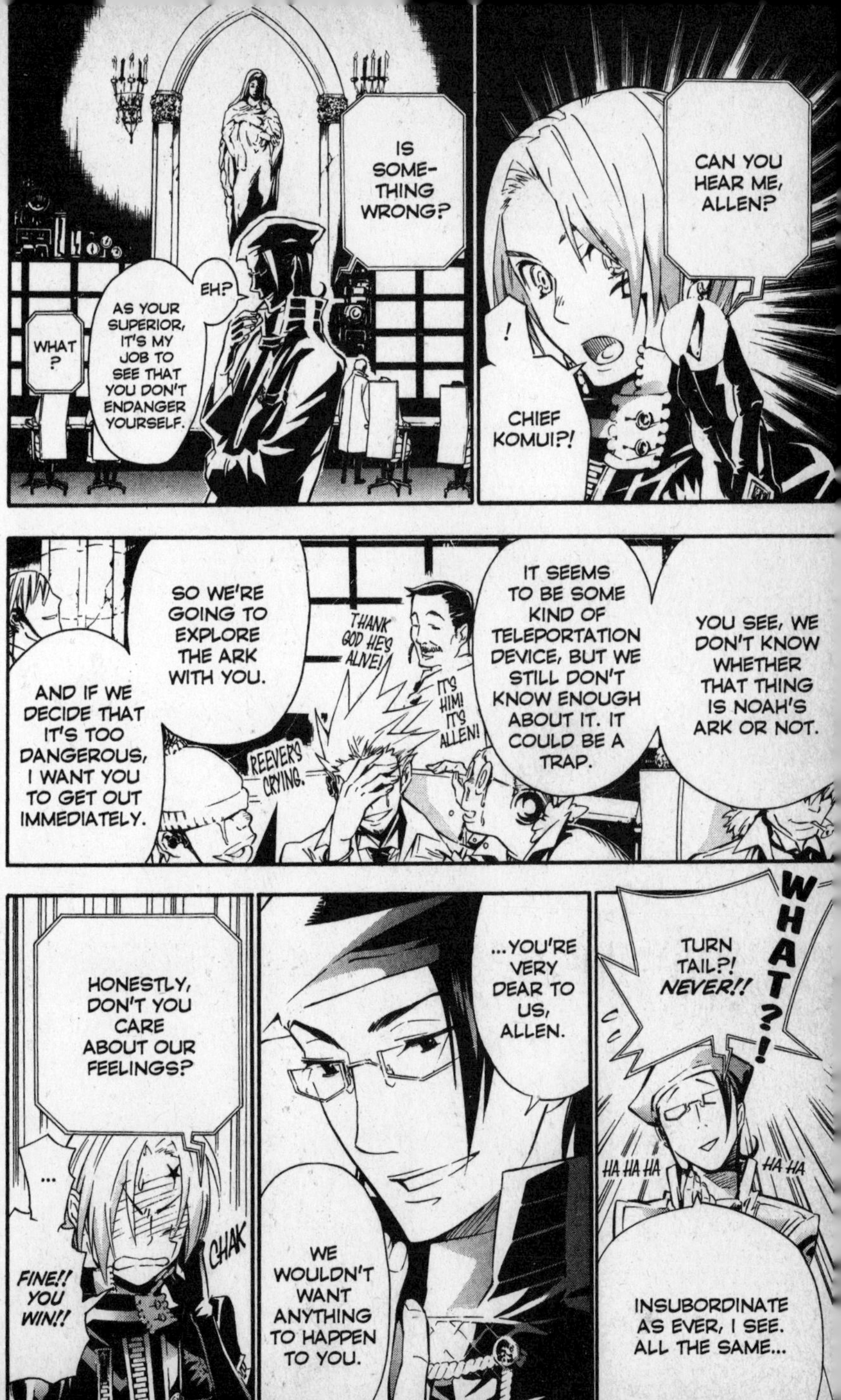
CAN YOU HEAR ME, ALLEN?
!
CHIEF KOMUI?!
IS SOMETHING WRONG?
EH?
AS YOUR SUPERIOR, IT'S MY JOB TO SEE THAT YOU DON'T ENDANGER YOURSELF.
WHAT?
YOU SEE, WE DON'T KNOW WHETHER THAT THING IS NOAH'S ARK OR NOT.
IT SEEMS TO BE SOME KIND OF TELEPORTATION DEVICE, BUT WE STILL DON'T KNOW ENOUGH ABOUT IT. IT COULD BE A TRAP.
IT'S HIM! IT'S ALLEN!
THANK GOD HE'S ALIVE!
REEVER'S CRYING.
SO WE'RE GOING TO EXPLORE THE ARK WITH YOU.
AND IF WE DECIDE THAT IT'S TOO DANGEROUS, I WANT YOU TO GET OUT IMMEDIATELY.
WHAT?!
TURN TAIL?! NEVER!!
HA HA
HA HA HA
INSUBORDINATE AS EVER, I SEE. ALL THE SAME...
...YOU'RE VERY DEAR TO US, ALLEN.
WE WOULDN'T WANT ANYTHING TO HAPPEN TO YOU.
HONESTLY, DON'T YOU CARE ABOUT OUR FEELINGS?
...
CHAK
FINE!! YOU WIN!!

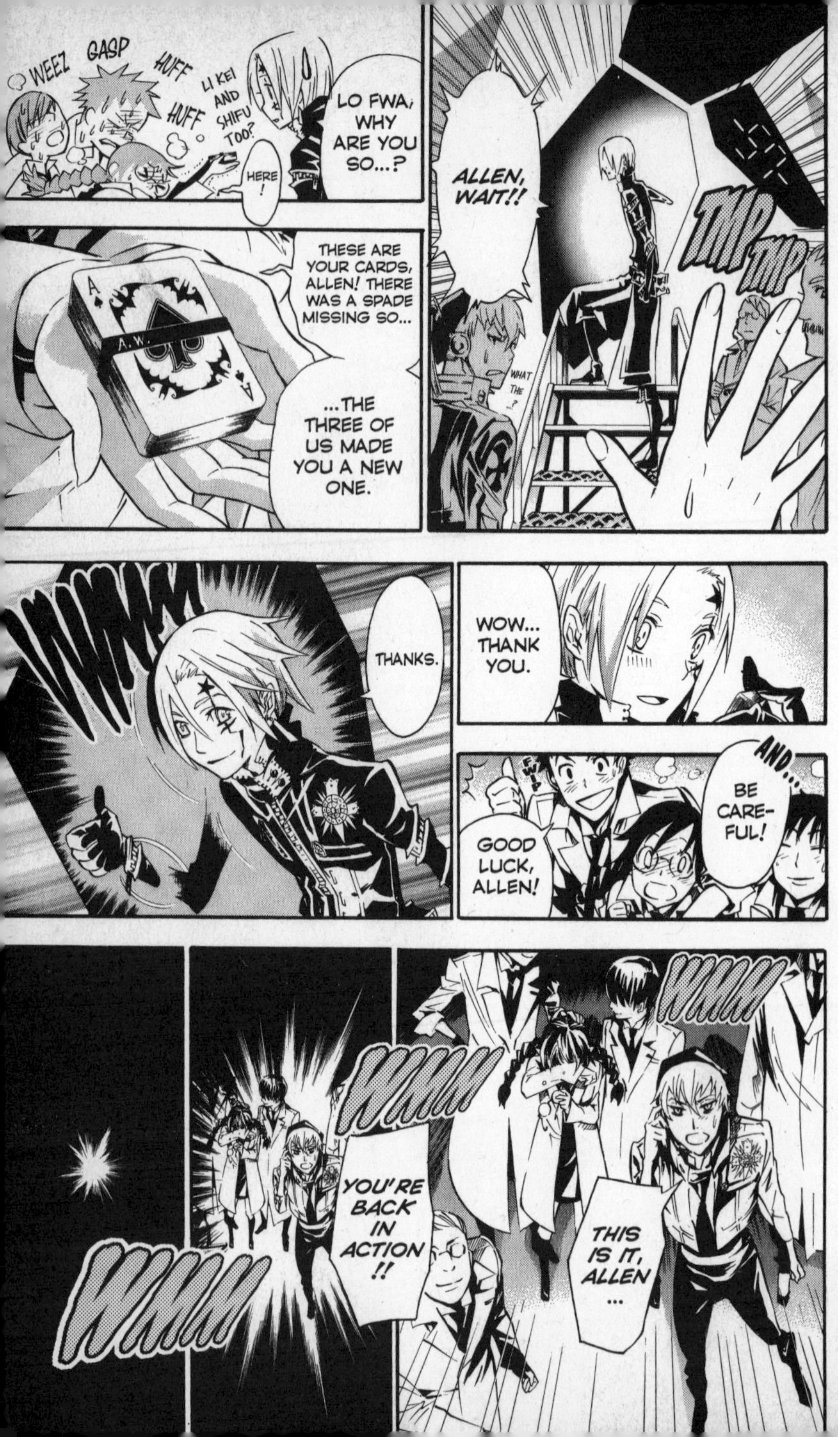

ALLEN, WAIT!!
TMP TMP
WHAT THE ...?
LO FWA, WHY ARE YOU SO...?
LI KEI AND SHIFU TOO?
HUFF
HUFF
GASP
WEEZ
HERE!
THESE ARE YOUR CARDS, ALLEN! THERE WAS A SPADE MISSING SO...
...THE THREE OF US MADE YOU A NEW ONE.
WOW... THANK YOU.
AND...
BE CARE-FUL!
FWIP
GOOD LUCK, ALLEN!
THANKS.
THIS IS IT, ALLEN...
YOU'RE BACK IN ACTION!!

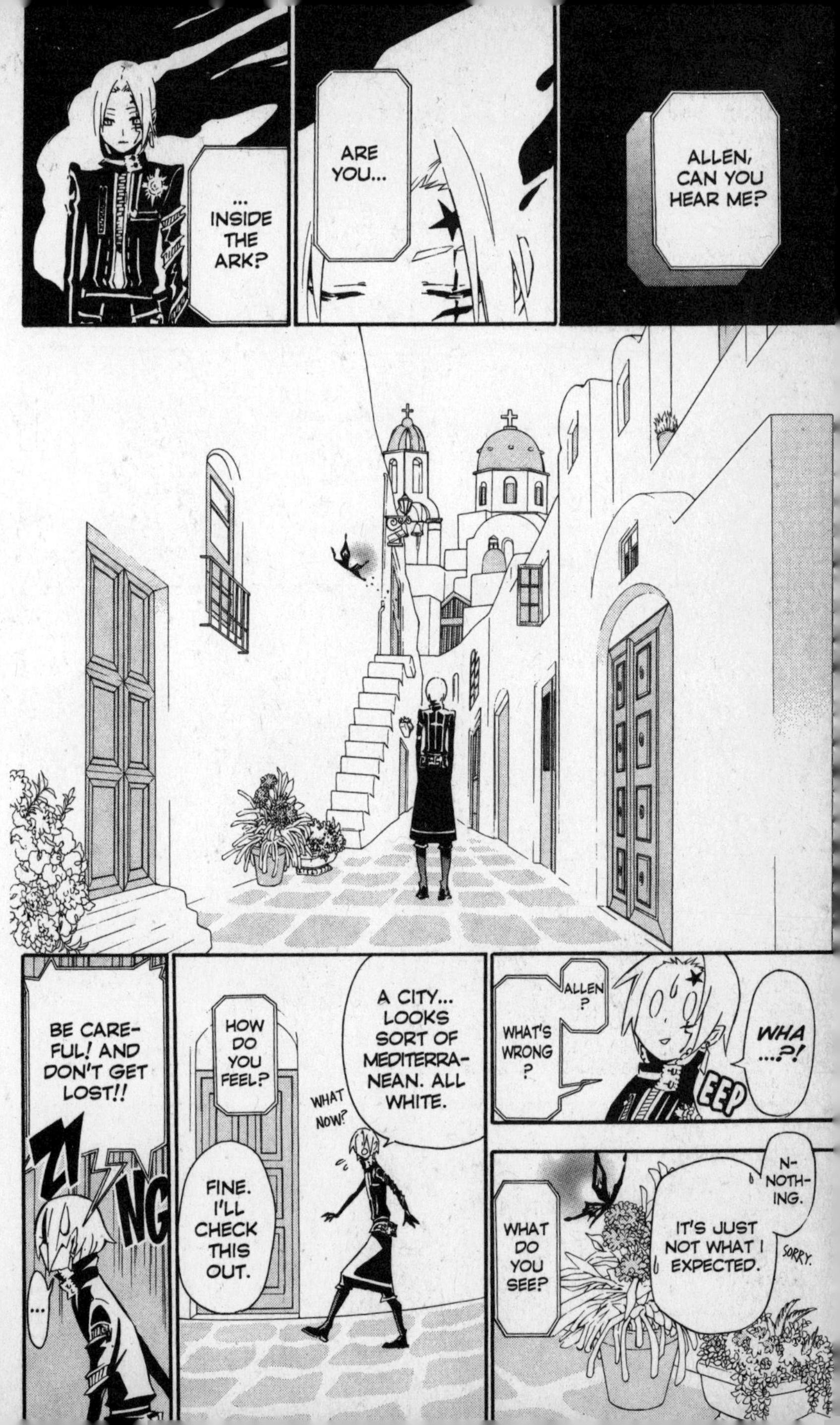
ALLEN, CAN YOU HEAR ME?
ARE YOU...
... INSIDE THE ARK?
WHA ...?!
EEP
ALLEN ?
WHAT'S WRONG ?
N-NOTHING.
IT'S JUST NOT WHAT I EXPECTED.
SORRY.
WHAT DO YOU SEE?
A CITY... LOOKS SORT OF MEDITERRA-NEAN. ALL WHITE.
HOW DO YOU FEEL?
WHAT NOW?
FINE. I'LL CHECK THIS OUT.
BE CARE-FUL! AND DON'T GET LOST!!
ZI NG
...

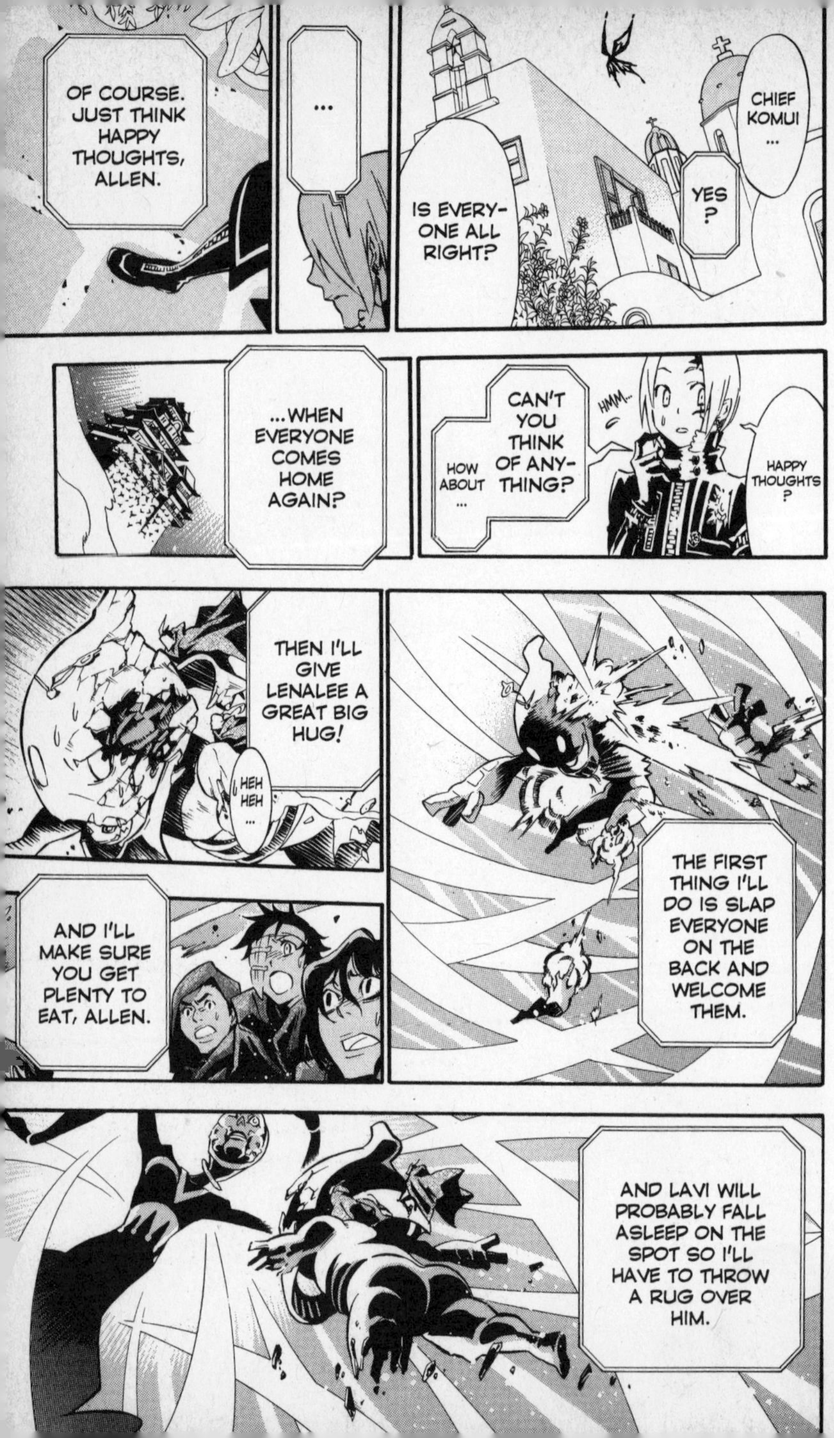
CHIEF KOMUI ...
YES ?
IS EVERY-ONE ALL RIGHT?
...
OF COURSE. JUST THINK HAPPY THOUGHTS, ALLEN.
HAPPY THOUGHTS ?
HMM...
CAN'T YOU THINK OF ANY-THING?
HOW ABOUT ...
...WHEN EVERYONE COMES HOME AGAIN?
THE FIRST THING I'LL DO IS SLAP EVERYONE ON THE BACK AND WELCOME THEM.
THEN I'LL GIVE LENALEE A GREAT BIG HUG!
HEH HEH ...
AND I'LL MAKE SURE YOU GET PLENTY TO EAT, ALLEN.
AND LAVI WILL PROBABLY FALL ASLEEP ON THE SPOT SO I'LL HAVE TO THROW A RUG OVER HIM.

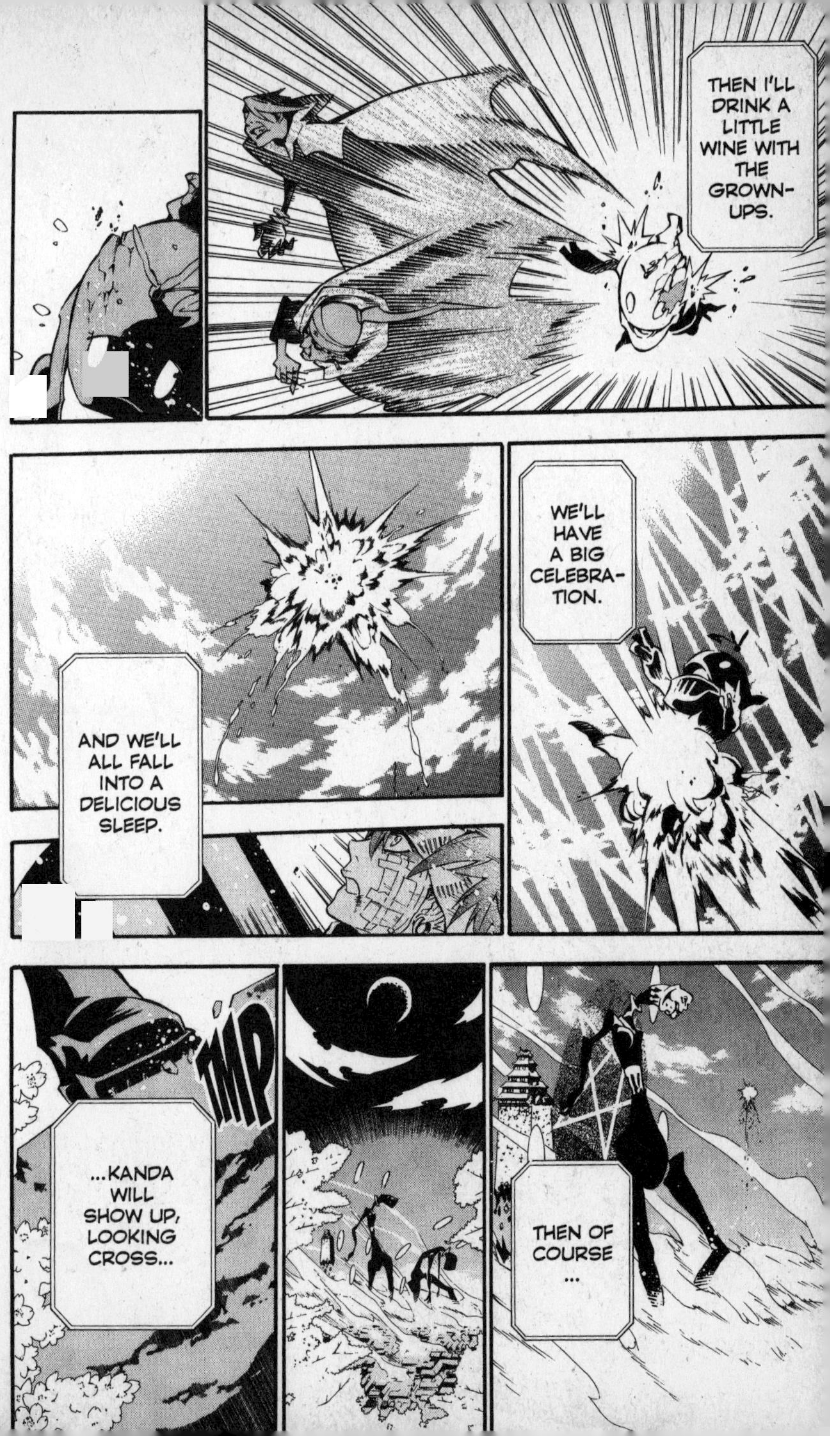
THEN I'LL DRINK A LITTLE WINE WITH THE GROWN-UPS.
WE'LL HAVE A BIG CELEBRATION.
AND WE'LL ALL FALL INTO A DELICIOUS SLEEP.
THEN OF COURSE ...
TMP
...KANDA WILL SHOW UP, LOOKING CROSS...

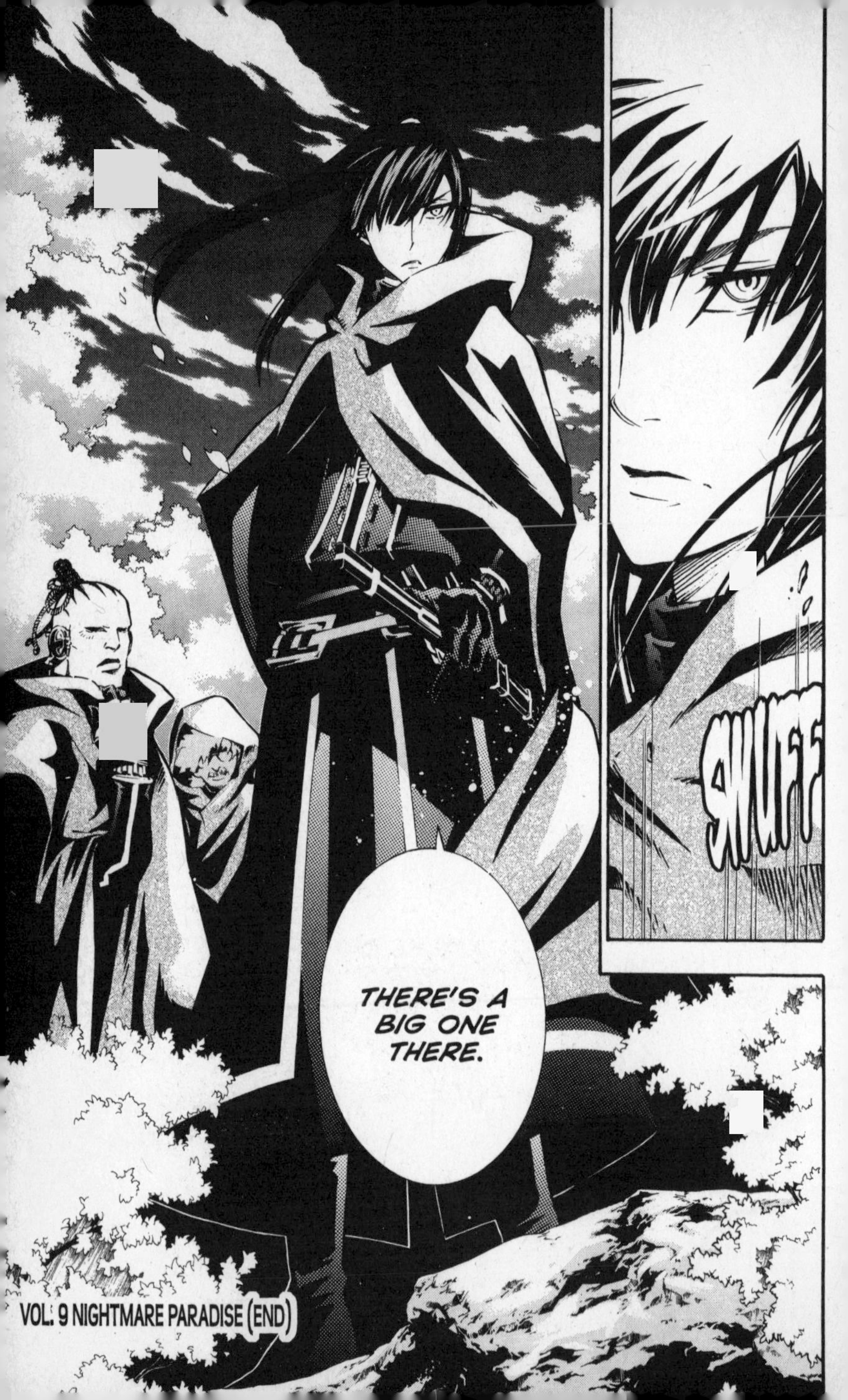
SNUFF
THERE'S A BIG ONE THERE.
VOL. 9 NIGHTMARE PARADISE (END)

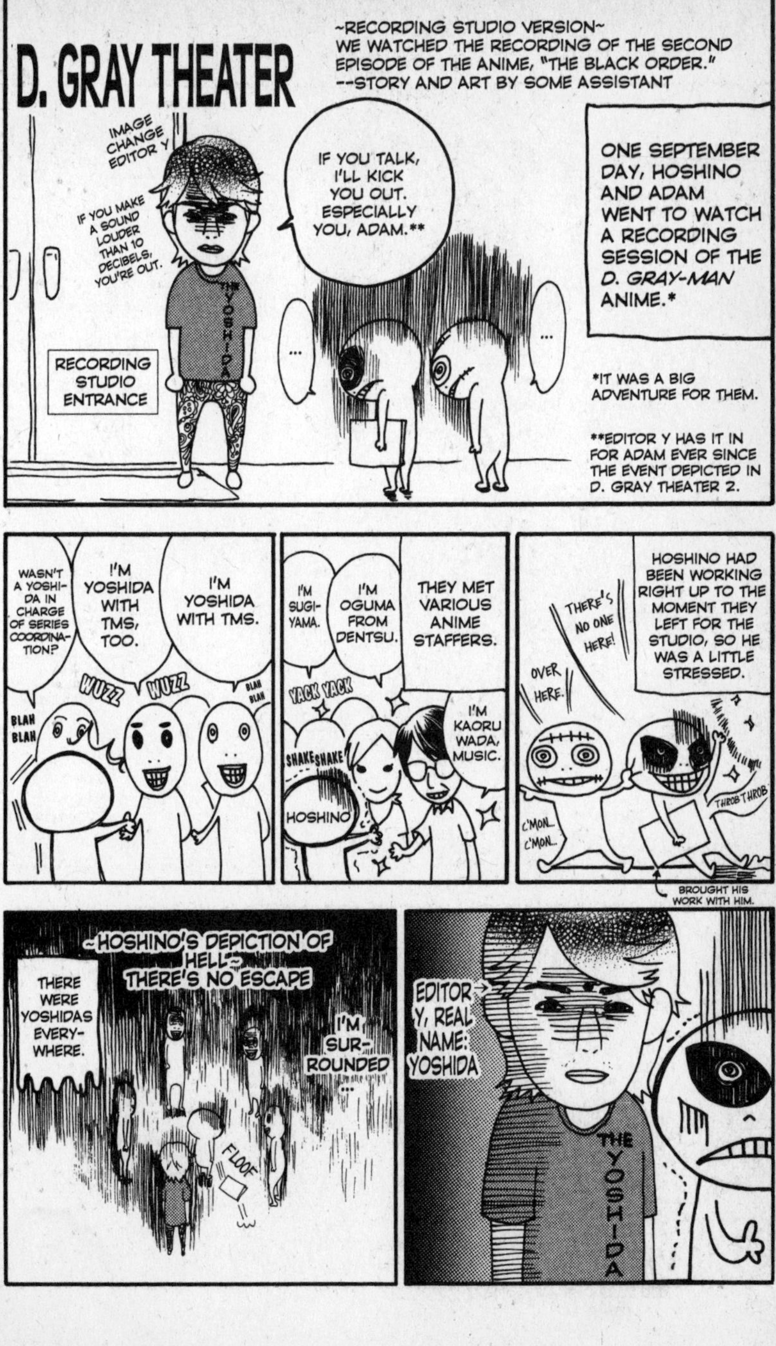
~RECORDING STUDIO VERSION~
WE WATCHED THE RECORDING OF THE SECOND EPISODE OF THE ANIME, "THE BLACK ORDER."
--STORY AND ART BY SOME ASSISTANT
D. GRAY THEATER
ONE SEPTEMBER DAY, HOSHINO AND ADAM WENT TO WATCH A RECORDING SESSION OF THE D. GRAY-MAN ANIME.*
IF YOU TALK, I'LL KICK YOU OUT. ESPECIALLY YOU, ADAM.**
IMAGE CHANGE EDITOR Y
IF YOU MAKE A SOUND LOUDER THAN 10 DECIBELS, YOU'RE OUT.
THE YOSHIDA
...
...
RECORDING STUDIO ENTRANCE
*IT WAS A BIG ADVENTURE FOR THEM.
**EDITOR Y HAS IT IN FOR ADAM EVER SINCE THE EVENT DEPICTED IN D. GRAY THEATER 2.
HOSHINO HAD BEEN WORKING RIGHT UP TO THE MOMENT THEY LEFT FOR THE STUDIO, SO HE WAS A LITTLE STRESSED.
THERE'S NO ONE HERE!
OVER HERE.
THROB THROB
C'MON... C'MON...
BROUGHT HIS WORK WITH HIM.
THEY MET VARIOUS ANIME STAFFERS.
I'M OGUMA FROM DENTSU.
I'M SUGIYAMA.
YACK YACK
I'M KAORU WADA, MUSIC.
SHAKE SHAKE
HOSHINO
I'M YOSHIDA WITH TMS.
I'M YOSHIDA WITH TMS, TOO.
WASN'T A YOSHIDA IN CHARGE OF SERIES COORDINATION?
BLAH BLAH
WUZZ WUZZ
BLAH BLAH
EDITOR Y, REAL NAME: YOSHIDA
THE YOSHIDA
~HOSHINO'S DEPICTION OF HELL~ THERE'S NO ESCAPE
THERE WERE YOSHIDAS EVERYWHERE.
I'M SURROUNDED...
FLOOF

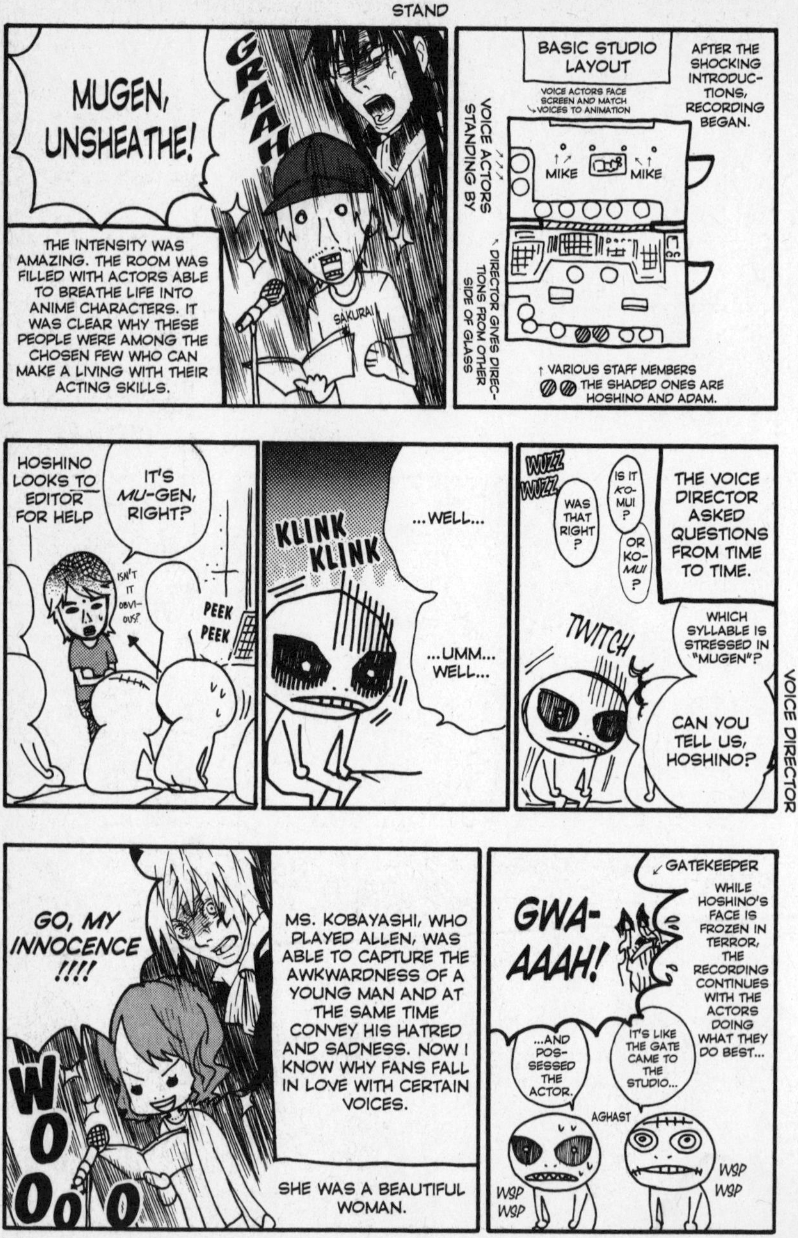

BASIC STUDIO LAYOUT
AFTER THE SHOCKING INTRODUCTIONS, RECORDING BEGAN.
VOICE ACTORS FACE SCREEN AND MATCH VOICES TO ANIMATION
MIKE
MIKE
VOICE ACTORS STANDING BY
DIRECTOR GIVES DIRECTIONS FROM OTHER SIDE OF GLASS
VARIOUS STAFF MEMBERS
THE SHADED ONES ARE HOSHINO AND ADAM.
STAND
GRAAH
MUGEN, UNSHEATHE!
SAKURAI
THE INTENSITY WAS AMAZING. THE ROOM WAS FILLED WITH ACTORS ABLE TO BREATHE LIFE INTO ANIME CHARACTERS. IT WAS CLEAR WHY THESE PEOPLE WERE AMONG THE CHOSEN FEW WHO CAN MAKE A LIVING WITH THEIR ACTING SKILLS.
THE VOICE DIRECTOR ASKED QUESTIONS FROM TIME TO TIME.
IS IT KO-MUI?
OR KO-MUI?
WAS THAT RIGHT?
WUZZ WUZZ
WHICH SYLLABLE IS STRESSED IN "MUGEN"?
TWITCH
CAN YOU TELL US, HOSHINO?
VOICE DIRECTOR
...WELL...
KLINK KLINK
...UMM... WELL...
HOSHINO LOOKS TO EDITOR FOR HELP
IT'S MU-GEN, RIGHT?
ISN'T IT OBVIOUS?
PEEK PEEK
GATEKEEPER
WHILE HOSHINO'S FACE IS FROZEN IN TERROR, THE RECORDING CONTINUES WITH THE ACTORS DOING WHAT THEY DO BEST...
GWA-AAAH!
IT'S LIKE THE GATE CAME TO THE STUDIO...
...AND POSSESSED THE ACTOR.
AGHAST
WSP WSP
WSP WSP
MS. KOBAYASHI, WHO PLAYED ALLEN, WAS ABLE TO CAPTURE THE AWKWARDNESS OF A YOUNG MAN AND AT THE SAME TIME CONVEY HIS HATRED AND SADNESS. NOW I KNOW WHY FANS FALL IN LOVE WITH CERTAIN VOICES.
GO, MY INNOCENCE !!!!
WOOOO
SHE WAS A BEAUTIFUL WOMAN.

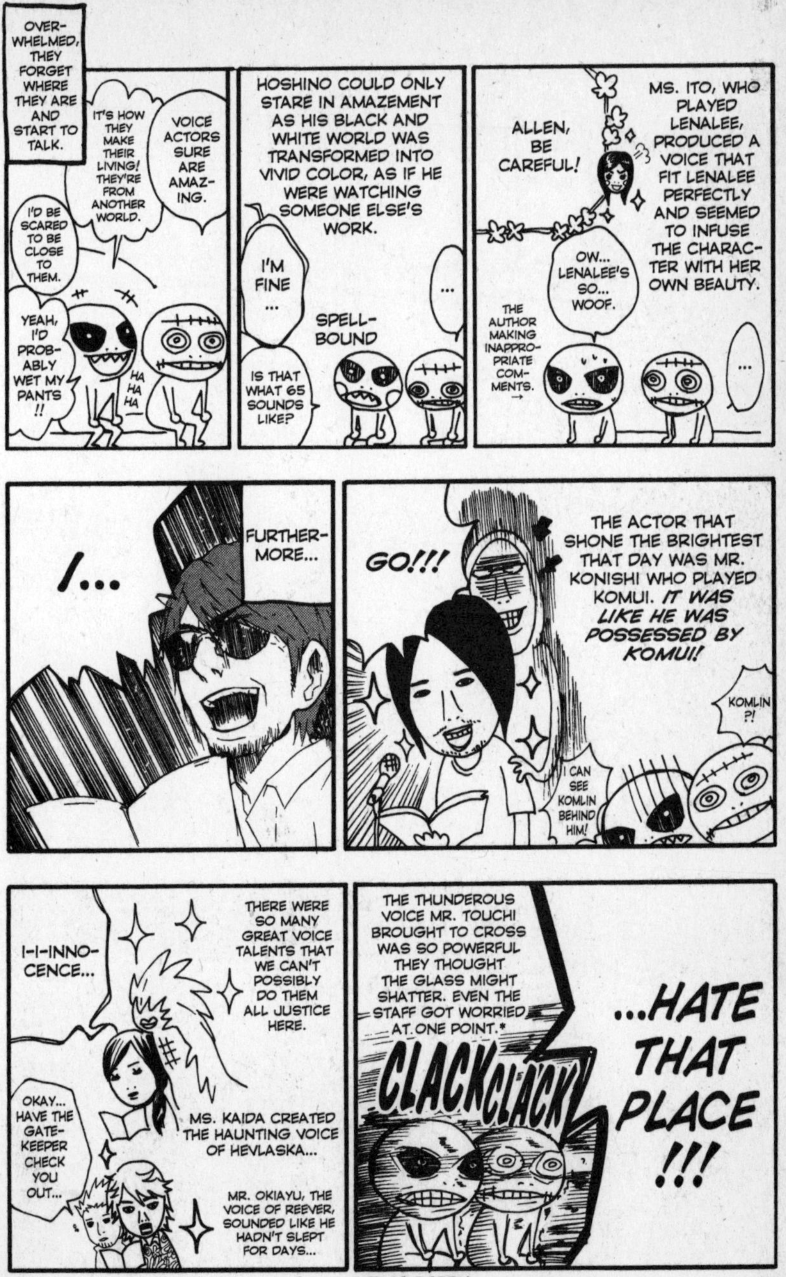
MS. ITO, WHO PLAYED LENALEE, PRODUCED A VOICE THAT FIT LENALEE PERFECTLY AND SEEMED TO INFUSE THE CHARACTER WITH HER OWN BEAUTY.
ALLEN, BE CAREFUL!
OW... LENALEE'S SO... WOOF.
...
THE AUTHOR MAKING INAPPROPRIATE COMMENTS. →
HOSHINO COULD ONLY STARE IN AMAZEMENT AS HIS BLACK AND WHITE WORLD WAS TRANSFORMED INTO VIVID COLOR, AS IF HE WERE WATCHING SOMEONE ELSE'S WORK.
...
I'M FINE ...
SPELLBOUND
IS THAT WHAT 65 SOUNDS LIKE?
VOICE ACTORS SURE ARE AMAZING.
IT'S HOW THEY MAKE THEIR LIVING! THEY'RE FROM ANOTHER WORLD.
OVERWHELMED, THEY FORGET WHERE THEY ARE AND START TO TALK.
I'D BE SCARED TO BE CLOSE TO THEM.
YEAH, I'D PROBABLY WET MY PANTS !!
HA HA HA
THE ACTOR THAT SHONE THE BRIGHTEST THAT DAY WAS MR. KONISHI WHO PLAYED KOMUI. IT WAS LIKE HE WAS POSSESSED BY KOMUI!
GO!!!
KOMLIN ?!
I CAN SEE KOMLIN BEHIND HIM!
FURTHERMORE...
I...
THE THUNDEROUS VOICE MR. TOUCHI BROUGHT TO CROSS WAS SO POWERFUL THEY THOUGHT THE GLASS MIGHT SHATTER. EVEN THE STAFF GOT WORRIED AT ONE POINT.*
...HATE THAT PLACE !!!
CLACK CLACK
THERE WERE SO MANY GREAT VOICE TALENTS THAT WE CAN'T POSSIBLY DO THEM ALL JUSTICE HERE.
I-I-INNOCENCE...
MS. KAIDA CREATED THE HAUNTING VOICE OF HEVLASKA...
OKAY... HAVE THE GATEKEEPER CHECK YOU OUT...
MR. OKIAYU, THE VOICE OF REEVER, SOUNDED LIKE HE HADN'T SLEPT FOR DAYS...

*TRUE STORY

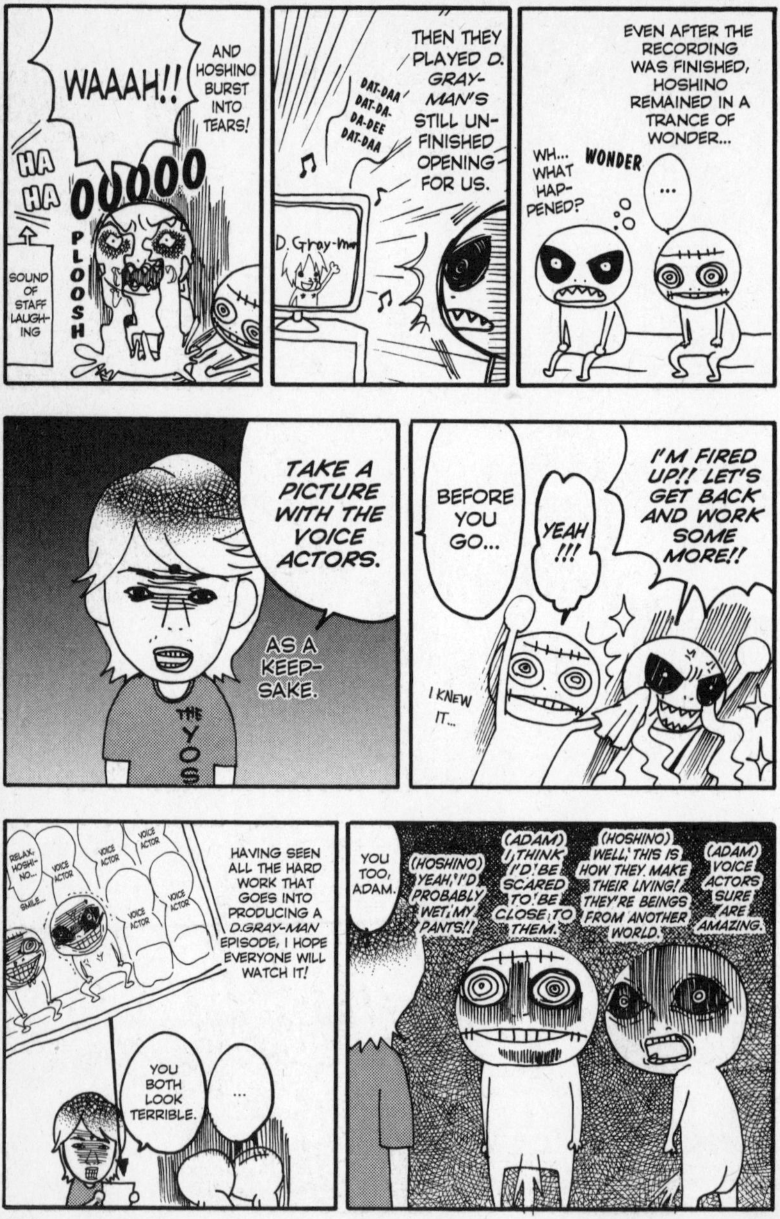
EVEN AFTER THE RECORDING WAS FINISHED, HOSHINO REMAINED IN A TRANCE OF WONDER...
WONDER
...
WH... WHAT HAPPENED?
THEN THEY PLAYED D. GRAY-MAN'S STILL UN-FINISHED OPENING FOR US.
DAT-DAA DAT-DA-DA-DEE DAT-DAA
D.Gray-man
AND HOSHINO BURST INTO TEARS!
WAAAH!!
OOOOO
PLOOSH
HA HA
SOUND OF STAFF LAUGH-ING
I'M FIRED UP!! LET'S GET BACK AND WORK SOME MORE!!
YEAH!!!
BEFORE YOU GO...
I KNEW IT...
TAKE A PICTURE WITH THE VOICE ACTORS.
AS A KEEP-SAKE.
THE YOS
(ADAM) VOICE ACTORS SURE ARE AMAZING.
(HOSHINO) WELL, THIS IS HOW THEY MAKE THEIR LIVING! THEY'RE BEINGS FROM ANOTHER WORLD.
(ADAM) I THINK I'D BE SCARED TO BE CLOSE TO THEM.
(HOSHINO) YEAH, I'D PROBABLY WET MY PANTS!!
YOU TOO, ADAM.
HAVING SEEN ALL THE HARD WORK THAT GOES INTO PRODUCING A D.GRAY-MAN EPISODE, I HOPE EVERYONE WILL WATCH IT!
VOICE ACTOR
VOICE ACTOR
VOICE ACTOR
VOICE ACTOR
VOICE ACTOR
RELAX, HOSHI-NO... SMILE...
...
YOU BOTH LOOK TERRIBLE.

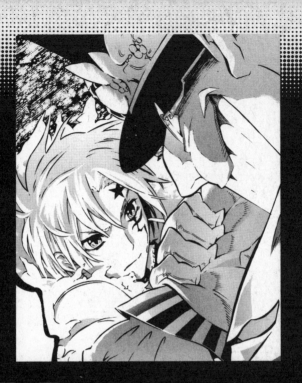

IN THE NEXT VOLUME...

Though heavily outnumbered, the Exorcists from Anita's ship decide to confront the Millennium Earl's forces in Japan. The struggle could not be more one-sided, and that's before the Noah arrive to make things even worse! With the Earl's plans so near completion, the Exorcists battle on with pure will, though there seems little hope they will emerge victorious!

Available August 2008!

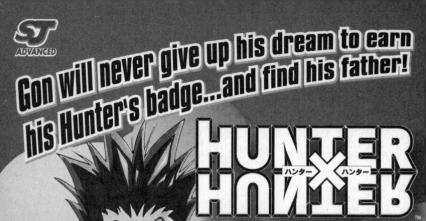
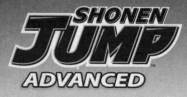

Tell us what you think about SHONEN JUMP

Our survey is now available online.
Go to: **www.SHONENJUMP.com/mangasurvey**

Help us make our product offering better!

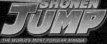

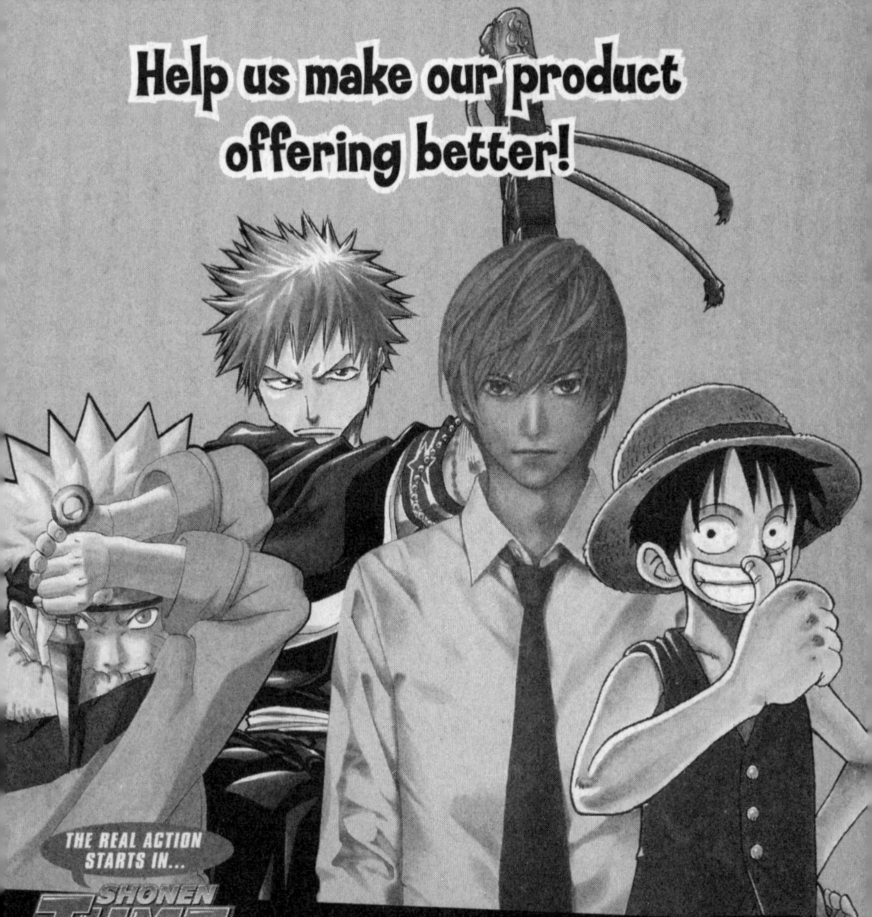

THE REAL ACTION
STARTS IN...

SHONEN JUMP
THE WORLD'S MOST POPULAR MANGA
www.shonenjump.com